Word by Word

CHRISTOPHER HAGER

Word by Word

EMANCIPATION AND THE ACT OF WRITING

HARVARD UNIVERSITY PRESS   Cambridge, Massachusetts, and London, England

2013

Excerpt from "The Idea of Order at Key West" from
The Collected Poems of Wallace Stevens
by Wallace Stevens, copyright 1954 by Wallace Stevens
and renewed 1982 by Holly Stevens. Used by permission of
Alfred A. Knopf, a division of Random House, Inc. and
Faber and Faber Ltd.

Library of Congress Cataloging-in-Publication Data

Hager, Christopher, 1974–
  Word by word : emancipation and the act of writing / Christopher
Hager.
     p. cm.
  Includes bibliographical references and index.
  ISBN 978-0-674-05986-3 (alk. paper)
  1. American literature—African American authors—History and
criticism.   2. Authors, American—19th century—Political and
social views.   3. American literature—19th century—History and
criticism.   4. African Americans—Intellectual life—19th century.
5. African American authors—Political and social views.
6. African Americans—Social conditions—To 1964.   7. Literature
and society—United States.   8. African Americans—Civil rights.
9. African Americans in literature.   10. Slaves—Emancipation—
United States.   I. Title.
  PS153.N5H17 2012
  810.9'896073075—dc23   2012016934

for Ali

Contents

Illustrations

The song and water were not medleyed sound
Even if what she sang was what she heard,
Since what she sang was uttered word by word.

—Wallace Stevens, "The Idea of Order at Key West"

Introduction: A Colored Man's Constitution

SOMETIME in the late summer of 1863, an African American man in New Orleans sat down with pen and ink, a few blank sheets of paper, and a copy of the U.S. Constitution. Born a slave, he had lived to witness the outbreak of the Civil War and Abraham Lincoln's historic Emancipation Proclamation—and to realize that freedom from slavery might not lead to racial justice. Through good fortune or force of will he had learned to write, but his misspelled words and strained sentences scantly reflected his intellect. Now, taking up his pen to write about the revolution unfolding around him, for page after page he mingled his own prose—in fine penmanship but faltering spelling and syntax—with passages impeccably copied from the nation's founding document.

As he filled blank sheets of paper with his fiery, disjointed treatise and then displayed the manuscript on a city street, he engaged in more than an act of writing. It was an act of learning: by transcribing excerpts from a printed document, he taught himself new vocabulary and practiced his penmanship. It was an act of protest: in his commentary on quotations from the Constitution, he chastised the government and argued for black civil rights. It was an act of invention and discovery: as he slowly strung sentences together, he struck upon new ideas and came to see himself in a new light. When he began expressing himself to an imagined audience and resolved to post his writings in a public place, it became an act of publishing. And when he adopted the pronoun *we*—an echo of "We the people," transcribed from the Constitution's first line to the top of his own blank page—he engaged in an act of political representation: he defined a community and dared to speak on its behalf. He signed his name "A Colored man," and what he had created was a new kind of constitution. Though many were its implications, all sprang from what was a daunting and laborious but exhilarating undertaking: to translate one's thoughts into words and write them down. His constitution epitomizes the way ordinary African Americans constituted their post-emancipation identity with pen on paper.

This book is about acts of writing by enslaved and newly freed southern blacks during the era of emancipation—a neglected episode in the history of African American writing and of American culture more broadly, as well as a crucial dimension of the history of slavery and emancipation. It tells the stories of writers most people have never heard of, because none of them became a professional author or played a leading role in the events of the time. Their names include "A Colored man," Maria Perkins, John M. Washington, William B. Gould, Abram Mercherson, Martha Glover, Garland H. White, and Peter Johnston. They were ordinary people who suffered the gravest injustice, and lived through the most dramatic social revolution, in American history: they were born into bondage in the antebellum South, and most of them took advantage of the upheavals of the Civil War to secure their freedom.

Somewhere along the way, they learned to write, but none received more than fragments of education. All struggled, to one degree or another, to do something a majority of white Americans at the time could take for granted. A Colored Man could read and write far more ably than the majority of southern blacks, yet his fledgling literacy sometimes proved barely sufficient to articulate his ideas. Few readers can effortlessly apprehend that this string of words—"the tel lies Sometimes and So dos all negro traders the get Drunk and lawiers and merchants"—asserts that some of the most common criticisms of black people were equally true of whites. Elsewhere the sense of A Colored Man's argument travels with striking clarity through his lapses in spelling and punctuation, as when he indicts the Union forces occupying southern Louisiana for treating black soldiers little better than rebel planters had treated them as slaves: "it is retten that a man can not Serve two masters But it seems that the Collored population has got two a reble master and a union master the both want our Servises one wants us to make Cotton and Sugar And the sell it and keep the money the union masters wants us to fight the battles under white officers and the injoy both money and the union." Whether he experienced his command of written English as fluent or slight, he recognized a difference between the words he wrote and those he copied from the Constitution, and he concluded his text by saying, "i am Sory that I am not able to write good."[1]

Nearly all the quotations in this book display such irregularities, and many of the writers were likewise moved to apologize for them. Misspelling and erratic punctuation are hardly the most meaningful bonds among these writers, though. After all, nineteenth-century manuscripts show that spelling remained unstandardized for writers of all social classes, and not many white Americans were educated enough to write as well as, say, James Madison.[2] For enslaved people, though, acquiring literacy usually entailed secrecy and subversion; it involved the haphazard lessons of individual initiative or, at best, an untrained teacher; and it rarely could be accomplished before adulthood, if it ever was fully accomplished at all. For those newly freed, learning how to write symbolized the end of their enslavement, but it also was a dizzyingly new part of their venture into an uncertain era. Virtually all who are reading this book learned to write in childhood and write during the normal course of their daily lives. They may not find the work of writing effortless, but they probably experience little anxiety about whether they are doing it right; they do not regularly stop to ask someone how to spell a word. Consider, though, the experience of public speaking for someone who almost never does it, of using a new piece of computer software, or boarding the subway in a foreign city. To do something new, or something one knows other people can do better or more easily, provokes a particular kind of worry and self-scrutiny, as well as a negotiation between originality and emulation.

Everyone learning to write has already learned to read; has seen how other people write; can, and often must, take from other texts cues both technical and substantive. For A Colored Man, the Constitution's sentences served as his copybook, and its meaning as his primer on political reality. By writing out the clause in Article II that begins, "the president Shall be commander in chief of the Army and navy of the united States," he taught himself to spell "president"; to that person he then directed this blunt demand: "Declare freedom at onc and give us Somting to fight for." Blacks all over the South were finding their own ways to mount resistance, weaken the institution of slavery, and seize freedom, but A Colored Man, dismayed by the racist abuses he was witnessing, believed the ultimate remedy must come from the president, the man in whom the Constitution invested the power to let black men fight their battle in uniform.

For A Colored Man, as for thousands of literate slaves and freed people, learning to read and write represented perhaps the greatest accomplishment of his life, and the *trait* of literacy symbolized his freedom. But the *practices* of literacy, for him as for any neoliterate person, were challenging and arduous. A Colored Man read the Constitution in his own way, finding in it meanings that not every reader would find, but it was in his act of writing that he had to negotiate between others' words and his own. Writing unleashed his mind, but it also compelled him to adapt his thinking to the forms and ideas already in use. It provided a means to explore the meaning of freedom, including the extent to which freedom might be bounded, contingent, and—all too often in post-emancipation America—illusory.

The writers and texts in this book merit attention not for the reasons historical figures or works of literature usually do. The texts are distinguished by neither their aesthetic accomplishments nor their cultural influence. By most accepted standards, they are not especially well written, and some are barely intelligible. Most of them remained unread during their author's lifetime and long after. The writers' experiences are not necessarily representative of broader social realities; about some, little is known beyond the scant details gleaned from a single surviving letter. But where this book's subjects stray outside certain conventional boundaries of the academic disciplines of literature and history, they converge on ground common to both. Literary scholarship seeks in large part to understand how meaning is created out of written language—but confines itself to the works of highly literate people. Historical research examines more capacious bodies of texts, including the writings of less-educated people—but looks primarily at the evidence such artifacts harbor about past events, rather than at how the texts were written. By applying methods of literary analysis to documents that previously have been regarded as a regrettably small data set, rather than as a genre of intellectual creation, I propose to broaden literary studies (to manuscripts in addition to printed works, marginally literate writers in

addition to the well-educated) and inspire new modes of interpreting historical sources.[3]

During the era of emancipation in the United States, when many thousands of literate slaves could begin writing openly and many thousands
more who had been denied literacy suddenly gained access to education,
the production of a written text, no matter what information it contained,
was itself a historic event. The manner in which an enslaved or newly freed
person expressed herself—the words she chose, her figures of speech, the
models on which she relied (polite letters? newspaper columns? the U.S.
Constitution?)—formed a key part of her transition from slavery to freedom. The countless accumulated hours former slaves spent seated at tables
composing their thoughts, setting pens to paper, generated a written record
of the experience of emancipation. Those hours also constituted a central
part of the experience, as important as the time spent migrating from plantations to Union camps and southern cities, looking for work, being drilled
in army camps, searching for lost family members, sustaining households,
raising children, or organizing religious and political communities. In fact,
acts of writing were integral to many of those activities.

This book, then, presents an intellectual history of a group that by most
accounts had no intellectual history: who were largely illiterate, kept no annals, and whose every move in such directions was brutally suppressed—
until the destruction of slavery supposedly released them to begin climbing
from primitive ignorance up toward literate civilization. In fact, there *were*
letters being sent, chronicles being kept, and art being made by American
slaves, beneath the South's repressive surface. And so it was that, in the
openings created by the Civil War, enslaved African Americans began writing
prolifically, revealing a culture of letters they had nurtured largely in secret.
The postbellum flourishing of African American culture and politics—a
rising class of professional black authors, a distinctive literary tradition, and
a tenacious, century-long struggle for civil rights—began well before the
dust of the war and Reconstruction had settled. As much as in the well-
known fugitive slave narratives published in the antebellum North, African
American literature had its prelude in the manuscripts of southern slaves
and freed people, in their unpracticed acts of writing.[4]

The story their writings tell is often hard to read. Only a fraction of what
they wrote has been preserved, and much of what does survive is misspelled, barely legible, or stripped of context. A Colored Man, whose name

probably will never be known, may have written much more than his seven-page "Constitution," but that document alone was found "in the public Street" by a New Orleans police officer, turned over to authorities at the local military headquarters, filed away in U.S. Army records, and consequently preserved in the National Archives. Such serpentine tales of provenance hint that writing was more prevalent among slaves and freed people than the quantity of extant documents suggests. If this text survived only through such a sequence of contingencies, imagine how many must have disappeared somewhere along the way—written but not finished, finished but not posted, posted but not taken, taken but not kept.

Those contingencies also make it necessary to acknowledge that the known corpus of writing by marginally literate freed people necessarily has certain slants and partialities. Some of the sources included in this study were held privately, passed down through generations of black families, but most were preserved by white people or institutions run by them—which is to say, most of them exist today because they were addressed to white audiences or otherwise fell into their hands. Intimate letters between individual slaves are much rarer in the archives than they would have been in enslaved people's lives. Some of the sources here come from local repositories, but most of them were preserved in a centralized national archive. In one way or another, they entered the province of the federal government's official business. Many of them did so inadvertently: A Colored Man's treatise because it was confiscated; various private letters between family members because they were turned over to military or governmental authorities. But the complete body of writings by ordinary freed people nevertheless over-represents written interactions with white authority figures.

One important corollary of these texts' public and national slant is that most were written by men. The relative paucity of writings by enslaved women and freedwomen reflects several historical realities. Enslaved men may have acquired literacy with somewhat greater frequency than women. Some wealthy slaveholders, for instance, found it convenient for male slaves who served as labor foremen to learn to read and write so they could keep accounts and send reports from outlying plantations. And freedmen who enlisted in the Union army definitely enjoyed greater opportunities for education than women. It would be a mistake, though, to suppose that women engaged in acts of writing as infrequently as surviving records suggest. Enslaved women who labored in domestic settings were among those most likely to receive instruction from philanthropically minded owners. In the paradigmatic instance, a white southern woman would regard it as her Christian duty to enlighten the black woman who was her maidservant and daily companion.[5] Many enslaved mothers then passed on surreptitiously acquired literacy to their children. Since they were the anchors of families that had been strained by slave trading, many women had particular need for the ability to bridge physical distance by writing letters. But the gender biases of nineteenth-century America at large, as well as of many African American communities, tended to discourage women's writing except for familial and otherwise private purposes. Even women who had managed to become literate while enslaved faced cultural strictures after emancipation. Sending a letter to a white official on a matter of business—producing the kind of text most likely to be preserved in an archive—was widely considered, regardless of race, the task of a man.

Despite its limitations, the trove of writings in this book, read carefully, reveals a rich and complex narrative of emancipation, a distinctive account of the experiences of the people emancipation affected most. A trend toward public engagement and national consciousness is not just an effect of archiving. As the chapters that follow will show, the transformations wrought by the Civil War not only allowed blacks' written literacy to emerge from hiding but also prompted African Americans to begin using writing to imagine new and more national forms of community, even in private journals and letters. At the same time, southern blacks' acts of writing, including those composed in a formal voice for an official audience, display an unfaltering preoccupation with the bonds of family. They betray staggering emotional anguish alongside celebrations of freedom. Women and children also occupy a more central role in the story than the volume of their surviving writings would indicate. In all, the texts included here represent emancipation as not only the end of slavery but also a profoundly complicated new challenge, the close of a horrific era as well as the inception of a new odyssey of struggle.[6]

We enter the relatively unknown world of enslaved people's writings through the gateway of nineteenth-century America's more familiar literary and political culture. Chapter 1 explores what white Americans, northern and southern, thought they knew about literacy among the slaves, as well the published slave narratives that heretofore have been the principal examples of "slaves' writings" (even though all were written by fugitives dwelling in the North). Through the sympathetic yet surprised eyes of Harriet Beecher Stowe, we look at our first manuscript: a barely legible plea for help from a marginally literate slave named Thomas Ducket, who had been sold away from his family to Louisiana. Such acts of writing could expose, reshape, and intensify the largely hidden affective experiences of literate slaves. An enslaved potter in South Carolina named Dave illustrates the tedium of forced labor in the short poems he etched into clay jars. And a Virginia slave named Maria Perkins—the focal point of Chapter 2—writes a letter to her distant husband in which she struggles to come to terms with the destruction of her family by the domestic slave trade.

Other enslaved people's solitary processes of composition came into greater contact with an outside world of inherited ideas about the uses of writing—including how to write the story of one's own life. In Chapter 3, Adam Plummer keeps a log of his daily life and makes a few, mostly abortive attempts to assemble details into a coherent narrative. John M. Washington fashions successive, differently inflected autobiographies, ranging from a diary he kept while a slave in Fredericksburg, Virginia, to an autobiography he began writing (through a process of revising his diary entries) while hired out in Richmond, to a full-fledged memoir composed after he had become free and moved to Washington, D.C. Washington's successive life narratives—two written prior to his emancipation, one after—represent the only surviving texts, so far discovered, written by the same individual both while enslaved and while free. As he practiced different ways of narrating his life on either side of that momentous boundary, Washington drew upon shifting rhetorical and structural models—first the romantic fiction of popular culture, later the established conventions of the slave narrative genre.

For Perkins, Plummer, and Washington, family life dominated their sense of identity, and their writings revolved around children and spouses, either as audiences or subjects. As slaves' flight from their owners accelerated during the Civil War, and emancipation became an undeniable revolution, the social and political worlds of southern blacks widened—and so did their uses for writing. Concerns for intimate bonds, especially families, never faded from the foreground of their attention, but they increasingly found themselves part of the larger drama of wartime emancipation, and thus of a community of nearly four million others. The role of literacy in forging new affiliations among freed people, as well as the ways writing could shape communal identity, occupy Chapter 4. In a journal he kept while a sailor in the Union navy after escaping from slavery in 1862, William B. Gould experimented with pronouns singular and plural, with ways of chronicling both individual and collective experience. As the pages of his journal filled and his knowledge of life as a freedman expanded, Gould's written representations of racial and interracial communities shifted from portraying his optimism about a new beginning toward voicing worry about the plight of African Americans in the reconstructed United States.

Across the Union-occupied South during and after the war, enslaved people were receiving mixed first impressions of freedom as they escaped the subjugation of owners and found themselves under the authority of the Union army and the federal government. They wrote letters trying to sway that authority toward addressing their most pressing concerns. The words from their pens now could travel all the way from Florida or Texas to Washington, D.C. As Chapter 5 reveals, these writers entered an unfamiliar realm characterized by a new group of people (northerners), arcane protocols, and numerous apparent hypocrisies in federal policy. Hundreds of African American men, especially soldiers, tried out the forms of the business letter or the petition and practiced the rhetoric of political protest. They wrote to military officials and political leaders, laying claim to civil rights, seeking aid for their families and communities. For black women, who were denied much of the opportunity and protection the military afforded to freedmen, written petitioning faced obstacles formidable but not insurmountable, as the ingenuity of a literate Missouri slave named Martha Glover demonstrates.

As the dismantling of slavery became an accomplished fact, southern blacks confronted profound uncertainties about their future. Although some envisioned freedom as a life apart from white people, either in colonies abroad or in largely separate communities within the South, the vast majority knew that race relations in the United States were entering a new phase—a more equal phase, they hoped, but possibly only subtler in its injustices. There were some reasons to expect sympathy and stewardship from northern whites and from the federal government, but evidence soon abounded that an abolitionist could also be a racist, that the most well reasoned and carefully written petitions could be met with indifference. If one thing was certain, it was that white society did much of its business in writing, and securing a place in the postwar United States would require navigating a world replete with texts. Chapter 6 examines cross-racial alliances transacted on paper, as well as the complex politics of race and class that followed the spread of black literacy, by focusing on the writing career of a former slave and army chaplain named Garland H. White. Between 1862 and 1866, White produced a few dozen compositions, including letters to white politicians, letters to the editor of a newspaper, reports for the military bureaucracy, and narrative descriptions of his regiment's wartime experience. Though an anomalous figure in African American history, White's manifold efforts to integrate into America's literate culture provide a sweeping view of how the act of writing might catalyze—but also sharply delimit—a former slave's vision of freedom at the dawn of Reconstruction.

This book concludes by contemplating the impact on American culture of former slaves' entry into literate society. In two case studies of the reception of freedmen's letters by white readers, the concluding chapter takes up the elusive matter of influence—the way Peter Johnston imparted his own vision of freedom to one white teacher from New England, for example, and the way a letter from Jordan Johnson chastened another. In the same way that Chapter 1 enters the domain of freed people's writings through the portal of relatively mainstream publications, the conclusion leads back out—with a glance at white writers in the late 1860s, including Louisa May Alcott and Rebecca Harding Davis—into a culture transformed. Slaves had become citizens under the Constitution and now could claim a place in the citizenry of letters.

For all the writers studied here, emancipation and the ability to write were somehow connected. One made the other possible, or both came within reach simultaneously. Each of them could spark a great transformation, and each could progress with frustrating slowness. To understand the complexities of the work by these little-known writers, we must first consider the central terms of this book's subtitle: *emancipation* and *writing*. Their historical meanings, and our current understanding of them, frame what *Word by Word* has to say about newly emancipated writers and their significance to American history and literature.

Emancipation did not happen all at once. Even the decisive stroke of the Emancipation Proclamation was months in the making. Abraham Lincoln confided to his cabinet in the summer of 1862 that he wished to issue an executive order of emancipation; he released the preliminary Emancipation

Proclamation on September 22, announcing his intention to issue an actual proclamation to the same effect one hundred days later, provided the rebel South did not lay down its arms in the meantime; and on January 1, 1863, he officially transformed the Union army into a force for slave liberation. When New Year's Day arrived at Tremont Temple in Boston, where New England's abolitionist luminaries gathered, and in the open air of Port Royal, South Carolina, where former slaves celebrated the "day of jubilee" in a Union camp, the ticking of the clock and the turning of the calendar seemed to change the world. But that moment was the epilogue not only to months of orchestration in the Lincoln White House but also to decades of political change across the United States. And it was the mere prologue for hundreds of thousands of African Americans enslaved in border states or deep in the Confederacy, where they would wait up to two and half more years to realize their nominal freedom.[7]

The long process of emancipation dates at least to the aftermath of the American Revolution, when New England states began legislating against slavery, if not to the very first time a North American slave ran away. It continued apace in the antebellum North even while southern states were solidifying a repressive slaveholding regime. The North's gradualist abolition laws left small numbers of African Americans in bondage until the mid-nineteenth century (Connecticut did not pass a measure of complete abolition until 1848), and although the North came to symbolize freedom and the South slavery, the idea of emancipation worried most white residents of both regions. When Alexis de Tocqueville toured the United States in the early 1830s, he observed with discernment and clairvoyance that "the prejudice against Negroes seems to increase in proportion to their emancipation, and inequality is enshrined in mores as it disappears from laws." Northerners may not have wished to have slaves in their midst, but they generally did not want free blacks living among them either; emancipation in their own states was necessary but not always cause for celebration. About the prospect of emancipation in the South they were likewise ambivalent. If northerners grew to dislike the southern system of slavery, most of them also feared the possibility that millions of African Americans, if liberated, would come to the North. Among southerners, for whom the institution had become the very foundation of their society, emancipation was virtually unthinkable, a practical synonym for violent insurrection and the collapse of civilization.[8]

Many southern slaves therefore rightfully doubted that their freedom would be handed down from white politicians. They would have to seize it however they could. Through numerous acts of resistance, even small and subtle ones, they had pushed and pulled at the conditions of their enslavement for years, and as the Civil War approached they foresaw a wider field for their campaign to become free. According to some historians, the federal government and its army simply created fertile conditions for a vast slave rebellion. By their very numbers, the thousands of enslaved people who made their way behind Union lines forced military officials to adjust their prosecution of the war, influenced Congress and the White House, and, in time, opened virtually all Americans' eyes to the reality that, barring Confederate victory, slavery was in its death throes.[9]

Like the federal policy of emancipation, the grass-roots revolution was slow in unfolding. Not all slaves had the same opportunities to emancipate themselves. In some areas of the border states that did not secede, little changed until the conclusion of the war. Deep in the southern interior, Union forces never disrupted the plantation order to the point that enslaved people could hope to survive an escape attempt. In those places, slaves suffered not only continued bondage but also the same privation their owners faced as the war dragged on. In parts of the South where the Yankees did provide a haven for "contrabands," African Americans ventured into the uncharted territory of life after slavery with their status ambiguous, their treatment by the military inconsistent and often unfair, their entire existence an experiment in which they had little say.

Despite what many white Americans have preferred to think, most enslaved people could not celebrate a single, decisive moment of emancipation. For northern magazine readers, Thomas Wentworth Higginson, the abolitionist commander of some of the war's first black soldiers, narrated jubilant scenes of liberation along southern riverbanks. Scanning the horizon of rice fields along the banks of southern rivers, he saw them "become alive with human heads" as scores of slaves emerged from every direction, ran toward the Union gunboats, and greeted their liberators, Higginson recalled, "as if we had been Cortez and Columbus." Surely the people emancipated on that day never forgot it, but what lay ahead for them, and for the many slaves whose freedom arrived less dramatically, mostly went unrecorded by white northern writers. Only in retrospect have historians recognized the extent to which emancipation "appears as a saga of persistence rather than change, stagnation rather than progress, the resiliency of an old ruling class rather than the triumph of a new order." At the time, it fell to writers like A Colored Man to dramatize emancipation's complexities—the winding path, fraught with uncertainty and hardship, that southern blacks hoped would lead from slavery to freedom.[10]

When he complained that New Orleans blacks remained in thrall to both "a rebel master and a union master," A Colored Man captured the untenable premise of federal occupation in places exempt from the Emancipation Proclamation. One of those places was Orleans Parish, because it had come under Union control prior to Lincoln's decree. The military government in southern Louisiana needed to enlist black troops but also was supposed to protect the "property rights" of local slaveholders. As a result, white soldiers might be found taking black men out of the city and returning them to their former owners' plantations, while others ventured into the countryside to press rebel planters' slaves into the service of the Union army.[11] The federal "recruiting officers" were "Drawing his Sword over us like we were dogs," A Colored Man wrote. Even when freedmen willingly signed up, in an army that allowed no black officers they faced potential abuse "under white officers which a great part of them has been in the reble army"— men who had converted to Unionism out of expediency and possessed little sympathy with the cause of emancipation. "I heard a federal officer Say," A Colored Man reported, "we will not want any more negro Soldiers go home to your master." In such a turbulent environment, a clear definition of freedom, not to mention freedom itself, seemed maddeningly elusive. With federal policy inconsistent and the attitudes of white soldiers unpredictable, A Colored Man condemned the entire war effort as a hypocrisy: "Before the fall of porthudson the white Preachers told us we were all free as any white man and in Less time than a month after you weare taking us up and puting in the lockups and Cotton presses giving us nothing to eat nor nothing Sleep. By those means you will Soon have the union north."

A Colored Man's attention to the disjunctions between rhetoric and action, between promise and reality, may have been a cause or an effect of his distinctive writing process. As he moved back and forth between the Constitution's text and his own blank page—juxtaposing the nation's ideals with the reality surrounding him, writing his own experience into the law of the land—he found little that lined up. Though possibly unsure how to articulate in his own words the realignments that justice demanded, he could instead realign other people's words to advance a political vision. On the second page of his manuscript, he assembled a collage of found text:

> the Constitution is if any man rebells agains those united States his property Shall be confescated and Slaves declared and henceforth Set free forever when theire is a insurection or rebllion agains these united States the Constitution gives the president of the united States full power to arm as many soldiers of African decent as he deems nescesisary to Surpress the Rebellion and officers Should be black or white According to their abillitys the Colored man Should guard Stations Garisons forts and mand vessels according to his Compasitys

None of what he introduces with the words "the Constitution is" actually is in the Constitution. The ensuing clauses intermix language from multiple other documents, including the 1862 Confiscation Act (which provided for the president "to employ as many persons of African descent as he may deem necessary and proper for the suppression of this rebellion") and the Emancipation Proclamation (which invited freed slaves into the Union army and navy "to garrison forts, positions, stations, and other places, and to man vessels of all sorts"). Those two documents were the most important legal underpinnings of black military service. Given that they appear in misspelled paraphrasings—rather than in perfect verbatim copy, like his excerpts from the Constitution—A Colored Man must have committed these parts of them to memory. After cobbling them together into one declaration and calling them "the Constitution," he returns to the Constitution itself and again transcribes selected passages: "A well regulated militia being necessary to the cecurity of a free State the right of the people to keep and Bear arms Shall not be infringed we are to Support the Constitution but no religious test Shall ever be required as a qualification to Any office or public trust under the united States."

Out of all 142 words in this section, which makes up most of his manuscript's second page, only 5 of them are A Colored Man's own words: "the Constitution is" and "we are." With these emendations as the ligatures, he effectively constructs an argument—a syllogism, to be exact. If the government has declared African Americans free and eligible to bear arms against the Confederacy (as it did in the Militia Act, the Second Confiscation Act, and the Emancipation Proclamation), and if the Second Amendment makes

bearing arms a "right of the people," then African Americans ought to enjoy the same rights as all who are spoken for in the Constitution's thunder-
ing "We the people"—including those rights implied by the last sentence,
excerpted from Article VI. The original sentence reads: "The Senators and
Representatives before mentioned, and the Members of the several State
Legislatures, and all executive and judicial Officers, both of the United States
and of the several States, shall be bound by Oath or Affirmation, to support
this Constitution; but no religious Test shall ever be required." A Colored
Man silently changes the long compound subject of this sentence, replacing
a compendium of those in political power with a simple "we." From fragments of American law, a few of them seemingly inhospitable to his cause,
he fashions a rationale not only for African Americans' citizenship but also
for their eligibility to govern.

In the revolutionary events of the preceding year—the institution of a
federal policy of emancipation, the advent of black military service—A
Colored Man could discern a path toward freedom and racial justice. As
he surveyed the textual landscape of the nation, though, he saw that the
path ran a crooked line—a line his own act of writing could only partially
straighten. Neither self-emancipation nor presidential emancipation alone
could guarantee meaningful freedom to African Americans in the South,
yet the forces of black self-determination and federal policy came together
uneasily. For A Colored Man, as for many of the people included in this
book, life on the margins of emancipation entailed written interactions between those forces, between an emergent community of freed people and
American society as they found it.

Just as *emancipation* denotes a process rather than a discrete moment, the
acquisition of literacy unfolds over time, and often slowly. Just as emancipation could entail uncertainty and oppression as well as confer freedom, the
act of writing can prove to be, for those new to literacy, as arduous and dispir-
iting as it is empowering.

Writing is both a mental process and a material product called a text, and
the text never exactly replicates what has transpired in the mind. Countless
readers and writers have indulged in "the dream of reducing writing to a
transparency"—the fantasy that writing can provide frictionless, unmedi-
ated access to someone's mind or to the truth. One of the authors of the

U.S. Constitution, Gouverneur Morris, believed the document's "unequiv-ocal provisions" should lie beyond interpretation because their written-ness endowed them with unimpeachable clarity—the predecessor myth to the enduring phrase, "right here in black and white." The fact is, text is a me-dium. Like any medium, writing can transmit as well as transform, or even scramble, its messages. Writing neither predetermines what one expresses nor leaves it entirely untouched. As thoughts journey to the written page, they cross the mediating filters of a given language (its vocabulary and its syntax) and a given context (the cultural and personal influences that consti-tute the writer's known and imagined worlds), not to mention the physical conditions under which the process occurs (on a computer in a cubicle, with pencil on the back of an envelope). Written language always is inflected by the spoken word. The sounds of speech, the echoes of conversations, often are visible in written words and phrases. But the act of writing a sentence previously heard or uttered inevitably reshapes it.[12]

Once set down in writing, sentences may not be worded or expressed ex-actly as they would have been had they never made that crossing, yet what happens along the way remains largely mysterious and almost always pri-vate. The solitary practice of translating thought into intelligible verbal form can be done, undone, and redone without anyone else knowing. It is virtually inconceivable that people ever would fill an auditorium to watch someone write—to look on as her words spread out across a large projection screen, as she crosses out or erases some words and replaces them with oth-ers, as she labors toward, perhaps without ever achieving, the articulation of some vision or idea. Not solely because our culture treats writing as a pri-vate activity, though, does the nature of the process remain obscure. The problem of understanding how writing mediates human thought, and to what effect, has proven intractable for centuries. Plato worried that the rise of writing would erode memory and weaken the intellect. Modern inter-preters of ancient Greece have argued that, on the contrary, memorization had fostered conformity but writing allowed individuals to criticize their so-ciety's traditions—that writing in effect made democracy possible.[13] Precisely because writing could extend and standardize human memory, it proved crucial to the rise and administration of nation-states in the ancient world as well as the coalescence of ethnic, religious, and political communities—which could be but certainly were not always democratic. Across centuries and in numerous societies, including the nineteenth-century American

South, social elites tried to maintain their power by withholding literacy from those they wished to marginalize. As a consequence, popular movements often have touted literacy as the lever of social advancement, and many modern thinkers have embraced the attractive position that written literacy represents "the origin of independent, analytic thought."[14]

Most current scholars of literacy find that position overly simplistic. Nothing intrinsic to the ability to write necessarily shields a person from discipline or repression, and there is little empirical evidence that literacy, if unaccompanied by other advantages, translates into social or economic gain. It is neither the technology of writing nor the possession of the skill that chiefly shapes the role written literacy plays in private or political life. It is, rather, the context in which writing is practiced, and such contexts, both individual and cultural, are innumerable. Some cultures value written expression for its originality, others for its faultless imitation of tradition. One student may experience learning to write as inspiring while another in the same classroom finds it exasperating. Written literacy may be instrumental to one poor craftsman's upward social mobility but ineffectual for another.[15]

While historians, linguists, and anthropologists, among others, may study the outward limits of written literacy, the interior limits—"the mysteries that often baffle or block us when we try to write," as a leading theorist of composition pedagogy puts it—are more resistant to investigation. Neuroscientists in Japan used functional magnetic resonance imaging to detect the brain regions activated by writing the two different scripts of the Japanese language. European researchers have tried to pinpoint the neurophysiological differences between handwriting and typing. Manufacturers of a pen that allows students to take notes while recording their teacher's voice relied on research in the cognitive process of written note-taking. A psychology experiment demonstrated that students got higher test scores when they wrote about their anxieties immediately before taking the test. Other research found that students writing an essay about a Van Gogh painting used different language depending on the computer interface they used to view the painting.[16]

Science surely has more yet to reveal about the mysteries of written literacy's cognitive workings, but it may never yield a complete understanding. Our frequent reliance on physical language to describe writing—*grabbing* our pencils, *sitting down* to write, *filling up* or *cranking out* pages—compensates for our incomprehension of the inward process. What happens during a person's individual act of writing—awakenings and demurrals, redoubled avowals and changes of heart, inventions fanciful, ingenious, and pedestrian—can neither be predicted by theory nor fully explained by context. Some irreducible element of thinking's transformation into words remains accessible only, if at all, through the artifact of the process: the text.

The known context of the nineteenth-century United States therefore takes us only a fraction of the distance toward understanding freed people's acts of writing, and even that context, despite its historical specificity, exhibits many of the same tensions and ambiguities as the theory. The culture of writing in the antebellum and Civil War–era United States was characterized by theoretical commitments to standardization, even as writers persisted in their tendencies toward invention and idiosyncrasy. Noah Webster famously tried to rationalize spelling at the end of the eighteenth century; the Spencerian system of penmanship endeavored to do the same for handwriting in the middle of the nineteenth. Formal education valued adherence to norms over individual distinction. Supporters of public schooling advocated literacy as the foundation of citizenship in a republic, but early American education, as one modern scholar concludes, "did not encourage students to create their own possibilities as much as it enumerated and defined those possibilities." Like education in most contexts, it served "as the induction of the young into the dominant literate practices of the larger society." At its most basic level, learning to write in the nineteenth-century United States entailed rigid physical discipline—carefully controlled arm movements, a precisely defined posture, perfect positioning of the pen in the hand.[17]

The cultural elite's aspirations for systematic literacy and writing pedagogy, though, never more than thinly concealed the fundamentally idiosyncratic nature of manuscript writing. Webster's orthography spawned as much anxiety as uniformity. No less a writer than Herman Melville, who lacked much formal instruction, frequently vented frustration as he strained for the "right" spelling of a word ("how the devel do you spell it?" he would exclaim in letters). John Quincy Adams thought he could tarnish Andrew Jackson's reputation by revealing that Jackson was a poor speller. Ideals of penmanship were observed mostly in the void, although writing students labored to achieve them, and women and men were instructed to hew to different models. At the ground level, writing happened in innumerable, scarcely predictable ways. Ordinary American readers wrote in the margins and flyleaves of their books. During the Civil War, consumers could purchase battlefield maps that came with red and blue pencils for adding their own updates and annotations as the war raged on. Many people who could not write, or were not encouraged to write, nevertheless found ways to produce original texts. Women and children, especially, created books of their own by cutting out and inventively rearranging snippets of magazines and newspapers. Until Congress lowered postal rates in the 1840s, Americans who could not afford to send letters took advantage of the cheaper rates for mailing newspapers and scribbled notes to loved ones in the papers' blank spaces, or even blacked out individual letters in the printed articles so that what remained visible conveyed their message.[18]

No people were more estranged from the formal culture of literacy, or more driven to improvisation, than those enslaved in the South. Under penalty of law in most places, and of white hostility virtually everywhere, southern blacks were not supposed to learn to read or write. Nevertheless, many of them did, and when they did they entered a realm dominated by white people. The materials of their tutelage, from purloined schoolbooks to the U.S. Constitution, could be as culturally alien and politically inhospitable as they were practically useful. For many slaves, and for the small number of southern whites who condoned or even encouraged black literacy prior to emancipation, literacy (mainly reading) served principally to provide access to the Bible, which countless southern whites held up as a justification for the system of slavery itself.[19]

Breaking through any of these bounds therefore could represent a political act of resistance and provide a tool for self-emancipation, exemplified by the forging of a pass that might allow a slave to escape. Frederick Douglass—after cunningly learning to read and write in slavery, fleeing to the North, starting an abolitionist newspaper in Rochester, New York, and becoming a highly accomplished writer—could in hindsight call his literacy "the direct pathway from slavery to freedom."[20] For many years the study of African American literature and history has focused on this relationship between literacy and liberation. Numerous scholars have advanced the view that, as Henry Louis Gates, Jr., has put it, "In literacy lay true freedom for the black slave," or, in another scholar's more ardent language, that "for the slaves, literacy was more than a symbol of freedom; it *was* freedom. It affirmed their humanity, their personhood. To be able to read and write was an intrinsic good, as well as a mighty weapon in the slave's struggle for freedom."[21]

But most slaves, even most literate ones, never escaped, never had a realistic hope of escaping, and never achieved Douglass's fluency with the written word. For those who remained enslaved or gained only the provisional freedom that came with wartime emancipation, forging passes might hold less appeal than communicating with family members. For the writers to whom this book is devoted, attending to practical and emotional immediacies often preceded the demonstration of their personhood to white audiences. The act of writing, though it brought them a sense of power unattainable while they were illiterate, could prove laborious and daunting. The widely accepted literacy-as-liberation thesis tends to neglect the multiplicities of literacy itself—reading and writing, not to mention innumerable degrees of proficiency and contexts of acquisition—as well as the complexities of how liberation occurred for most enslaved Americans.[22]

This book focuses on writing (occasionally using the shorthand "literacy" to refer to this single component of a larger set of skills) in part simply because the act of writing leaves visible traces. Many scholars have been rightfully circumspect about privileging historical evidence that comes in the form of textual records. Documents capture only a portion of lived experience and usually overrepresent the experiences of powerful, well-educated people. For precisely that reason, a key strain of African American studies has resisted a common presumption that written texts represent the height of expressive culture or the most reliable form of evidence. Studies of nineteenth-century African American oral culture have incalculably deepened our understanding of slavery and emancipation by recovering what was ignored or dismissed by most white Americans of the time, as well as most historians well into the twentieth century.[23]

The realm of oral expression does not exist entirely apart from writing, though. As one scholar of literacy has observed, "When men learn to write they do not then forget how to speak." To study the writings of slaves and freed people is not to exclude oral culture, for acts of writing constantly overlap with acts of speaking. A freedman in the army asks a comrade how to spell a word he wishes to write. An enslaved woman's letter to her husband makes a veiled allusion to a conversation they had before they were separated. A literate petitioner writes down the grievances voiced by the less literate people gathered around him. Numerous times in the pages that follow, we will observe writers mingling words they said and heard, ones they thought and read. And in their capacity to record interior experience, if only as one track among several, written texts do offer something irreplaceable.[24]

The layers of provenance and meaning in the primary texts examined here—expressions of feeling, imitated phrases, aftereffects of conversations—are precisely what require the kind of attention works of literature typically receive. Indeed, that layering is the most important reason for this book's focus on the act of writing, which always involves a convergence of voices, a mixture of conformity and originality, a balance of structure and play. In its theoretical dimensions and in nineteenth-century American culture at large, but to an unparalleled degree among enslaved and newly freed people, writing encompasses both a submission to norms and the assertion of new meanings. It can entail adopting the words of the Constitution and also reinterpreting them.[25] Even one of the most powerful conjunctions of literacy and freedom—the moment at which a former slave, long denied the dignity of a surname, writes his or her own full name—might be overseen and mediated by a wartime bureaucrat recording that name on a government form. In short, writing harbors within it a tension between freedom and bondage. It can be freeing, and it can also frustrate and constrain.[26]

If literacy did not always and everywhere translate into liberation for American slaves, the act of writing could spark new conceptions of one's self and one's freedom—sometimes despite, sometimes precisely because of, a writer's struggle to express himself on the page. The writers in this book, whom I categorize as "marginally literate" or "neoliterate," were not necessarily handicapped in their expressive abilities.[27] Some of them could barely write intelligible sentences, but several had an impressive vocabulary, elegant penmanship, and a distinct writerly flair. In all cases, their literacy remained a work in progress. For good and ill, they received a more or less ad hoc education, bypassing the formal schooling that might have not only endowed them with greater technical skill but also initiated them into a system of protocols, genres, and idioms—into ways of seeing the world. Their writings are peculiarly revealing precisely insofar as they are peculiarly difficult to read.

No matter how revealing, of course, these writings cannot reanimate their authors. Many times in the chapters to come, I endeavor to reconstruct an enslaved or newly emancipated person's thoughts and feelings based on a brief manuscript—a difficult and complicated undertaking, to say the least, and one in which I suffer from at least a few personal limitations. In this regard, my own act of writing is a nearly impossible one. But if it may, even a little, enrich our knowledge of an elusive history—a history of loss, hiding, and near silence—it is worth undertaking.[28]

A Colored Man, during the course of composing his constitution, made two separate tries at narrating an anecdote from his recent experience. On one page, in the midst of an account of racism among Union officers, he writes, "i my Self went to ª union lawyer on Some Buiness the first question are you free or slave." On a different page, he writes an expanded version of the same conversation: "I heard one of most Ables and distinhgush lawiers Say that the Colored population was all free and Had as much liberty in the union as he had in four or five days after I went to him to get him to atend Some business for me he Said to me Are you free or Slave Sir Said i am free By your own speeches was you born free no Sir Said i we have been made fools of from the time Butlers fleet landed hear but I have remained At my old Stand and will untill i See what i am dowing."

The sequence of these two passages' composition is unclear (A Colored Man numbered only some pages of his constitution). Whichever one he wrote first, his repeated attempt at crafting this small narrative provoked a rethinking. Perhaps he could not find a way, the first time around, to describe his tense and probably infuriating interaction with a lawyer who insisted on knowing whether he ever had been a slave. Even in the fuller version, he barely manages to make the conceptually difficult point that the lawyer proved a hypocrite for asking the question. In this version, A Colored Man resigns himself to claiming only a qualified form of freedom conferred by a white man's authority—"i am free *By your own speeches*." On the other hand, he may have written out the conversation first and then decided to redact it, in its second iteration, as he became more mindful of his public audience (the abbreviated anecdote appears in a section of the constitution written on two letter folios collated to resemble a small book or pamphlet). His interview with the lawyer having taught him that his formerly enslaved status would be held against him—as it was in federal pay rates for black soldiers—he may have decided to stop avowing it and focus only on the fact that the question was put to him.

Either way—and no matter that A Colored Man was unable to create a literary autobiography akin to Frederick Douglass's—his act of writing catalyzed an inward reckoning with his identity and experience. "Free or slave" remained an open question for countless African Americans in occupied Louisiana, and—perhaps more profoundly than he realized when he sat down and began to write—it persisted as a frustrating uncertainty for A Colored Man himself. Having listened to speeches, read the Constitution, witnessed the arrival of the Yankees, half-memorized the Emancipation Proclamation, and woven all that accumulated knowledge into an argument for black equality, he still confronted ambiguities about what freedom was and whether he could possess it except by the authority of other people's words—the Constitution's, the lawyer's. The very form of the document he produced, half his own and half not, exemplifies the central tensions of both emancipation and the act of writing. Freedom is not the total absence of constraint or peril; the written word is no perfect translation of original thought. For countless enslaved Americans, becoming free happily involved learning to read and write. It also involved—as did reading and writing themselves—coming face to face, like A Colored Man in the lawyer's office, with a culture not of their own making.

African American literature arguably always has revolved around such confrontations—of a community and its members defining themselves against the prevailing headwinds of white society's other definitions, navigating between assimilation and protest.[29] The known history of African American writing, though, is predominantly a history of publishing. The texts modern readers know and college students study are those that made their way into print—whether by dint of a slaveholder's patronage (as in the case of the pioneering black poet Phillis Wheatley), through the support of an abolitionist organization (as with Frederick Douglass's first autobiography), or with an author's own meager financing (William Grimes arranged for the publication of two editions of his slave narrative). Whether one locates the origins of African American literature in its earliest major works, in the genre of the fugitive slave narrative, or in the broader "discursive worlds" in which black voices first resonated, the literature in question consists of printed works.[30]

The chapters that follow turn our attention to the manuscript writings of marginally literate African Americans who were enslaved, not because such texts are less mediated or somehow more authentic than published works, but because their authors had different, hitherto unaccounted experiences of both emancipation and the act of writing. In the work of their hands is registered an inner experience of mass emancipation, much different from the solo flights toward the North Star that excited readers of published slave narratives. Most ordinary African Americans in the South, even those who had learned to write, could not pinpoint, and had no literary aspiration to portray, a dramatic moment of jubilee. Living amid profound uncertainty, the men and women we are about to meet used writing to pursue, doggedly if not always successfully, some modicum of justice; some security for themselves and their families; some deeper understanding of themselves and their world.

chapter one

Black Literacy in the White Mind

THOMAS DUCKET INSISTED he was innocent. After slave catchers seized the schooner *Pearl,* which was carrying seventy-six fugitives down the Potomac River, slaveholders in Washington, D.C., scoured the city for conspirators. Desperate to know who had funded and orchestrated one of the largest escape attempts in the history of American slavery, they interrogated the fugitives, put the ship's captain on trial, and harassed other slaves. Ducket was guilty by association: his wife and children had been captured aboard the *Pearl.* His owner suspected he was among the plotters of the escape, or at least knew who they were, and resolved to sell Ducket to the Deep South—the severest of punishments in the eyes of most enslaved Washingtonians. The accused slave's protests of innocence came to nothing, nor did his single plea: if he must be sold away, might he at least be sold to the same person who purchased his family? Ducket's owner may have openly rejected his request or he may have feigned to honor it, allowing Ducket to depart Washington with false hope of a reunion with his wife and children.[1]

By the time he arrived on a plantation in southern Louisiana, Ducket no longer harbored illusions about his fate. He had indeed suffered what the domestic slave trade portended for most of its victims from the Upper South: consignment to grueling labor and a diminished life expectancy in the Lower South's cotton or sugarcane fields; the near impossibility of escape; and, what Ducket most dreaded, permanent separation from family and friends. In the antebellum American imagination, as in the well-founded fears of millions of slaves, to be sold farther south was to descend into greater suffering, isolation, and enforced ignorance—including illiteracy. As Harriet Beecher Stowe's Uncle Tom was carried down the Mississippi River and away from his family, he found fewer opportunities to practice his reading and writing. In the barbaric domain of Simon Legree, even the marked passages in Tom's own precious Bible no longer reached his "failing eye and weary sense."[2]

Abolitionists regularly denounced white southerners for withholding the light of knowledge from their slaves, but the institution's pall of mental darkness, though nearly overwhelming, was not total. Even on the banks of the lower Mississippi years before emancipation, a slave might take up a pen and write. Thomas Ducket did it on February 18, 1850. Desperate to find his lost family, Ducket wrote a faltering plea to Jacob Bigelow, a white abolitionist back in Washington:

> Mr Begelow dr sir I rit to you to let you no how i am get in a long had times her I have not Had one our to go out sid of the place sence I hav bin on et i put my trust in the lord to halp me I long to hear from you all I ret ten to hear from yo all Mr Begelow i hop yo will not for me you no et was not my falt that I am hear I hop you will nam me to Mr Geden Mr chaplen Mr Baly to healp me out of et I be leve that if Would mak the les move to et that et cod be Don i long to hear from my famaly how the ar Geten a long you will ples to rit to me jest to let me no how the ar Geten a long you can rit to me I re main yous yo umbl servent
>
> *thomas Ducket*
>
> you can Ded rec you let ters to thomas Ducke in car of Mr samul t harisin lusana nar byaGoler of is for God sake let me hear from you all my wife and children ar not out of my mine day nor night[3]

Evidently Ducket was acquainted with Bigelow back in Washington and also was familiar with other opponents of slavery ("Mr Geden Mr chaplen Mr Baly": Jacob Giddings, William Chaplin, and Gamaliel Bailey, each of whom was thought to be implicated in the *Pearl* affair), which may suggest that Ducket indeed was involved with the escape plot. Nevertheless, the injustice of his punishment remains: "you no et was not my falt that I am hear." Exiled to a plantation near Bayou Goula, Louisiana, Ducket is not allowed "one our to go out sid of the place," and his forsaken "wife and children ar not out of [his] mine day nor night."

Whether Ducket found his family, or even received a reply, remains unknown. Only against long odds has his letter even survived. A barely intelligible missive scrawled by an enslaved hand, improbable to begin with, would not have struck many people at the time as an artifact worth preserving, and the original manuscript indeed does not survive. We have Ducket's letter only because Harriet Beecher Stowe wanted her millions of readers to see it. Following vociferous attacks by southerners on *Uncle Tom's Cabin*, the best-selling novel of its time, Stowe undertook to present the reading public with evidence that would validate her novel's representation of slavery. She gathered various sources, ranging from letters to newspaper clippings to legal papers, that provided a glimpse inside the institution, and she published her findings in 1853 as *A Key to Uncle Tom's Cabin; Presenting the Original Facts and Documents upon Which the Story Is Founded, Together with Corroborative Statements Verifying the Truth of the Work*. While she was working on *A Key*, Stowe received additional materials from friends and supporters, including Jacob Bigelow, who passed along the letter he had received from a marginally literate slave.

A text penned by someone still suffering in slavery was scarcely thinkable in the 1850s, and to Stowe, the surprising example that arrived on her desk remained largely unreadable. Intent on conveying Ducket's palpable suffering and the depth of his devotion to his family, Stowe regularized the letter's prose when she transcribed it into a chapter of *A Key*. She added punctuation, corrected spelling, and supplied a few missing words ("I hope you will not forget me" for "i hop yo will not for me," and "if they would make the least move" for "if Would mak the les move"). In addition to making the letter easier to read, though, Stowe insisted on showing just how poorly written it originally was. She took the unusual step of having a reproduction of the handwritten letter published along with her transcription. Convinced that the material document revealed as much as its text, Stowe introduced it with these words: "We give a *fac simile* of Tom's letter, with all its poor spelling, all its ignorance, helplessness, and misery."[4]

not allowed to talk with the other servants, his master fearing a conspiracy. In one of his letters he says, "I have seen more trouble here in one day than I have in all my life." In another, "I would be glad to hear from her [his wife], but I should be more glad to hear of her death than for her to come here."

In his distress, Tom wrote a letter to Mr. Bigelow, of Washington. People who are not in the habit of getting such documents have no idea of them. We give a *fac simile* of Tom's letter, with all its poor spelling, all its ignorance, helplessness, and misery.

Facsimile of Thomas Ducket to Jacob Bigelow, February 18, 1850, from Harriet Beecher Stowe, *A Key to Uncle Tom's Cabin* (Boston: John P. Jewett, 1853), 171–172. Courtesy of the Watkinson Library, Trinity College, Hartford, Connecticut.

long to hear from my famaly
how the ar Geten a long you
will ples to rit to me jest
to let me no how tha ar geten
a long you can rit to me I re
main yours ye until servent

       thomas Ducket

You can Ded ree you let ters
to thomas Duck in car of
Mr sam ul t har is in
lusana nan byagoler of is
for god sake let me hear
from you all my wife and
children ar not out of my
mine day nor night

[February 18, 1852.

MR. BIGELOW. DEAR SIR:— I write to let you know how I am getting along. Hard times here. I have not had one hour to go outside the place since I have been on it. I put my trust in the Lord to help me. I long to hear from you all.

As Stowe implies, Ducket's crooked lines and shaky penmanship testify to the anguish of his enslavement at least as forcefully as the story he tells. His "poor spelling" and "ignorance" are part and parcel of his "misery," and what Stowe finds appalling is not that Ducket has been deprived of literacy but that his literacy has been deformed. In a gruesome counterpoint elsewhere in *A Key to Uncle Tom's Cabin*, Stowe quotes slaveholder Micajah Ricks's 1838 newspaper advertisement seeking the return of his fugitive slave: "Ran away, a negro woman and two children; a few days before she went off, I burnt her with a hot iron, on the left side of her face. I tried to make the letter M." Stowe comments: "It is charming to notice the *naïf* betrayal of literary pride on the part of Mr. Ricks. He did not wish that letter M to be taken as a specimen of what he could do in the way of writing. The creature would not hold still, and he fears the M may be ilegible [*sic*]." Stowe finds that both these texts, the terrible alphabetic wound and Thomas Ducket's labored supplication, have power precisely because they are difficult to read. Arrested literacy shows the suffering and sentiments of the enslaved—the "helplessness" in Thomas Ducket's dual inability to spell or to find his family; the terrified, fierce resistance (she "would not hold still") revealed in the attempted *M* on the runaway's cheek. The written word proves less important for what it says than for what it falls short of saying.[5]

In preparing her compendious documentary account of southern slavery, Stowe encountered evidence of slave literacy that few northerners had ever seen, and that even she found challenging to understand. To most white Americans of the antebellum era, writing by those who were currently enslaved was scarcely conceivable. From a northern perspective, the chances for slaves' writing were buried in the abyss of slavery's brutality or the supposed backwardness of southern culture. For many southerners, the possibility of slave literacy was covered over by their own illusions or their slaves' secrecy. Whether sympathetic or indifferent to the plight of slaves, free Americans before the Civil War knew they were living within a paradox: their society valorized education, abounded in books, and relished the written word, yet it tolerated the legal prohibition of literacy for millions of African Americans. In myriad ineffable ways, that contradiction affected the imagination of writing in the mid-nineteenth-century United States. Unmistakably, it obscured the role writing actually played in the lives of enslaved people, and that obscurity, passed down with the rest of our cultural inheritance from antebellum America, continues to inform our thinking. Most scholars today esteem slaves' literacy as a form of resistance and a means of escape but neglect the ordinary acts of writing—often faltering and agonized—that were part of life in slavery. To begin the process of making those acts intelligible, we first need to unravel the misapprehensions of white observers.[6]

Between 1830 and 1860, the political debate over slavery intensified, with both sides becoming radicalized. By the 1850s, slaveholders and their apologists, once apt to characterize the institution as a necessary evil, now painted an idealized picture of it as a "positive good"—a divinely ordained relation of harmony between benevolent masters and puerile slaves. Meanwhile, abolitionists amplified their condemnations of slaveholders' mendacity and barbarousness. To acknowledge that some slaves enjoyed the limited autonomy necessary to acquire a modicum of literacy, not to mention to commit their thoughts to paper, would have tempered both sides' characterizations. Anti- and pro-slavery forces constructed narratives about literacy that served their political ends better than they represented slaves' experiences.[7]

Ironically, many slaveholders ranked among the nineteenth century's most committed believers in the importance and liberating potential of the ability to write. They tacitly acknowledged a form of racial equality that almost no one else did: if African American slaves acquired literacy, they could be expected to use it more or less as white people did—to communicate with each other and speak their minds. They especially would use it, southerners feared, to rebel or escape. Soon after Frederick Douglass began receiving elementary reading lessons from his white mistress, Sophia Auld, her husband forbade her to continue teaching Douglass, calling it "unsafe." Most significantly, as one reader of Douglass's autobiography points out, Mr. Auld "does not say, as public racist discourse of the period would dictate, that Mrs. Auld's efforts are futile because of Frederick's innate biological inferiority."[8]

In Harriet Beecher Stowe's 1856 novel, *Dred: A Tale of the Great Dismal Swamp,* Anne Clayton, a well-to-do North Carolina woman, teaches her slaves to read and write, in defiance of the laws of her state. When a family friend, Mr. Bradshaw, visits her to discuss the matter, their conversation sketches out two common views of slave literacy. Affecting politeness,

Bradshaw speaks on behalf of worried and angry plantation owners in Clayton's neighborhood:

> "We appreciate your humanity, and your self-denial, and your indulgence to your servants. Everybody is of opinion that it's admirable. You are really quite a model for us all. But, when it comes to teaching them to read and write, Miss Anne," he said, lowering his voice, "I think you don't consider what a dangerous weapon you are putting into their hands. The knowledge will spread on to other plantations; bright niggers will pick it up; for the very fellows who are most dangerous are the very ones who will be sure to learn. . . . You see, Miss Anne, I read a story once of a man who made a cork leg with such wonderful accuracy that it would walk of itself, and when he got it on he couldn't stop its walking—it walked him to death—actually did! Walked him up hill and down dale, till the poor man fell down exhausted; and then it ran off with his body. And it's running with its skeleton to this day, I believe."
>
> And good-natured Mr. Bradshaw conceived such a ridiculous idea, at this stage of his narrative, that he leaned back in his chair and laughed heartily, wiping his perspiring face with a cambric pocket-handkerchief.
>
> "Really, Mr. Bradshaw, it's a very amusing idea, but I don't see the analogy," said Anne.
>
> "Why, don't you see? You begin teaching niggers, and having reading and writing, and all these things, going on, and they begin to open their eyes, and look around and think; and they are having opinions of their own, they won't take yours; and they want to rise directly."[9]

Perhaps Anne Clayton is merely being coy. She may grasp Bradshaw's analogy entirely but refuse to credit the implication that black literacy will "walk" white slaveholders "to death." Perhaps, though, she genuinely does not "see the analogy"—does not understand how black literacy resembles the cork leg. Clayton, like Stowe's sympathetic readers, wants her slaves to know how to read so they can study the Bible and achieve Christian salvation. As she sees it, literacy is not an instrument of rebellion, perhaps not of any kind of autonomy; it serves to integrate readers into a religious community. To conceive of black literacy as a prosthesis with a life of its own is to understand the act of reading and writing as a catalyst of individual development and resistance. Like Mr. Bradshaw, pro-slavery interests recognized—and feared—that possibility. Like Anne Clayton (an anomalous southerner), white northerners were generally unable or unwilling to see it the same way.

In the experience of most abolitionists—most middle-class northerners, in fact—learning to read and write did not foster radicalism. On the contrary, literacy brought children into the fold of Christian belief, taught them morality and manners, and generally helped them assimilate their culture's values. Accordingly, anti-slavery rhetoric tended to decry the forced illiteracy of slaves not because it violated their individual rights but rather because it excluded them from the broader community of Americans and Christians. Only the most extreme abolitionist would have argued that slaves should be granted an education so that they would be empowered to revolt against their masters. Most of slavery's white opponents believed in literacy's more benign advantages.[10]

Most commonly, anti-slavery arguments pointed out that slaves' illiteracy deprived them of access to religious scripture—an appalling fact in a society increasingly dominated by evangelical Protestantism. An abolitionist children's book from the 1840s lists slavery's evils, apparently in ascending order of their outrageousness: "It reduces man to a beast—a thing— defaces the image of God on the mind, takes away the key of knowledge, robs man of the Bible and his soul!" Some northern activists launched a "Bibles for slaves" campaign in the late 1840s, but this effort succeeded only in revealing how divided white northerners were on the subject of black literacy, and how little they contemplated slaves' own perspectives. The American Bible Society, reluctant to become embroiled in the politics of slavery, refused a sizable donation earmarked for providing Bibles to African American families. Meanwhile, some abolitionists objected that slaveholders might actually welcome and exploit the endeavor, pointing out that pro-slavery thinkers already used cherry-picked passages from the Bible to defend their position in public discourse, and now it was proposed to put into slaves' hands the very tools with which slave owners would legitimize their bondage. From a cravenly pragmatic angle, other northern activists worried that, if slaves had access to the Bible, the abolitionist movement would lose a valuable arrow from its quiver of charges against the institution. Frederick Douglass decried the Bibles-for-slaves plan as a cruel mockery, given the widespread illiteracy of slaves; it would be like "throw[ing] a drowning man a dollar," he wrote. Scarcely anyone voiced the conviction that slaves had a right to literacy, or their own uses for it.[11]

Even among strident abolitionists, discussions of slave literacy primarily expressed white northerners' image of their own civilization. One historian sees an "anti-individualistic and restrictive" streak in the anti-slavery movement's conception of freedom, a tendency to stress "social and moral orderliness" as much as liberation. Indeed, for Theodore Dwight Weld, one of the leaders of the American Anti-Slavery Society, the problem with forced illiteracy was that it undermined the rule of law. Weld castigated slaveholders for a "blacker infamy" than Caligula's tyrannical ruses: "They prohibit their slaves acquiring that knowledge of letters which would enable them to read the laws; and if, by stealth, they get it in spite of them, they prohibit them books and papers, and flog them if they are caught at them. Further— Caligula merely hung his laws so high that they could not be read—our slaveholders have hung theirs so high above the slave that they cannot be seen—they are utterly out of sight, and he finds out that they are there only by the falling of the penalties on his head."[12]

However strongly worded, Weld's attack notably takes aim only at the prohibition against reading. Slavery's critics generally were mute on the subject of writing. Virtually no one contemplated equipping African Americans with a skill that was closely related to voting and governance, and not even universally encouraged for white women. Abolitionism and literacy acquisition may have come closest together in a children's book called *The Anti-Slavery Alphabet* ("S is the Sugar, that the slave / Is toiling hard to make, / To put into your pie and tea, / Your candy, and your cake"), yet even this text, expressly designed for white children becoming literate, does not contemplate the possibility that slaves might do the same. "Although quick to point out the ironies in the differences between a monarchy and a democracy, and between an eagle and a slave," one scholar writes, the alphabet book "seems blind to its own irony of advocating literacy to only one group."[13]

Northern outrage at the South's anti-literacy laws often seemed motivated less by concern for slaves than by pride in New England's vaunted culture of education. At the broadest level, anti-slavery agitation doubled as regional evangelism. Not all abolitionists were New Englanders, but in public perception the movement was firmly rooted there, in a region convinced of its "moral and cultural preeminence" and resolved to "imprint its regional values on the nation."[14]

Northerners' comments on slave literacy usually served to dramatize the disparity between literate cultures in the two sections of the country. From their perspective, slaves' inability to read and write was symptomatic of the pandemic ignorance wrought by the South's backward ways, or it was a blight that was infecting white southerners as well. Whereas Stowe's Mr. Bradshaw characterized literacy as a disease that would "spread on to the other plantations," northern critics portrayed the *absence* of literacy as the region's spreading affliction. During the 1850s, numerous writers in the northern press compared literacy statistics for New England and southern states. One anonymous writer jeeringly juxtaposed a southern educator's boast that only 1 in 7 adults in North Carolina was illiterate with the corresponding statistic for Massachusetts: 1 in 446. Another cited similarly divergent figures on school attendance and attributed the disparity to "the paralyzing influence of slavery." After the Civil War broke out, the abolitionist Moncure Conway struck the same note with even greater fervor:

> Virginia received from that Dutch [slave] ship a curse which chained back the blessings which her magnificent resources would have rained upon her, and the sun of knowledge shining everywhere has left her to-day more than eighty thousand white adults who cannot read or write. It was at an early period as manifest as now that a slave population implied and rendered necessary a large poor-white population. . . . It gives but a poor description of the "poor-white trash" to say that they cannot read. The very slaves cannot endure to be classed on their level. They are inconceivably wretched and degraded.[15]

As often as anti-slavery writings lamented the injustice of slaves' illiteracy, they deplored the mental condition of southern whites. Theodore Weld cited unflattering literacy statistics for Virginia, Kentucky, and Georgia, and proclaimed that "a majority of the slaveholders are ignorant men, thousands of them notoriously so, mere boors unable to write their names or to read the alphabet." Stowe devoted a whole chapter of *A Key to Uncle Tom's Cabin* to the subject, titled "Poor White Trash." There, she borrowed from Theodore Parker another litany of statistics on southern illiteracy and concluded, "The institution of slavery has produced not only heathenish, degraded, miserable slaves, but it produces a class of white people who are, by universal admission, more heathenish, degraded, and miserable." A writer in the *New Englander and Yale Review* fulminated in 1845: "The Cimmerian intellectual darkness of the *poor* whites of the slave states, is proverbial.

Compared with it the intellectual condition of the *free negroes* at the North is effulgence itself."[16]

Northern educational materials tacitly disparaged the intellectual condition of the South. A variety of antebellum spelling books, including *Cobb's Spelling Book* and Comly's *New Spelling Book,* both reprinted numerous times during the first half of the nineteenth century, featured lists of "vulgar" pronunciations or "improprieties that occur in common conversation." Though superficially the equivalents of what we would recognize today as guides to commonly misused words, these lists appear to have another agenda, for they decidedly resemble African American and poor southern white dialect. Comly's extensive catalog warns against using, for instance, "acrost" for across, "ax" for ask, "bime by" for by and by, "cotch" for caught, "fust" for first, "hos" for horse, and "nigger" for negro. The list of erroneous spellings includes diacritical marks keyed to a "Scheme of the Vowels" at the front of the book, so that the industrious reader may discover exactly how to pronounce these improprieties—a curious necessity for the student being warned against them. The guide seems to function less as an aid to students than as a work of armchair sociolinguistics, allowing northern readers a glimpse of the pitiable deficiencies in learning elsewhere.[17]

The self-congratulatory statements of white northerners implied that slaves—in fact, all southerners—inhabited a dark age. Even Harriet Beecher Stowe, who listened "more deeply and thoroughly than most other whites of the time . . . to what African Americans had to say about slavery," remained preoccupied with black illiteracy's effects on white southerners.[18] One of the most ubiquitous illustrations for *Uncle Tom's Cabin* depicts the scene in which Tom and Eva sit together in the arbor, reading the Bible. In many versions of this image, Little Eva is shown holding the book (the text says it "lay open on her knee"); almost invariably, she resembles a ministering angel of literacy, enlightening the humble slave.[19] But in a different scene in the novel, a more detailed representation of literacy that never became an iconic image, Stowe shows Eva and Tom as peers, united in their unrealized wishes to write: "Tom's home-yearnings had become so strong, that he had begged a sheet of writing-paper of Eva, and, mustering up all his small stock of literacy attainment acquired by Mas'r George's instructions, he conceived the bold idea of writing a letter; and he was busy now, on his slate, getting out his first draft. Tom was in a good deal of trouble, for the forms of some of the letters he had forgotten entirely; and of what he did remember, he did not know exactly which to use." Eva discovers Tom absorbed in this labor and sympathizes: " 'I wish I could help you, Tom! I've learnt to write some. Last year I could make all the letters, but I'm afraid I've forgotten.' "[20]

The privileged child and enslaved man stand at identical levels of literacy: both have learned to write the alphabet but forgotten much of it. The two collaborate, "and, with a deal of consulting and advising over every word, the composition began, as they both felt very sanguine, to look quite like writing. 'Yes, Uncle Tom, it really begins to look beautiful,' said Eva, gazing delightedly on it." When Augustine St. Clare, Eva's father and Tom's owner, enters the room, he judges their composition differently: " 'I wouldn't discourage either of you,' said St. Clare, 'but I rather think, Tom, you'd better get me to write your letter for you. I'll do it, when I come home from my ride.' " St. Clare may be uncomfortable seeing his daughter engaged in the forbidden activity of helping a slave to write; he may simply find their letter sadly unintelligible. In either case, Tom's dictated letter goes into the mail that evening. The slaveholder takes the task of writing out of the hands of both his wards, the child and the slave.[21]

By the time Stowe wrote her next novel, *Dred,* she had completed *A Key to Uncle Tom's Cabin* and been exposed to such materials as Thomas Ducket's letter. Perhaps as a result, *Dred* featured numerous literate African American characters (Dred, Harry, Milly's deceased son Alfred, and Clayton's slave Dulcimer), as well as a pair of southern slaveholders who willfully violate anti-literacy laws. Nevertheless, the novel remains fixated on the arrested literacy of white slaveholders. Its white heroine, Nina Gordon (who, like Eva, succumbs to an untimely death), repeatedly declares her distaste for books and makes a show of her disregard for letters and paper. Nina throws letters around the room, stores receipts in a bonbon box, and uses a merchant's bill for "for curl-papers."[22] When she tries to orchestrate a private conversation with one of her suitors, Edward Clayton, she leads him to the window of her library:

> The room lay just above the one where they had been sitting, and, like that, opened on to the veranda by long-sashed windows, through which, at the present moment, a flood of moonlight was pouring. A large mahogany writing-table, covered with papers, stood in the middle of the room, and the moon shone in so brightly that the pattern of the bronze inkstand, and the

color of the wafers and sealing-wax, were plainly revealed. The window commanded a splendid view of the river over the distant tree-tops, as it lay shimmering and glittering in the moonlight. "Isn't that a beautiful sight?" said Nina, in a hurried voice.[23]

Nina refers to the shimmering river, but Stowe's description of the scene pays more attention to the writing desk—a physical detail of no narrative purpose, in that it plays no role in the balance of the chapter. Neither Nina nor Edward Clayton refers to the desk or its papers, picks anything up from the desk, or bumps into it on the way out, yet the implications of the idle writing desk inflect their entire conversation. The tools of writing lie neglected in a dark room, illuminated only by moonlight, and Nina's disinclination to write turns out to be central to her romantic troubles. Nina and Clayton discuss their engagement (which Nina does not exactly want to end, though she regrets having entered into it hastily) as a matter of writing letters. Nina feels that she "cannot be bound," that she "want[s] to be free," that she resists engagement's feeling of "constraint"—but, she says to Clayton, sounding a single note of encouragement, "I like to get your letters." Clayton responds that they may defer their engagement without discontinuing their correspondence, but Nina then confesses, "I don't think I write very good letters! I never could sit still long enough to write." Clayton encourages her: "Write exactly as you talk," he says; "Say just what comes into your head, just as you would talk it." With this advice, Clayton invites Nina to do what Thomas Ducket did in his phonetically spelled letter—compose a written text "just as you would talk it." Meanwhile, Nina's half-brother, Harry—who is also her slave—manages the entire plantation, handling the paperwork with which Nina cannot be bothered. Even with an elite girl's education and this well-stocked mahogany desk, Nina Gordon, like Eva St. Clare, is scarcely more literate than a black slave. The tableau of the unused writing table attests that her privilege and leisure do not make her immune to the deleterious effects of illiteracy in the slave South.[24]

At root, Nina Gordon simply finds writing to be very hard work, at odds with her youthful restlessness: "I never could sit still long enough to write." One might sooner expect to hear those words from an overworked slave. Stowe's representations of literacy, as of life in the South more broadly, reveal a New Englander's disapproval of slaveholders' proverbial indolence. Anti-slavery rhetoric frequently extolled the virtues of honest labor, making the point that slavery was not only unjust for forcing slaves to do their masters' work; it also deprived slaveholders of the salutary effects of laboring for them-selves. If writing requires sitting still—something slaves are not allowed to do and slave owners cannot do when they are, like Nina Gordon, undisci-plined and distractible—then everyone involved is unable to write.[25]

Northern cultural values, from universal education to individual self-reliance, offered the antidote. As both a teacher and a professional writer, Stowe consistently recognized the arduousness of writing. In *A Key to Uncle Tom's Cabin,* she rejected claims that African Americans could not learn, arguing that all students, regardless of race, require coaxing and discipline: "In the process necessary to acquire a handsome style of hand-writing, to master the intricacies of any language, or to conquer the difficulties of math-ematical study, how often does the perseverance of the child flag, and need to be stimulated by his parents and teachers." Years later, in her columns as editor of *Hearth and Home,* Stowe continued to stress the hard work of learning to write, advising fledgling writers that they "must go through a great deal of practice." She displayed her disciplined pedagogical approach in a letter to Mary Edmondson, a young former slave whose northern edu-cation Stowe sponsored. Upon receiving her first letter from Mary, Stowe replied with a cordial missive—and a list of Mary's misspellings. At the bottom of her letter, Stowe writes:

harde	is spelt hard
Studys	is spelt studies
presant	is spelt present
wate	is spelt wait
too — for 2	is spelt two

In correcting her spelling, Stowe tells Mary, she is doing precisely "as I do for my own children when they write to me." Mary Edmondson (who was between nineteen and twenty-two years old at the time) suffers the embar-rassment of having exited the darkness of slavery but not yet entered the ad-vanced literacy of the northern middle class. Stowe encourages her, though, to keep up the hard work: "I shall keep your letters & six months hence compare what you write then & if I am not much mistaken we shall see great improvement—you write now much better than I expected."[26]

In Harriet Beecher Stowe's depictions of an intellectually enervated South, as in the representations put forth by northern abolitionists in general, the act of writing is in crisis. Southerners enslaved and free languish in a climate that denigrates labor and stunts the mind, brought on by the southern states' attempts to legislate slaves into illiterate submission. According to abolitionist thought, slavery anywhere jeopardized freedom everywhere. A line from a hymn summed up the sentiment: "While there breathes on earth a slave, no man is truly free and brave."[27]

Likewise, selective and unequal access to education in the South threatened to hobble literate culture. The explicit proscription of slaves' literacy was therefore an extraordinary wrong, and abolitionist publications painted the South's legal landscape in broad strokes: "It is a crime in the Southern States, for any person to undertake to teach a slave how to read and write"; "in all the principal Slave States, teaching a slave to read or write is rigorously prohibited." The anti-slavery movement described the South in categorical terms—a place of unmitigated intellectual darkness, presided over by a monolithic anti-literacy regime—but, in law and in fact, the state of black literacy in the antebellum South was more complicated than northern critics alleged.[28]

By 1830, the American South had become a full-blown slave society—a place where "slavery stood at the center of economic production, and the master-slave relationship provided the model for all social relations." Large-scale staple agriculture had spread west from the tidewater region, creating the cruel economy known as the internal slave trade. Slavery became not only a labor regime but also "a system of capital accumulation." In the early 1830s, an economic boom brought flush times both for planters in the newly cultivated interior (from western Georgia to the Mississippi River and beyond) and for slaveholders in Upper South states like Virginia and North Carolina, where prices of slaves rose with the demand for "export" to the labor-hungry west.[29]

At the same time, two events combined to remind slaveholders about the fragility of their lucrative economic system. The commodities, it turned out, had minds of their own. First, David Walker published his *Appeal to*

the Colored Citizens of the World in 1829 and succeeded in distributing it to
black communities in the coastal South, an act white southerners saw as "a
conspiracy to effect the emancipation of the slaves." Then, in the 1831 slave
rebellion at Southampton, Virginia, led by Nat Turner, they saw their fears
confirmed. The circulation of the *Appeal*—Walker explicitly charged literate blacks to read it aloud to their "more ignorant brethren"—together with
Turner's own ability to read and write focused panicked southerners' attention on slave literacy as one of their greatest worries.[30]

Southern states fashioned a repressive legal architecture to protect the
political economy of slavery, and a key target of those laws was black literacy. Alarmed by Walker's *Appeal,* coastal states like Georgia and North
Carolina passed "quarantine" laws to prevent black sailors on northern
ships from disembarking in southern port towns, where they might distribute pamphlets or otherwise spread insurrectionary ideas to local slaves and
free blacks. Virginia responded to the Southampton rebellion with laws
forbidding slave assembly. Even states farther removed from those sensa-
tional events passed anti-literacy statutes (Alabama in 1831, for example),
for as the domestic slave trade made the South an increasingly intercon-
nected economic region, the planter class consolidated to protect its shared
interests.

Northern abolitionists were thus partly justified in characterizing southern slave codes as a unified anti-literacy regime, but the actual status of slave
literacy in southern law and slaveholder opinion, like most aspects of American slavery, defies generalization. Even if economically interdependent, the
antebellum South was not a monolith. Famously committed to states' rights
in principle and characterized by an intense localism in their legal culture,
southerners actually adhered to no party line on the education of slaves.[31]

The letter of the law varied considerably across the South. As the leading
historian of slave literacy has pointed out, "Laws banning the teaching of
slaves were only in effect in four states for the entire period from the 1830s
to 1865: Virginia, North and South Carolina, and Georgia. . . . Two other
southern states passed literacy restriction laws in the 1830s but did not
maintain them as part of legal codes."[32] Virginia prohibited "meetings or
assemblages of slaves" for the purpose of learning to read or write, and Mississippi likewise banned such assemblies of slaves "above the number of
five," but both states remained silent on any less organized form of slave
education, thereby allowing slave owners to teach their slaves if they wished.

Some states legislated with notable idiosyncrasy. Alabamians followed up on their anti-literacy law with a special dispensation for the education of "Certain Persons of Color"—children of the free Creole community in Mobile—because the Creoles had "heretofore conducted themselves with uniform propriety and good order." Virginia made an exception for a young, blind white man named Henry Juett Gray, who required a literate assistant, "which object cannot be permanently secured otherwise than by the education of a young slave named Randolph, the property of said Henry Juett." The legislature allowed Randolph to be educated, on the condition that Gray's father would indemnify the state "against any improper use by said slave of the art of reading and writing." In short, anti-literacy laws "were surprisingly vague, inconsistent, and ineffective, and were poorly enforced."[33]

The effects of anti-literacy laws may have varied even more than the laws themselves. Records reveal few prosecutions for teaching slaves to read or write. One of the few white people to be punished for teaching African Americans to read, Margaret Douglass of Virginia offered the timeless defense that everybody else was doing it, too. "All the churches in Norfolk were actually instructing from books both slave and free colored children," she wrote in 1854, "and had done so for years without molestation." The texts of anti-literacy laws themselves reveal that the genie was out of the bottle: statutes in Georgia, North Carolina, and South Carolina all expressly forbade *slaves* from teaching other slaves to read and write. (In earlier years of North American slavery, one small subgroup had arrived from Africa already literate—Muslims who could read and write Arabic.) During the mid-nineteenth century, outside observers readily voiced what state legislators had tacitly acknowledged. According to Scottish traveler James Stirling, "Many slaves have learned to read in spite of all prohibitions. . . . In Richmond, I am informed, almost every slave-child is learning to read. Even in Columbia, the capital of South Carolina, hundreds of slaves can read, and twenty or thirty negroes regularly teach reading in the evenings to their fellow-slaves, receiving a fee of a dollar a month. Other slaves are taught by friendly whites. I have myself seen this going on in the corridors of an hotel. On plantations the slaves teach one another."[34]

Some southerners reluctantly confirmed what Stirling witnessed. A petitioner to the South Carolina legislature reported that "the ability to read exists on probably every plantation in the state; and it is utterly impossible for even the masters to prevent this—as is apparent from the cases in which servants learn to write by stealth." Examples abound of newspaper advertisements for the capture and return of runaway slaves whose owners announced their slaves' literacy. Fugitive-slave advertisements that Harriet Beecher Stowe reprinted in *A Key to Uncle Tom's Cabin* refer to runaways who "can read print," "can write some few words," and "can read and write." Thomas Ducket's owner evidently tolerated his marginal literacy. In his letter to Jacob Bigelow, Ducket seems confident that he will receive letters addressed to him "in car of Mr samul t harisin" (in care of Mr. Samuel T. Harrison), whose sugar plantation near Bayou Goula was home to nearly one hundred slaves. Ducket, who was not allowed "out sid of the place," probably could not even have sent his letter without Harrison's assistance. (From Harrison's point of view, that assistance probably functioned mainly as surveillance.)[35]

Even on the general principle underpinning anti-literacy law, no consensus prevailed among slaveholders. Not everyone agreed that literate slaves threatened the institution. As Frederick Douglass's *Narrative* shows, there could be differences of opinion within a single southern household, as when Sophia Auld's husband upbraids her for teaching Douglass to read. Many slave owners, especially women, did teach their slaves out of religious principle or simple compassion; Stowe's Little Eva may be unrealistic in many respects, but her desire to help Uncle Tom read the Bible is by no means far-fetched. Even some less magnanimous slave owners found reasons to condone slave literacy. One Georgia planter, writing on the subject of "The Negro and His Management" in an 1860 issue of *Southern Cultivator,* believed anti-literacy measures overestimated African Americans' capacities. Slaves might as well learn to read, he explained with shifting pronouns, because they would never gain anything from their reading: "I encourage them to spell and read; I know of no possible injury that can result from this course—it is very convenient at times in weighing cotton, building, &c. His native stupidity and indolence are effectual barriers to his ever arriving at any proficiency in the art, and it would amount to corporal punishment to force him to listen to the reading of a chapter from Helper or Spooner." The same palpable cockiness—the Georgia planter claims he would as soon read abolitionist propaganda to a slave as whip him—appears in less crude form in John Belton O'Neall's commentary on South Carolina's anti-literacy statutes. O'Neall, an eminent legal thinker and "part of a regional elite with strong national ties," likewise thought forbidding slaves to read and write amounted to an unseemly confession of weakness: *"Such laws look to me as rather cowardly. It seems as if we were afraid of our slaves. Such a feeling is unworthy of a Carolina master."* Though on the surface very unlike Stowe's Anne Clayton, these writers shared her inability to see any life in the cork leg of black literacy.[36]

To acknowledge that white southerners, in law and in practice, took complicated positions toward slave literacy is not to say that large numbers of slaves actually were being taught or encouraged to learn. (In one striking exception, Cherokee slaveholders looked to their literate black slaves to teach them English.) Many white slave owners resolutely, even brutally suppressed slaves' efforts to educate themselves. Even in states that did not outlaw the teaching of slaves, even in the absence of a complete consensus among white southerners, even for slaves whose owners may not have punished them for learning to read or write, the force of ambient anti-literacy ideology could squelch the will to learn, if not wreak psychological terror. Janet Cornelius's analysis of the ex-slave interviews conducted by the Federal Writers' Project (FWP) in the 1930s found that some former slaves recalled more stringent anti-literacy statutes than actually existed. Several of them mistakenly believed that antebellum laws in their states prescribed amputation as the punishment for learning to write. Undoubtedly they imbibed those beliefs from slave owners who at least threatened to, and probably in some instances actually did, cut off the fingers of slaves who endeavored to learn to write. Although punishments that heinous were rare and never had legal sanction, slaves' widespread fear of such consequences surely had as chilling an effect on incipient literacy as law or punishment itself.[37]

Nevertheless, as historians have amassed evidence of the complicated and uneven nature of the South's anti-literacy regime, they have opened our eyes to the possibility that slaves learned to read and write in larger numbers than most people think. Early African American historians, though intuitively sure of slaves' fervent will to learn, initially could point to little proof of literacy acquisition. Carter Woodson lamented in 1919, "We are anxious to know exactly what proportion of the colored population had risen above the plane of illiteracy. Unfortunately this cannot be accurately determined. In the first place, it was difficult to find out whether or not a slave could read or write when such a disclosure would often cause him to be dreadfully punished or sold to some cruel master of the Lower South. More-over, statistics of this kind are scarce and travelers who undertook to answer this question made conflicting statements." Woodson ventured a guess, though, based on a fuzzy averaging of white observers' qualitative accounts. Counterbalancing the reports of white abolitionists—who "would make it seem that the conditions in the South were such that it was almost impos-sible for a slave to develop intellectual power"—with those of travelers who found literate slaves to be ubiquitous, Woodson concluded, "it is safe to say that ten per cent. of the adult Negroes had the rudiments of education in 1860."[38]

W. E. B. Du Bois, somewhat less optimistic, averred that anti-literacy laws "were explicit and severe. There was teaching, here and there, by indul-gent masters, or by clandestine Negro schools, but in the main, the laws were followed." Du Bois extrapolated an estimate of slave literacy from a sample of African Americans in South Carolina, where "a majority of the nearly 10,000 free Negroes could read and write, and perhaps 5% of the slaves." Forty years later, Eugene Genovese wrote, "The estimate by W. E. B. Du Bois that, despite prohibitions and negative public opinion, about 5 percent of the slaves had learned to read by 1860 is entirely plausible and may even be too low," for, as Genovese found, "literate slaves appeared everywhere, no matter how unfavorable the atmosphere."[39]

Indeed, Du Bois's and Woodson's estimates have proven to be more ac-curate than their sketchy evidence would have predicted. When Janet Cor-nelius revisited this question with the added evidence of the FWP interviews, she arrived at similar figures. Among the former slaves in that sample, 5 percent "stated that they had learned to read or to read and write during slav-ery." Such a number is undoubtedly low, as Cornelius points out, because most of the African Americans interviewed had been enslaved in rural areas of the Lower South and remained there after emancipation; they were less likely to have become literate than slaves in urban areas and border states, while slaves with the advantages of some education were among the most likely to have left the rural South by the 1930s.[40]

To discover, then, that 5 percent of even the men and women inter-viewed by the FWP had acquired some literacy before the Civil War would seem to confirm Genovese's supposition that, among all slaves, a 5 percent literacy rate is too low. Cornelius counterbalances that figure by citing an old study of slavery in Kentucky, in which a survey of 350 advertisements for runaway slaves revealed that 20 percent of the fugitives could read and 10 percent could write. These figures, in contrast, are probably too high, because slaves who had become literate would have been somewhat more apt to run away. (Additionally, Kentucky had no anti-literacy law.) At the same time, such sources may underreport the number of literate slaves. Slave owners may not have been aware of their slaves' literacy in every case, and they would have had limited incentive to broadcast it when they were.[41]

This tug-of-war between figures thought too high and too low represents the clearest answer we are likely to get. Measuring historical literacy has never been easy. Governments and census takers sort people into the clear-cut categories of "literate" and "illiterate" using necessarily vague criteria and often relying on self-reporting. In 1951, a UNESCO committee for statistical standardization offered this definition: "A person is literate who can, with understanding, both read and write a short, simple statement on his everyday life." Though a serviceable description, it is of limited use in assessing the literacy of people who are not present to be examined. Quantitative historians have relied on shrewd though imperfect methods for determining how many people in a social group could read and write, such as counting library borrowers or calculating the proportion of people who signed their own names on official documents. Of course, neither technique reveals the "understanding" with which anyone reads or writes, and both reflect only people who enjoyed certain civil rights. The oppression of American slaves makes their literacy even less traceable than that of other historical groups.[42]

The already gray area between low and high estimates of slave literacy becomes even grayer when we consider the range of ways in which slaves may have been literate. With respect to written literacy, that range extends from the ability to sign one's name, to the ability (which Thomas Ducket achieved) to write a reasonably lucid short statement or letter, to the ability (which Frederick Douglass ultimately possessed) to write the narrative of one's life. It is impossible to know the numbers of people who acquired any of these more precisely defined skills while enslaved, but it is beyond question that a very large number fell within the span. If literate individuals composed at least 5 percent and perhaps upwards of 10 percent of the entire slave population, then at least 200,000 and possibly almost half a million people achieved literacy while they were enslaved.

That is to say, the act of writing mattered—whether as a triumphant exercise of self-determination for an able penman, the frustratingly elusive aspiration of a beginning reader, or something in between—to a very large group of American slaves. However impossible it may be to quantify that community of writers more precisely, it is both possible and illuminating to examine the artifacts of their varied acts of writing. Because so much of this history is obscured, it is especially important to study the texts that survive.

Studying the writings of slaves traditionally has meant studying slave narratives, approximately sixty-five of which were published in the United States before the Civil War. These invaluable texts provided antebellum Americans—and continue to provide readers and scholars today—with reliable and incomparably insightful representations of enslaved people's experiences. Published slave narratives are not, though, the artifacts of slaves' acts of writing—not, like Thomas Ducket's letter, dispatches from within the abyss. Slave narratives were written almost exclusively by *former* slaves looking back on their lives in slavery, and they sometimes were not written at all but narrated aloud and transcribed by others. Most often writing to support political abolitionism, these authors usually portrayed their lives in accord with the values of their white northern audience (although there were exceptions both subtle and startling). The hallmarks of the genre include an account of how the author learned to read and write, and slave narratives tend to associate literacy acquisition with a yearning for freedom, knowledge, and Christian salvation—and, just as often, with simple hard work. Though they offer an incomplete picture, these texts provide a glimpse of the conditions under which enslaved people wrote; they prepare us to understand, as Stowe and her contemporaries perhaps could not, the full meaning of a text like Thomas Ducket's letter.[43]

Some of the most famous slave narratives emphasize the shrewdness required for slaves to acquire literacy in the face of legal and social obstacles. Frederick Douglass and William Wells Brown both describe the stratagems they used to sneak bits of education from their white peers. "When I met with any boy who I knew could write," Douglass recalls, "I would tell him I could write as well as he. The next word would be, 'I don't believe you. Let me see you try it.' I would then make the letters which I had been so fortunate as to learn, and ask him to beat that. In this way I got a good many lessons in writing." Douglass also made surreptitious use of conventional educational materials. When left alone in his owners' Baltimore home, Douglass reports, "I used to spend the time in writing in the spaces left in Master Thomas's copy-book, copying what he had written. I continued to do this until I could write a hand very similar to that of Master Thomas."[44]

William Wells Brown describes a similarly cunning tactic in the autobiography appended to his 1853 novel, *Clotel:* "I carried a piece of chalk in my pocket, and whenever I met a boy I would stop him and take out my chalk and get at a board fence and then commence. First I made some flourishes with no meaning, and called a boy up, and said, 'Do you see that? Can you beat that writing?' Said he, 'That's not writing.' . . . I said, 'Is not that William Wells Brown?' 'Give me the chalk,' says he, and he wrote out in large letters 'William Wells Brown,' and I marked up the fence for nearly a quarter of a mile, trying to copy, till I got so that I could write my name. Then I went on with my chalking, and, in fact, all board fences within half a mile of where I lived were marked over with some kind of figures I had made, in trying to learn how to write."[45]

In these examples, the enslaved narrator is both writing student and trickster figure. His performance of knowledge he does not possess, calculated to provoke an informative comeuppance, not only dupes his audience of white schoolboys but also reveals to his reading audience the superior knowledge he *does* possess—how to extract education from a society that refuses to provide it. This acrobatic self-representation depends on highly developed literacy, and both Douglass and Brown emphasize the success of their efforts to learn to write—and, in Brown's case, the sheer volume of what he wrote, with the work of his hand dominating the neighborhood.

Many of the less widely read slave narratives place their emphasis not on social ingenuity but rather on hard work, practical knowledge, and the travails of simply acquiring and learning to use the tools of writing.[46] Substitutes for books, pens, and paper abound in slave narratives because the legal and cultural obstacles to slaves' literacy necessitated them. Douglass learns the letters marked on timbers in the shipyard where he works; Noah Davis, apprenticed to a shoemaker who "used to write the names of his customers on the lining of the boots and shoes," tries to imitate those letters; Juan Manzano "used to station [him]self at the foot of some painting whose title was in capital letters" and assiduously copy them; and Peter Randolph states simply, "I had no slate, so I used to write on the ground."[47]

Forced to such resourcefulness by deprivation and the threat of pun-ishment, many former slaves came to conceive of written literacy as primar-ily a physical skill. In contrast with Douglass and Brown's social and theat-rical scenes of learning, "Uncle Tom" Jones portrays himself alone and methodical at his makeshift writing desk, keenly attentive to the tools of the craft:

> Jacob showed me a little about writing. He set me a copy, first of straight marks. I now got me a box, which I could hide under my bed, some ink, pens, and a bit of candle. So, when I went to bed, I pulled my box out from under my cot, turned it up on end, and began my first attempt at writing. I worked away till my candle was burned out, and then lay down to sleep. Ja-cob next set me a copy, which he called pot-hooks; then, the letters of the alphabet. These letters were also in my new spelling-book, and according to Jacob's directions, I set them before me for a copy, and wrote on these exer-cises till I could form all the letters and call them by name. One evening, I wrote out my name in large letters,—THOMAS JONES. This I carried to Jacob, in a great excitement of happiness, and he warmly commended me for my perseverance and dilligence.[48]

Other narratives represent the practice of writing as an almost industrial process of taming the raw materials for pen and ink—the task of penman-ship as itself an obstacle to literacy. Solomon Northrup "appropriate[s]" a sheet of foolscap while on an errand for his mistress, and "after various ex-periments," he recalls, "I succeeded in making ink, by boiling white maple bark, and with a feather plucked from the wing of a duck, manufactured a pen. When all were asleep in the cabin, by the light of the coals, lying upon my plank couch, I managed to complete a somewhat lengthy epistle." Wil-liam Hayden describes a similar procedure: "My ink, I made by boiling walnut bark and coperas, and having obtained some paper, abandoned my copies in the sand, and took to pen, ink and paper. In this manner, I suc-ceeded in writing a tolerably legible hand."[49]

By saying he achieved success "in this manner," Hayden expressly links learning to write with the practical matter of making ink and pens—as if simply to make the tools is, at least in some measure, to know their use. His sense of accomplishment upon "writing a tolerably legible hand," which one might dismiss as mere penmanship, should not be gainsaid, though, and not only because Hayden faces the peculiar obstacles imposed by slavery. Those of us who learned to write as children, and have foggy memories of the process, are apt to underestimate the challenges of learning to form letters with pen or pencil. The more advanced abilities we associate with written literacy—creation, self-expression, critical thinking—may follow far in the wake of writing "a legible hand." In the slave narrative of Henry Bibb, the gap between writing as manual labor and writing as intellectual activity appears especially pronounced: "Whenever I got hold of an old letter that had been thrown away, or a piece of white paper, I would save it to write on. I have often gone off in the woods and spent the greater part of the day alone, trying to learn to write myself a pass, by writing on the backs of old letters; . . . by so doing I got the use of the pen and could form letters as well as I can now, but knew not what they were."[50]

To write letters and words without knowing what they signify had no place among the all-or-nothing images of literacy purveyed by white Americans swept up in the debate over slavery. Neither the abject darkness of illiteracy nor the sophisticated facility needed for spiritual devotion, fugitive connivance, or violent insurrection, Henry Bibb's marginal literacy conjures the dogged and ordinary acts of writing that have largely disappeared from the annals of American slavery. Long-dissolved pages of penmanship practice, texts inscribed on the backs of old letters, missives that never reached their destination or carried out their office: these writings did not spark dramatic transformations, but the untold hours slaves spent creating them form a crucial part of their experience—a part that the scant surviving archive can reveal.

Perhaps owing to the relative advantages of life in the District of Columbia, or to his own sheer tenacity, Thomas Ducket had by 1850 pushed beyond the state of literacy Henry Bibb described—not so far beyond, though, that his letter could pass without difficulty before a white reader's eyes. As Harriet Beecher Stowe wrote in *A Key to Uncle Tom's Cabin*, "People who are not in the habit of getting such documents have no idea of them." Stowe's strange locution—to "have no idea" of a letter—suggests precisely what white Americans' presumptions about black literacy predict: they would have trouble not only reading Ducket's misspelled words and poor handwriting but also comprehending that such a document even exists. All the letter's readers—from Jacob Bigelow, its recipient, to Stowe and her vast reading public—were a part of an educational culture that had considerable coherence, in form and ideology, compared with the fractured community of American slaves.

When Ducket's missive issued from the offices of a Boston publisher, it became an embassy from a foreign state of literacy. Stowe could overcome her audience's disbelief, could give them some idea of such a document, by reproducing the manuscript. Her only way of making it intelligible, though—of finding meaning in it—was to translate it into standard English. Yet the text of Ducket's letter exactly as he wrote it, "with all its poor spelling," can reveal as much about how he learned to write as the recollections in slave narratives. In what it says and what it struggles to say, Ducket's letter reveals not only the "misery" Stowe saw in its visual qualities but also a pale history of literacy acquisition—a history that intensifies the poignancy of his plea.

Ducket's letter appears to be the work of a writer who has learned from a spelling book, as most children and many slaves did, but whose education has been arrested. Ducket knows the whole alphabet, graphically and phonetically, but he has very little practice writing and likely has not received the guidance of a teacher, who might have alerted him, for example, to the pitfalls of the silent *e*. Most spelling books of the time, including Noah Webster's *American Spelling Book,* the ubiquitous "blue-back speller," progressed first from the alphabet to pronunciation tables (in Webster, for example, "ab eb ib ob ub"), then to words of one syllable, then to words of two syllables. So many slaves taught themselves from the blue-back speller that it became a part of the vernacular: many former slaves report having learned to "spell to baker"—*baker* being the first of the two-syllable words printed in Webster's text—meaning that they got through only the monosyllabic words.[51]

Ducket, too, evidently could spell only to baker. Silent consonants, which mostly elude him (as in "write," "know," and "could," although not in "night"), were not introduced in the blue-back speller until after words of three syllables, and most of Ducket's two-syllable words are broken into single syllables: "ret ten" for written, for instance, "be leve" for believe, and "Ded rec" for direct (a word that Ducket may have only heard a few times but understood was necessary in postal parlance).[52] Ducket knew how to sound out words, and his phonetic writing at times seems to reveal how he talked (his substitution of "sence" for since is actually one of the "improprieties" listed in Comly's spelling book). But besides broken-down words and proper names, with which he clearly struggles, Ducket uses only three words of two or more syllables: "famaly," "children," and "servent."

If Ducket indeed has studied the first several lessons in a spelling book, he has achieved a stronger foundation in literacy than most slaves ever did. Nevertheless, he was little prepared to write a letter with a purpose as serious and potentially delicate as trying to persuade white abolitionists to purchase his freedom and orchestrate a reunion with his family. Spelling books and primers were not intended to teach students to write, after all; there were copybooks and penmanship books for that. Ducket must have received some form of writing instruction, because he knows cursive (and he may have had easier access to ink than by boiling walnut bark), but he plainly stretched himself to write this letter. He may have attempted it multiple times before completing the copy he mailed.[53]

Where he navigates the treacherous terrain of propriety, where he senses the need to show tact without servility, his writing shows the strains on his literacy. On the verge of scolding Jacob Bigelow for his inattention, Ducket drops a syllable that nearly sinks his message: "i hop yo will not for me"— which Stowe reasonably glosses as "will not forget me," but which Bigelow may just as reasonably have failed to comprehend. In making his greatest request—for Bigelow and the other abolitionists to rescue him from the Louisiana plantation—Ducket apparently tries to minimize his imposition by suggesting it would take little effort on their part, and he pens one of the letter's most stilted and unclear clauses: "I be leve that if Would mak the les move to et that et cod be Don." Ducket's writing appears most confident, meanwhile, in those multisyllabic words. One of them, "servent," is both an epistolary convention (people of all social stations might sign themselves "your humble servant") and a term Ducket may have heard applied to himself. The other two, "famaly" and "children," confirm what we already know to be Ducket's abiding worry. As he says in his most lucid sentence, the last thing he writes, "my wife and children ar not out of my mine day nor night."

There may be many reasons the language of the home comes more easily to Ducket than the language of petition and negotiation, but he surely did not expect to need literacy for the latter purpose. Ducket's efforts back in Washington to learn to write—alone or with a teacher; more or less covert; apparently successful, if interrupted—sprang from aspirations of some other kind: to assist his family in escaping, to keep a diary, to lead a fuller spiritual life, or simply for self-improvement, but not to plead for the charitable intervention of white abolitionists a thousand miles away. Only after he was sold did writing become this tragic exigency, his only hope of re-union with his family. As the strains of his writing reveal, he may never have composed a letter to a white person until the anguish of separation drove him to apply his germinal skills to this unlikely enterprise. The la-bored prose of Ducket's letter thus records the traumatic impact of sale and displacement, his hard-won literacy wrenched from his own designs and set to use in bare desperation. Intertwined in this act of writing are both the persevering spirit of resistance and the stolen autonomy that defines slavery. The image of Thomas Ducket's penmanship may show the oppression of an education withheld, and Stowe's transcription may show the misery of his longing, but only together with the turns of his knotted sentences—the full artifact of his act of writing—can they begin to suggest the totality of his enslavement.

chapter two

The Private Life of the Literate Slave

WHEN THE WORK of Thomas Ducket's hand traveled from southern Louisiana to the New England desk of Harriet Beecher Stowe and into the pages of her *Key to Uncle Tom's Cabin,* readers glimpsed the iceberg-tip of a culture of writing among supposedly ignorant slaves. If anti- and pro-slavery thinkers at the time lacked political motivation to look deeper, modern historians have discovered the outlines of that broader culture, finding evidence that acts of writing figured in enslaved people's daily lives, collecting the surviving letters slaves wrote to each other and to the white people who owned them. From this epistolary culture—partly known to white southerners of the time, partly kept hidden within slave communities—would spring many of the ways of writing practiced by ordinary freed people during the emancipation era.[1]

   Scholars have mined slaves' letters for what they reveal about the conditions of southern slavery, but the letters' composition remains largely unconsidered as an experience unto itself, an often practical, sometimes creative act not only of resistance but also of reflection and inner transformation. To read the writings of enslaved people as unfolding processes of composition is to discover the complex role of written literacy in their lives. Knowing how to write could confer the liberating and empowering ability to record experience, to declare *this is what is happening to me,* and it also could intensify the isolation and totality of enslavement, deepening the affective impact of what was happening. In the case of Maria Perkins, the act of writing this single surviving letter was, as for Thomas Ducket, an act of desperation:

Charllotesville Oct 8th 1852

Dear Husband I write you a letter to let you
know of my distress my master has sold albert to a trader
onmonday court day and myself and other child is for sale also
and I want you to let hear from you very soon before
next cort if you can I dont know when I dont want you to   5
wait till chrismas I want you to tell dr Hamelton or
your master if either will buy me they can attend to it
know and then I can go after wards I dont wa^{n}t a trader to
get me they asked me if I had got any person to buy me
and I told them no they told me to the court houste too they   10
never put me up a man buy the name of brady bought albe
rt and is gone I dont kow whare they say he lives in scott
esville my things is in several places some is in staun
ton and if I sould be sold I dont kow what will be
come of them I dont expect to meet with the luck to get   15
that way till I am quite heart sick nothing more I
am and ever will be your kind Wife Maria Perkins

To Richard Perkins

Though clearly a testimonial to the domestic slave trade's ravaging of African American families, Maria Perkins's letter also, less obviously, demonstrates how the act of writing catalyzes thought and feeling.[2]

A lot can happen during the writing of a short text. When one sits down and writes a page of a letter, or of any sort of document, it does not turn out exactly as one had planned. New thoughts occur, unforeseen complexities are confronted, different associations emerge. The process of composition has special importance for marginally literate writers. We readily acknowledge the greater significance of a year in the life of a child than a year in the

Charlottesville Oct 8th 1852 =Oct 8?, 1852?

Dear Husband I write you a letter to let you
know of my distress my master has sold albert to a trader
on monday court day and myself and other child is for sale also
and I want you to let hear from you very soon before
next cort if you can I dont know when I dont want you to
wait till chrismas I want you to tell dr Hamelton or
your master if either will buy me they can attend to it
know and then I can go afterwards I dont want a trader to
get me they asked me if I had got any person to buy me
and I told them no they told me to the court houste too they
never put me up a man buy the name of brady bought albert
and is gone I dont how whare they say he lives in scottes
ville   my things is in several places some is in staun
ton and if I should be sold I dont how what will be
come of them. I dont expect to meet with the luck to get
that way tell I am quite heart sick   nothing more I
am and ever will be your kind wife Maria Perkins
To Richard Perkins

Maria Perkins to Richard Perkins, October 8, 1852, Ulrich Bonnell Phillips Papers (MS 397), Manuscripts and Archives, Yale University Library.

life of a fifty-year-old, and the act of writing a single letter is likewise a
graver undertaking for an uneducated person, and may constitute a larger
step forward in her facility with the medium, than for a seasoned writer.
Additionally, the basic challenges facing an untrained and inexperienced
writer make the act of putting pen to paper an arduous process, far from
automatic, and (as we are apt to forget in the age of digital word processing)
very time-consuming. It takes me six and a half minutes to write out the text
of Maria Perkins's letter with the convenience of a modern pen and without
pauses to reflect or review, much less to decide what to say. In short, her letter is no snapshot of a single instant. Much may have happened in her mind
as she made her way from the top of the page to the bottom. The errors, omis-
sions, and idiosyncrasies of Perkins's manuscript, far from obfuscations,
testify that, for marginally literate enslaved people, writing involved a confrontation with continuing acute limitations on both their education and
their freedom. In literacy was power, but not the power to keep your family
from being broken apart. For Perkins, the act of writing provoked and
sharpened that agonizing tension.[3]

Nothing is known about Maria Perkins's life or the surrounding influences
that may have shaped her act of writing, beyond what her letter and its
dateline can reveal. She and her husband, Richard—enslaved in different
parts of Virginia, separated by a forty-mile journey over the Blue Ridge
Mountains—would have had little opportunity to see each other in person.[4] Exchanging letters offered a way to hold their family together and
may have been Maria's principal motivation for learning to write, as it was
for many slaves separated by sale from their loved ones. Perkins might never
have had the chance to become literate had she not lived in Charlottesville,
home to the University of Virginia and to a sizable African American community. The town was one of three Virginia municipalities with a black
majority, according to the 1850 census, and free and enslaved blacks would
have mingled in workplaces and at church (by the mid-1840s, the Charlottesville Baptist Church had a growing congregation of almost 400 black
members). For many, daily labor brought them tantalizingly close to the
very learning of which they were deprived. Some Charlottesville slaves were
held to domestic service in the households of university faculty, and some
arrived as students' personal servants. Although some university professors

treated their slaves just as harshly as did unlettered farmers, others taught their slaves to read and write.[5]

Perkins could have been taught to write by a sympathetic white person or in a free black teacher's covert schoolroom, or by a fellow slave who had learned by such means. The fine, steady penmanship of the letter implies that she benefited from someone's individual tutelage, as opposed to picking up what she could from contraband spelling books. Her use of the "long *s*" (*ſ*)—which persisted in manuscripts of the period but carried a tinge both archaic and genteel, since it had disappeared from print typography—suggests that her tutor was an older white person or a black person who had received relatively formal instruction.[6]

However she learned to write, Maria could not have corresponded with Richard without having access to the mails or another network of communication, and in this respect she was likewise well situated. Charlottesville was not only a college town but also a bustling county seat, the nexus of business for Albemarle County and a regular site of "court days." Though centered around the proceedings of the circuit court, court day offered an occasion for people to congregate informally on the periphery of official events. They came from all over the county to transact business; they reported news from home and shared gossip. But as Perkins's letter attests, court day in a southern town was a fearful scene for enslaved people. Much of the business done outside the courthouse consisted of transactions in slaves—the hiring-out agreements that would determine the fates of local slaves for a year's term, or the buying and selling that could send them away forever.[7]

By 1852, Perkins had not only learned how to write and direct a letter to its destination; like most enslaved letter-writers, she had picked up, either by instruction or imitation, some of the conventions of epistolary writing. A date, a place, and a first line that announces her reason for writing are not inevitable elements of a message she might send to her husband. However private, even secretive, slaves' correspondence with each other often needed to be, their letters participate to a surprising extent in the letter-writing customs of the time.

Those customs were notably robust and widely observed. Dramatic reductions in postage rates encouraged Americans to send letters at unprecedented rates—the volume carried by the U.S. Post Office nearly quadrupled between 1840 and 1860—and this boom in manuscript culture made letters probably the largest single category of textual production in the country. Even barely educated farmers and factory workers, people who may never have undertaken to write anything else, wrote letters to their distant friends and relatives. Handbooks proliferated to help them, and a set of remarkably stable epistolary conventions took root. One guide directed young students to use this "skeleton" for writing letters:

Dear Sister,

 I take this opportunity to write you a few lines.
1. Mention the state of your health, and that of your friends.
2. Of your school and how you like it—of your studies—the progress you make in them—how you like each, and which the best—and why.
3. Use of these branches—and which the most useful.
4. Particulars.

As such templates suggest, composing a letter involved balancing self-expression with the prescriptions of a guidebook or the unspoken dictates of politeness. The "particulars" that comprise personal experience might occasion inward reflection, but only in the context of socially accepted protocols.[8]

Despite being the products largely of informal education, despite often circulating through an underground network, slaves' letters nevertheless display many of the same conventions that marked the correspondence of educated people. In letters to loved ones as well as to white owners, they employed the sentimental rhetoric of domesticity that pervaded antebellum American culture.[9] They used traditional epistolary frameworks, including standard opening sentences: "I Take my penn in hand to write you a few lines"; "I now tak this oportunity to let you kow that I am well"; "I take this oppertuinty of writeing you a few lins in answer, and I to inquire how you and your Childrens are"; "i Rite you A fuw lines for to let you knoo how we ar." When John M. Washington recalled learning to write as a young slave in Fredericksburg, he described a lesson from his uncle, who wrote out this copy text: "My Dear Mother, I Take this opporteunity to write you a few lines to let you know that I am well." "When you can do that much," Washington's uncle told him, "you can write to your mother." Becoming literate here implies not only learning to form the words but also knowing the proper things to say in a letter—yet writing to one's mother requires only "that much," the generic opening, not necessarily embellished with original thoughts or "particulars."[10]

Letter writing, in short, entails not only—sometimes, not even very much—spontaneous self-expression. It involves working within received forms, seeking out bridges between an inner world—craving connection with distant loved ones—and an outer world, potentially alien to someone marginally literate, that can be traversed in writing. For a writer like Abream Scriven, a slave in Savannah, Georgia, a commonplace lament about the inadequacy of words carries special import. He wrote to his wife, Dinah, "My Dear wife for you and my Children my pen cannot Express the griffe I feel to be parted from you all." Doubtless no one's pen could fully give voice to Scriven's profound sadness upon being sold away from his family, but he must sense the limits of his pen in particular, held tentatively in hand as he deliberates how to spell "grief." The solitary undertaking of writing a letter taps into private feelings and also puts them in negotiation with an exterior framework of language and form; the act of epistolary writing can both "fortify a self" and "consolidate a relationship." Such negotiations could be generative as well as disheartening, as a close reading of Maria Perkins's letter suggests.[11]

As a historical artifact, the letter comes to us almost like a manuscript in a bottle, washed up on an archival beach—but not quite. It is unknown whether it ever reached Richard, much less whether it helped keep the family together. The manuscript did not resurface until 1929 when, like Harriet Beecher Stowe almost eighty years earlier, the historian Ulrich Phillips looked upon "a letter which lies before me in the slave's own writing." Phillips included a full transcription of it in his book *Life and Labor in the Old South* (which proved influential for decades and a subject of controversy for decades more). He had acquired most of the primary sources he used in writing *Life and Labor* during his travels through the South in the mid-1920s, and the Maria Perkins letter was most likely one of the thousands that came out of the attic of one remote farmhouse in Augusta County, Virginia— somewhere outside Greenville, about fifteen miles south of Staunton, near where Richard Perkins once lived.[12]

The house belonged to an aged farmer named George Armentrout, whom Phillips's friend Herbert Kellar knew to be an avid collector of old papers.

When Phillips, Kellar, and a colleague arrived at the Armentrout house, they learned that George had died, but his sister agreed to sell them his collection of papers—five large sacks that proved to be filled with about 25,000 documents—for five dollars a sack. (The Maria Perkins letter probably cost a tenth of a cent, it turns out.) The three historians repaired to a hotel in nearby Lexington to find out what they had purchased. As Kellar recalled in his journal, "The guests in that somewhat sedate establishment were greatly astonished to see two colored boys, bending and staggering under the weight of five huge gunny sacks, proceeding through the front door, solemnly followed by three scholars, disheveled in appearance, but with the light of victory glowing in their eyes." The three men sat on the floor of a hotel room, drank contraband whiskey (it was the middle of prohibition), and pored over old letters, some dating as far back as the early eighteenth century. Each of the men gathered piles of noteworthy documents and, at the end, exchanged them based on each scholar's interest. All the slavery materials—about two thousand items—went to Phillips.[13]

So came Maria Perkins's plea for help before our eyes: from the attic of an eccentric southern collector, borne on the shoulders of "colored boys," and traded, finally—as Perkins had feared she and her child would be—among white men.

Among the surviving letters written by American slaves, circuitous and poignant tales of provenance are legion. The improbable explanations for many such documents' existence reveal the suggestive outlines of a vibrant epistolary culture of which only a few traces remain. A small packet of letters from Harriet Newby, a slave in Brentsville, Virginia, was plucked from the pocket of her deceased husband. Dangerfield Newby had saved the letters, stretching back over six months, and carried them with him into battle with John Brown at the Harper's Ferry arsenal in 1859. A Virginia slave named Sargry Brown (no relation to John) wrote with concern to her husband, "this is the third letter that I have written to you . . . and dont no the reason that I have not received any from you." She probably never did learn the reason: her letter was pulled from the Dead Letter Office in Washington (and printed by the editor of an anti-slavery newspaper). Other letters are preserved in the papers of southern slaveholding families—in at least some instances, because owners intercepted and withheld letters to or from their slaves. George Hobbs's letters to his wife, Agnes, found safekeeping with their daughter, who published one in her postwar memoir. "I have wrote a greate many letters since Ive beene here," George wrote, "and almost been reeady to my selfe that its out of the question to write any more at tall: my dear wife I don't feeld no whys like giving out writing to you as yet and I hope when you get this letter that you be Inncougege to write me a letter." It is impossible to determine the number of times enslaved people sat down and labored over missives that never reached their intended readers, or that arrived successfully—and were read, pondered, and replied to—but long ago disappeared. Most white southerners would have been little inclined to preserve writings by slaves even if they had come to their attention (and slaves often had ample reason to ensure they did not), and enslaved people themselves had not the luxury of being archivists.[14]

If Maria Perkins's letter is exceptional for having survived to the present day, it is in another sense quite ordinary. A substantial number of the surviving writings of enslaved people are letters between family members, despite the fact that such documents had slim chances of being preserved compared with slaves' letters to white recipients, such as abolitionist benefactors, owners, or, after emancipation, public officials. For those slaves who had the ability, writing letters to distant family members apparently was one of the most common uses of their hard-won literacy.[15]

Though our understanding of slavery has been enriched each time such documents have come to light, scholarly attention to slaves' letters has been incommensurate with the role writing played in many enslaved people's lives. When Ulrich Phillips transcribed Maria Perkins's letter into his book, he brought it to the attention of countless twentieth-century historians of American slavery, but he also laid the foundations of a scholarly tradition of overlooking slaves' own writings. Phillips's book, a methodological innovation in its time, relied on an array of sources to reconstruct daily life on southern plantations—contemporary newspapers and periodicals, letters by slave owners and overseers, travelers' diaries, even gravestones—but virtually all of those sources reported from the perspectives of whites. The views of black slaves were inaccessible, Phillips maintained, because enslaved people had left too few records. (The Federal Writers' Project interviews were undertaken soon after, on the premise that some former slaves' experiences had not yet disappeared into that historical black hole; African Americans who had been born during the final decade of slavery were about eighty years old during the 1930s.) Forty years later, Kenneth Stampp aggressively challenged Phillips's overall characterization of plantation slavery yet maintained the same dismissive stance regarding sources: "Direct evidence from the slaves themselves is hopelessly inadequate."[16]

The 1970s witnessed transformational efforts to recover the perspectives of enslaved people, but their acts of writing remained peripheral. John W. Blassingame launched a monumental project to document slaves' points of view, but his anthology, *Slave Testimony,* included mostly oral sources, such as interviews. When he discussed written sources, Blassingame focused on slave narratives, and he tended to depreciate them for being written by "exceptional" individuals. "An overwhelming majority of the narrators were among the most perceptive and gifted of the former slaves," Blassingame wrote, while "many scholars insist that more of the average slaves should be heard." A florescence of scholarship about African American oral and material culture responded to that call. By turning to the study of folklore, songs, material artifacts, and the archaeology of slave quarters, scholars from the 1970s to the present have supplied much of what early historians left out. In this way, the project of restoring enslaved African Americans' perspectives has responded to, but ultimately not challenged, a consensus that written sources are too few (or too unreliable, too distant from the authentic experiences of "average" slaves) to be revealing. As a consequence, modern historical scholarship by and large has not developed a methodology for maximizing what we *can* glean from the slaves' letters that have survived. Since the Maria Perkins letter came to light in 1929, many writers and editors have reprinted and quoted it, and they have avoided the subject of Perkins's imperfect writing, apologized for it, even tried to rectify it, but generally not sought to use the letter's idiosyncrasies as reflections of Perkins's experience.[17]

The ambiguities and occlusions of texts by marginally literate writers indeed can prove frustrating if one looks to them mainly for direct reportage.[18] When Maria Perkins wrote, "my master has sold albert to a trader onmonday court day and myself and other child is for sale also," why did she write "other child" instead of using the child's name? Perhaps she intended to use an article or a possessive pronoun to further identify this "other child," but because she did not we cannot glean potentially valuable evidence about families in slavery. Has Richard Perkins never met this child? Could it be that Albert is the child of Maria and her husband while the "other child" has a different father? Might Perkins refer simply to some other child whom her owner sold, unrelated to any of them?

The authors of a college textbook, presumably trying to make the Perkins letter more accessible to student readers, reprinted it with half a dozen
words inserted in square brackets, including one that invented parentage:
"My master has sold Albert to a trader on Monday court day and myself
and [our] other child is for sale also." By intruding the pronoun "our," the
textbook sharpens its readers' sense of the internal slave trade's devastation
of families. The conjecture that the "other child" belongs to Richard and
Maria Perkins together subtly invokes a more customary image of a nuclear
family, with which many students can more easily identify, in danger of
being further broken up. At the same time, the speculative "our" elides the
complexity of actual family relations in slave communities, including the
possibilities that the "other child" is Perkins's by a different black man (a
suggestion that might invite students' uninformed moral judgments) or the
offspring of rape by Perkins's owner.[19]

The textbook's editorial license crystallizes a tendency to treat Maria
Perkins's marginal literacy as an obstacle that must be surmounted or evaded.
Rather than contend with the hazards of missing pronouns and their meanings, many readers of the letter have refrained from interpreting it—Ulrich
Phillips offered just seven words of commentary: "We cannot brush away
this woman's tears"—or have disassembled it into more cogent parts. Snippets of the letter appear in studies of the African American family as well as
works of women's history; in histories of the domestic slave trade; and,
because of Perkins's expression of concern for her "things," expressed near
the end of the letter, in studies of economy and property within slave
communities.[20]

Predictably, the differing reasons Perkins's words have been quoted put
different shadings on the cloudy image of her that the letter begins to reveal. Even transcription is an act of interpretation: different translations of
the manuscript into print have shaped the emerging character of its author.
When John Blassingame reprinted the letter from the original manuscript,
he transcribed it slightly differently than Ulrich Phillips had. To enhance
the text's readability, he followed the reasonable editorial practice of introducing spaces between what appear (despite the letter's total lack of punctuation) to be separate sentences, and he took the further step of introducing
a paragraph break, making the line "I don't want a trader to get me" stand
out as the first sentence of a second paragraph. In addition, he rendered the
writer's name "Marie Perkins." Such details may seem the merest arcana,

but the different names conveniently mark two threads of interpretation—a double life of the letter, and of previous readers' understandings of it, that guides our attention toward the crux of the overlooked story this letter has to tell.[21]

From one angle, "Maria" Perkins is an afflicted mother expressing her emotional anguish (as she was in the first place for Phillips, who noted only "this woman's tears"). A women's history textbook reprints the letter under the heading, "Maria Perkins, 'I am quite heartsick . . . ,' " and the historian Elaine Tyler May, in a book on infertility, distills the original text into the following quotation: "I write you a letter to let you know my distress my master has sold albert to a trader on Monday court day and myself and other child is for sale also . . . a man buy the name of brady bought albert and is gone I don't know where. . . . I am quite heartsick." By isolating the last clause from its context (a particularly convoluted phase of Perkins's syntax), May joins with the textbook in making "I am quite heartsick" the touchstone of the letter.[22]

From another angle, "Marie" Perkins is distinguished less by heartsick-ness than by her canny if desperate strategy to mount resistance against her owner. Readers in this vein have gravitated toward a different sentence as the letter's marquee passage—"I don't want a trader to get me," the line Blass-ingame highlighted with a paragraph break. One writer quotes the letter only up through that sentence; another quotes just that line along with Per-kins's request that her husband talk to Dr. Hamilton (as his name is spelled in Blassingame's transcription). Both cite the Perkins letter as evidence that slaves could exercise a limited form of control over their fate. As one writer puts it, "A number of slaves, both male and female, resisted the more arbi-trary nature of slavery by taking an active part in determining who their new owners would be."[23]

These two portrayals of the letter's author—Maria's anxiety and an-guish, Marie's willfulness and sense of power—are not merely the inven-tions of historians with differing agendas. They are the traces of a conflict Perkins herself experienced during the act of composing her letter—an emotional crucible's impression on the page, born of the epistolary form's endemic tension between self and other, and Perkins's own conjoined expe-rience, as a literate slave, of autonomy and bondage.

The first two-thirds of her letter—the parts reporting the sale of Albert, describing Perkins's fear of being sold herself, and appealing to her husband

for assistance—have usually attracted the most notice from modern readers. The last part of the letter typically receives less attention, probably for
two reasons: first, and most simply, Perkins's syntax becomes more difficult
to parse in the final lines; second, her concern for the plight of her "things"
strikes some readers as jarringly unlike the image of Maria as a heartsick
mother. There are several indications that Perkins, like most writers, wrote
more carefully and deliberately on first sitting down than near the end of
her letter. At least twice in the first half of the letter, she corrects small errors. At the beginning of line three, she evidently had omitted the word
"on" before "monday" and went back to insert it ("on" barely squeezes in between the edge of the page and "monday," and it is the only text on the page
that lies to the left of an imaginary line drawn at Perkins's left margin).
Also, she initially wrote, in line eight, "I dont wat a trader to get me," and
subsequently added a small *n* above the line to turn "wat" to "want." These
changes could have been almost immediate—she may have added the "on"
as soon as she reached the end of "monday," and the *n* as soon as she had
crossed the *t* in "wat"—or they could indicate that Perkins paused somewhere during the composition of her letter and reread it from the beginning,
editing as she went through. In either case, the early stage of Perkins's composition was not fevered or automatic but rather self-conscious, attentive to
detail, and punctuated by pauses of some duration.

Toward the end of the letter, by contrast, there are no such corrections,
and there are signs that Perkins sped up. She runs out of room at the ends
of four lines; lines eleven to fourteen all break midword—something that
does not happen earlier in the letter. At line twelve, if nowhere else, she is
sufficiently absorbed by what she is writing to neglect her pen, which runs
almost completely out of ink before she stops to dip it midway through the
word "whare." She also misspells "know" in lines twelve and fourteen, even
though she can spell it correctly (see lines two and five), and makes no effort to supply missing *n*'s, as she did with "want" in line eight. She twice
repeats an earlier word in place of the one she presumably intends: "told"
for "took" in line ten, and "buy" for "by" in line eleven—possibly errant
mistakes, possibly instances of looking back through her own letter for
copy text.[24]

Any one of these details by itself appears inconsequential, but all of them
together form a pattern—fastidiousness in roughly the first ten lines of the
letter, haste or distraction in the last eight. Those final lines are precisely the

ones many historians have neglected in quoting this letter, and they constitute the transition from "Marie" Perkins's trademark sentence—"I dont
want a trader to get me" (lines eight to nine)—to Maria's "I am quite heartsick" (line sixteen). Perhaps most crucially, they represent a transition away
from an epistolary mode of outreach to her husband and toward a diaristic
mode of private reflection.

For a person enslaved, "private life" might be imagined as one's only inviolable refuge—the haven of free will and the spirit of resistance—but also
the place where the traumas of bondage ultimately lodge, where its agonies
are felt. Perkins's letter charts the interaction of those two possibilities. Previous readers of the letter have recognized its affective significance but
seemed reluctant to interpret it. One historian introduces the letter by re-
servedly saying, "It is seldom that the historian finds recorded the personal
emotion of the *victims* of the internal slave trade." Others call the letter "an
eloquent and moving cry of distress"; "one of the rare instances in which
the cries of the victims of slavery have come to us in their own voices";
and a representation of "a personal aspect of slavery." What those personal
emotions were, what the moving cries actually say, one can never know
fully and with certainty, because language—and especially the written language of a marginally literate person—always mediates expression. There
are many registers of feeling, from the fidgets of anxiety to the furrowed
brow of confusion, and writing is privileged among them only because, in
its material form, it lingers after the fact and, while it lingers, responds to
interpretation.[25]

Even to begin to speak about a private life is to summon countless cave-
ats and questions, including some of the most intractable problems in hu-
manistic thought. Does "the self" exist in itself, or is it a role performed?
Does the self well up from within, or is it molded by forces without? Whether
articulated as nature versus nurture, as essential versus socially constructed,
or in other terminology, this classic debate represents only the widest aper-
ture on a host of more intricate questions. When and why, for instance, do
we imagine the self as a wellspring of novelty (the originality of artists and
courage of heroes, who transcend or defy the habits of the mass), or as the
prey of ideology and conformity (the locus of "false consciousness," in a
Marxist thinker's view, of Freudian repression, or of Foucaultian subjection

to discipline)? Is the self exemplified by Marie Perkins's will to control her surroundings, or by heartsick Maria's vulnerability to others' control?[26]

Such questions have special acuteness in the context of slavery. In the nineteenth century, the ontological problem of human interiority—is the self produced from within or by its environment?—lay at the center of white racism. Some people believed African Americans' minds were innately inferior to those of whites, and various pseudo-scientific inquiries endeavored to prove it. More egalitarian thinkers generally conceded the "degraded" mental condition of African Americans but attributed it to environment rather than biology—to the brutalizing effects of slavery rather than intrinsic racial differences. A different contingent, "romantic racialists," took an essentialist view of black interiority without defending slavery. They did not see blacks as wholly inferior but did see them as intrinsically different— naturally "childlike, affectionate, docile, and patient," a feminine contrast to the supposedly masculine and domineering Anglo-Saxon race. Romantic racialists believed these traits gave African Americans the potential to be ideal Christians, but they did not envision for slaves any very rich or complex intellectual life. Despite their disagreement about causes, most white Americans tacitly agreed that enslaved people's mental lives were stunted.[27]

Frederick Douglass, whose whole existence gave the lie to charges of black inferiority, testified in just such terms to slavery's power to dehumanize the slave. Of his suffering under the harsh overseer Covey, Douglass wrote, "My natural elasticity was crushed, my intellect languished, the disposition to read departed, the cheerful spark that lingered about my eye died; the dark night of slavery closed in upon me." Douglass's life in slavery included intense moments of solitary reflection—standing alone upon the Chesapeake's shore on a summer Sunday, he recalled, "I would pour out my soul's complaint, in my rude way, with an apostrophe to the moving multitude of ships"—but such moments became apprehensible to others only years later, after Douglass escaped to the North, became practiced in rhetoric and writing, and composed his autobiography. His apostrophe to the ships was no play-by-play account of his thoughts at the time but rather the construction of an older, no longer enslaved Douglass, not merely recollecting a past experience but also shaping it for an audience.[28]

Because African Americans' inner lives were, like all people's, unknowable, they were also—expediently, for those who wished to rationalize slavery—ignorable. Their written literacy threatened the slaveholding regime not only, maybe not even most of all, because it portended rebellion or escape. Writing was particularly provocative because it made manifest the intellectual and affective activity of people whose supposed inner vacancy justified their servitude. In actuality, of course, the written word has no monopoly on providing access to human interiors, but antebellum America, like the modern West overall, tended to regard private writings as the most reliable indexes of autonomous selfhood. A white observer could witness a slave reading a book and deny that he or she really understood it, much less thought or felt anything about it; could trivialize a slave's spoken language on account of its dialect or dismiss it as the imitative performance of a mental inferior. Such delusions are more difficult to sustain in the face of a letter like Maria Perkins's.[29]

For the enslaved North Carolinian George Moses Horton, "writing" mattered more as a mental activity than as words on the page. Horton, the first black man to publish a book in the South, authored a volume of poetry *before* he learned to write. Though he learned to read at a young age, he "knew nothing about writing with a pen" until much later in life. That did not stand in the way of his aspiration to create poetry: "I fell to work in my head, and composed several undigested pieces." Many of his poems, Horton reports, "I composed at the handle of the plough, and [I] retained them in my head, (being unable to write,) until an opportunity offered, when I dictated, whilst one of the gentlemen would serve as my emanuensis."[30]

Elsewhere, Horton actually substitutes the word *writing* for the wholly interior process called "composing." When he created a memorial poem for the child of Caroline Lee Whiting Hentz (a southern novelist who also was Horton's frequent patron and benefactor), Horton remembered, "She was extremely pleased with the dirge *which I wrote* on the death of her much lamented primogenial infant, and for which she gave me much credit and a handsome reward. *Not being able to write myself,* I dictated while she wrote." In Horton's view, to write is to think; he can do it without setting pen to paper, can do it "at the handle of the plough." Whether he wrote his poems down himself or got someone else to do it for him, they attested that he led an active inner life even while at forced labor.[31]

More striking is the example of an enslaved potter named Dave, who labored for three decades in South Carolina and etched short verses, many of them rhyming couplets, into the clay of his pots before firing them in the kiln. If he ever wrote with pen and paper, no evidence of it survives, but more than a hundred of his pots do survive, most of them bearing the signature *Dave,* and about a quarter of them inscribed with simple phrases or short poems. In technological terms a throwback to ancient Sumerians' cuneiform writing, Dave's clay texts represent an ingenious circumvention of the travails other slaves met with ink and paper, in favor of a craft at which Dave obviously excelled and which his owner sanctioned.[32]

Some evidence suggests Dave learned to read and write while he was employed as a typesetter at an Edgefield, South Carolina, newspaper. If true, that means he became literate, like most students, by imitation—looking at either manuscripts or printed texts in front of him, then setting those same words in type—but with comparatively little practice in penmanship. (Georgia's anti-literacy code, passed in 1833, explicitly forbade white citizens' using slaves or free blacks "in the setting up of types, or other labour about the office, requiring said slave or free person of colour, [to have] a knowledge of reading or writing," suggesting that such practice was common enough to arouse legislators' concern.) For a marginally literate slave, the temperamental demands of typesetting bear some similarity to those of the learning process described in slave narratives such as Thomas Jones's: the work was slow, repetitive, often done by rote, perhaps without full awareness of all the words' meanings.[33]

The patience Dave would have had to muster in that job would have served him well in pottery. By all accounts, his skill as a ceramic artist was extraordinary, and art historians continue to be impressed in particular by his ability to make extremely large vessels—well over twenty gallons in volume—on a throwing wheel. Dave's largest extant piece holds forty-four gallons and may be the largest wheel-thrown pot produced in the nineteenth-century South. Making pots this large was slow, methodical work. Dave would have started with as much as forty pounds of clay, centered that mass on a rotating wheel—which he kept spinning by working a foot treadle at the base of the throwing wheel's supporting axis—then molded and pulled the clay upward at the sides to form a cylinder. Pulling must happen slowly, lest the clay's center of gravity get too high too quickly and topple the growing form. Dave's largest pots would have been created by throwing multiple cylindrical sections, stacking them one by one, and fusing them on the turning wheel—a process that requires letting the bottom section dry partially for about an hour in the sun, because if fully pliable the clay would collapse under the weight of the next section.[34]

These are the basics of the craft, and during a thirty-year career in which Dave enjoyed local fame for his pottery, they undoubtedly became as automatic for him as the use of a pen is for an educated person. He even developed a distinctive style: "The walls flair boldly to the shoulder, near the top of the vessel. Above the shoulder of the jar, the walls break sharply inward to the mouth, leaving a distinct ridge." That "distinct ridge" became Dave's writing surface, and Dave's writings, though spare and often cryptic, reveal that he frequently meditated on the slow and solitary passing of time that defined his art and labor. A pot created in 1858 reads, "A very large jar: which has 4 handles = / pack it full of fresh meat—then light : candles." The second line likely refers to the practice of filling pots with salted meat and sealing them with candle wax. Dave suspends his couplet at the brink of waiting: the lit candles burn while the reader, the user of the pot, slowly accumulates enough melted wax to seal the jar.[35]

Dave's poems also reveal a preoccupation with permanence, including the permanence of writing itself (which is reinforced, of course, when words are etched in wet clay and then fired). A rather sardonic 1854 inscription reads, "LM says this handle will crack." That terse note incorporates the entire object as a part of Dave's text: the handle, in whatever form it appears at the moment someone reads the line, constitutes as important a part of Dave's meaning as the six words. "LM" denotes Lewis Miles, Dave's owner, and if Dave is recording a wager about the durability of the loop-handled jug on which he etched this sentence, then the jug—whose handle remains intact today—is its own proof that Dave won the bet.[36]

Sometimes the idea of permanence takes on a bleaker aspect. An 1836 pot reads, "Horses mules and hogs / all our cows is in the bogs / there they shall ever stay / till the buzzards take them away." In the poem most overtly about Dave's enslavement, he writes, "Dave belongs to Mr. Miles / wher the oven bakes & the pot biles." The former verse dwells—with sadness and sympathy, one senses—on the permanence of the livestock's captivity; the latter presents an iterative narrative of Dave's abiding condition. Business goes on—baking ovens, boiling pots—and all the while Dave "belongs" to another person, same as the livestock. To be enslaved is to endure time, with little hope that time's passage will bring any change.[37]

Dave's writing most directly considers his mental life in a couplet on an 1858 vessel that reads, "making this Jar : I had all thougts / Lads & gentlemen : never out walks." The duration of "making this Jar" may not be so long that the potter literally can think *all thoughts,* but Dave's pansophical claim certainly evokes the long duration of throwing a large pot—a creative process that would have taken hours from start to finish. The particular vessel upon which Dave wrote this poem is among his largest and most broad-shouldered—twenty inches tall and more than sixty inches around at its widest. Consider the act of "making this Jar": Dave's arm is through the mouth of the pot, his hand held against the inside. He cannot see his hand, but he can watch the shoulder of the pot broaden very gradually as the pressure of his fingers forces the clay wall outward, a little more with each revolution of the wheel. He watches the blank tablet for his stylus come into being. After the pot is finished, he composes this couplet—or, more appropriately, he writes it. He could have composed his poem on the pot—and even revised it by wetting and smoothing the clay to "erase"— but as George Horton would remind us, he also could have composed it while he worked at the wheel, holding it in mind until he could etch it in the clay.[38]

Dave's act of writing seems designed less to express something than to register a still-hidden act of thinking, simply to declare the fact that he *had thoughts*—their moment past, their content opaque—that now, translated into this word, "thougts," are cast in material form like a finished pot. To write this poem was partly to make an indexical mark, to act out his ability to write (like the signature Dave made on most of his pots, or the enigmatic nonalphabetic marks that appear on many of them), and partly to signify his consciousness during the process of making the jar. Even regardless of what it says, the writing signals the elapse of time—the clay must have been soft once, but now it is not—and in its specific reference to the maker's "thougts" the poem discloses what the pot itself conceals. Only a trained potter can look at one of Dave's vessels and instantly understand how long it took to make; but by writing this verse upon it, Dave challenges everyone who sees the pot to acknowledge that a thinking person spent time—in fact, a lot of time—making it.[39]

Amid the nearly all-encompassing racial ideology of the slave South, few white people would look at a slave driving a plow across a field and wonder what he was thinking (unless they had heard George Horton recite the poetry he composed during that supposedly empty time). It requires a greater depth of denial, though, for someone to confront the material product of a literate person's time-intensive labor and not so wonder. In the words of the French philosopher Henri Bergson, "Duration . . . implies consciousness," and for Dave the inward experience of time crystallizes both the agony of enslavement and the yearning for freedom. His time was systematically stolen from him and yet also partly his to use for cogitation and reflection. The poems George Horton composed as he traversed the fields testify to an interiority hemmed in but autonomous—the simultaneous forced labor of his body and chosen work of his mind. Likewise, Dave's thoughts while working indicate his double consciousness of the duress of production and the duration of the wheel. For both men, literacy is not an instrument of freedom—both remain enslaved—but it is a sign of freedom's writing beneath the oppression of slavery. Their acts of writing, unusual in a variety of ways, serve less as tools for bettering their condition than as outward markers of the tenacious exercise of their private lives: composing poems behind the plow, thinking all thoughts while making the jar.[40]

Maria Perkins takes up her pen first and foremost to tell Richard about the events of court day. Like most letters between family members, hers reports the news. Even though the news is urgent and terrifying, the first ten lines of the letter are relatively free of error, apparently carefully composed; furthermore, they indicate Perkins's own composure in this state of crisis. She provides a highly structured account of her own mind: "I want you to let [me] hear from you very soon . . . I dont want you to wait till chrismas I want you to tell dr Hamelton or your master if either will buy me . . . I dont wa^{n}t a trader to get me." Each pair of sentences composes a single unit of logic, a balanced articulation of what she wants and its opposite: I want to hear from you soon, not as late as Christmas; I want Dr. Hamilton or your master to buy me, not a trader. One can imagine these determinations taking shape in Perkins's mind, perhaps anxiously repeating on a mental back channel as she went about her daily toil, for hours or days before she found the chance or the resolve to write them out. (She is writing four days later, on Friday.) Her steady back-and-forth between "I want" and "I dont want" shows the expressiveness of a capable writer and the confidence that may derive from her own literacy or her trust in Richard's partnership. It shows the practicality and willfulness that define "Marie" Perkins.

After line eight, though, her self-avowals weaken, shrinking first from what she knows she wants to what she knows simply about her circumstances, and finally to what she does not know at all. Lines nine to twelve constitute narrative exposition of the events of Monday, the information she gathered on the scene at the courthouse: "they asked me if I had got any person to buy me and I told them no they told me to the court houste too they never put me up a man buy the name of brady bought albert and is gone I dont kow whare they say he lives in scottesville." As she comes to the end of this sentence, Perkins comes also to the limits of her own knowledge—from what she witnessed to what she only gleans from rumor—and to the end of her resources. Not knowing where Albert is, she has no further course of action to suggest to her husband. This first, relatively clear section, the practical phase of epistolary communication, is bounded off at the end by the letter's closest thing to punctuation: a long space in line thirteen, between "scottesville" and "my things," twice as long as the next longest space between words anywhere in the text and longer even than the space following the salutation, "Dear Husband."

It is near this apparent transition that more frequent errors begin to appear in Perkins's writing. Possibly she now is writing faster, or is simply less certain of what to say. The first two-thirds of the letter may have been composed as a rough draft and then recopied; they may have been to some degree mentally rehearsed before Perkins took up her pen, or they might represent the low-hanging fruit of her limited literacy—what she knew in advance she possessed the words to express. In any event, the letter's final passage leaves behind the epistolary business of reportage and the joint concerns of family. It veers inward, takes up her individual preoccupations—the fate of her "things"—and, notably, addresses no longer her quandary's present tense or recent past but rather a contemplated future.

The letter is, from the start, fundamentally about the future—the impending sale of Perkins and her (or the) other child—but the future tense scarcely appears until this closing movement: "my things is in several places some is in staunton and if I sould be sold I dont kow what will become of them I dont expect to meet with the luck to get that way till I am quite heart sick." The last clause of this passage is difficult to parse. What exactly is the meaning of "till," or until, in this context? Would the (unwelcome) achievement of heartsickness somehow earn her "the luck" to get to Staunton? If she does meet with that luck, would she not then be somewhat less heartsick? Besides, isn't Perkins already deeply heartsick? That, certainly, has been the interpretation of many previous readers, who link the line "I am quite heart sick" with the earlier passages of the letter about the (already past) sale of Albert, even though Perkins's own syntax marks this heartsickness as conditional and anticipated. Is her despair of meeting with that luck so unrelenting that it has made or will make her heartsick?

Perhaps the most reasonable paraphrase is, *By the time I get the opportunity to go to Staunton (if I ever do), I will have become quite heartsick.* Why did Perkins not write that? Among other conceivable reasons, the future perfect tense almost certainly was not in her grammatical repertoire. It is, though, crucial to the mood of her letter. The future perfect is a staple of epistolary form generally; to write any letter is to envision the future moment of an addressee's receipt of the letter, and an anticipated reply or reaction. For an enslaved letter writer, the future perfect is similarly inescapable but unusually fraught. Perkins writes with the hope that she and the other child *will not have been sold* by the time Richard receives the letter and can solicit a purchaser. Her closing gesture is a devastating counterpoint to the hope that she invests in her husband: "till I am quite heart sick" projects the certainty of the future perfect, unlike the optimistic conditional of line seven ("if either will buy me") or even the pessimistic conditional of line fourteen ("if I sould be sold"). Heartsickness looms unavoidable.

The letter progresses, in short, from an assertive beginning to a nearly hopeless end. The relative buoyancy of her connection with Richard and her confidence in her own resourcefulness begins to fade, we imagine, as Perkins sits alone with the pen in her hand, meditating on her isolation and coming face to face with the limits on both her expressive abilities and her power to prevent the tragedy's unfolding. As she finishes describing the aggravating gap between her knowing and not knowing—"a man buy the name of brady bought albert and is gone I dont kow whare they say he lives in scottesville"—her hand and slightly lifted pen glide across the blank space before her next sentence, or she rests them on the table. In that silence, Perkins may have reflected on how little she really had to go on. She had gleaned some information (Brady) from the court-day crowd—Charlottesville friends, or fellow slaves more knowledgeable about the trade—but Brady's residence in Scottsville is only hearsay. Besides, it may not matter where

Brady lives. He is a trader, as Perkins reported at the outset. Albert may be destined almost anywhere in the South. His sale in October is consistent with post-1830 patterns of interstate slave trading: traders traveled through Upper South states such as Kentucky and Virginia in the summer and fall to purchase slaves, then transported them to the labor-hungry states of the Lower South or the West and sold them after harvest time to planters who were thinking about next season and had the proceeds from their crops to invest in slaves.[41]

After diligently and with some confidence expressing first what she wants and second what she knows (what she learned at court day), Perkins reaches a point at which her knowledge seems ineffectual: Brady may live in Scottsville, but so what? What can she or Richard do about it? Albert by this time could be plodding across the Virginia countryside in a coffle, in transit at least to Richmond, perhaps ultimately as far as Alabama or New Orleans. It may be that by the time Richard reads Maria's letter, Brady will have sold Albert to someone else—the unspeakable future perfect. The resolve to send a letter to Richard for help, surely animated by something like hope, slowly diminishes as Perkins moves down the page, following the thread of her envisioned salvation to its logical end, where she finds, as she thinks through it in writing, little for which she might realistically hope after all.

Perkins's lamentation for "things," on the heels of sizing up the grim reality of Albert's sale, redirects what she cannot otherwise articulate: a private dread of distance and loss. The geography of Maria Perkins's known world extends no farther than forty miles over the mountains to Staunton. The prospect that Albert will be carried even farther away than that represents a cognitive black hole—a place, and a maternal grief, unknown, unknowable, and unfathomably hard for even a gifted writer to express. When Perkins writes that her things "is in several places some is in staunton," she envisions a map that depicts her family as well as it does her things— already distant husband, imminently unreachable children—and forges a subtle metaphor: the anguish of separation is as acute as if her child, as if she herself, were actually dispersed "in several places."

After all, her tragic plight is precisely that she and her children have no legal status except as things. When she adds, "and if I sould be sold I dont kow what will become of them," Perkins imagines her very life slipping off that disheartening map—her things, her family, and her self scattered beyond her ken. In her rapid outpouring of barely articulable feelings, she seems literally to forget herself. In writing, "till I am quite heartsick," she initially omits the "I" and begins to write something beginning with the letter *a,* as if the struggle to write has led her to the brink of surrendering to the slaveholder's epistemology: Is there really anything in there, any *I* in her interior? Is she really not as fully human as someone who can eloquently complete every sentence she begins? But Perkins quickly brushes away with her finger the wet ink of that *a* and regains her *I.*

It may be that "I dont expect to meet with the luck to get that way till I am quite heart sick" is not a single, clotted sentence, but rather two, the first of them aborted. In the midst of writing, "I dont expect to meet with the luck to get that way till a . . . ," Perkins may simply have given up in despair. Contemplating some future too painful to describe, or realizing the futility of continued wrangling with the minutiae of her "things," she simply stops writing, brushes away the incipient next word, and takes a breath. Her letter's conclusion bespeaks the resignation of a writer for whom writing has come up empty. "I am quite heart sick" sums up the entire situation: her inmost feelings are resurgent, but into the outward form of the letter she can project, finally, "nothing more."

The act of writing this letter, of composing these thoughts as she moved down the page, may have made an already aggrieved Maria Perkins even more disconsolate. Her desperate recourse to pen and paper—tools with which she was not entirely comfortable and may have had to use in secret—unravels her initial pragmatism, her belief that something can be done, and provokes an emotional outpouring she cannot fully capture in writing. The enigmatic ending of the letter registers a twin confrontation with freedom's limits. Despite all the knowledge she has gathered, all the ingenuity she can muster, and all the tenacity of her improbable education in writing, she cannot save Albert, and she cannot find the words to express the feelings her own act of writing has bought forth. Slavery has rent her family and fractured her sense of herself—the greatest agonies of Maria and Marie both.

Perkins's literacy figures as a source of empowerment in the sense that she, unlike many enslaved women, could contact her distant husband and attempt to influence the plight of her family. She could declare on paper the awful truth about what was being done to her; could refuse to cede literacy to the slaveholding regime's definition of selfhood. But the act of writing also catalyzes, and the written artifact makes visible, a private affective experience.

As it does for all writers, it enables Perkins to get to the bottom of what she thinks and feels. Through that portal lies the inexorable darkness of being enslaved—not knowing what will become of things, staring into a future of certain heartache.

It could be otherwise, of course. A decade later, John Boston, among the first slaves to seize freedom during the Civil War, wrote to his wife, Elizabeth, from whom he had been separated not by sale but by his own flight: "it is with grate joy I take this time to let you know Whare I am i am now in Safety in the 14th Regiment of Brooklyn this Day i can Adress you thank god as a free man I had a little truble in giting away But as the lord led the Children of Isrel to the land of Canon So he led me to a land Whare fredom Will rain."[42]

Boston's act of writing begins with epistolary decorum, Christian thanksgiving, and careful penmanship. On the back of the page, it spills over into an array of postscripts and afterthoughts one is tempted to read as the verbal effusion of unbridled elation. "Dear Wife i must Close," he writes as he approaches the end of his available space; "rest you self Contented i am free i Want you to rite To me Soon as you Can Without Delay." He signs himself "Your Affectionate Husban, John Boston," implores his wife one more time to "Write my Dear Soon," and makes sure to let her know how: "Direct your letter to the 14th Reigment New York State Malitia Uptons Hill Virginea In Care of Mr Cranford Comary." As if unwilling to let any part of the paper go unused, he proceeds to fill in the blank space around his signature with cramped remembrances: "Kiss Daniel For me," he writes in small script above his own name. At the paper's bottom edge, he squeezes in the words, "Give my love to Father and Mother." What began as a declaration of individual independence became, in the course of its composition, a profession of his continued attachment to his distant family—a textual representation of the affective bonds that literally encircle his signature. If slavery's strains upon those bonds incited the epistolary writing of people like Maria Perkins, emancipation's promise to relieve those strains would call forth new reasons and new ways to write.

chapter three

Writing a Life in Slavery and Freedom

ADAM PLUMMER, ENSLAVED in Prince George's County, Maryland, kept an eccentric diary that was part family chronicle, part commonplace book and notepad, part autobiography. He wrote down receipts and payments (on July 5, 1853: "Christa Lee pants & shirtes $1 piad"). He recorded the births, marriages, and deaths of members of his family, his owner, and Abraham Lincoln, among others. He compiled a "Cat a Log of things and wares" that includes a "blue flowered suger bole," "tow stone ware Dishs," and a "Look en Glass." He copied down parts of the letters he exchanged with his wife, Emily. And three times within the few dozen pages that survive, Plummer brought his pen to the top of a clean page with grandly self-reflective ambition. "The Life of Adam Plummer and Emily Plummer," he wrote at the head of two pages; "This is the History of Adam Francis Plummer," began another. Each time, the marginally literate Plummer followed with only a few faltering lines, consisting mostly of dates and references to letters received.[1]

The book Plummer's descendants preserved for a century clearly does not form a narrative in any usual way, but Plummer's strained and laconic writings, like Maria Perkins's letter, show not only the limits of the writer's literacy but also the challenges of giving voice to suffering. In its gaps and false starts, the diary tells the story of Plummer's struggle to come to terms with his separation from his family. He tried repeatedly to narrate what was undoubtedly his life's signal affliction: on one page of his diary, he wrote in uneven lines, "1849 the 24 of March Emily and 4 Children for Sale" and "November 25 Day 1851 Emily Plummer and five Childrens who whous sold publick." On the facing page, in steadier hand and straighter lines, he wrote: "March 24—1849 Emily plummer and four Child wose fore sale but She being Sick at the time she wouse not. . . . Emily plummer and four Childrens on November 25, 1851 Sold at publice sale. The said woman was bought by Mrs M A Thomson in the Washington City 16 street North to the plac Meaderen Hill. there she loeh for a short time. a bout four years and banished form my Eyes. 1855. of thn wote shorte letters to See or hear forme her. but I hear form not."

Adam and Emily did exchange letters after they were separated. From Meridian Hill, where Adam could still visit her occasionally, Emily was transferred to a new owner at Ellicott Mills, Maryland, thirty miles distant from Adam and thus "banished" from his eyes. Emily could not write, but she dictated a few letters to someone. Adam replied to Emily and saved the precious missives he received from her. He also wrote about her letters in his diary and recopied pieces of them. His first effort to write "The Life of Adam Plummer and Emily Plummer" begins by reciting a sequence of three letters from Emily, from each of which he quotes the opening lines: "in March 2nd 1856 it Reads Thus as follows I write to you Adam that Emily s earnest desiere she has felt very unhappy and Gaine I Get a nother Letter date Mt Hebron July 2nd Dear Plummer I am sorry that I have Not been able to write to you before and Gaine I Get another Letter dated March 20th 1857 wood Lawn Near Ellicotts Mills I take this opperuneity of writ-eing you a few Lins and hope that they may find you better than I am."

Later, when he undertakes to write "the History of Adam Francis Plum-mer," he revisits one of those letters. Four events make up Plummer's brief life-narrative: his birth in 1819, his marriage to Emily in 1841, his separa-tion from her in 1855, and his receipt of her first letter. Why the letter should be singled out as one of his life's great watersheds is not immediately clear, but Plummer's closing comment on it provides a hint: "After five month Loocking I Get a Letter date March 2nd 1856 De ziers to see me at

Mount Hebron ^{near} Ellicotts Mills, 20 milds no and to and form me I think that I shall Never be comme able a Gain but o my God." This obscurely poignant lament with which Plummer trails off, halfway down the otherwise blank page of his unfinished history, seems interrupted—*shall never become able again* to do what? Emily's letter has not survived, but in her next one Adam found, in the clear prose of the person taking her dictation, this wrenching line: "I cannot think that we are parted for life."[2]

If the fourth defining event of Adam Plummer's life is the unbearable and inexpressible realization of "Never"—the finality of "for life," the overwhelmed "o my God" of seeing his marriage permanently consigned to the realm of letters—it represents also a turning point in his relationship to writing. Although learning to write meant developing a precious and powerful ability, putting that skill to use in letters with Emily seems to remind Adam Plummer of the *dis*abling effects of slavery's trade in persons. The act of writing becomes the prosthetic limb in which he feels the pain of what's missing—all that he will never be "able a Gain" to do with his wife and their children.

Plummer evidently understood that written literacy served more than the utilitarian function of allowing him to communicate. He also could use it to fashion a self-image of the sort the slaveholding regime sought to foreclose. Plummer's life history might be narrated in a variety of ways—he was, notably, the personal servant of Charles Benedict Calvert, founder of the Maryland Agricultural College, which later became the University of Maryland—but as he chose to represent it, everything revolved around Emily. He insisted on being defined by the people he loved, not those who claimed ownership of him. Though Plummer continued to keep terse records of daily business for years after the war, the surviving pages of the diary show no further efforts to narrate his life. Perhaps the grim prospect that he would "Never be comme able a Gain" to live the life he yearned for, alongside Emily, initially made it impossible to craft any more complete "history." But by the time the Civil War and emancipation had run their course, he may have found it unnecessary. Adam and Emily no longer needed writing to stay connected: both were free and had been reunited.

Autobiography is the dominant form of antebellum African American literature. As early as the eighteenth century, formerly enslaved people wrote or dictated the stories of their lives, and these slave narratives became one of the first literary genres indigenous to anglophone America, as well as a crucial element of the abolitionist movement. In ways both literal and conceptual, though, slave narratives are artifacts not so much of enslavement as of escape and of entry into the public world of white America. Black autobiographers may have become literate either while enslaved or once free, but getting their narratives published almost invariably required first fleeing to the North and then finding a white sponsor. More abstractly, too, to publish a slave narrative was to become part of a white person's world, for better or for worse. Authorship conferred a mark of personhood that, throughout the history of modern Europe and the United States, had been denied to people of African descent; at the same time, it distanced the writer from "the domain of experience constituted by the oral-aural community of the slave quarters."[3]

Whether or not composing and publishing an autobiography had these effects—bringing one closer to selfhood, taking one further from an "authentic" view of slavery—it was necessarily a work of memory, a reconstruction of past events. In the words of one of the most influential scholars of slave narratives, writing an autobiography constituted "a search for language through which the unknown self and the unspeakable within slavery might be expressed." That search presumably begins only once the writer has left behind the "unspeakable" darkness of slavery and become free to know or invent him- or herself. For all they reveal about slavery, then, the well-known narratives of writers like Olaudah Equiano, Frederick Douglass, and Harriet Jacobs leave important questions unanswered. For a writer who remains in slavery, can the self be known and the experience of slavery expressed? Could a person, while still enslaved, wrest from a white-dominated culture the rhetorical authority to craft an autobiography?[4]

Adam Plummer obviously could try, even if the agonies of enslavement thwarted his autobiographical efforts. A Virginia slave named Fields Cook penned a thirty-two page manuscript in 1847, telling the story of his life up to the moment of writing, including "the way I obtained my little education with which I am porsested at this time." Such rare texts belong in a category apart from the published, retrospective autobiographies known as fugitive slave narratives—a category we might call the *enslaved narrative*. As a self-conscious representation of an individual's life written while still in slavery, an enslaved narrative is, like Maria Perkins's letter, a revelation of mind. But it also uses writing to tell a story about the author's experience and place in the world. Even though unpublished and probably never expected to be published, it seeks to make the author's life intelligible, perhaps to an audience, perhaps only to himself. In such writings, the intellectual history of enslaved people comes forth from an epistolary underground and, though still mostly hidden, flirts with the publicity of the literary realm.[5]

The fullest and richest example of this genre was written by John M. Washington, who came to light very recently by way of his (retrospective) slave narrative, "Memorys of the Past," a manuscript he wrote in 1873, a decade after his emancipation. Washington was also the author of an enslaved narrative. Prior to achieving his freedom in 1862, he wrote a different story of his life, based on a diary he kept while a slave in the late 1850s. This autobiography, and the diary that was its rough draft, remain unpublished. Taken all together, these works represent something unique in the annals of American slavery: autobiographical writings, in manuscript, by the same individual both in slavery and after emancipation. This remarkable set of texts makes it possible to study not only how one slave acquired literacy and understood the uses of writing but also how his writing process—and his conception of himself, wrapped up in it—evolved on the way from slavery to freedom. Writing may have intensified the pangs of isolation for Maria Perkins and Adam Plummer, but for John Washington—more fortunate in his marital life, possessed of a realistic hope for emancipation—the act of writing helped him imagine his plight anew.[6]

Washington's writings are oriented toward family and community, in which his literacy itself had its origins. His mother, Sarah Tucker, had learned to read and write by the time she gave birth to him in 1838 in Fredericksburg, Virginia. She briefly ran away when he was three years old but was soon recaptured. When he was four she began teaching him the alphabet from *The New York Primer*. "I was kept at my lessons an hour or Two each night by my mother," he recalled, and he could read proficiently by the age of eleven or twelve. His domestic schooling was interrupted, though, when Sarah Tucker was hired out around the end of 1850 and sent to Staunton, Virginia, nearly one hundred miles away (and, incidentally, close to Maria Perkins's husband).[7]

The agony and injustice of Washington's separation from his mother, he later recalled, sparked in him an outrage at slavery and a yearning for freedom: "Then and there my hatred was kindled secretly against my oppressors, and I promised myself If ever I got an opporteunity I would run away from these devilish slave holders." It also sparked Washington's desire to learn to write: "We wrote often to each other as circumstances would admit. of course, the white people had to write and read all the letters that passed between us. About this time I began seriously to feel the need of learn to write for myself. I took advantage of every opporteunity to improve in spelling." Washington received a few lessons from two young white men, but he made limited headway. "For it positively forbidden by law to teach a Negro to Write," he recalled, "So I had to fall back upon my own resources."[8]

What he calls his "own resources," though, might better be called the resources of the whole African American community of Fredericksburg. Not only is communication with his family Washington's principal motivation to learn to write; it is his connection with an extended family and a broader social network that enables him to learn:

> My Uncle George, Mothers Brother was one day in the lot where I lived with Mr Ware and noticed me trying to copy the writing Alphabet as shown in "Comleys Spelling Book," of that time, prinicipally used by those trying to learn to read or write. So he asked me what I was trying to do. I replyed, I am trying to write, see here and seizing the pen he wrote the following lines, on a peice of wallpaper
>
> "My Dear Mother,
>   I Take this opporteunity to write you a few lines to let you know that I am well,"——
>
> Now said he when you can do that much you ~~can do that much~~ you can write to your mother. He was at best a poor writer, but the copy that he had Just given me was as good as the best penmanship would have been because I could not get a teacher of any kind, or a Copy Book that I could understand.

Washington does not divulge how he acquired his first printed spelling book—did he buy it, steal it, borrow it from a white child?—and without hesitation he puts the book aside in favor of his uncle's homemade copy text.[9]

If Washington had believed in literacy as the pathway to personhood in the eyes of white society, he might have stuck with Comly's *New Spelling Book*—a standard mode of instruction, as he seems to know, for untold numbers of white children. For the twelve-year-old Washington, though, function was more important than symbolism. His uncle's "poor" copy text was "as good as the best penmanship would have been"—first because Washington, by his own admission in the final line, could not understand the copybooks, and further because his uncle's lesson took him directly where he wanted to go: to "My Dear Mother." Unlike the printed spelling book, Uncle George's copy text not only taught Washington to write in the sense of developing his basic literacy; it also tutored him in the social conventions of the particular form of writing in which Washington was most interested— the personal letter.[10]

The next episode in Washington's education repeats the sequence of an unsatisfying experience with a published text followed by help from a black teacher:

> However I availed myself of the first chance I had to buy a 12 cent copy book. which was a most wretched concern, and with its help I was most successful in laying the foundation of a very bad writer, for there was nothing like form or system about the thing. About this time I, by some means or other, attracted the attention of the Rev. Wm. I. Walker, who was one day hanging paper in the house where I lived. And seeing my efforts at writing he kindly stoped, and wrote me a very good copy of the alphabet from which I soon learned to write some kind of an inteligable hand.[11]

Many enslaved people had difficulty simply finding paper on which to practice, but Washington and his teachers—in one of the small strokes of good fortune that may come to those enslaved in an urban locale—enjoyed access to a lot of wallpaper. Washington's attention to this material detail conjures suggestive images of the duality of black life in a southern town, of partly hidden streams of activity running beneath the surface of white society. Though only a wallpaper hanger in the eyes of white townspeople, Walker is, to the black community, a preacher and a writing teacher. He transforms a scene of manual labor into one of literacy instruction. Along with the initial reclamation of wallpaper for writing paper by Uncle George, this scene raises the possibility that some of John Washington's earliest writings were preserved for decades, adhered text-side down to the walls of white Fredericksburg's parlors and dining rooms—a transcript of black life hidden in plain sight. Washington's education follows this same doubled pattern. He twice takes up the educational materials of white society before abandoning them in favor of ad hoc lessons from black copymasters. The process mirrors his original motivation to write: to create a closed-circuit channel of communication with his mother, shielded from the surveillance of white owners.[12]

Washington may have received an underground education in the basics of forming letters and words, but for his further development he drew upon a wider frame of reference. Like any writer, he learned from what he read, and in his reading Washington tapped into the mainstream of American culture. He found copies of *Harper's Magazine* in the room of his owner's son, and he enjoyed the magazine so much that he would "look for [it] with lively interest each month." Though he likely could read *Harper's* only in stolen moments, Washington evidently came to possess his own private stash of reading material. His diary and enslaved narrative are sprinkled with snippets of light verse, invariably free from misspellings or erratic punctuation; evidently Washington did not memorize them but rather had books or magazines at hand while he wrote. He copied into his diary this verse from an old Isaac Watts hymn:

> How Long dear Saviour oh how long
> Shall that bright hour delay
> Fly swiftly round ye wheels of time
> And bring the welcome day

Washington could have found the hymn reprinted in numerous places, but one likely source is an 1857 collection of uplifting Christian prose and poetry called *The Angel Visitor*. The stanza quoted appears in a short sketch called "A Visit to Dream-Land," whose evangelical rhetoric echoes throughout the same section of Washington's diary.[13]

Washington also copied into his enslaved narrative a poem titled "Scorn Not the Lowly," which appeared in *Merry's Museum*, a children's periodical:

> Many a bright bud perished
> Neglected and alone

When had a word been spoken
In a kindly gentle tone
The bud had bloomed unbroken
The gem had graced a throne.[14]

Elsewhere, Washington's early writings show the influence of popular nineteenth-century literature. In a florid turn that resounds with the language of sentimental fiction, he writes of himself in the third person: "He continued his visits to the young Lady. for a long time after his first and each time with increasing pleasure. untill there remained. no doubt" of his [love] for her. but did she love him.—time alone must prove."[15]

In short, Washington's reading before his 1862 emancipation appears to have consisted of ordinary and, from a slave owner's perspective, fairly benign literary fare—religious literature, texts for children, and large-circulation periodicals. It is highly unlikely that Washington had ever read a slave narrative. No matter how much relative autonomy he enjoyed as a literate slave in an urban area, he would not have found Frederick Douglass's *Narrative* among his owner's issues of *Harper's,* nor at a Fredericksburg bookseller. Though Washington certainly became a more proficient and prolific writer than Adam Plummer, his literary education was necessarily piecemeal and sheltered; his sense of the uses of narrative was unlike that of an escaped slave in refuge among northern abolitionists. Having derived his literacy from the aid of his community and from traces of sentimental fiction, Washington created an autobiography that focuses on his immediate surroundings in the present tense, on the travails of his emotional life, on his friends, and most of all on the woman he would marry.[16]

When John Washington was a teenager, he met Annie Gordon, a free black girl four years his junior. By the time he turned twenty, he had begun keeping a diary. Taking up his pen sometimes every day, sometimes only once in a few weeks, Washington committed to paper the sentimental ruminations of a love-struck young suitor. He chronicled parties, gossip, whispers outside church, and walks through the streets of town with his friends. Most of all, he wrote about Annie—their flirtations and love letters, jealousies and quarrels, and halting march toward engagement. He never mentioned forced labor, punishment, separation from his mother, or any plans for escape.

In the twenty surviving pages of this diary, Washington never once referred to slavery. He never indicated his own race or legal status, nor those of the many friends and acquaintances who form his cast of characters. To read the text unaware of its author's identity, one would have no reason to think it was written by someone enslaved.[17]

Did Washington avoid controversial subjects in case a white person were to find and read his diary? Was he self-consciously writing a utopian version of his life in Fredericksburg, creating a picture of himself in a world without slavery? Did Washington experience enslavement as something so totalizing, so obvious and inescapable, that he would no more think of writing about it than about breath or sunlight? Or is the experience of freedom—the one thing every slave narrative's author possessed that Washington, at the time, did not—somehow prerequisite to creating a literary representation of slavery? Whatever initially motivated the boundaries of Washington's subject matter, if anything consciously did, the ultimate effect is a narrative that centers, like his education, on connections with the people around him. To discern his experience of enslavement depends not on explicit expressions of personal feeling, of which there are few, but on the details of his writing process—how he shaped this narrative and, most revealingly, how he *re*-shaped it, for Washington began revising his diary a few years later to produce a more self-consciously crafted text.

Like any piece of writing, Washington's enslaved narrative came into being with the contact of a pen and a piece of paper. But in this case, that paper lay side by side on Washington's writing table with the other papers he was recopying and revising. That table sat in the tavern where Washington was hired out, and that tavern stood in Richmond, Virginia—the biggest city he had ever seen and, in late 1861, the capital of a renegade nation, the Confederate States of America, at war with the United States. Washington's enslaved narrative is the product not only of his experience and his mind but also of this process and its context.

On January 1, 1861, in the thick of the secession crisis, Washington began a year's term of labor in Richmond. For the first time in his adult life, he lived away from Fredericksburg, away from his many friends there, and away from Annie, with whom he corresponded throughout the year. Love letters were not all that kept him at his writing desk, though. Washington had brought the pages of his diary with him, and he revised them to create a narrative of his courtship back in Fredericksburg. With evident aspiration to produce a formal literary representation of his life, Washington took the penciled pages of his diary, recopied them in ink on finer white paper, and translated the diary's narrative into more dramatic form, with fancier rhetoric. He organized the dated diary entries into chapters, sometimes with titles and verse epigraphs. He occasionally wrote about himself in the third person ("Let us return and see What is become of our young Lad") and adopted theatrical language ("The Scene now changes").[18]

That Washington wrote the enslaved narrative by revising his diary is evident from the surviving diary pages. Washington kept his diary in pencil on ordinary blue letter paper, of which five folios (twenty pages) remain, covering the period from July 5 to December 29, 1858. At the top of the first folio, which comprises entries for July 5, 6, and 7—material that appears, lightly revised, in the narrative—Washington has written, in ink, "Copied." The second folio does not bear this mark because Washington evidently never finished the project of working up his diary into a literary autobiography. That manuscript leaves off at July 16, 1858, with several pages of his diary remaining as an unrevised rough draft. Those pages carry the story forward to December, when Washington was preparing (for the second time) to propose marriage to Annie.[19]

The narrative is an unfinished and incomplete work—eighteen pages of it survive, numbered in Washington's hand up to twenty-three, with five missing—but its outline clearly reveals the story's preoccupation. It begins in the mid-1850s, on the occasion of Washington and Annie Gordon's first meeting, and it wraps up as their courtship approaches its traditional conclusion. Their engagement seems to have been understood by the time he left for Richmond, and in October of 1861, Washington sent a letter saying, "I think we might be married soon next year"; indeed, they wed almost immediately after he returned to Fredericksburg. Washington's diary records a young man's uncertainty and anxiety about his unfolding romance, but once he begins turning these writings into an autobiography, he knows how the story will end. Annie becomes the destination of the narrative's rising action. At the same time, Washington knows that historic changes are afoot, as did many slaves keenly attuned to the progress of the war. Writing about impending marriage to Annie becomes his way of giving voice to a

1

Copyed

July 5th   For Noon.

All of the girls and Boys are going to fishing to-day
up at the falls. I wish I could go too but I can not because
I have not any Holiday: well I am not by myself. that is one
consolation, at any rate. — how I would like to see the
Boat leave her wharf, filled with happy hearts. no doubt,
though I should much rather go to fishing this Evening. with the
girls to tell the truth. only to be with Annie is the
most that I care about. the fishing-party.
I will go up to the Robertsons, to-night before I go to practice
and hear how the Fishing Party enjoyed themselves!
"Night.—   I went up to The Robertson's.
They Enjoyed their walk. but they did not catch
any fish but one. So I was disappointed. in
my Expectations. Poor Annie has gone home with
the head ach. I wish I could cure her: would at I
hasten to her relief. — as fast as my feet could carry
me. O why was I not a Doctor. but I will wait
until to-morrow-night and then go after her and go
with her down to her Practice — So I will make myself
contented with these noisy Girls Sallie Buckley, Bettie
and Susy.   Oh ain't I happy here is Sally sitting as
close to me as the chairs can with, and her cherry red lips
is in 3 inches of my own. — never mind I will sharpen
a kiss presently before she knows it.
And here is Bettie with her charming big arms around my neck
they feel just like [annie's] oh don't squeeze me
me So. Oh me, I'm cho— cho— choking.
but it makes me feel so good to See that I am loved

dawning vision of freedom from the bondage he never names. Crafting the narrative of his courtship describes a path toward emancipation.[20]

Washington enjoyed enough free time in Richmond to write to Annie on a regular basis, perhaps even once a week. "I did hope for a letter from you saturday," he wrote to her in October, "but no it did not come. I can hardly Expect one to-morrow for I never get your sweet letters before tuesday or Wendesday." In composing a narrative of their courtship, Washington found an additional way to use his literacy to stay connected with Annie, and revisiting his diary was a chance to reminisce about her and everyone he had left behind. When Washington looked back on this period later in life, when he wrote "Memorys of the Past," he made no allusion to homesickness for Fredericksburg or to his literary endeavors, but he did describe the atmosphere in Richmond: "I was living there when the Southern Slave holders in open Rebellion fired on Fort Sumter, little did they then think, that they were Fireing the Death-knell of Slavery, and little did I think that my deliverence was so near at hand."[21]

The outbreak of war may not have immediately portended emancipation, but Washington's residence in Richmond surely did expose him to freedom's possibilities. Slavery in Richmond, more than in Fredericksburg and far more than in the rural South, revolved around the practice of hiring out, and that practice often provided enslaved people with new forms of autonomy. Most other slaves Washington would have met in the city were, like him, laboring for wages outside their owners' immediate control. Some were even at liberty to "hire their own time"—to negotiate their own employment and receive their wages in cash, though they would have been forced to surrender to their owners most if not all of what they earned. Employers of slaves had broad authority to mete out punishment, but they could not discipline a slave with the same abandon as an owner, and the large enslaved population—almost 12,000 in 1860, in a city of less than 40,000—made complete supervision and surveillance of slaves an impossibility.[22]

Though he might have given little thought to emancipation back in April, Washington followed the progress of the war carefully, and after the Battle of Bull Run in July, he began to realize the conflict's potential impact on people like him: "Already the Slaves had been Escapeing into the union armys lines and many thereby getting of to the Free States. I could read the papers and Eagerly watched them for tidings of the war which had began in earnest. almost every day brought news of Battles. The Union troops was called 'Yankees and the Southern 'Rebs,' It had now <u>become</u> a well known fact that Slaves was daily making their Escape into the union lines." By October, Washington had decided that he would not spend another year in Richmond. Annie feared that his owners would send him back after the Christmas holidays, but Washington assured her, "I Think your fears groundless about my comeing back to Richmond. I'd do most any thing first. no Indeed I can not. you know they don,t force me. any where."[23]

His insistence on returning to Fredericksburg no doubt was motivated by his desire to be closer to Annie, but he probably also expected emancipation to come sooner to Fredericksburg—only fifty miles from Washington, D.C.—than to the Confederate capital. When the working year ended at Christmas in 1861, Washington embarked for Fredericksburg by train, leaving his Richmond employer under the impression that he would return on January 1. When he arrived back home, he revealed his true plans. "My Master was not pleased when he heard of my intention to remain in Fredericksburg that year," Washington recalled; "he seemed to think I wanted to remain too near the 'Yankees.'" As the new year dawned, Washington was convinced of the "well known fact" of emancipation's unfolding, and he eagerly anticipated something else. On January 3, 1862, he and Annie Gordon were wed at Fredericksburg's African Baptist church.[24]

During the last half of 1861, as Washington sensed the approach of these twin transformations—his impending marriage and the chance of freedom—he was working on the fourth and fifth chapters of his enslaved narrative. These chapters, based on diary entries from July 1858, describe a tumultuous time in his relationship with Annie. As Washington copied and rewrote, he subtly reshaped the diary's uncertain chronicle into a narrative that would culminate in marriage, as he now felt assured it would. His revisions also turned the one story he tells openly—the tale of his courtship—into another story, barely visible on the page, about slavery and freedom. When Harriet Jacobs narrated her life, she concluded with this observation: "Reader, my story ends with freedom; not in the usual way, with marriage." John Washington, writing in hopeful but uncertain anticipation, brought those two endings together. His autobiography represents something little published literature of slavery does, and something historians have only recently begun to understand. It draws an imaginative and logical connection between emancipation and romantic love.[25]

In the first and most aggressive revision of his diary, Washington changes the chronology of his relationship with Annie. According to the diary, Annie rejected his first marriage proposal on September 26, 1858. As a jilted twenty-year-old diarist, Washington recorded his bitterness at some length: "if She intended this from the first. She was wrong to encourage my visits. wrong to recive my addresse's wrong in permiting me to Trust her so confidantly. as I did (though I do not regret any thing. I ever told her in confidence) yet it was not Lady-like in her to permit. me to hope thus far. without warning me. which she could have done very easely if she had, wish to do so. No. Lady would permit a young man's advance so long without Discurageing him, unless she positively wished to trifle with his affection's." In rewriting this episode for chapter 4 of his autobiography, Washington situates it three months earlier, in June of 1858, and in his revised version of the same complaint against Annie, he adopts a different rhetoric: "In return, what should I expect from her. Simply <u>her love</u> or still less ~~he~~ a <u>candid refusal.</u> or an Entire discuragement. but to deceive me was cruel. Then why should I still press on and be her slave. any longer. in a word To be first encouraged then slighted. When I pay her a visit to be treated not as a Friend nor a Brother, much less a <u>lover</u>. is too unkind. Have not I the common feelings of man kind?"[26]

To express all his bitterness "in a word," Washington employs the word that never came up in his diary. Its usage here marks the only appearance of the word "slave" in all his surviving pre-emancipation writings, which amount to more than 10,000 words. Hints of anti-slavery rhetoric, too, have crept into Washington's prose at this point. The motto emblazoned on the abolitionist movement's iconic badge—a kneeling slave and the words, "Am I Not a Man and a Brother?"—reverberates in Washington's phrase, "not as a Friend nor a Brother," and in his plea, "Have not I the common feelings of man kind?"[27]

Living in a major city, Washington was exposed to a wider range of reading material than he had ever seen before. When he read newspaper articles on the progress of the war and its attendant political turmoil, even if they were the slanted pro-Confederacy reports of Richmond papers, he undoubtedly picked up some "opposition" rhetoric—which he apparently found resonant with his memory of a rocky courtship, or with the portrait of that courtship he wished to paint. By altering the sequence of events, he makes Annie, whom Washington now knew to be the central figure in his life, also the centerpiece of his story. With her rejection taking place three months earlier, he can construct a figure of himself as an afflicted protagonist who spends the summer of 1858 on an emotional journey toward winning her over—and by calling himself a "slave" in suffering the tyranny of her coquetry, Washington makes that journey an allegory of emancipation.

Washington's enslaved narrative remains, like the diary, silent on the subject of his legal status, but in this revised narrative of his romantic pursuit, Washington begins to hint at the afflictions of his enslavement. The obstacles between him and Annie fill him with a sense of injustice, the feeling that he suffers an unfortunate plight for no good reason. His fourth chapter, devoted to a week-long "painful misunderstanding" between them, is recopied almost verbatim from the diary, but the few sentences Washington inserts in 1861 consistently stress that he suffers unfairly—that mere accidents (like the accident of his birth to an enslaved mother in antebellum America) determine his fate. When he loses a chance to talk with Annie, or when she seems "offended" and he "wonder[s] what I have done," he augments the diary's text with brief laments like "Devil take My Luck," or "if it had of been any one else that would not have happened"; he twice adds the phrase, nowhere used in the diary, "Just my luck."[28]

He also slightly lifts the curtain across his enslavement by making reference to another kind of obstacle in his quest for Annie's hand—his work obligations, which the diary never mentions. The diary entry for July 6 relates Washington's excitement about a musical performance in town that evening: "I may have the pleasure of going with Annie," he writes, "but I am afraid I shall not have an opportuneity to go atal. and I have hardly time to think about it After noon—Just as I feared after all I can't go." When he revises this passage for the autobiography, Washington amplifies his grievance and makes clear it was the obligations of labor that detained him: "I do wonder if I can get off and have the pleasure of going with Miss Annie. but I am afread I can not. get off. and I hardly have time to think about it. Night. Just as I feard we have company and I can t go after her."[29]

Washington added to his enslaved narrative one more word he never used in his diary. In an offhand description of a pleasant moment at a social gathering, he writes, "ain,t I a happy 'nigger.'" The sole betrayal of his racial identity in anything he wrote before his emancipation, this peculiar self-reference suggests that what may have been too obvious to remark in 1858 has become salient by 1861. Now that he has sensed the contingency of slavery, Washington realizes the subjugated status that attends his race is not permanent and immutable.[30] He can put quotation marks around the identity the slave South has assigned him, can even be "happy" therein. Alternative realities now were imaginable, if still frustratingly out of reach. For an enslaved man in Richmond at the dawn of the Civil War—hopeful yet forced to wait, for his wedding and his freedom alike—an ebullient optimism springs forth, tempered by the sour awareness that injustice persists. These are the emotions of a writer whose hard work at literacy mostly has come to fruition—who is literate enough to write imaginatively, to control nuances of narrative structure and rhetorical emphasis—but who remains deprived of the time, the freedom, and the literary education to develop his talent.

It is no wonder, then, that he left off his narrative—perhaps tired of copying his diary, perhaps packing up to depart Richmond—at a moment of ambivalence about the act of writing. In the next diary entry Washington would have copied, had he continued revising it in Richmond, he records the events of July 17, 1858. At the end of several agonizing days of hoping to hear from Annie, and not hearing, he finally relents and decides to contact her: "I made up my mind this morning to write her a note much against my will. If I had of known that I should have to write her after all before we could understand each other, I would have written the next day, but as I don't think notes can always be understood properly, I did not write untill I was compeled to do so." For the lovesick Washington, writing is plagued by the possibilities of miscommunication, but he is compelled to do it by the exigencies of his affective life. It sounds like something from which he might prefer to be liberated. Annie Gordon provoked a grudging note from him in 1858, and it was she also who inspired him, in distant Richmond, to write an autobiography, a love story whose intricate composition tells that a life with her might be as longed for as emancipation.[31]

John Washington may have enjoyed privileges most slaves lacked, but he did not hesitate to seize his freedom when he saw the opportunity. Just as the Richmond newspapers had led him to believe it would, the progress of the war unsettled the slaveholding regime, and enslaved people increasingly seized the chance to escape their bondage. When the Union army approached Fredericksburg from the north, Washington flew to its refuge. A decade later, when he told the story in "Memorys of the Past," he crafted an explicit image of emancipation, notably individualistic, to succeed the one that lay submerged, coded as marriage, in his enslaved narrative—yet he also would return to the writerly ways and imaginative mien of his early diary.

In Richmond in 1861, Washington had spent untold hours, probably alone, seated with pen in hand. He was surrounded by letters from Annie, reading material like *Merry's Museum,* the pages of a diary (written in pencil) that recorded his interior experience of a few years before, and the accumulating pages of an autobiography (written in ink) that adapted that interior experience to a story about his new expectations for the future. In 1873, as a free man in Washington, D.C., married to Annie and surrounded by their five children, John Washington again spent many hours in the act of writing. He filled the pages of a composition book with recollections of his early life in slavery and, most of all, the story of his escape in 1862. He began writing "Memorys of the Past" with pen and ink, but by the end he had reverted to pencil. That seemingly mundane material difference reveals his still-evolving understanding of how to use his written literacy and how to depict his emancipation. As we will see, his writing practices show how blurry the boundary might sometimes have seemed, to Washington, between writing a life in slavery and writing it in freedom.

By the time he wrote "Memorys," Washington evidently had read some classic slave narratives. The best-known characteristics of the genre mark Washington's own narrative, including the archetypal first line that opens dozens of prior slave narratives. "I was born (in Fredericksburg Virginia: May 20th 1838)," he writes, his parentheses even seeming to bound off the sentence's particularity from its formulaic portion, as if Washington were filling in the blank of a template he has internalized. Like other authors of slave narratives, he discusses his early life, his separation from his mother, his education, and finally his escape. One unusual feature of "Memorys" is that it involves two distinct and equally dramatic moments of emancipation. Many slave narratives describe returns to the South, as fugitives either were recaptured or boldly returned to help family members escape, and a second journey to the North. Washington, though, as he narrates his two flights north across the Rappahannock River, experiments with different ways of articulating himself and different perspectives on the meaning of

freedom. His account of his initial escape, written in pen, has the individu-
alist tenor he might have encountered in other slave narratives. The description of his second flight, on the other hand, written in pencil, returns to the
interior immediacy of his diaristic writing. It reflects an abiding concern for
his family commitments and a mixed set of emotions about leaving behind
his Fredericksburg community.[32]

Washington's initial escape takes place on April 18, 1862—Good Friday—
as Union forces advance toward Fredericksburg. Most white residents evac-
uate the town in a panic: "a rumor had been circulated among them that
the Yankees was advancing but nobody seemed to believe it, until Every
body was startled by several reports of cannon. Then in an instant all was
wild confusion as a cavalry man dashed into the Dining Room and said
'The Yankees is in Falmouth.' Every body was on their feet at once. . . . In
less time than it takes me to write these lines, every white man was out of
the house." Washington and some friends head north out of town along the
banks of the Rappahannock River until they are hailed by Union soldiers
on the opposite shore, who row across to pick them up. The narrative rises
to an understandably stirring pitch:

> A Most Memorable night that was to me the Soilders assured me that I was
> now a free man and had nothing to do but stay with. . . . Before Morning I
> had began to fee like I had truely Escaped from the hands of the slaves master
> and with the help of God, I never would be a slave no more. I felt for the first
> time in my life that I could now claim Every cent that I should work for as my
> own. I began now to feel that life had a new joy awaiting me. I might now go
> and come when I pleased So I wood remain with the army until I got Enough
> money to travel further North. <u>This was the First Night</u> of my Freedom. It was
> good Friday indeed the Best Friday I had ever seen Thank God—xxxx.

In this passage, Washington writes in a way he rarely has before. For one
thing, he explicitly addresses slavery and freedom, as he never did in his
earlier writings. He also abandons his graceful cursive in favor of heavy
printed letters.[33]

His careful lettering attests that Washington has continued to be an avid
reader, growing well enough acquainted with print culture that he can easily replicate the shape of a typeset *g,* knows the appropriate use of serifs,
and perhaps has imagined his own writing ending up in print. The printed

as My own. I began now to
fell that Life had a new Joy
awaiting me I might now go and
come when I pleased So I wood
remain with the army until I got
Enough Money to travel farther
North This was the First Night
of My Freedom. It was good
Friday indeed the Best Friday I
had ever seen. Thank God — xxxx
———————— We were all astire very
early next Morning for the Soilders
had a Sad duty to perform.
The night before they captured Fal-
Mouth, they, while advancing
Suddenly in the darkness found
the road Barracaded, and its
Rebels concealed, close by who
fired upon the advancing troops
Where the Road way cut through
a hill and killed and wou
7 and

Page 91 of "Memorys of the Past," John Washington Papers, Massachusetts
Historical Society. Courtesy of the Alice Jackson Stuart Family Trust.

letters also offer a close-up glimpse of Washington's writing process. Anyone who has doodled in the margin of a notebook knows the meditative
sensation of the slow, back-and-forth movement of the pen when making
and retracing the heavy lines of letters or shapes. Of the words "First Night
of my Freedom," one can say nothing with greater certainty than that Washington spent more time inking them than he did any other words on the
page. Exactly how long he lingered over them is impossible to know, but
the slowness or quickness of writing is not merely a matter of tempo. It can
represent, as the art historian Michael Fried explains, a transformation in
interior experience, turning a verbal exercise into a graphical one: "A manner of writing that shaped individual letters with extreme slowness would
maximize the likelihood of diverting the writer's attention away from the
larger flow of meaning in his prose to the letters themselves, or say to the
letters as variously configured, conspicuously legible (almost an oxymoron),
and undeniably material marks on a sheet of paper, inscribed there by the
metal point of a pen dipped repeatedly—every several words—in a container
of ink."[34]

Whether or not Washington lost sight of the "larger flow of meaning,"
his stream of thought certainly could have run on faster or further in these
moments than his hand was moving—dwelling over and reliving a scene he
cannot fully reproduce; recalling, as his pen doubles back over the thick
lines of the letter *N,* flashes of firelight on the faces of Union soldiers; pon-
dering the abstract joys of being, for the first time, beyond an owner's ken;
or just wandering unaccountably over present distractions (a crying child in
the next room, the cost of ink for a man living on a housepainter's wage).
Only a few pages earlier, Washington had contemplated the duration of
writing, its slowness compared with thinking and acting: "In less time than
it takes me to write these lines," he mused as he described white Virginians'
flight from the Yankees. That temporal lag between physically forming letters and witnessing or thinking through events stretches to an extreme in
the four small *x*'s at the end of the passage: "It was good Friday indeed the
Best Friday I had ever seen Thank God—xxxx." Here, Washington wields
his pen yet fully occludes his thoughts, setting down on the page what are
unquestionably nothing more than "material marks on a sheet of paper."

Whatever he was thinking as he inscribed those deterrent *x*'s—perhaps
almost nothing at all, perhaps so much that it overwhelmed his ability
to express it—his account of his first night of freedom culminates with a

reminder that his interior is ultimately inaccessible. In its composition, word
by word and letter by letter, Washington's emancipation remains largely
private, and in his express recollection, it is likewise a transformation for
one person within himself. The meaning of freedom—to "claim Every cent
that I should work for as my own," to "feel that life had a new joy awaiting
me," and to "go and come when I pleased"—resides with the individual (and
reflects Washington's apparent assimilation of the free-labor ideology of
President Lincoln's Republican Party). This representation of emancipation,
though, is not the climax of "Memorys of the Past." When Washington depicts a second moment of transition from slavery to freedom, he composes it
differently and gives it a different resonance; there, the individual self fades
from prominence.[35]

Washington's "First Night of Freedom" occurs less than two-thirds of
the way through his manuscript. He goes on to narrate his four months as
a "contraband." Though technically a ward of the Union army, he proved to
be an enterprising free agent. He secured gainful employment as a cook in
General Rufus King's kitchen, earned the confidence of military commanders by providing intelligence on local people and geography, and marched
with the infantry, occasionally even mounting a horse, as the army roved
through northern Virginia. For a time, while General King maintained headquarters at Fredericksburg, Washington lived among his old friends. He
reports that "Hundreds of colord people obtained passes and free transpor-
tation to Washington and the North. And made their Escape to the <u>Free
States.</u>" He never says why he waited to do the same, but the reason becomes
clear in the final chapters of "Memorys," in which he narrates his second
emancipation.[36]

The tenth and penultimate chapter begins, like Washington's old diary
entries, with a dateline: "Sunday morning August 10th 1862 dawned bright
and warm." In this chapter, as Washington narrates one of the more action-
packed sequences in the entire text, he approaches a suspenseful moment—
"Woods on both sides of the road here was densely thick and we did not
know what moment the rebels might fire on us"—and it is exactly then that
he abandons pen and ink in favor of a pencil, the same instrument he used
to keep his diary in 1858. Though the portions of the narrative written in
ink show signs of careful editing, what Washington wrote in pencil seems
to be both first and final draft, and "Memorys" proceeds, from this point,
at the brisk narrative clip that composition with a pencil enables.[37]

Washington receives news that cuts short his time with the army: "A Reward of $300.00 had been offerd for my head in Fredericksburg and knowing if I should be captured by the rebels I should be taken to Richmond Va where I was well known and no doubt be immediately hung or shot for being with the 'Yankees.'" He therefore leaves the army in the field and returns to Union-occupied Fredericksburg. He "had intended now to stay at home and make a living while after a while, perhaps, to go north some where," but he can sustain that intention only a week, because he soon learns that Union forces plan to withdraw from Fredericksburg. "My wife and friends advised me not to let the Yankees leave me Behind," Washington writes, because "they firmly beleived the rebels would take my life."[38]

Washington's friends' fears probably were warranted. Confederate policy on African American prisoners of war was unsettled and incoherent for much of the war, and in August of 1862, with formal enlistment of black Union soldiers just getting under way (in southern Louisiana and coastal South Carolina), southern leaders had scarcely begun to consider the matter. Individual commanders in the field did not necessarily act in accordance with policy, though. The Confederate army generally denied African Americans the rights of prisoners of war, and in several instances, including the notorious Fort Pillow massacre, southern troops murdered black soldiers who surrendered to them. Washington had not technically enlisted in the Union army (he was not allowed to, at this early stage of the war), but a Confederate officer might not make that distinction. Having fled from his owner and spent four months effectively in the service of Yankees, Washington very likely may have faced retribution if captured.[39]

In even more haste, then, than he displayed upon his initial escape in April, Washington prepares to flee the city. The eleventh and final chapter of "Memorys" carries the diaristic heading, "Sunday afternoon Aug 31st 1862 about 4 oclock P. M." He looks across the river and discovers Union troops are breaking camp. With his protectors departing, he knows he must leave, too. "With a sad heart, I returned to tell my wife the bad news." He seeks a pass from a colonel who advises him to be across the bridge and out of Fredericksburg within fifteen minutes. Without Annie—who "was not in a condition to travel far," presumably because she was pregnant with their first child—Washington departs. He and his fast-moving narrative pause one last time:

After crossing the Bridge I hastened to the Top of the Hill at the East end of the Bridge. and looked back at the town that had given me birth and with a sad heart and full eyes thought of some of the Joys I had felt within its limits—But now compelled to fly from it for my life, for daring to make my Escape to the Union army, and with a price fixed upon my head if caught. I could not help weeping, (though it was not manly) as I looked back, and thought of my poor young wife, who could not fly with me. The Rebels was at that very minnit swarming the Heights, West of Fredericksburg. And I know not, but they might take vengence on her as I had Escaped they could lock her up in jail or any thing else and who would protect her.

My Solequay was interrupted by a tremendous Explosion that could be heard for Miles around, and shook the Earth like an Earthquake. The Flames shot upward hundreds of feet into the air—and as suddenly all was Silant as death.

The retreating army had destroyed the bridge behind them. Twenty-four hours later, Washington would be in the District of Columbia—one of forty thousand slaves who fled to the capital city during the first three years of the Civil War, one of almost thirty thousand African Americans who would settle there permanently by 1870.[40]

This passage represents the moment of his flight from Virginia, the final break with his past in slavery, and it differs considerably from the "first night" of his freedom. Annie has moved to the center of Washington's attention, where she was in his diary and enslaved narrative, and he revives the sentimental voice of his earlier writings ("sad heart and full eyes," unmanly weeping). In narrating his first escape, Washington used the first-person pronoun thirteen times in the space of 150 words; the second account of escape contains just seven *I*s in a longer passage. His earlier celebrations of personal freedom (to come and go as he pleases, to claim the wages of his labor as his own) here give way to bittersweet reflections on "the town that had given me birth" and "Some of the Joys I had felt within the limits"—the joys of friendship and romantic love documented in his diary and first autobiography. "Compelled to fly" from his home, as he was "compeled" to write to Annie, Washington registers an ambivalent embrace of the freedoms of literacy and escape to the North.

If the slow penwork of the "First Night of Freedom" conceals some interior richness, poignantly veiled by the materiality of Washington's letters, this concluding section swings the other way, toward writing quickly with a will to keep up with the rush of his recollections. Whereas his pen and ink tended to hide what he was thinking, Washington's pencil narrative almost overflows, his effusive "Solequay" (soliloquy) interrupted only by the remembered blasting of the bridge. Words erased and rewritten reveal a process in which writing frequently outpaces thought and reaches a moment of reconsideration. Immediately preceding the passage quoted above, Washington has torn out a page of his composition book. His writing evidently ran on too quickly for him—his penmanship lapsed into illegibility, or he second-guessed too many words to erase, or he expressed more than he thought appropriate or necessary—and he went to a new page and began again.[41]

In the closing passage of "Memorys," writing still in pencil, he describes his first night in his new home in a free land. No longer a lone freedman in the protection of the Union army, he is now his own family's guardian:

> I then came out and arrived Safe at 6th Street Wharf in Washington, D.C. on the Night of September 1st 1862, in a hard rain. My Grandmother, Aunt and her 4 children all Slept on 14th St that Night and next morning walked to Georgetown Where we had friends My Grand mother aunt and the children Soon found Some place to Stay, and I obtained board at Mrs. Boons at $2.50 per Week. My next object Was to obtain Work in order that I might pay my board and get a change of clothing for I was sadly in need of them. I had no trade then and knew not what to do. But soon learned to turn my hand to most any thing light. There was a plenty of heavy work. Such loading and unloading vessels and steamers but that was mostly to heavy for me as I was not very strong but finally obtained a place Bottleing Liquor for Dodge &c at $1.25 per day which lasted for some time.

With this different kind of soliloquy, this quiet recollection of practicalities—board and wages and places for the children to stay—John Washington concludes his post-emancipation slave narrative.[42]

The figure of a liberated self that Washington constructed in his first moment of escape—using the self-conscious language of ink's careful permanence—harmonizes with the many other slave narratives he may have taken as models. It displays a commitment to the realism that largely characterizes that genre. The second escape, meanwhile, revolves around Washington's interrelationship with his former community in Fredericksburg, exhibits a complex mixture of nostalgia and fear, and participates in the conventions of romantic fiction. By its conclusion, "Memorys of the Past" reveals itself to be a hybrid of the two literary genres that shaped Washington's development as a writer, and the text defies any attempt to associate one way of writing with slavery, one with freedom. Emancipation, in turn—the result of both escapes—appears less as slavery's antithesis than as the sum of Washington's experiences, his being bound (in slavery, in marriage) as well as his being free.[43]

As a thirty-five-year-old husband and father composing a life story for at least the second time, John Washington was still—as when he was a slave—learning to write. Of course, for someone with no formal education, he had achieved stunning technical proficiency. Not just capable of making himself understood in writing, he had even undertaken the unusual and ambitious project of experimenting with different ways of narrating his own life. In this he resembles some of the most talented writers of his age, including Frederick Douglass, who rewrote and augmented his autobiography three times between 1845 and 1892, and Mary Boykin Chesnut, who spent years revising her Civil War diary into a first-person epic of the South. Though surely gratified by his literary ability, and by seeing his experiences made real on the written page, Washington still wrote with an awareness of his limitations, and the autobiographical act transported him back to their source.[44]

In "Memorys of the Past," when telling the story of how he learned to write, Washington recreated his Uncle George's copy text—"My Dear Mother, I Take this opporteunity to write you a few lines to let you know that I am well"—and recalled his uncle's encouragement: "when you can do that much you ~~can do that much~~ you can write to your mother." The struck-out words reveal that Washington had composed a draft of this episode and was recopying it. Doubling a phrase is precisely the error one makes when losing one's place in a copy text (the repetition begins at a line break in the manuscript). Even the most accomplished writers recopy drafts and lose their place, but Washington's slip occurs at what for him must have been a vertiginous and affecting moment. Only an instant before, he was reproducing his uncle's model—that is, writing the same few lines he had copied repeatedly when he was twelve years old, arduously trying to become literate. Gripped by the déjà vu intensity of that memory, he might well be expected to lose track of the *you*s in his draft, a copy text of his own making in place of his uncle's exemplar on wallpaper.

If the beginnings of his literacy seemed like only yesterday, or if he took pride in observing just how far he had come, Washington nevertheless knew as he wrote these pages that his skill as a writer remained hobbled. He ends the chapter on "Learning to Write" by asserting precisely that: "[I] am Still trying to improve—But having never had a regular course of spelling taught me. I am in consequence very defficent in every branch of a common and edocation." Washington's assessment of his literacy may seem to place undue weight on spelling, especially given that irregular orthography is far from uncommon in nineteenth-century manuscripts. Whether free or enslaved, white or black, educated or not, writers misspelled many words. But Americans of the post–Noah Webster era came to view correct spelling as a virtue; educational practice and the mores of society treated the ability to spell as a crucial marker of literacy and breeding. Not knowing how to spell a word could provoke great anxiety in a writer (as it did for the likes of Herman Melville). Washington had to have been acutely aware that he was misspelling words on the very pages that narrate how he learned to write many years before.[45]

Washington did see redeeming value, though, in the uncomfortable fact that his education remained "defficent" even in 1873. He concludes the self-deprecating remarks on his literacy with these lines: "So those who may be tempted to read thees pages may possibly learn for the first time the disadvantages of of Slavery. With some of its attending evils." Other slave narratives commonly include prefatory apologies; Harriet Jacobs, for instance, writes, "I trust my readers will excuse deficiencies in consideration of circumstances," and her sponsor, Lydia Maria Child, adds that although she has edited Jacobs's text, "both the ideas and the language are her own." Usually, the verbal facility such narratives do exhibit serves to demonstrate African Americans' intellectual abilities and supports their claims to equality. Washington, conversely, offers his own verbal imperfections as a testimonial to the "disadvantages" and "evils" of slavery—a form of political instruction from which his reader "may possibly learn." His manuscript's imperfections, far from obscuring or invalidating its content, he suggests, harbor a significance beyond the words they struggle to represent.[46]

The act of writing an autobiography is an unfinished reckoning with past events, and John Washington, still learning to write a decade out of slavery, finds that bondage hobbles him long after its shackles are unlocked. In his first autobiography, Washington both imagined freedom (as an adjunct of romantic love's fruition) and exercised it with pencil and pen. In composing "Memorys of the Past," he not only offers an account of his life in slavery but also—taking up the familiar pencil, inscribing some long-remembered words—senses the ways in which slavery's oppressions remain a part of his life.

chapter four

The Written We

AS JOHN M. WASHINGTON stepped ashore in Washington, D.C., on a September evening in 1862, Abraham Lincoln was headed northward out of town, returning to the Soldier's Home after a day's work at the White House. At the presidential summer retreat, Lincoln had spent several evenings and weekends writing an executive order on slaves in the rebel states. He had produced the first draft in July but, at his secretary of state's suggestion, decided not to issue it until the Union's military position improved. At the beginning of September, that prospect seemed more distant than ever. The withdrawal from Fredericksburg that compelled John Washington to leave the place of his birth was part of a series of setbacks connected with the Union's demoralizing defeat at the Second Battle of Bull Run. The same federal soldiers who had cheerfully greeted Washington on the banks of the Rappahannock River in April now found themselves hastily retreating to defend the nation's capital against possible Confederate attack.

Within a few weeks, those soldiers had marched seventy miles north to meet Robert E. Lee's invading army near Sharpsburg, Maryland. By the end of the day on September 17, more than twenty thousand American soldiers had been killed or wounded, but the incomparably bloody Battle of Antietam seemed at last to have brought Lincoln the victory he was looking for. Once he received definitive news of Lee's retreat, he would issue the Preliminary Emancipation Proclamation without delay. On Sunday, September 21, he sat down with his draft, "dressed it over a little," and, in preparation for his Monday morning cabinet meeting, wrote out a clean copy of the four-page manuscript that would officially make the Civil War a battle to end slavery.[1]

After Lincoln retired for the night, eight enslaved men in Wilmington, North Carolina, stole a boat on the Cape Fear River. They rowed thirty miles downstream, desperate to remain unseen, racing against the coming of dawn. By the time the president's cabinet assembled at the White House the next morning and listened to Lincoln read the historic document he was about to make public, twenty-four-year-old William B. Gould and his seven compatriots had reached the Atlantic. One of the Union's blockading naval vessels picked them up off Fort Caswell around eleven o'clock in the morning. These eight men, who knew nothing of Lincoln's proclamation, had freed themselves.[2]

Two meanings of emancipation—an individual's passage to freedom, a revolution in the life of the nation—converge in the experience of William Gould and in his writing. Five days after he rowed into the Atlantic, while still aboard the ship that rescued him, Gould began keeping a diary—the only surviving diary by a newly self-emancipated African American. On October 3, Gould wrote: "all of us ship'd to day for three years. first takeing the Oath of Allegiance to the Goverment of uncle Samuel." He wrote in his diary regularly during his three years of service in the U.S. Navy, not only chronicling the advent of his own freedom but also crafting a collective history of "all of us," the freedmen and sailors with whom he shared the trials of war and service to "uncle Samuel."[3]

In time, the act of writing in his diary became a way for Gould to figure out his place in the succession of communities to which emancipation seemed to open a door: the ship, the navy, a national citizenry. If John Washington experimented with ways of translating an individual life into written language, Gould did the same with his life's intersection with others' lives. As an artifact of a freedman's political consciousness taking root, the diary shows how quickly on the heels of freedom's promise might come anxiety about the problems of race in the post-slavery United States.

It may have been with a thrill and a ceremonious gesture that Gould opened the cardboard cover of a composition book, brought his pen to a fresh page—perfect icon for his own new beginning—and began chronicling his life after slavery. Here is what he wrote:

Sun. Sept. 27th
At Beaufort, N.C. We coald ship all night and until ten Oclock. we then up anchor. hauld alongside of the store ship (Wm. Badger.) for the purpose of takeing more Coal. and stores on board.

Mon. Sept. 28th
At Beaufort. finishd Coaling to day. took in stores. fine day

Tues. Sept. 29th
At Beaufort. takeing in stores. all day. made preperation. to convey some paroled prisoners to Wilmington.

Wens. Sept. 30th
At Beaufort. finished takeing in stores. we were visited to day by. Major General. Foster and staff. (commander of the Department) fine day.[4]

This astonishing artifact, the diary of a just-escaped slave, can sometimes seem, as here, surprisingly dull. Of course, the life of a sailor whose ship lies at anchor to load supplies—like that of a soldier set to drills all day, or a woman doing an army hospital's laundry—could be tedious, too. In this regard, Gould's wartime diary may be a model of verisimilitude, a crystalline account of freedpeople's wartime experience. Still, what he writes is striking for its understatement and impersonality. Even on occasions more momentous than the taking in of stores, Gould proves peculiarly inexpressive. In early 1863, he writes, "came to anchor. at 4 bells Quarters and Serveace. Read the Articles of War. Also the Proclamation of Emancipation, verry good." Relative to his usual staid manner, "verry good" may seem almost effusive, but it nevertheless reveals little of Gould's thinking about Lincoln's historic decree.[5]

Gould's literacy, though not perfect, is too highly developed to account fully for his reticence. Just as John Washington, in his diary, could have discussed slavery instead of courtship, had he wished, Gould clearly is capable of expressing his thoughts about emancipation, at least in some plain form, rather than logging the monotonous activities of his ship. But the purpose of his act of writing, the implicit rationale for the diary, changes during the three-year period in which Gould encountered a world beyond North Carolina's shores, watched the drama of the Civil War unfold, and became a more adept writer.

Gould's initial decision to devote his diary to outside events more than his own thoughts reflects an experience of wartime emancipation, and of a freedman's military service in particular, defined by the assembly of new communities. It is only the first intimation of Gould's literary project that he uses the pronoun *we* three times in his first four days' entries, the pronoun *I* not once. (Even when he drops the subjects of sentences, the implied nouns are plural. Gould's arms and back probably bore part of the load—though, tellingly, he does not say so—but it would not have been he alone who "finishd Coaling.") With his diary's *we,* Gould fashions a written representation of his own belonging in a larger collective—something many formerly enslaved men began to forge, through writing, as they came together in the military. In the tumult of wartime emancipation, its jubilation and its trials, literacy served freed people not only, perhaps not even very much, as a tool for individual self-expression. Writing mattered as a medium for the new relations of communities—as a literal interaction among black soldiers or, as for Gould, a verbal reckoning with the possibilities and problems of collective bonds. Several recent histories of African American life in the postbellum period have highlighted the importance of formal organizations—political, religious, social, educational, literary—that black communities developed during Reconstruction and after. William Gould's diary bespeaks the more nebulous bonds of companionship, the real and imagined affiliations that manuscript writings, more than the published literature of a public sphere, may both depict and create.[6]

When the Union army entered the Confederate States, slaves could see northern forces in a variety of ways: as a host of liberators, as an employer offering jobs in manual labor, as just another set of white people seeking to control and exploit them. By late 1862, with the Emancipation Proclamation officially allowing black enlistment, African American men could see in it an opportunity to prove themselves and claim their dignity, to fight for the liberation of those still in bondage, and to take the first steps toward freedom, self-sufficiency, and citizenship. One of those steps, as they themselves knew and some of their commanders acknowledged, was to become educated. During the years of wartime emancipation—from 1861, when the first "contrabands" arrived at Fortress Monroe, until 1865, when the Freedmen's Bureau was created—the army took scattershot measures to teach black soldiers basic literacy, in part because literate men were needed as noncommissioned officers in black regiments. As thousands of men, women, and children fled from their owners and flooded Union army camps, military leaders also cooperated with northern aid societies to set up schools for the freed people, even if for no better reason than to keep contrabands out of their hair. The federal government, northern missionaries, and southern blacks themselves would soon begin organizing a major system of formal education for the freed people. But in the meantime, this great congregation of former slaves—in and around the African American regiments and in contraband camps, their "first great cultural and political meeting grounds"—also meant that those who had become literate while enslaved now could openly teach others to read and write.[7]

The literacy of the enslaved emerged from hiding with great rapidity. Susie King Taylor was teaching her fellow ex-slaves as early as the summer of 1862. Born into slavery in Georgia, Taylor had surreptitiously learned to read and write from a free black woman in Savannah. She walked the streets of the city with her books "wrapped in paper to prevent the police or white persons from seeing them." As Union forces encroached on coastal Georgia, Taylor's uncle carried her and his own children to one of the outlying islands, where they were taken up by a Union gunboat. The commander of the vessel espied the fourteen-year-old Taylor and struck up a conversation with her. He asked her first if she could read, and when she told him she could, persisted in asking if she knew how to write. "As if he had some doubts of my answers," Taylor later recalled, "he handed me a book and a pencil and told me to write my name and where I was from." The black girl's demonstration earned her a spot teaching other freed children and, later, the men of the First South Carolina Volunteers, the earliest African American regiment.[8]

Even outside of such makeshift schools, the pursuit and practice of literacy drew former slaves together. Frances Beecher Perkins, a white northerner in Florida who taught black soldiers stationed there, observed: "Whenever they had a spare moment, out would come a spelling-book or a primer or Testament, and you would often see a group of heads around one book." A white visitor to a hospital for black soldiers saw that men "would all gather about" whichever men in the ward could read. The commander of the First South Carolina Volunteers, Thomas Wentworth Higginson, learned that some of his men set out to form "a literary association, with the end chiefly, of learning the art of writing." Elijah Marrs, a literate freedman from Kentucky, could often be found "surrounded by a number of the men, each waiting his turn to have a letter written home." Indeed, once a few freed people in a contraband camp had learned to write, they became amanuenses for everyone around them. According to one account, a group of military recruits just escaped from slavery produced a "brisk correspondence" by enlisting the help of students in the nearby school: "Three quarters of the letters came from camp in the well-known chirography of Sammy Simmons, Jerry Polite, or others of the schoolboys who had learned their alphabet since emancipation."[9]

We generally suppose that writing occurs in solitude, and undoubtedly it often did. Higginson described a freedman of his regiment setting up "a little table" for writing in the corner of a tent, and some soldiers' letters suggestively capture the inward and absorbing quality of writing. Zack Burden evidently sat a long time alone with his barely intelligible letter to President Lincoln spread in front of him. After he had signed his name, this novice writer fastidiously inscribed dozens of small dots in a cloud around his signature, his mind perhaps dreamily wandering, or just captivated by the alchemy of ink and paper. Less meditative, but probably just as engrossed in the act of writing, Warner Madison relentlessly punctuated his protest against the harassment of blacks by Freedmen's Bureau agents in Memphis, stabbing the page after nearly every word, as if to vent his anger: "i think, it is, one of the most. obnoxious. and foul, and, mean. thing. that exsist on, anny. part. of. the. Beauraur. Why My Children has, to, get. passes, now. to, go, to. schooll."[10]

Solitude was not the norm, however, for soldiers and sailors. In a military unit or a contraband camp, not only learning how to write but also putting literacy to use could become a communal undertaking. Dictating

and let me no how you
feel so No More this
time N E E
stat of N raggenne in Cit of John
To A Lenkin
r my Wife is left A long
and no help and they Wont let
me go home Direct you letter
to City Saint 8 Reg. U.S.C.T.
25 Corps 2n Brig gaeb 2nd Division
Com. B. & Deriet to
Zack Burden

Zack Burden to Mr. Abebrem Lenkin, February 2, 1865, B-110 1865, Letters
Received, ser. 360, Colored Troops Division, Record Group 94, National
Archives, Washington, D.C.

to a more literate peer, like Elijah Marrs, obviously entailed cooperation and forging new acquaintances; taking up the pen oneself also could spark the kinds of interactions and alliances that had been suppressed under slavery.

The legal and ideological regime that had driven black literacy underground had also discouraged assembly. If the idea of slaves forging passes nagged at antebellum slaveholders, visions of secret councils of insurrectionary slaves drove them entirely to distraction. Slave-state statutes that prohibited slaves' education often took special aim at their gathering together for that purpose—or for almost any other reason. An 1823 Mississippi law prohibited "all meetings or assemblies of Slaves, or free negroes, or mulattoes, mixing and associating with such slaves, above the number of five, at any place of public resort, or at any meeting house or houses, in the night, or at any school or schools, for teaching them reading or writing, either in the day or night, under whatsoever pretext." Virginia legislators, with the repetition of the obsessed, used the words *assembly* and *assemblage* eight times in a single section of its 1849 slave code. In South Carolina, whites' particular terror of what slaves might do under cover of darkness led them to ban slave meetings—even for religious purposes, even when white people were present—"either before the rising of the sun or after the setting of the same."[11]

As with anti-literacy laws, these measures had mixed effects. They could be difficult to enforce; many slaveholders wished to make exceptions for religious instruction (usually by white preachers); and enslaved people managed to form social ties and exchange information anyway. Just as they could learn, covertly, to read and write, slaves could find ways to lead active and complex social lives outside their owners' supervision—certainly when they lived or were hired out in urban areas, but on large plantations, too. Slaves in the rural South gathered for worship on their own (sometimes blending aspects of African religious practices with Christianity) and even held large barbecues and dances. These gatherings often remained a secret, but some owners merely turned a blind eye, regarding them as harmless outlets for energies that might otherwise lead to escape or rebellion. Many slaves were allowed to travel between plantations to visit spouses and children nearby—or made the excursion without permission—and so became part-time members of another slave-quarter society. Though more common in the eighteenth century than during the height of plantation slavery, maroon colonies—small groups of runaways secreted in wilderness areas of the South, occasionally along with Native Americans—provided some escaped slaves a chance to build semi-independent communities in the shadow of the institution.[12]

Such exceptions notwithstanding, there is no question that slavery ravaged African American communal life, forcing incipient social relationships behind veils of secrecy and toward the margins of daily activity. One reason state legislators paid special attention to nighttime gatherings is that long hours of forced labor and extensive white surveillance during the day already denied slaves much chance to assemble. Most important, the domestic slave trade imposed the constant threat and frequent reality of separation, making social connections tenuous and transient. Emancipation therefore not only allowed ordinary African Americans' acts of writing to come into the open but also enabled new forms of affiliation. Whether they migrated to a new home, as John Washington did, or remained linked by choice or economic exigency to the land where they had been enslaved, freed people could begin to think anew about their places in communities—communities with some hope of permanence, no longer exclusively formed and often broken up by white owners' inscrutable dealings.[13]

The formerly enslaved men who enlisted in the U.S. military encountered particularly novel forms of collectivity. In the army, they met fellow African Americans from different places and backgrounds. They met white men who were not their owners—but could still give them orders. (In the navy, they could serve on nominally equal terms with white sailors, though only at the lower ranks.) Their wives and children, if they had them, may have encamped nearby along with numerous others fleeing slavery for the protection of Union lines. This strange social landscape was for thousands of African Americans their first experience of freedom. Some, like William Gould, were slaves only days or hours before they enlisted, entering into their first contract, receiving their first promise of wages they could keep, and often finding their first opportunity either to learn to write or to employ their literacy with impunity.

In this setting, the new freedoms of literacy and assembly came together. The act of writing could be an occasion for face-to-face cooperation among marginally literate men, as well as a medium for imagining the new communities that emancipation's social revolution made possible. Some collaborations were small and incidental. A soldier stationed in South Carolina wrote a letter using a piece of paper on which someone else had been practicing penmanship. Rows of cursive lowercase *y*'s and *g*'s run across the bottom of the page, in pencil and in different handwriting—perhaps that of a fellow soldier the letter writer was tutoring, or of an industrious tentmate who borrowed paper and then gave it back half-used.[14] Rufus Wright was literate enough to write a letter to his wife in April of 1864, but he still was learning from the people around him. When he wrote to his wife again the next month, he wanted to tell her about his comrades who had been killed in recent fighting. He evidently had to ask someone how to spell the name of "Sergent Stephensen," and his latest discovery in the quirks of English spelling made an impression on him: he now signed his name "Ruphus."[15]

In other, more concerted joint efforts, collaboration in writing was also a form of political action. Scenes of writing by committee—a group of freedmen funneling ideas to an appointed penman—might culminate in a letter of petition bearing multiple signatures in the same handwriting (or seventeen signatures in the handwriting of two or three people, plus a notation of "fifty outher"). Black soldiers came together to register their shared complaints through the pen of a secretary: "Wee have been on Dayley fetig from the Last of Juli up to this Day without a forlough or any comfort what ever." Some letters arrived on the desks of authorities with no names attached but still speaking in chorus. Perhaps at the urging of one of his fellow noncommissioned officers, the writer of an 1864 petition added a postscript across the top margin of the page, presumably in hope of convincing the authorities to pay attention: "this Letter are wretten by fficers." One petition entailed not only confabulation about the content but also some creative procurement of writing materials: it is written on a blank form used by the Confederate quartermaster, appropriated (under official or unofficial auspices) by men of the advancing regiment, who adapted it to their purposes. Squeezed in around blank lines for dates and signatures, preprinted text about "the articles specified in the foregoing list," and the imprimatur of the "Quartermaster, C.S. Army," the most literate man in the group writes: "And So this is from Co A. 99th U.S.C.T. and we All Enhope that we weill Recieve Some Satisfaction from you Ser And we Enhope that you will think Nufe of us as to Answerd this Letter Ser if you please Ser."[16]

If the physical act of writing was an occasion for affiliation, the mental undertaking became a medium for expressing new bonds of friendship. After William Guy was killed in action at Petersburg, Virginia—the disastrous "Battle of the Crater," in which African American regiments suffered espe-

cially heavy casualties—two of his friends took up their pens to memorial-
ize him. One, in a tentative schoolboy's hand, wrote a dispatch to the *Lyceum Observer,* a black newspaper back home in Baltimore. "[Y]our unworthy
coresponde[nt] of these few lines feels his incapa bility of the task which he
has undertaken," writes Zacharia Jefferson. Nonetheless, he wishes the
newspaper's readers to know "the galantry of my young and valiant friend
Corpoal William Guy this noble young man died fighting to defend stars
and stripes of the noble 30th of Maryland Corpal W[m] Guy was one of the
Color guards of the 30th Rg I must say ^to ^much credit ~~it due this~~ ^cannot be given
this noble young man who so nobly so valliantly fought for the liberty and
equality of the human race." Another friend, James H. Freeman, accepted
the task of answering a worried letter from his fallen comrade's mother: "I
am sarry to have to inform You that thear is no dobt of his Death he Died
A Brave Death in Trying to Save the Colors of Rige in that Dreadful Battil
Billys Death was unevesally by all but by non greatter then by my self ever
sins we have bin in the Army we have bin amount the moust intimoat
Friend wen every our Rige wen into Camp he sertan to be at my Tent and
meney happy moment we seen to gether Talking about Home and the Prob-
ability of our Living to get Home to See each other Family and Friend."[17]

Driven by the emotional impact of Corporal Guy's death, both writers
stretch themselves to apply their literacy to new ends. Jefferson may never
have written for a newspaper before (there is no evidence that his letter was
published, but he hoped it would receive "the careful revision of the editors
of the Lyceum Observer"). He is undoubtedly a reader of newspapers,
though, and from the *Observer* or other sources he has imbibed the rhetoric
of wartime journalism ("to defend stars and stripes"; a heavy reliance on the
word *valiant*). Fastidious about his phrasing, anxious about his writing's
fitness for its subject and for public consumption, he reviews, crosses out,
and revises what he has written.

Where Jefferson strives to live up to a standard of public discourse, Freeman must use written language to convey something very personal. To con-
sole Corporal Guy's mother, he suggests that he sympathizes with her grief
because he too has lost, if not a son, an "intimoat Friend." The abstract language of emotion is only barely available to Freeman: he struggles to spell
"intimoat" and (elsewhere) "Simppathy," he omits some crucial verb following "Billys Death was unevesally" (universally *mourned* or *grieved?*), and he
lacks words for his own feelings toward his friend. Though Freeman may be

limited in his lexicon, he can use the stuff of elementary learning—*see, saw, seen*—to accomplish a deft narrative maneuver dramatizing his bond with Corporal Guy. He transports Mrs. Guy into the army camp that was the scene of the men's friendship. In describing "meney happy moment we seen to gether Talking about Home," Freeman trains a camera eye on himself and his friend. If he cannot articulate just how much those conversations meant to him privately, he can express their significance by declaring that they *were seen*—that the bond of friendship was strong enough to show forth publicly. In effect, Freeman enlists the whole assembled army, the men who saw him and Corporal Guy together talking, in his written expression. What he cannot by himself translate into words, his community can bear witness to.

In a subtler yet more insistent way than the memorials to Corporal Guy, William Gould's diary ponders the bonds among newly freed men brought together in military service. If John M. Washington reflected on emancipation indirectly by writing about marriage, Gould does so by writing about community. In his first year of diary keeping (as we will see, the diary has two distinct phases), not only is Gould reserved regarding his own thoughts, preferring to log the daily activities of his ship, but he scarcely ever writes about other individuals, either. The diary has few "characters." All are always one, and one word stands for all. By aggregating himself and everyone around him into a unified *We,* Gould creates out of grammar and rhetoric a picture of freedom's promise—personhood, integration, equality. As his three years in the navy stretch on, though, Gould both becomes a more skillful writer and also witnesses the sometimes dismaying realities of post-emancipation life. His writing more nuanced, his politics more subdued, Gould in the diary's second phase begins to contemplate his individual place in the community of the ship, and that community appears more complex and stratified. The *We* crumbles slowly into fragmentary, and occasionally racialized, *Is* and *thems.*

During Gould's first year of freedom, his diary serves as a venue for adjusting to, and sometimes celebrating, the novelty of life after bondage. His daily writings in 1862 and 1863 record an unfolding education in things unknown to him as a slave, new sources of fascination and uncertainty. Gould learns the idiom of the navy (going ashore "on Liberty") and tries out the seamen's vernacular (referring to the end of shore leave as a return to "Prison life"). He develops a command of basic nautical terminology ("we sat up and tared down Rigging") but struggles with more rarefied vocabulary: "took A look at the (Devel or What do you call it) submariene Batry cigar shape that is propell'd by A Screw and fires A gun under watter after being submerged." (Maybe Gould wanted the word *submersible*, or maybe he was so unsure about his spelling of "submariene" that he felt it necessary to clarify with a definition.) Becoming acquainted with more northerners than he likely knew previously, he learns to call Massachusetts "the old Bey state." Inspired perhaps by an abundance of new reading material, or by the romantic language of quaint "old tars," Gould pens a few isolated bursts of florid maritime rhetoric: "There is nothing like the whistling wind and the danceing Bark on the Bounding Billow"; "all hands were calld to up Anchor and we were soon plowing the Briney deep."[18]

As his vocabulary gets its sea legs, Gould also experiments with his new freedom to write. In a moment of curiosity, or boredom, or slightly giddy exuberance, he tries out his left-handed penmanship. As he grows more comfortable with the physical act of writing, he also samples its different applications. His diary mentions numerous letters he sent to relatives and friends scattered from North Carolina to Boston. Later in the war, he would write a few articles for the *Weekly Anglo-African*, a black newspaper to which he and some of his comrades subscribed with their pooled resources. And the diary itself, from its inception, partakes of different genres. Part journal and part history, the text reveals a writer both uncertain of how to keep a diary and bold enough to invent a literary form.

The most common attributes and purposes of diaries do not readily apply: given Gould's almost studied exclusion of his own thoughts and feelings, his diary clearly is not motivated by an interest in self-expression or contemplation of its author's hopes and worries. It contains nothing particularly secret. For the playful diarist writing left-handed—or, elsewhere, drawing a picture of a ship on a blank page of his book—the task may simply be an enjoyable diversion or a celebration of his literacy; but for the frustrated writer who wonders what the devil to call a submarine, it probably is neither. Indeed, Gould evidently regarded diary keeping as a duty—to himself, to his comrades, or to history—rather than a way to occupy each day's unfilled time. When his daily entries lapsed, he usually made sure to catch up—to go back and record something for each of the days gone by. In

Off Gloucester, quaters at 1 bell. Served out clothing, went ashore and spend the evening, verry cold received two papers from Boston.

Wensday Dec 2nd

Off. Gloucester. A heavy Gale. blowing nearly all day. quaters at 3 bells A.M. and 1 bell P.M.

Thursday. Dec. 3rd

Off. Gloucester. quaters. at 3 bell A.M. Shipd two men. and two deserted

Friday Dec. 4th

Off Gloucester. fine day. arrest the two men. who deserted yesterday. received A letter from Act. Jones.

Saturday. Dec. 5th

Off. Gloucester. Shipd one man write home.

Sunday. Dec. 6th

Off Gloucester. verry cold. Service at 5 bells pray at 1 bell. our Lieuts Wife. dined on board

Monday. Dec. 7th

Off Gloucester. verry cold. Received A letter from E. W. R. maild A letter for home.

Entries from December 1–7, 1863, William Benjamin Gould Diaries, Massachusetts Historical Society. Courtesy of the Massachusetts Historical Society. Entry for December 1 is written left-handed.

this, too, Gould's text differs from the strict form of a diary, for which, it has been said, "the only rule . . . is its explicit submission to a regulating calendar."[19] The entry for December 7, 1862, reads: "This is the coldest day of the season. Salt watter freezed. We hear of the Battle of Fredericksburg, Va and defeat of our troops." In fact, the battle would not begin for another four days, and news of its outcome could not have come sooner than December 15. Not only did Gould write his December 7 entry sometime later; he must have written it so much later that he could not remember which week, much less which day, had brought news of the Union loss at Fredericksburg.[20]

That erratum notwithstanding, Gould was scrupulous about the accuracy of his chronicle. He reread the diary periodically and corrected or expanded it, sometimes inserting new sentences in the margins or overwriting them crosswise on an already filled page.[21] With an eye to narrative development, he would return to earlier portions of the diary to fill in the background for events that only later proved significant. His entry for November 18, 1863, reports the verdict of a court martial that sentenced "the Engineers Stwerd" to "thirty days in Double Irons on bread and water" for "smugeling Liquor on board." Perhaps struck by the punishment, Gould not only recorded it but also turned back three pages in his composition book and added the necessary prologue in tiny script at the bottom of the entry for November 7: "the Engineer stwerd was detected in bringing Liquor on board and was placed in confinement."[22]

Sometimes he went back and made changes because he had gotten ahead of himself. On a summer morning, docked at Antwerp, Gould evidently seized the daylight to compose his entry for the new day: "coald ship all Morning until about 10 Oclock when we unmoor'd ship and got ready to sail." But the day did not unfold as Gould anticipated. The crew's work was interrupted for a ceremonious twenty-one-gun salute to visiting dignitaries. Coaling remained unfinished, and the ship did not leave port. Gould crossed out what he had written for July 1, 1864, and inserted a new account: "coald ship all ~~Morning~~ day . . . We saluteed the American minister . . . we are orderd to sea on tomorrow. A great many visiters came on board." In the entry for July 2, Gould reports that the crew finally, a day later than expected, "unmoor'd ship and got ready for sailing." The diary gives no indication of whether Gould found this delay enjoyable or disappointing.[23]

Although Gould is certainly not the only diarist ever to fill in gaps or make changes after the fact, his writing protocol reinforces what his decisions about content suggest: his diary is less about his own thoughts and feelings than about his community's history. As his grammar favors *We* over *I*, his process values the fullness and accuracy of a historical record over the recording of one man's real-time impressions. To follow the calendar religiously, as a diary is supposed to do, is to privilege the individual writer's vision, subject to change, in all its particularity. To respect events, on the other hand—the fact that visitors interrupted work on July 1, for instance, rather than what Gould thought would happen, or how he felt about it—is to create a public record, to acknowledge that individual perception is not the whole story, and, like a historian, to pursue the clearer vision hindsight makes possible. Of the events Gould records, those relevant primarily to himself rarely clear the threshold for inclusion. On the day his ship passes just offshore from the North Carolina plantation of his former owner, Gould writes: "Took A good look at the place that I left in (62)." This remarkable occasion to reflect on his past in slavery provokes only twelve words, stirring the diary's placid surface no more than men loading coal or an anonymous sailor smuggling liquor. The kinds of events about which Gould writes most faithfully and in most detail are not those that concern him alone but those that constitute shared experience.[24]

Why Gould decided to apply such parameters to his act of writing is impossible to know for certain. He may have held the same conviction some historians have attributed to newly freed southern blacks in general, "that freedom, in reality, would accrue to each of them individually only when it was acquired by all of them collectively." In a sense more local, his seven partners in escape and enlistment may have looked to Gould and his literacy with particular respect, encouraging him to begin writing down their experiences and inspiring him to write partly on their behalf. Though we cannot know Gould's motivation for creating a collective chronicle rather than a personal diary, we can discern from his writings who he means by "We," and what story he tells about them—how he imagines the national and racial communities to which he belongs, or might soon belong, in the aftermath of slavery.[25]

During the first year of his service, Gould's first-person plural pronouns have a shifting definition. He writes most often in the voice of a generic *we* that obviously includes everyone on board the U.S.S. *Cambridge:* "we had Muster and inspection," "we came to anchor," "we had Target Practice."[26] In other instances, he applies a similarly all-embracing *we* to things not as clearly universal. When he writes "we feel the approach of Winter," or "our pet squirrel got drownd," he seems to extrapolate a common experience from his own sensation of cold or his particular interest in the squirrel (which well may have been a mascot of sorts for the whole crew but surely was not a pet equally in everyone's care). Nevertheless, Gould is not using a royal or editorial *we.* In numerous notations about mail delivery, he separates himself from the mass: "We received A Mail. I received three letters"; another ship "took A mail from us. I sent three letters." When he writes, "we all have the Blues," his insistent "we *all*" makes the point that others commiserate with his mood, but this rare foray into the realm of interior feeling also makes it difficult to believe Gould really could be speaking for nearly a hundred other men.[27]

While Gould's definition of his community remains obscure, his aspiration to belong shows through clearly. In its first week, reporting that "All of us ship'd to day for three years," the diary expresses the solidarity of the eight fugitives as they enlist. In the weeks thereafter, Gould begins to situate himself within the broader—and, presumably, interracial—*we* of the whole ship's crew. His occasional overreaching locutions ("we all have the Blues") may evince the recently freed slave's aspiration to full membership in that larger community—his sense that, if he has freedom in common with those who until recently were strangers, then they all may be bound by sympathies deeper still. In the dozens of instances when "we" dispatched a mail of which "I" sent a letter or two, Gould portrays his individual life, his private attachments committed to paper, coursing through the ship's umbilical with the world on land, the work of his own pen merged with a great concourse of free men's correspondence.[28]

That hopeful communion—as well as its tenuousness—becomes most palpable in moments of crisis. On November 10, 1862, the constitution of Gould's community is shaken: "At Beaufort. verry fine day. went asshore. to day. three Men Deserted. one of them George P—e. I am verry sorry for it. searched all Night for them but found them not." *We,* presumably, "went asshore," but not everyone returned to the ship. The day's entry tells a story of the group's fragmentation: "three Men Deserted," and among them, assuming "George P—e" refers to George Price, was one of the original eight fugitives. Gould's usually expansive attention narrows from an inclusive whole who went ashore, then to the "three" who deserted, the "one" he knew best, and finally to the unaccustomed *I*, who feels "verry sorry for it."[29]

Following this cascade from a communal to an individual perspective, Gould resumes his diary's plural voice—but something has changed. The implied subject of Gould's closing sentence—*we* "searched all Night for them"—must not be the same as the implied *we* who went ashore, for it is doubtful that the whole crew participated in the search; Gould himself may or may not have been among the party. Regardless, Price and the other two deserters are no longer among the official *we* of the ship. Not only AWOL from the navy, they now also stand outside the bounds of the diary. Gould's elision of his friend's last name may reflect simply that he has picked up this literary convention from his reading, but its effect is to reinforce Price's removal from the group. Gould's general habit, on the relatively rare occasions that he refers to specific individuals, is to provide the full name of fellow crew members and to indicate people on land—his correspondents—by their initials. The dashed elision of Price's name, almost unique in the diary, marks him as being between categories.

However sorry Gould may be, however much he may miss George Price, he preserves the diary's focus on the community to which he wishes to belong. It is not implausible to suppose that Gould contemplated desertion himself but cast his lot with the ship, not with his friend. In any event, the diary's point of view, like Gould himself, will not follow the deserters but rather will stay with the ship. In the entry for the next day, November 11, the undisturbed surface of Gould's *we* rolls on: "about 7 Oclock a.m. we up Anchor. and stood out for sea. boun to the Cape Fear. we arrived off our station at New Inlet. about 5 Oclock. all well."

The departure of one compatriot might rattle Gould's project but not sink it. He goes on expressing in a plural voice his sense of affiliation with a shipful of men. When he contracts the measles, though, and is sent to a military hospital—where he remains, unattached to any ship, for more than four months—that project evidently becomes impossible. Gould writes not a single entry while ashore on sick leave, and all that he does *not* write about—especially the tumultuous events of the summer of 1863—underscores how studiously he has confined his diary to life aboard ship, how firmly he thus far has staked his post-emancipation identity on his place among his fellow sailors. After that summer, neither his writing nor his sense of community would be the same.

At the end of March, 1863, the U.S.S. *Cambridge* docked at Boston. Its crew was transferred to a "guardo," or receiving ship, the *Ohio,* which sat permanently at anchor to accommodate sailors awaiting new assignments. On the first full day he and his fellows spent among the hundreds of sailors on the massive ship, Gould wrote, "Here we meet with all Kinds and all classes of men." For nearly two months, Gould's crew remained in limbo, expecting to be shipped out (together or split up) at any time. They were frequently given liberty to go ashore in Boston. Gould did not write about their explorations of the city or speculations about their next tour of duty; in fact, his diary falls silent for long periods as the spring progresses. On May 29, 1863, still aboard the *Ohio,* he showed signs of measles and promptly was sent to the Chelsea Naval Hospital, on the Mystic River just north of the city.[30]

Gould may have been too ill to read newspapers or to strike up conversations about current events, but a spectacle from the previous day would have been on the lips of many Bostonians around him. On May 28, the Fifty-Fourth Massachusetts Infantry—one of the first African American army regiments, and one of the most celebrated collectives of black men in American history—marched through downtown Boston and departed for battle. An estimated 20,000 people filled Boston Common and lined the streets of the city to witness what not long before had been unthinkable: armed African Americans wearing the uniform of the federal government, headed south to fight the rebel army.

Local newspapers described a "sea of heads" gathered along the parade route; "the sidewalks were crowded, and the windows and balconies were thronged" with "an immense number of people such as only the Fourth of July or some rare event causes to assemble." The *Christian Recorder,* an African American newspaper in Philadelphia, called it "one of the most enthusiastic, exciting, and demonstrative local military events of the war." Massachusetts governor John Andrew, who had authorized the regiment, inspected the troops. Frederick Douglass, who had helped recruit the men, including two of his sons, saw them off from Boston Harbor. From the home of fellow abolitionist Wendell Phillips, William Lloyd Garrison looked out at the marching soldiers, reportedly leaning on a bust of John Brown and weeping. The annual meeting of the New England Anti-Slavery Society adjourned to allow its members to join the crowd. On the streets, vendors sold souvenir pamphlets bearing the quotation from Lord Byron that Douglass used in the recruiting campaign: "Those who would be free, themselves must strike the blow." That stirring phrase circulated both in the printed memorials of the day and in onlookers' memories. Among the assembled thousands was a former slave, now a relief worker in the war and the author of a pseud-onymous autobiography, *Incidents in the Life of a Slave Girl.* Harriet Jacobs recalled, "How proud and happy I was that day, when I saw the 54th re-viewed on Boston Common! How my heart swelled with the thought that my poor oppressed race were to strike a blow for freedom!"[31]

During the summer of 1863, as they waited for news of the Fifty-Fourth's exploits, the citizens of Boston—indeed, of the whole nation—were witnessing the visible effects of emancipation as a federal policy. Black military enlistment was changing the course of the war, and it portended change for American society, too. As Frederick Douglass said in a speech in Philadelphia on July 6, "Once let the black man get upon his person the brass letters US; let him get an eagle on his button, and a musket on his shoulder, and bullets in his pocket, and there is no power on earth or under the earth which can deny that he has earned the right of citizenship in the United States."[32]

Such suggestions of coming racial equality infuriated Confederates, who threatened that captured black soldiers would be re-enslaved, or worse. They also inflamed white racism in the North. Working-class immigrants feared emancipated slaves soon would flood the labor force in northern cit-ies, and many whites decried a war to liberate African Americans. In a week-long outbreak of rioting across the North, free blacks became scape-goats for anger over the latest round of Union conscriptions. The violence was worst in New York, where mobs terrorized Manhattan's African Amer-ican population, burned an orphanage for black children, and lynched eleven black men. In Boston, civil unrest followed only a day after the out-break of rioting in New York. After nightfall on July 14, a thousand-person mob attacked the Cooper Street armory; hundreds of rioters raided gun shops in Faneuil Hall Square. Governor Andrew wanted to call in federal troops to preserve order, but he quailed when he learned that the only unit available was the Fifth-Fifth Massachusetts Infantry—the state's second African American regiment—and concluded it was not safe to send in black soldiers among white rioters.[33]

Only days after the violence subsided, Bostonians began receiving news of the Fifty-Fourth. African American soldiers had shown their valor by leading the charge on Fort Wagner on July 18. They also suffered terrible casualties. Almost half the men in the regiment—272 out of 600—were killed or wounded. Robert Gould Shaw, the white commander of the Fifty-Fourth and a favorite son of Boston's abolitionist elite, was among the fallen.[34]

If William Gould, with nearly a year of naval service under his belt, did not already see himself as part of a larger historic transformation, his time in Boston likely expanded his vision. The events of that summer saw a vast corps of African American men, far more numerous than Gould's partners in escape or his shipmates on the *Cambridge,* taking up arms to destroy the institution of slavery. Even if Gould did not follow the news, his daily life brought him face-to-face with a larger community of black servicemen. Though he made no diary entries while in the hospital, once he was released he wrote a long paragraph summing up his time there. He mentions receiving attentive care from the staff of the hospital, and he also reveals that, as his health improved, he "acted as A nurse." Attending to sick and injured sailors—he refers to them as "my Patients"—Gould formed new attachments.

He made special mention of two men who died while under his care: "there names are respectfully Henry. Burrows. of Hamilton. Canada. west. and Louis. B. Hoagland Brooklyn. N.Y. both were Burried in the Grave Yard attatchd to the Hospital."[35] Though Gould does not say so, both men were African American (naval records list their "complexion" as "mulatto"). Burrows entered the navy at the rating of seaman, indicating he had considerable prior experience as a sailor (perhaps on the Great Lakes, since he was born in Buffalo and evidently later moved to Hamilton, Ontario). Lewis Hoagland, a ship's cook, was seven years older than Gould.[36] From both men, Gould could have learned about the lives of African Americans in the North, heard tales of the merchant service or the antebellum navy, and discovered free blacks' motivations for fighting in the Civil War.

Gould also may have heard them recount instances of racial discrimination, and he surely witnessed some. However much the North, and Boston in particular, symbolized freedom, white northerners—even those who opposed slavery on political grounds—were capable of a racism more blind and virulent than what prevailed in Gould's birthplace, as July's draft riots painfully demonstrated. Whether Gould grew close to Burrows and Hoagland through racial solidarity or a sympathy irrespective of race, he probably met them in the first place because hospital staff matched him, by design or unconscious habit, with other African American patients. Meanwhile, the attention focused on the Fifty-Fourth Massachusetts during the summer of 1863 highlighted something Bostonians found normal but that may have surprised Gould: unlike the *Cambridge,* the Union army was segregated.[37]

When Gould had fully recovered and shipped out from Boston aboard the U.S.S. *Niagara* on October 13, 1863, he ceremoniously recommenced his diary, taking up a new notebook and inscribing its front page with the words:

> Journal of W. B. Gould.s
> cruise in the U.S.
> Frigate Niagara
> Commenceing
> Oct. 13th /63

In its second volume, Gould's diary remains an understated chronicle of events aboard ship, but its *we* becomes more nuanced. No longer the mark of an aspirational communion, the first-person plural now denotes a limited solidarity, influenced by racial division and more frequently interrupted by Gould's sense of his own separateness. In his second two years of service, following the memorable summer in Boston, Gould uses writing to record and reflect on his individual place in the community of his ship, and the place of his fellow freedmen in the national community. As he realizes during these years—which saw the climax of the war and the dawn of Reconstruction—the collective African American future is unsettled and uncertain, and the diary becomes his forum for an emergent politics. Gould's *we* begins to voice the protestations of A Colored Man's *We the people.*

Though he could depict a relatively stable collective aboard the *Cambridge,* Gould faced a more complicated task in chronicling the life of the *Niagara,* a larger ship on which the crew's membership was a troubled matter from the outset. Rated for a complement of 250 men—more than twice as many as the *Cambridge*—the *Niagara* struggled to enlist that number of sailors. For almost two months after Gould joined it, the ship remained anchored at Boston, waiting to fill its ranks. The entire crew of another vessel, the *Sabine,* was transferred to the thinly populated *Niagara,* but more men still were needed. Gould fastidiously recorded in his diary the slow pace of further enlistment: "ship'd one recruite to day," he wrote on October 29; four days later, "we shipd two men to day"; and on November 14, "ship'd four men. one of the Boat crew deserted."[38] Other days, the *Niagara's* ranks swelled not at all, or shrank: "shipd two Men. and two deserted"; "One man deserted last night with bag and Hammock. ship'd one man"; "A man that deserted from the Army and ship'd in the Navy was reclaimd"; "discharges four men unfit for duty. we shipd two men"; "three men were sent to the Hospital."[39]

Long separated from his original seven compatriots and the rest of the *Cambridge* crew, Gould now belonged to a community whose constitution changed from day to day, with men coming and going as if through a revolving door. Concerns about the size of the crew are a public and official matter, the sort of collective circumstance the diary has always included, but Gould's particular attention to the *Niagara's* numbers appears to provoke, in turn, keener observations about the composition of the crew.

Dwelling in this complex community, and possessed now of the broader perspective his summer in Boston afforded him, Gould qualifies his *we* at every turn, factoring in experience, rank, and demography. During the ship's first storm, he observes the difference between himself and the new recruits: "the greater portion of our Crew. being Landsmen's. on thair firs cruise thare is A large number of them sea sick. you can see them trying to get forward by crawling and helping eachother. they do not like thair first feelings of A seafareing. . . . I was realy amuseing to see the Landsmans trying to keep thair feet." Twice, the ship receives large groups of former Confederates—fully a hundred on one occasion, another time fifty "repentant Rebels," as Gould calls them, who "have takeen the oath of Aleigeance and now will fight for uncle sam." On St. Patrick's Day, Gould notes that "thare is lively times among the Irish portion of our crew." Sometimes the terms and travails of enlistment apportion the men into subgroups: in April 1864, three years after the war's beginning, many sailors' three-year terms begin to expire, and large numbers of men receive discharges. "[E]very day thare is some leaveing," Gould writes, "with A general exclamation that they will never enter the Navy again." As the word *they* begins to appear more frequently in Gould's vocabulary, his *we* becomes a shape-shifting entity that can watch some of itself ("our men") peeling away and becoming *them*.[40]

From seeing the crew as an assemblage of "portions" and subgroups, it takes only one further step to see it as a collection of individuals—and to record individual experience and perspective, as the *Cambridge* diary almost never did. Aboard the *Niagara*, Gould begins to isolate his personal relationship to "public" events—to remark whether he was participant or observer, for instance, or simply the recipient of secondhand news. "[I]t was reported that we pass'd an Iceberg last night," Gould writes near the Grand Banks of Newfoundland, "but I did not have an opportunity of seeing it being asleep at the time." The next day he notes, "some of the Boy's reported A Whale this afternoon but I did not get A sight."[41]

Gould also now departs occasionally from his detached, journalistic mode of writing and becomes a first-person narrator. In one moment of narrative action, while the ship is docked at New York, Gould tells of seeing his own ship from the outside: "as we intended to have company to day I was obliged to go to New York after some of the Indespenciables. as I was leaveing the Ship the Band from the 'North Carolina' came on board I returnd about 12 Oclock to find quite A number of Ladies assembled and Danceing goin on." Few readers can visualize the scene aboard the *Cambridge* when Gould writes, "finishd Coaling to day," but it is relatively easy to plot out this sequence: Gould walks down the gangplank and encounters a military band coming his way; later, walking back along the wharf, he hears music wafting ashore, and as he steps aboard his ship, he finds the unusual sight of women and dancing. As a newly freed former slave harbored within the confines of the *Cambridge,* Gould might have written simply, *we passed an iceberg,* or *had visitors and dancing.* Now, more experienced, entrusted with special responsibilities, he narrates both what others saw (but not him) and what he (and no one else) has seen.[42]

At the same time, Gould begins to write more about individual fellow sailors, almost creating a cast of characters. During ten months aboard the *Cambridge,* he mentioned the names of fifteen shipmates, and all but a few were officers, identified by their titles and associated with some event of official interest—"Act. Masters Mate Nickerson," for example, who "resignd on the account of ill health." Gould seemed to suppress references to ordinary sailors who bore a particular relationship to him, as when he elided his fellow fugitive's name as "George P——e."[43]

In entries for the two years on the *Niagara*, the diary refers to a proportional number of shipmates (forty), but roughly half are ordinary sailors like Gould. Sometimes he mentions them because they become subjects of the whole ship's attention—as when Henry Baxter falls from the mast and dislocates his shoulder, or a court martial convenes to try Michael Simmons for desertion—but often they warrant inclusion in the diary only because they matter to Gould personally. When the *Niagara* prepares for an Atlantic crossing, Gould as usual explains what affects the whole ship—"all the men haveing less than three months to serve were transferred to the North Carolina"—but he also details the larger event's personal implications: "Among them was Charles E. Ross and Charles H. Scott." It is not immediately apparent why he should name these two in particular—he does not say he will miss them—but an entry more than seven months earlier disclosed a then-burgeoning bond of companionship when Gould mentioned that he "commenced to study French in company with C. Ross of N.Y."[44]

Many of Gould's friends appear to have served, as he did, in the ship's wardroom, the officers' dining room. Though initially enrolled on the *Cambridge* as a "boy" (the rating of most contrabands), aboard the *Niagara* Gould achieved the ratings of "landsman" and "assistant steward, Ward Room" (at some point he went back in his diary to cross out "landsman" and insert his new title in a different ink).[45] At least some of the compatriots named in the diary served alongside him there. Gould identifies the two Charleses as "Ward Room Serveants," and others, whose enlistment records list their occupations as "waiter" or "cook," would have been likely candidates for wardroom service.[46] Accordingly, the diary, though always chronicling the life of the entire ship, begins paying particular attention to the life of the wardroom. Gould notes, for instance, that the wardroom's steam conductors broke one day in early November, leaving it without heat. When recording crew changes, he sometimes accounts the wardroom separately: "two hundred and fifty (250) of our crew were transferd to the Hartford. out of nine boys in the Ward Room six (6) were sent away"; "Eighty of our crew that was transferd. were returnd. among them five of the Ward Room Boy's."

Amid his routine coverage of infractions and punishments, Gould notes when it was "one of the W.R.B."—Ward Room Boys—who "was punishd for breaching his liberty."[47]

If the wardroom was the center of Gould's social world, it was not so by chance. A Union navy ship may have been racially integrated, but the various roles and domains within the ship were not. Cooks and stewards were almost exclusively African American. In the wardroom, black men served white officers.[48] Indeed, Gould does not seem to have had many cross-racial friendships. Every one of the enlisted men he names—Charles Ross, James Thompson, Michael Simmons, Henry Smith, Charles Scott, Hutchinson Allen, Henry Belt, Charles Johnston, Jeremiah Jones, Richard Johnson, William Morris—is African American.[49]

Gould's propensity to name his African American comrades may not by itself indicate a sense of racial solidarity, but as the diary's entries for 1864 and 1865 slowly build a roster of black fellow sailors, they also exhibit an increasing sensitivity to race and racism. The disturbing news from Fort Pillow, Tennessee—where Confederates under the command of Nathan Bedford Forrest, a future leader of the Ku Klux Klan, reportedly murdered Union soldiers who had surrendered—prompted a somber diary entry: "we also heard of the capture of Fort Pillow. by the Rebels and the Mascare of all the troops, both White. and Colard. Still the Govermet do not Retaileate." The following day's entry reads: "Quite A fine day but we cannot enjoy the day." All Union sailors undoubtedly were angered and saddened by the news from Tennessee, but Gould and his friends would have been particularly dismayed by reports that Forrest's men targeted black soldiers for execution. The "we" who are cast down and "cannot enjoy the day" could refer to everyone aboard the *Niagara,* but it more likely represents the smaller circle of Gould and his fellow African Americans.[50]

That group's separate racial identity was coming to the fore—especially as the racial hostility displayed by white Confederates was being mirrored, if in milder form, among Union forces and even on Gould's own ship. When an African American army regiment came on board the *Niagara* for an evening, Gould writes, "they were treated verry rough by the crew. they refused to let them eat of the Mess pans and calld them all Kinds of names. one man his watch stolen from him by these scoundrels. in all they was treated shamefully." A few weeks later he writes, "At night there was A malee on Deck between the white and colard men." On a page of the diary that has deteriorated around the edges, effacing a few words, Gould records in typically terse language an unusually harrowing event: "This Morning four or fiv white fellows beat Jerry Jones (co he was stab'd in his left shoulde verry. bad." In the parenthetical note that has worn away, Gould presumably makes clear that Jones is "colored."[51]

It is difficult to tell from Gould's descriptions whether these encounters with racism on the *Niagara* sparked feelings of outrage or of isolation, whether they intensified or taxed his sense of community with other African American sailors. It is clear, though, that Gould was developing connections with a broader black community on land, and his writings reveal his growing interest in issues affecting African Americans nationwide. Around the time of Fort Pillow, Gould spearheaded an effort among his black shipmates to purchase a subscription to the *Weekly Anglo-African,* a New York–based black newspaper. Gould already received occasional copies of the paper with the sporadic comings and goings of the ship's mail; this new subscription, sponsored by men of the *Niagara,* was to be sent to freedmen serving in the army. Though his diary does not expound on exactly what Gould wished the newspaper would offer black soldiers, it does evince an obvious concern for a group of people he had never met—but with whom he shared a racial identity, a common past of enslavement, and an initial experience of freedom defined by military service. As Gould increasingly wrote in the voice of a *we* thus composed, he displayed an intensifying concern about the future African Americans might face.[52]

The very act of reading a newspaper—learning of far-flung events of the war, imagining himself part of the community of the paper's readers—undoubtedly contributed to Gould's broadened consciousness.[53] The virtual connections forged by the *Anglo-African* may have been less significant, though, than Gould's mobility and his rapidly expanding social world. He had met and become part of a network of black men from all over the country; he had seen Boston in 1863 (though he did not write much about it), and in 1864 he saw New York City. There, with a fervor and wonder almost like that felt by Southern migrants who arrived in Harlem sixty years later. Gould joined a vibrant African American community. Whereas he never mentioned the Fifty-Fourth Massachusetts in his diary, he did describe taking "A stroll up Broadway" and witnessing the "Departure of the 20th Regmt. of U.S. (colard) Volunteers, the first colard Regement raised in New York pronounce by all to be A splendid Regement." At least five times while the *Niagara* was docked at New York, Gould visited the offices of the *Weekly Anglo-African.* He heard lectures by prominent abolitionists, including the British parliamentarian George Thompson and the black minister Henry Highland Garnet. He attended a performance by the African American singer Elizabeth Greenfield, known as "the Black Swan." When Abraham Galloway, a fellow North Carolinian, fugitive slave, and activist, came to New York leading a delegation in support of African American suffrage, Gould met Galloway at the *Anglo-African* offices and then listened to him speak in a nearby African Methodist Episcopal church. Perhaps keeping a promise made to Lewis Hoagland, the dying sailor he nursed in Boston, Gould paid several visits to Ann Hoagland of Brooklyn.[54]

As if inspired by his Manhattan experiences but also troubled by his growing awareness of the obstacles to black equality, Gould evinces a more complicated political sensibility during his final year of service, and his diary betrays a more downcast sense of himself and his place in the navy.[55] Where he once trained a journalist's eye on daily events, touching on them lightly with a dispassionate pen, Gould now gazes through the lens of his own racial identity and sees a world in which all are sorted by skin color. In his usual spare inventories of arrivals and departures, Gould explicitly isolates African Americans: "one colard Jentleman from Brussels. came on board the first that I have seen. belonging to the Country"; "one Man Deserted. The first Colord Man that left. on this side of the watter." He mentions the minstrel performances that were commonplace among sailors of the time—though he does not say that he attended them.[56]

Sometimes without comment, sometimes with slight editorial interjection, he writes about racial politics on a national stage. He finds causes for optimism in the Union's military successes: after the fall of Richmond, he reports "the Glad Tidings that the Stars and Strips had been planted over the Capital of the D̶a̶m̶ nd Confedercy" and calls fallen federal soldiers "mayrters to the caus of Right and Equality." He also pays particular attention to the progress of emancipation: "We have an account of the passage of the amendment to the Con[sti]tution prohibiting slavery througho the United States." After the war's official end at Appomattox, though, and "the awful tidings of the as^{a}s^{a}ination of President Lincoln," Gould's political outlook turns skeptical, worried, and at times indignant. He becomes restless to leave the European coast and return home. Over the summer of 1865, the diary registers Gould's concern about the new presidential administration's Reconstruction policy. At first glad to learn that Jefferson Davis would be tried for treason, Gould soon laments, "we see. that the Rebels are being pardon'd verry fast. and that quiet will soon reighn throughout the states." The tenor of Gould's sarcastic critique—to the Johnson administration, white reconciliation and "quiet" were more important than racial justice—elsewhere takes the form of bald outrage: "we see by. the papers. that. the President in A speech. intimates. Colinization. for the colard people of the United States. this move of his must and shall be. resisted we were born under the Flag. of the Union and we never will know no other. My sentement is the sentement of the people of the States."[57]

To whom exactly "the people of the States" refers is hard to tell; Gould's opposition to the deportation of freed people was *not* shared by all Americans. It may be that the diary here not only speaks in an African American *We* ("we were born under the Flag") but also concerns itself with the "people" of one race in particular. William Gould in 1865—devoted reader of the *Anglo-African,* intimate of black activists in New York—has come to identify himself less as part of his ship's crew than as a member of a community on land, the fellow hopeful citizens with whom he shares his racial identity and his "sentements."[58]

Accordingly, the diary in its final months does not so much chronicle shipboard life as register Gould's impatience with it. About a week after receiving news of Lincoln's assassination, Gould begins writing down thoughts startlingly unlike his earlier dutiful logs of quotidian details: "Nothing of note occurd," he writes one day in mid-May; the next week, "Nothing of much much importance," and "Nothing of great importance transpireing." Seven times Gould sums up the day's events by saying that nothing important happened; twice he complains that he and his fellows are "just killing time." With the restiveness of a seasoned sailor—and, at times, the lyrical dexterity of a more seasoned writer—he laments that "time passes verry heavaly" amid the "monotony of Sea Life." "How slowly the time passes," he muses, "or that we in our anxiety are unconscious of its flight."[59]

The man whose first days of freedom carried a broad promise of camaraderie and belonging, who confined his writings to collective experience, now dwells more often on his own isolation and inward thoughts. Of a beautiful September night, Gould writes, "The moon shone forth in its splendor and one could sit for hours and medetate apon the works of nature. Myself I devideed my thoughts between Nature and the loved ones at Home and longs for the hour of our meeting." While the ship cruises off the Iberian Peninsula, Gould shows that he has picked up some Spanish, writing, "We received A mail from the states. Yo no receba nada." Where the movements of the mail once seemed to describe a commingling of *we* and *I,* here Gould's *I* (or *yo*) stands distinct, having received nothing, and preoccupied, as his Spanish-language diversion suggests, with his distance from home. On a day when he is "A little at leasure" but has "nothing to read," Gould reports, "I amuse myself by overhauling my Corospondancees." Whatever it might mean to overhaul correspondences—presumably Gould copied out some of his past letters, or perhaps he engaged in some form of literary revision and creation, as when John Washington crafted a memoir by rewriting his diary—it clearly is an activity both self-directed and private, a mode of writing concerned not with his ship but with the community he anticipates rejoining on land.[60]

After a slow Atlantic crossing, the *Niagara* sighted Nantucket on September 20, 1865, adjusted its course northward, and dropped anchor at Boston the next day. Gould went ashore exactly three years after he stole away from slavery in North Carolina. The next morning, three years almost to the hour since he had first climbed aboard a naval vessel in a moment of emancipation, he stepped back aboard the *Niagara* and this time found himself chafing against naval discipline and the incompleteness of his freedom: "I returnd on board this Morning. got scolded for remaining on shore." Not altogether sanguine about his place in post-emancipation America but attuned to the emergent politics of a national black community, Gould concludes his diary, as John Washington ended "Memorys of the Past," mindful of practicalities. In the final entry, dated September 29, 1865, Gould writes, "at five Oclock I received my Discharge. being three Years and nine days in the serveace of Uncle Sam. and glad am I to receive it paid of $4.24.00. So end my serveace in the Navy of the United States of America." He settled in Dedham, Massachusetts, raised eight children with his wife, Cornelia, and worked as a mason and plasterer until his death in 1923.[61]

Gould crossed the Atlantic in both directions, but neither passage symbolized enslavement or freedom. The journey that began with a stolen boat did not follow a straight line toward the North Star, nor did literacy prove a straightforward instrument of uplift. In the many hours Gould spent inscribing pages with his daily ink, his act of writing sparked imaginings as winding and sometimes stormy as his passage—a future, for him and his fellows, sometimes bright with emancipation's potential, sometimes darkened by uncertainty.

chapter five

Petition and Protest in the Occupied South

AT DUSK on August 12, 1864, Abram Mercherson was at home in Mitchelville, South Carolina, a self-governing town of freed people, newly constructed on Hilton Head Island under the auspices of the federal military. An alarmed neighbor broke the evening's sultry quiet, beckoning Mercherson to a nearby house. When Mercherson arrived, he faced an appalling scene: the neighbor's wife had been raped by three white soldiers. The rapists were officers in the Union army, and they were drunk. Though a respected leader among the African American residents of Mitchelville, Mercherson was helpless to control these men; how he finally convinced them to leave is unknown. Mercherson returned to his own house at a later hour, probably too infuriated to sleep, intent on seeking justice. The course he chose required him to do something with which he had limited experience: He sat down and wrote a letter.

To his exelency
    Maj Gen J G Foster

Dear Sir a bought (8) this evening I was Call a pon by a Man Who Stated that thair was three men in his house trubling his wife on the Pretence of hunting Recrutes which he Ses that he have paper indors by you on my a Rival at the house i saw the 3 men who had commited wrape on the Person of his wife there are as i Suppose to be officers of the 25 ohio Reg & was under the influent of Licor thay also took thair Sholder Straps of there Coat & Pin it on the inside i have 4 or five witness if requierd: We have been trubled very often by these officers & Sailers & i think a Stop aught to Put to it

    Gen I Have the Honer to Remain your obediant Servant
                                        Revd Abram Mercherson[1]

A reader struggling through this letter's more obscure words and labored sentences can sense that Mercherson himself struggled as he wrote, perhaps frustrated that he did not know how to spell a word, could not express this or that a little more clearly. The paper at times grew wet with ink as Mercherson doubled back with his pen, correcting words, trying to get it right. The act of writing recreated some of the helplessness he felt at his neighbor's house, even as it embodied his best hope and greatest power to seek redress.

It is harrowing to consider the many southern blacks who had as much cause as Mercherson to write such a letter, without even his modest recourse to written literacy; stirring to wonder how many did write letters of which no trace remains. Still, many letters of protest and petition were written and have survived, and they capture the astonishing range and complexity of American slaves' experiences of emancipation: the faith in northern liberators that led a woman named Mary Ann to write a Union general seeking release from a New Orleans slave jail; the hopes that families long separated by the slave trade now could be reunited, expressed in freed people's letters asking government officials for help finding their enslaved spouses and children; the confusion about blacks' actual legal status that prompted Annie Davis to address Abraham Lincoln in 1864 with the succinct request, "please let me know if we are free"; the pride black men felt on enlisting in the Union army, but also the mistreatment of which they complained in letters to military commanders; the difficult transition to free labor and self-sufficiency, reflected in letters asking Freedmen's Bureau agents to adjudicate disputes or settle land claims.[2]

Some of these letters, poorly written, barely intelligible, or mistakenly addressed, were ignored by their recipients.[3] Some of them sparked action, or at least brought the realities of slave emancipation more vividly before the eyes of white readers. In the aggregate, these letters represent the work freed people did, in writing, to make sense of their transformed world. From small circles of friends like William Gould's to social experiments like the all-black town of Mitchelville, emancipation's newly formed communities met with surprising treatment—violent at worst, inconstant at best—from white Americans who found their own view of the world drastically altered. Southern slaveholders felt aggrieved by the passing of the old order. Federal officials and military commanders tried, often in vain, to grip the reins of a social revolution. And northern missionaries ventured south wielding both good intentions and flawed assumptions about African Americans.

When freed people mustered their burgeoning literacy and wrote letters to these audiences—lodging grievances, asserting rights, petitioning for justice—they practiced a form of power they rarely had as slaves. At the same time, they addressed themselves to people with power much greater—more educated readers and writers, figures of authority, icons of the prevailing image of humanity from which African Americans ever had been excluded. For numerous southern blacks like Abram Mercherson, the act of putting outrage into writing, struggling with pen and paper to make a claim to justice, provided a way of reckoning with the upheavals of wartime emancipation. It also brought forth new ways of conceiving former slaves' nascent rights as free citizens. Their letters were one crucible of emancipation's tensions—the triumph of freedom, the retrenchments of racial oppression. From that crucible emerged some of the hallmarks of African American politics after slavery, including, as we will see, intractable problems of gender. Rarely did the process of emancipation lead straight from slavery to freedom; for black women it would follow an especially troubled path.

To most white Americans, northern as well as southern, emancipation portended nothing but trouble. To Confederates it meant the collapse of civilization. Racists and slavery apologists in every region predictably found the idea horrifying. Even people who deplored enslavement in principle had apprehensions about the institution's demise. Thomas Jefferson had famously described slavery as a "wolf by the ears"—terrible to hold but worse to let go—and as the Civil War made black freedom imminent, many whites feared that the evils previously confined to southern plantations now would be unleashed on the whole nation. Four million former slaves, accustomed to being treated as beasts of burden, would migrate northward and take the jobs of the white working class. The obligation to care for a dependent people, no longer borne by paternalist slaveholders, now would fall on the American taxpayer. Freed blacks brutalized by slavery and deprived of all moral influence would become a permanent criminal underclass. A handful of racist thinkers predicted, with callous nonchalance, that the slaves would prove too helpless to survive out of captivity—that worries about life after emancipation were overblown because the American Negro would simply become extinct.[4] To comparatively temperate observers and politicians, the best solution appeared to be colonization, or mass deportation. Some proponents of colonization thought blacks incapable of economic self-sufficiency or democratic citizenship. Others esteemed blacks' abilities more fairly but doubted that any group of people, however enterprising and intelligent, could overcome a disadvantage as formidable as American racism. The only hope for African Americans, they believed, lay outside the borders of the United States.[5]

Anxieties about how emancipation would play out in theory often withered, or at least changed, in the face of reality. The white northerners who ventured into the occupied South as soldiers, missionaries, and government agents confronted the monumental challenges that lay ahead—determining the legal status of the hundreds of thousands of slaves escaping behind Union lines, where they would live, how they would be educated and earn a living—but many of them found the freed people to be, however disadvantaged, also industrious, smart, religious, committed to the Union war effort, and eager to learn to read and write. When they had direct and meaningful contact with black southerners, white northerners often were won over to optimism about the future for freed people. Cornelia Hancock, a nurse from New Jersey, began her work in a contraband hospital observing that slavery had left this "class of beings" without a high "standard of morality" and "totally ignorant of the mere rudiments of learning[;] not one in one hundred can read so as to be understood." After a single week teaching in the neighboring contraband school, Hancock revised her opinion: "you would be astonished at the little blacks," she wrote to her niece; "They are very much smarter than the children of the [white] people in our neighborhood who dislike them so much." Such optimism fueled the government's and missionary organizations' wartime experiments, including the town of Mitchelville—as it would, for a time, underwrite radical Reconstruction.[6]

In nearly all these visions of emancipation, from the apocalyptic to the utopian, freed people's futures hinged on the intervention of white America—colonization programs to remove them, military commanders to seize land for them, government agencies to aid them, missionaries to teach them and preach to them. That African Americans might shape their own future, author their own place in post-slavery America, was scarcely contemplated among the prevailing meanings of emancipation. Whatever else white Americans expected from the destruction of slavery, they did not foresee the emergence of black politics any more than they had appreciated, before the war, the possible extent of literacy among the slaves. In their acts of writing, freed people worked out their own new conceptions of freedom, and they also made themselves, and their claims to civil rights, newly visible to a society whose scales were starting to fall from its eyes.

In many places, emancipation was heralded by the coming of the Union army, which altered the social landscape wherever it went. Slaves left plantations, and the slaveholding regime teetered or toppled. Recurrent fighting and shifting battle lines destabilized many parts of the South, casting both white and black southerners into uncertainty. In areas that remained under federal control for the duration of the war—such as southern Louisiana, where A Colored Man lived, and the Sea Islands of South Carolina, where Abram Mercherson did—the arrival of the Yankees ushered in a new social order, with new structures of authority. Military rule, the sometimes idiosyncratic fiats of individual generals, and, later, a large government agency called the Bureau of Refugees, Freedmen, and Abandoned Lands, or Freedmen's Bureau, touched every aspect of life in the occupied South. Freed people perceived these authorities sometimes as forces of liberation and sometimes as "new masters"; an enlisted man in the First U.S. Colored Cavalry wrote, "Wee are said to be U S Soldiers and behold wee are U S Slaves." The spectrum of northern soldiers' conduct—from heroic to abusive—and of official policies—from benevolent to indifferent, or overtly racist—justified both views.[7]

Since the Yankees' arrival meant freedom for literate former slaves to write, as well as ad hoc schools in which the illiterate could learn, many freed people tried to make sense of this complex environment through writing. In fact, the new structures and cultures of authority put a premium on written literacy. Enslaved people in the antebellum South had possessed limited means to protest wrongs and seek redress, generally through oral interchange at the local level. Slaves' political action for the most part involved activities kept secret or at least separate from whites. The few and anemic modes of petition available to them involved talking to people in the neighborhood or perhaps venturing to a court-day gathering in a town square. Both because of the legal proscriptions on their literacy and the decentralized nature of southern legal culture, sending a letter to a distant politician was neither permissible nor, even if it were, likely to have effect.[8]

With wartime emancipation, African Americans not only gained nominal freedom to speak and act; they also became part of a wider sphere of speech and action. The legal and political world they inhabited, which had rarely extended far beyond their owners' domain, now extended to Washington, D.C. As Confederate territory fell to advancing Union forces, the old social order of a county or an individual plantation gave way to the authority of a distant federal government. Freed people understood this transformation. By 1864, many had begun writing letters to the highest echelons of power. A black soldier named William Mayo knew that the president had jurisdiction even over a court martial proceeding in Florida, and he wrote to Abraham Lincoln, "I Apeal to a Great Man a man that is governing this Nation to govern the Justice and punishment that is delt out to one of its Faithfull subjects." Lucy Bailey, the wife of another black soldier, tried to locate her husband by writing to Edwin Stanton, the secretary of war, with high expectations of the war effort's centralization: "I wish you would look oar your Books and see if he is alive."[9]

Appealing to Washington, of course, was not an option without written literacy. Just as the physical separations of the domestic slave trade provoked much of slaves' letter writing, the new geography of power in the occupied South called forth a new epistolary culture. Hundreds, probably thousands of letters wended their way through the mail, from the front lines of emancipation to the desks of white authorities. Letters to public officials surely were less common than those between family members (they are far more numerous in the records today, thanks to government archiving), but they are in certain ways more illuminating. One historian has averred that only letters "written by blacks to their relatives can be accepted as literally true. These familial letters generally have a high degree of credibility because of the element of unconsciousness in them." Yet it is precisely the *consciousness* of unsolicited petitions to distant strangers—of writing for the eyes of the law, the army, the government—that registers this crucial part of emancipation: African Americans' complex, often troubled integration into new communities, new social systems, new modes of political action. Whether or not what freed people wrote to white leaders was "literally true," it reveals how they saw themselves and their freedom in the context of a nation organized around white people and their rules.[10]

Not all formal appeals from freed people were directed to officials in Washington, but even when they wrote to military officials and government agents stationed nearby, they encountered the unfamiliar ways of northerners and entered into the novel worlds of bureaucracy and the military. They found themselves not only in a changed social and political landscape but also in a new rhetorical culture. Some of their hallmark tactics for survival and resistance under slavery—secrecy, cunning, dissimulation—remained valuable in dealing with the Yankees, but they also discerned that federal officials, whether to be trusted or regarded with caution, were an audience apart from slave owners. The Yankees had different values, a different culture, and, in ways, a different language. Even barely literate former slaves quickly became adept at using the idioms of bureaucratic correspondence, understanding the ways of the military, and invoking the language and logic of legal contracts and civil rights.[11]

Like enslaved people writing to their distant spouses, wartime petitioners carefully observed the epistolary conventions that pervaded American culture, opening their letters by saying, "i Seat myself to Rite you a few lines," "I will rite you A few Lins to let you now that I am not Well," or "I take my pen to inform of my Case." Many adopted the more deferential salutations appropriate to business correspondence: "Suffer me to address you a few lines"; "i Am under the nisaty of Adressing thous few lines to you"; "I take the liberty to address you this humble request." Frequent variations on "taking the liberty" to write, though a commonplace of letters at the time, surely had special resonance when the act of penning the letter was, in no commonplace sense, a mark of the writer's liberty. At the same time, frequent usages of "humble"—as in "this humble request," or the valedictory phrase, ubiquitous in letters by people of all races and classes, "your humble [or obedient] servant"—signaled the limits of epistolary "liberty." Many petitioners underscored their humility by concluding letters with self-deprecating remarks on their literacy: "Pleass to Excuse bad writing & also mistakes"; "Sir I cant mot write very well an I lives so agreat wais of from eny one that can wrigh So I have to try an do it my self"; "please excuse my bad writing as I never went to School a day in my left"; "my writing is none of the best for Slaves are poorly learned."[12]

Formerly enslaved writers evinced anxiety and self-consciousness about various aspects of writing and various definitions of literacy, from the technical to the cultural. John Dennis, freed from slavery in 1863, could write a clear hand and produce a neat manuscript for his 1864 letter to Edwin Stanton, but he could not spell reliably. In fact, Dennis's spelling was little worse than that of many nineteenth-century Americans, but he likely had no way of knowing that, and he judged his own literacy harshly for this single defect. Misspellings such as "untell" for *until* or "letle" for *little* hardly clouded his letter's meaning, but he nevertheless concluded by saying, "please excuse my Miserable writing."[13]

Other freed people could scarcely worry about spelling while they struggled with the mechanics of pen and paper. An anonymous black soldier in Florida wrote to Washington in barely legible cursive, stringing together badly misspelled words ("Shud B" for *should be*, "Calala" for *Carolina*), but he took pains to put forward the best penmanship he could muster. On the first page of the letter, his sentences waver up and down, somewhat heedless of the blue lines on his ruled letter paper, and his tremulous letters vary widely in size. But by the end of the letter—perhaps with the aid of a friend or a ruler, perhaps simply growing more relaxed with the pen—he has managed to write in comparatively straight, even lines. When he signs off with a flourish of regimental pride, proclaiming the 35th U.S. Colored Troops the best in the army, he makes four attempts to get the number just right— first forming just the upper half of the 3 and blotting the ink, then forming a whole 3 and brushing the ink away with his finger, and then moving to a new line and inscribing another 3, which he crosses out, before finally inking the 35 to his own satisfaction.[14]

Newly literate former slaves were not only concerned with measuring up to real and imagined standards for a formal letter's appearance. They also strove to achieve the appropriate language. Especially when they leagued together to write formal petitions, freed people often adopted—even if they were unsure how to use—the rhetoric of legal documents. In scenes of collective composition, the several signatories of a letter may have in effect pooled words and phrases they had learned from speeches and court proceedings, which their designated penman then had to write out. A group of "Colored Citizens" in North Carolina protested to General Benjamin Butler that they were "oppressed by the military authurities in this Vicenity" and—although these next words proved more difficult to spell, they struck the official tone that the men evidently sought to produce—"Respeckfuley pitision you . . . for a redress of grievunces." An aggrieved soldier named Prince Albert complained of his punishment in the stilted language of a legal document, referring to himself and the commanding officer who punished him not as "I" and "he" but rather as "said Prince Albert" and "said Comdg. offr." Albert also evidently had observed that it was customary in epistolary prose to denote dates as "ult." or "inst." (from the Latin *ultimo* and *instante*—either *last* month or *this* month) but had not learned what either term meant. His letter refers variously to "the 27. inst.," "the 28th Ult.," and "the 28th inst." in the course of narrating a sequence of events apparently confined to a single two-day period—not spanning two different months.[15]

Each writer's struggle with the act of letter writing is idiosyncratic, but all of them show the effects of a particular combination of constraints: the halting literacy of the uneducated, the uncertain grasp on protocol of the uninitiated. If nineteenth-century letters in general shared fairly uniform conventions, the petitions of newly literate freed people, faced with this distinctive confluence of challenges, may have seemed a predictable genre— even, to white officials who suddenly were receiving scores of such letters, an imitable one. In late 1864, the White House received written complaints from two people at Freedmen's Village, a contraband camp that derived fame from the symbolism of its location—right across the river from Washington on the seized plantation of Robert E. Lee.[16] According to letters addressed to President Lincoln and signed by freed people living in the camp, a superintendent at Freedmen's Village jailed residents without cause, swore at them, and shipped the bodies of dead residents north for dissection. "[A]fter we are ded they put us into Barrels and send us to the Nor-th for the New York and Philadelphia Docts to cut up," wrote Sally Brown. "[T]he commissaries *Curse* and Sware at us Call us Black Biches Black Buggars and tell us to go to Hell." Freedman John Robertson implored "Mr Presedent

Linkin," "Will you not rid us of a cruel and hated man named Ridenor he is assistant Superintendent he is a very Cruel man and treats us very bad puts us in the gard house without cause." Both writers spoke up for the "good Superintendent Mr Johnson."[17]

The army official charged with looking into these claims, Captain J. M. Brown, presumably noticed that the handwriting of the two letters appeared identical. Upon investigating the situation, he deduced that they had been written by a white man. Brown reported to the Freedmen's Bureau that both letters in fact were authored by J. J. Johnson, the supposedly "good Superintendent" of Freedmen's Village, who recently had been dismissed. The disgruntled Johnson had set out to discredit his successor, and reclaim his old job, by ventriloquizing abused contrabands. Brown secured affidavits from no fewer than eight people, who worked at Freedmen's Village and had seen Johnson's handwriting, attesting that the letters were his. Brown's final report not only presented this hefty file of evidence but also added the fatuous claim that, besides, "none of [the contrabands] can read or write."[18]

The designing Johnson, however base in his ploy, knew the state of freed people's literacy better than Brown. He probably had read numerous letters from marginally literate black writers in the daily course of his work at Freedmen's Village, and he clearly thought it possible to write in such a way that he could pass, on paper, as a former slave. His letters represent both a surprising act of sympathy, as he inhabits freed people's perspectives, and a great betrayal (love and theft, like all forms of minstrelsy).[19] To some extent Johnson's imposture gives itself away. The handwriting in the two letters is not erratic, as in many neoliterate freed people's writings, but shaky in a measured—we now know, intentional—way. Freed people rarely used profane words in letters to authority figures, nor is a woman likely to write—as "Sally Brown" did to Lincoln—"they say you are a friend to the Black Man." But even if Johnson's performance of marginal literacy does not convince us, even if it convinced no one at the time (although the White House's response suggests it may have), he obviously believed former slaves had a way of writing that could be mimicked and that high-ranking federal officials would recognize. Indeed, six months later, a Freedmen's Bureau official at a different contraband camp, North Carolina's Roanoke Island, referred with some exasperation to the waves of freed people's "letter-writing, petitioning, and [claims of] abuse by their superintendents." Johnson, like other readers of former slaves' petitions, had come to see them as a genre, distinctly a part of the textual landscape of emancipation.[20]

If freed people's petitions seemed to follow a pattern, it is not easy to say why or to what effect. The formality and earnestness with which the vast majority of these writers addressed authority figures—palpable even when grammar and spelling are badly muddled—can be understood in a variety of ways. It reveals a key aspect of literacy acquisition itself, in that learning how to write a letter involves not only mastering letters and words but also assimilating a culture's epistolary mores. It perhaps shows African Americans adapting an old mode of dissimulation—playing the faithful slave, on paper, and telling white folks what they want to hear. Or it may instead, even at the same time, reflect a genuine embracing of a new reality: freed people seizing the tools of the American citizen, displaying the conviction that they can express themselves and be heard. It likely marks many of these letters as products of collaboration, direct or indirect, as new affiliations allowed ideas and advice to circulate more openly. The oral culture of the freed people made its way onto written pages in countless if not always traceable ways, as letter writers no doubt shared the names of authorities to whom petitions might be addressed, had and overheard conversations that inspired phrasings and arguments for those petitions, and, in helping each other spell words, propagated a shared lexicon.

Any letter belonging to the genre may bolster one or more of these general explanations, but each act of writing reveals an idiosyncratic cognitive process—a reckoning with the newfound faculty of literacy, the formerly forbidden spaces of the writing desk and the blank page, and the radically new social order of the post-emancipation South. Amid such tumult and novelty, it is not surprising that expressive tendencies might evolve, that writers might develop new thoughts, even within the confines of a single piece of paper. Petitioners could move with great rapidity from what they understood to be proper decorum to fervent desperation or outrage. The early months of 1863 found Gorgener Roman dwelling in legal uncertainty in southern Louisiana, where the Emancipation Proclamation technically had no effect but the Union occupation seemed to promise freedom. As for many slaves in areas where the army could not or did not fully enforce a policy of emancipation, the coming of the Yankees proved inauspicious for Roman: he remained enslaved, and his owner had him beaten for conversing with a Union officer. Roman wrote to General Nathaniel Banks, the commander of the Department of the Gulf: "I Gorgener Roman wright a fue lines to you to ask you if you will be so kind as to send some one to my assistence as soon as posable." By the end of his short letter, after Roman had spelled out in his slow, neat hand the "cruel treatments" of lashes and chains, his polite request ascended to a higher pitch of urgency: "I beg you for God sak pleas to sen some as soo as posable before they kill me."[21]

Others, more fortunately situated, argued for justice rather than mercy. General Banks was keen to hear evidence of rebels' bad behavior, even if it came to him in Gorgener Roman's irregular spelling, but an anonymous freedman serving in the Union army in North Carolina had much less reason to expect his audience's sympathy: he took a complaint about his own superior officers over their heads to the secretary of war. This writer based his petition on a sense of fairness, and he took care to establish his hard-won knowledge of the new order: "i Know that it tis not milertary to Keepe men on guard Longer 48 Hours at the Longes . . . i have Read the Reagulations Enough to Know that it is Rong but i Supose that because we are colored that they think that we Dont no any Better." For this soldier, literacy encompasses both the means of assimilating to military life and a tactic for holding military leadership to account.[22]

Newly literate and newly free, these ordinary African Americans crafted their own modes of political action. As they set their pens to paper and asserted their rights, they wove together not only epistolary conventions but also their fast-growing knowledge of the world's new ways, the ambient rhetoric of political culture (one letter of grievance concluded, "This is not the persuit of happa ness"), and, of course, their individual experiences and convictions. This fertile mix of intellectual raw material meant that even barely literate writers could arrive at arguments of striking originality and force.[23]

When Abram Mercherson insisted that "a Stop aught to [be] Put" to the abusive rampages of white soldiers in Mitchelville, he struck the tone of a town elder, as indeed he was. The experiment of a federally sponsored, self-governing freed people's community was not even two years old, and Mercherson had been present at its creation. As a slave in Savannah, Georgia, he already was somewhat literate, and was a preacher among his fellow slaves, when the Civil War broke out. In late 1861, when Union forces captured several of South Carolina's Sea Islands, including Hilton Head, the prospect of freedom came tantalizingly near—barely twenty miles from Savannah, as the crow flies, across the snaking rivers and marshland of the lowlying seacoast. Mercherson did not wait long to seize his opportunity. By springtime in 1862, and possibly earlier, he was behind Union lines on Hilton Head.

The Sea Islands were the vanguard of emancipation and black military enlistment. The low country southwest of Charleston already was anomalous in the antebellum South, isolated by its topography, noted for its aristocracy of firebrand planters, and remarkable for its demographics. In 1861, enslaved African Americans made up more than 80 percent of the islands' population. When Union gunboats sailed into a relatively defenseless Port Royal Sound on November 7, the plantation owners evacuated. In a virtual instant, the slaveholding regime of the islands vanished. When federal troops landed on Port Royal Island, they found it deserted by white people— and they found ten thousand African Americans, many already celebrating their freedom. As news of the Yankees' arrival spread, enslaved people from surrounding islands and the mainland flocked to Port Royal and Hilton Head. If the black community believed it saw a liberating army, though, military leaders were not at all sure they had liberated anyone. Federal policy had scarcely contemplated what came to pass in the Sea Islands—large numbers of slaves abandoned by their owners (who generally were surprised that their slaves did not willingly follow them to the interior of the state). The people here did not exactly fit the prevailing definition of contrabands, since they had not been employed in the Confederate war effort, yet they were in some ways better prepared for independence than the fugitive slaves who arrived behind Union lines elsewhere. Accustomed to the task system of low-country plantation slavery, these men and women had usually labored out of their owners' sight, under the supervision of black drivers and foremen, and had been allowed to cultivate small crops of their own. They became, then, prime subjects for an experiment in emancipation—what one historian aptly dubbed a "rehearsal for Reconstruction."[24]

The experiment captured the attention of northerners who thought it might reveal the freed people's fitness for citizenship. Could they learn to read and write from the missionary teachers headed to South Carolina? Would they acquire military discipline in the new black regiment commanded by abolitionist Thomas Wentworth Higginson? Were they capable of governing themselves in a community like Mitchelville? When General Ormsby Mitchel addressed the gathered residents of the town that would bear his name, he faintly echoed John Winthrop's famous admonition to the Puritans aboard the *Arbella* in 1630: "The whole North, all the people in the free States, are looking at you and the experiment now tried in your behalf with the deepest interest. . . . Supposing you fall down here; that will be an end of the whole matter. . . . [B]ut if you are successful, this plan will go all through the country. . . . Upon you depends whether this mighty result shall be worked out, and the day of Jubilee come to God's ransomed people." Among those Mitchel called to build an African American city upon a hill was Abram Mercherson. In fact, he probably had the best seat in the house. The occasion of Mitchel's speech was the dedication of the town church, and Mercherson had just been named its first pastor. By the end of the war, "Mr. Merchurson" would be remembered as "the founder of the settlement."[25]

Though his single surviving letter may not display perfect fluency in writing, Mercherson likely felt a well-earned confidence in his command of spoken language. He was by all accounts a captivating preacher, and the scant traces of his history suggest he had a knack for self-promotion and public outreach, too. Even six months before his appointment as pastor of the Mitchelville congregation, he already was perceived as a leader of the fledgling free community on Hilton Head. He somehow had come to the attention of General David Hunter, who decided (without War Department approval) to try organizing enslaved men into a military regiment. In early April 1862, Hunter called on Mercherson for advice and assistance, and in what was most likely the earliest instance of organized black military recruitment, Mercherson spoke to a meeting of freedmen on April 7. He explained that each man willing to take up arms in the Union cause, who could "prove that he has been employed, by command or consent of his master, in aid of the rebels," would be emancipated by General Hunter's order. According to a correspondent for the *New York Times* (the nation's eyes already were on the Sea Islands experiment), Mercherson "addressed his brethren in language of great feeling and power." More than a hundred men signed up on the spot, and within a week Mercherson could present Hunter with 150 recruits. Thomas Wentworth Higginson began his classic memoir, *Army Life in a Black Regiment,* by distinguishing the men he commanded, the First South Carolina Volunteers, as "the first slave regiment mustered into the service of the United States," and to establish its precedence, he wrote a fastidious chronicle of the unit's history dating back to May 7, 1862, when a white officer was charged with recruiting. In fact, the "Hunter Regiment," which Higginson identifies as the seedling of his own, began its path to service a month earlier, at Abram Mercherson's recruitment meeting.[26]

Mercherson's central role in these historic events made him a figure of modest local fame, as well as an object of curiosity among northerners who came to the Carolina coast to witness the dawn of emancipation. White travelers who wrote down their impressions of Mercherson applied many of the same stereotypes with which they imagined southern blacks in general. In their eyes, Mercherson's literacy was not enough to make him educated, much less refined. They called him "an intelligent negro, very black," "a man of ability and character," possessing "earnest eloquence, a vigorous and clear expression of his views, deep piety, and a powerful influence over the coloured people." But these same observers qualified their admiration with mixed assessments. One wrote that Mercherson "could read somewhat," another that "Abram, though able to read and write, is not polished in his manners."[27]

The journalist Charles Carleton Coffin listened to one of Mercherson's sermons in the Mitchelville church and described it as "a crude, disjointed discourse, having very little logic, a great many large words, some of them ludicrously misapplied." The *New York Times* correspondent called him "a remarkable Negro," comparable to "Mrs. Stowe's ideal 'Uncle Tom,'" and assessed one of his sermons more favorably—it was "marked by considerable originality and a closeness of logic that surprised me"—yet when this reporter transcribed his interview with the preacher, he rendered Mercherson's speech in a belittling caricature of black dialect he might have learned from Mrs. Stowe. Asked his impressions of General Hunter, for example, Mercherson reportedly replied, "Dat a berry smart General, sah; I know he be a fightin' General, by he looks!" A dispatch in a Boston newspaper devoted four paragraphs to unrestrained mockery of Mercherson's presiding over church proceedings; doubted whether Mercherson actually read from the hymnal or "or merely recited [from memory] with the book before him"; and concluded that he was "a man of no great mental resources, but of considerable fluency of speech, and of an extreme, and sometimes even ludicrous assumption of dignity."[28]

Abram Mercherson might initially have felt some pride in the attention he received, but as a backdrop to the sensitive task of writing to a high-ranking official about white-on-black sexual violence, white northerners' condescending scrutiny of Mercherson's verbal abilities could not have boosted his confidence. If nothing else, Mercherson's relatively high profile increased the pressure on him that warm August night to demonstrate skill and professionalism in his letter to General Foster. After all, as General Mitchel had said, the eyes of the whole nation were upon him. It is not surprising, then, that from the beginning of his halting composition, Mercherson engages in what linguists call hypercorrection—the tendency, especially common among people speaking a new language or aspiring to a higher social class, to overdo or misapply something they have only barely learned. Many marginally literate people, former slaves included, employ a phonetic spelling that captures their speech patterns (witness "fambely" for *family* or "amejeately" for *immediately*).[29] Not so with Mercherson: in writing "a bought" for *about* and "wrape" for *rape,* he misapplies a nascent understanding of written English's peculiarities—namely, silent letters.

Like many people excluded from full and formal education, Mercherson was a more proficient reader than writer. Armed with a preacher's knowledge of the Bible, Mercherson probably had become a habitual reader of newspapers and, as his role in Mitchelville grew, dispatches from military personnel. Accordingly, his letter presents flawless spelling and standard English when it comes to words and phrases that pervaded his daily life—standards of epistolary protocol, such as "your obedient servant," and military terms, like "officers." Mercherson tried at least twice to spell "recruits." After his first attempt, he doubled back and slowly overwrote the word, spelling out "Recrutes" in ink built up so heavily it suggests Mercherson spent more time on this word than any other in the letter—as well he might have, with hypercorrecting zeal, since this was an important word to him. It was, after all, as a recruiter that Mercherson first became acquainted with high-ranking military officers, got his name in a national newspaper, and began accruing the social authority on which he relied in sending this letter. His past success delivering stirring orations to potential recruits had gained him the ear of Union generals, and he lingers here over a word he has spoken aloud countless times, perhaps frustrated to find the written page more forbidding than the speaker's platform, but evidently determined to get it right.

Mitchelville S C
August 12 1864
To his Excelency
Maj Gen J G Foster
Dear Sir a bought (8) this evening
I was Call a fou by a man Who
States that thair was three men in
his house trubling his wife on the
Pretence of hunting Recrutes which
he Ses that he have passes indors by
you on my a Rival at the house i Saw
the 3 men Who had Commited norape
on the Person of his wife there are as i
Suppose to be officers of the 2.5 Ohio
Reg I was under the influent of Licor
thay also took thair Sholder Straps
of there Coat & Pin it on the inside
i have 4 or five witnes if Requiered
We have been trubled very often
by these officers & Sailers & i think
a Stop aught to Put to it

Page 1 of Abram Mercherson to Major General J. G. Foster, August 12, 1864,
M-268 1864, Letters Received, ser. 4109, Department of the South, Record
Group 393 Part 1, National Archives, Washington, D.C.

The word *rape* presents fewer tricks for the novice writer than several words Mercherson spells correctly ("officers," for example, in which one must differentiate a soft *c* from an *s*), but Mercherson is less likely to have seen it in print or written correspondence. It appears nowhere in the text he probably spent the most time reading, the King James Bible. Mercherson carefully spells out "wrape," inscribing a slightly wobbly *w* and awkwardly leaning *r* that suggest tense, wrist-driven penmanship, in contrast to the sweeping arm movements American educators of the period inculcated. Whether physically tense or not, Mercherson's hand faltered at least subtly as he conjured up a needless silent letter (lest he appear uneducated) to produce this most damning word in his charge against the white soldiers. The extremity of the unvarnished word *rape* may have sparked questions in Mercherson's mind about the propriety of using it in a letter to a general. Writing it down brought to mind a loathsome image. But the word was crucial, not only as information Mercherson wished to convey to General Foster but also as part of an unfolding narrative, within the letter, of Mercherson's own composition and thinking.[30]

Once Mercherson takes the step of using the word "wrape," it becomes possible to understand his earlier verb, "trubling," as a euphemism: "a bought (8) this evening I was Call a pon by a Man Who Stated that thair was three men in his house trubling his wife." The soldiers who were "trubling" the woman in Mercherson's first sentence are more explicitly identified, halfway down the page, as rapists. When Mercherson uses the same word again at the bottom of the page—the freed people in Mitchelville "have been trubled very often" by white servicemen—he ties up a delicate rhetorical thread. The repetition of the word and its spelling (correct except for the missing *o*) are not inevitable. Other parts of the letter show that Mercherson does not spell the words *soldier* and *sailor* the same way from page to page or even line to line. For his second use of "truble," on the same side of the same sheet of paper as the first, he may have looked back up the page for an exemplar and reproduced it. Copying models, after all, is the stock-in-trade of the writing student, and a writer who encounters difficulty with well-established elements of his vocabulary, like "recruits," may be reluctant to pass up a suitable verb, already before him in black and white, and cast about for synonyms.

Whether Mercherson's use of "trubled" stems from the habits of penmanship practice, the unpracticed writer's exigency, or a deliberate expression of protest and anger—which he well might have felt, as he wrote this letter sometime between eight o'clock and bedtime, flushed with outrage on his return from the victimized woman's home—the repetition forges a link. What rogue white soldiers in general were doing to the people of Mitchelville was comparable to what three of them in particular did to one black woman. The outrage over the individual assault calls forth the act of writing, which becomes, as Mercherson moves slowly down the page, a statement about a prevailing condition. Perhaps not despite but because of his limited literacy—his need to labor over the page in this way, choosing among a small stock of words—Mercherson strikes on something like a metaphor: the rape of the Mitchelville community by racist interlopers.

Neither the language nor the substance of Mercherson's critique is unusual. "Trouble" aptly described much that was afoot in the wartime South, and that highly elastic word proved useful to freed people trying to discuss emancipation's turbulence in the formal language of their petitions. It could stretch from epistolary niceties—"please excuse me for troubling you"—to written warnings of mass violence—"I blive without the intervention of the General governmt in the protection of the (col) popble that there will be trouble in *Miss.* before spring"—to the straightforward "I am in truble." Frequently and with special intensity, though, black southerners were troubled by the abuse of women—as in Mercherson's indictment, both its literal occurrence and its evocation of the broader community's adversities.

As the scope of African American enlistment widened and black regiments mobilized, increasing numbers of men were separated from wives and children, many of whom remained in bondage and subject to brutal reprisals by slaveholders who resented the men's desertion to the hated Yankees. Only somewhat more fortunate were black soldiers' families who had escaped to freedom and were living in contraband camps or near their men's units. They suffered severe poverty and privation, partly owing to the federal government's neglect of black soldiers' wages, and unhealthy, often appalling living conditions. A black recruiting agent in Indiana reported to the secretary of war in 1865 that "the hardships and troubles of Colored Soldiers Wives" also included being kidnaped and carried back into slavery in Kentucky. These very real vulnerabilities, combined with a gendered culture's presumption that women were helpless, made the suffering of wives and children both a common subject of freedmen's petitions and a touchstone of their thinking about emancipation in general.[31]

When it came to definitions of family and marriage, freed people in the occupied South found themselves caught in a clash of cultures. Marital bonds and "nuclear" families were far from universal. Slave owners, of course, had rarely given credence to slaves' affective relations, and masters who recognized slave marriages usually did so only when they found it convenient. The vow commonly used in white-sanctioned slave wedding ceremonies, " 'Til death or distance do us part," openly signaled that a marriage might be sundered by sale, and owners also imperiled slave marriages in a variety of less overt but no less serious ways. They could force enslaved men and women to mate irrespective of their feelings, prevent them from visiting spouses on other plantations, and commit sexual violence themselves against enslaved women. Many slaves developed and defended bonds of love in spite of it all, and solemnized those bonds in their own ways. Their marriages, though, did not match the norms of Victorian America. As African Americans arrived behind Union lines, white northerners were dismayed to find that the contrabands were not "really" married at all. Some of the ways they had coped with slavery's assaults on their romantic lives—by "taking up" with a second husband or wife after the first was sold away, for instance, or by steering clear of such a vulnerable attachment as a slave marriage—struck northern missionaries as evidence of the slaves' moral dissolution. Weddings abounded in contraband camps: many freed people clamored for the long-overdue chance to secure legal recognition for their marriages, and the missionaries fervently championed them, seeking to shepherd former slaves into Christian propriety. Meanwhile, formalized marriages helped federal authorities integrate former slaves into civil society and bring them under the rule of law. Exercising the right to marry was, for many freed people, the first step toward claiming broader civil rights. At the same time, as black families became a matter of the white public record, individual freed people became subjects of the state, and their marital bonds became entangled in the complexities of American contract law.[32]

In these respects as in many others, the transformations of emancipation affected men and women very differently. Without military service as a ticket to liberty, black women usually lagged behind men—geographically, legally, practically—in the transition out of slavery, and the blessings of freedom were slower in coming. Even when safely beyond slaveholders'

control, black women continued to face the terrors of racism and sexual violence, as Abram Mercherson attested. In subtler ways, black women felt the
consequences of colliding ideologies of gender in the occupied South. As
their relations to their husbands were brought within the province of law,
black women—who often had been the anchors of slave communities—
now found themselves encumbered by white Americans' preconceptions
about women's roles. Many officers in the Union army regarded black soldiers' wives and other female contrabands as simply a drain on resources,
the irksome price of filling the ranks with former slaves. And in legal and
cultural terms, freedwomen were beholden to their husbands in many of
the same ways they had been beholden to their masters in slavery.[33]

It was not only white people who saw it that way. For many freedmen,
emancipation signaled the long-overdue awakening of their masculinity,
the open door to a dominion slavery had denied them. They who had been
mastered now would be masters of their own wives and children. Antebellum abolitionists, steeped as they were in the gender ideology of their day,
had often decried slavery precisely for its emasculation of black men and its
desecration of proper, male-headed families. In the era of emancipation,
sympathetic military leaders, northern missionaries, and Freedmen's Bureau
officials, many of them abolitionists, were eager to see those ills remedied—
more eager, in many cases, than to attend the concerns of freedwomen—
and fostered a patriarchal view of the black family after slavery.[34]

Northern ideas, and sometimes the direct aid of white northerners, helped
embolden freedmen to assert their authority as heads of families by rescu-
ing wives and children from bondage. At the same time, they were only re-
inforcing a set of attitudes that freedmen—who were, after all, southerners—
already had absorbed from the world around them. Patriarchal marriages
and households were a pillar of the antebellum South's social order, and at
the dawn of the Confederacy, the manly duty to protect women and children suffused secessionists' rhetoric about the conflict. The slave foremen
and house servants who bent their ears toward owners' political conversations listened most keenly for news of the Yankees and black freedom, but
they could not help hearing, too, a gendered understanding of the war: men
fought, and they fought to protect women.[35]

With the private matters of marriage and family becoming increasingly
public, with the nature and definition of those relationships in upheaval,
the task of writing about them could prove unusually complicated. Beyond

meeting the basic challenges of letter writing, freed people petitioning white authorities had to consider multiple audiences and manage potentially volatile reactions to sensitive subjects. Not all freed people were married, nor did they belong to unbroken families, but the officials to whom they appealed could not be counted on to understand the injury and duress through which their emotional lives had traveled. The act of writing always entails urging one's thoughts across certain mediating filters—the limitations of marginal literacy, the strictures of social discourse—but these petitioners faced an especially difficult task. Along with the hopeful prospect that marriages and families now could be made whole, freed people faced an immediate reality in which—amid the conflagrations of war, in a fiercely racist South—both remained gravely threatened. In taking up their pens to meet those threats, they used the words *wife* and *husband,* and invoked the rhetoric of families and households, for a variety of purposes—to give voice to real affective bonds, to lay claim to a legal relation and a cluster of rights, and also to speak a language white people expected to hear.

Marriage and family loom particularly large in the surviving correspondence of slaves and freed people in the occupied border state of Missouri. There, black enlistment happened somewhat late but with unusual speed. Once a change in federal policy opened the door, enslaved men rushed en masse into the army, and the effect of their departure rippled across the Missouri countryside, where women and children remained in slavery. In the space of only a few months, from November 1863 through early 1864, nearly 40 percent of the state's military-age black men signed up. Almost all had been slaves. Their chance to serve initially was forestalled because Missouri, though a slave state, had remained in the Union, and the federal government began the war vowing in return to honor Missourians' property in slaves. Even among the border states, Missouri teetered especially precariously between North and South. In Maryland and Delaware, state legislators formally rejected secession; the state of West Virginia came into existence in 1862 because the states' westerners were so ardently Unionist they refused to follow the rest of Virginia into the Confederacy. Missouri was another story. The state's own leadership split, with a pro-secession faction of politicians, including the governor, fleeing the state capital and setting up a rebel government in exile. Many Confederate sympathizers refused to recognize federal authority, and a chaotic, vicious guerrilla war raged across the state. In numerous respects, Missouri was rebel territory under Union

military rule, a far more unstable place than the Sea Islands, where Confederates simply evacuated.[36]

As the war progressed and the army's need for soldiers became more
pressing, federal officials became less solicitous of Missouri slaveholders'
interests. In the summer of 1863, Colonel William Pile, a white abolitionist
and Methodist minister who joined the army as a chaplain, was charged with
limited recruiting among Missouri's free blacks, of whom there were very
few. This tepid approach did not last long. Enslaved men in effect forced the
government's hand. Despite the nominal proscription on their service, they
began escaping in large numbers and trying to sign up. In November, the
commander of the Department of the Missouri relented, and one day after
receiving the War Department's approval, he announced the army would
begin enlisting "all able-bodied colored men, whether free or slaves." With
the gates unblocked, thousands of men made their way to Union encampments, most of them to the huge installation north of St. Louis known as
Benton Barracks.[37]

The suddenness of the exodus provoked alarm among white farmers and
had dire repercussions for the enslaved people left behind. Like slave owners
in many parts of the South, Missouri farmers tried to deter men from fleeing by warning them about the travails of army life and the wickedness of
the "Yankee devils." Some, perhaps less rhetorically inclined, simply locked
up their male slaves' clothing and shoes each night. When the men left anyway, enslaved women and children were forced to take over their demand-
ing labor, or, in retaliation, they were deprived of food or evicted. Some slave
owners, seeing the institution of slavery crumble in Missouri, decided to
"salvage their investment" by sending or selling their remaining slaves to
more stable Kentucky—much farther away from enlisted husbands and
fathers—where emancipation remained in check. Since Missouri had none
of the large plantations emblematic of the Deep South, enslaved women
usually found themselves without the support of a large slave community.
Alone with those who enslaved them, many became even more vulnerable
to physical violence than they were before their husbands joined the army.
They would find ways to mount resistance, nevertheless; though less free
than men to write letters, the efficacy of their acts of writing would not
depend, as we will see, on the quantity of their words.[38]

As these changes roiled the countryside, the men gathering in St. Louis
got a toehold in the post-slavery order. Their numbers initially overwhelmed

military resources, and the prevalence of disease forced the army to convert the 2,000-bed Benton Barracks hospital into an all-black facility. Despite their hardships, these men also found the boons of freedom. "[T]he nurses are teaching their men to read, write, and, in some instances, to cipher," reported Emily Parsons, who managed more than 200 nurses at the hospital. "The poor colored men are very grateful and so anxious to learn it is very touching." As more men arrived, northern aid organizations began to formalize such impromptu lessons. The American Missionary Association set up a school for St. Louis contrabands as early as May 1863. The Western Sanitary Commission ordered 3,000 copies of *Sargent's Standard School Primer* for the freedmen at Benton Barracks, and by 1864 they had set up a school for children living in the adjacent contraband camp.[39]

The enlisted men also found that William Pile—now General Pile, superintendent of black recruitment for the state of Missouri—was highly sympathetic to freed people's concerns. Availing themselves of their white sponsors, their own advancing literacy skills, and their new authority as soldiers, these men attended to their first order of business: protecting wives and children still in slavery. For Sam Bowmen, a soldier recuperating in the Benton Barracks hospital, the task involved the tricky business of writing a letter for two audiences—his enslaved wife and the slaveholder from whom he sought to free her (and who may have been Bowmen's own former owner). He addressed his May 1864 letter, "Dear Wife," and began with customary epistolary pleasantries: "it is my prayer that when this comes to you it may find You in the enjoyment of good health and in the love of God." Though surely well meant, Bowmen's greeting is at least partly a performance, since he knew his words must pass first before the eyes of her owner, for Bowmen's wife evidently could not read. Bowmen therefore shifts quickly from the tone and form of a family letter to the real business at hand: convincing Goodridge Wilson to liberate Bowmen's wife. To make that shift, Bowmen does not at first address Wilson himself but rather ventriloquizes William Pile. In the sentence in which the letter pivots from one audience to the other, Bowmen writes: "If You donot want to stay tell Mr Wilson in a decent manner than You do not and General Pile says if You Mr Wilson is as good a Union man as [he was reported] to be you will let her come on good terms and give her a piece of writing to shew that You are what you profess to be, and if you do not this, we will shew You what we intend to do." Three times during the section in which he shifts his address from his wife toward

Wilson, Bowmen refers to the general's "orders" or to what "General Pile says." Having used that borrowed authority as his entering wedge, Bowmen then confronts Wilson directly, in his own voice, making strident demands and even overt threats: "You know that a Soldiers wife is free read this letter to her and let her return her own answer I will find out whether this has been read to her in afull understanding with her or not, and if I should find out that she has never heard her deliverance I will undoubedly punish you. . . . You can See I have power."[40]

Spotswood Rice, also a patient at the Benton Barracks hospital, wrote two separate letters, one to his enslaved daughters and one to his daughter Mary's owner, Kitty Diggs. Rice had recently received a letter from his daughter Caroline, who was owned by Diggs's brother, saying that Diggs had accused Rice of trying "to steal" Mary. In Rice's letter to Diggs, he responds to that charge in fiery language:

> now I want you to understand that mary is my Child and she is a God given rite of my own and you may hold on to hear as long as you can but I want you to remembor this one thing that the longor you keep my Child from me the longor you will have to burn in hell and the qwicer youll get their for we are now makeing up a bout one thoughsand blacke troops . . . and when we come wo be to Copperhood rabbels and to the Slaveholding rebbels . . . I want you to understand kittey diggs that where ever you and I meets we are enmays to each orthere I offered once to pay you forty dollers for my own Child but I am glad now that you did not accept it Just hold on now as long as you can and the worse it will be for you you never in you life befor I came down hear did you give Children any thing not eny thing whatever not even a dollers worth of expencs now you call my children your proty not so with me my Children is my own and I expect to get them and when I get ready to come after mary I will have bout a powrer and autherity to bring hear away and to exacute vengencens on them that holds my Child . . . this whole Government gives chear to me and you cannot help your self[41]

Though he wrote separate letters, Rice must have expected that, as with Bowmen, his personal message to his daughters would be read by the owner. And it was: both letters, interpreted as threats of violence, were forwarded by Diggs's indignant brother to General William Rosecrans. Accordingly, what Rice wrote to Caroline and Mary mostly amplifies the main points of his letter to Diggs: "If Diggs dont give you up this Government will and I feel confident that I will get you Your Miss Kaitty said that I tried to steal you But I'll let her know that god never intended for man to steal his own flesh and blood. . . . I want her to remember if she meets me with ten thousand soldiers she meet her enemy. . . . And as for her cristianantty I expect the Devil has Such in hell You tell her from me that She is the frist Christian that I ever hard say that aman could Steal his own child especially out of human bondage."[42]

The differences between Rice's two letters are less rhetorical than material: both appear to have been written on the same day, September 3, 1864, but whereas Rice wrote to Diggs by himself, he solicited help for his letter to his daughters. Only the first several lines are in his hand. A short distance down the page, cross-outs and repeated words begin to proliferate, and his penmanship grows labored. After that, someone else took over—someone also not highly educated but clearly more adept with the pen. Rice was in an army hospital suffering from rheumatism (possibly brought on by his work as a tobacco roller while enslaved), and he probably found it physically challenging to write this letter to his daughters, especially if he had just finished his three-page philippic to Diggs.

Even before Rice sought the aid of an amanuensis, he already had set about distinguishing the personal letter from the communiqué to a slaveholder. Whereas he wrote to Diggs on plain paper, he began his letter to his daughters on stationery provided by a northern aid organization active in his hospital. Alongside the image of a bird carrying an envelope, the letterhead carries the printed message:

> The U.S. Christian Commission
> sends this as the soldier's messenger to his home.
> Let it hasten to those who wait for tidings.
> "There is a Friend that sticketh closer than a brother."

Rice made sure his daughters got the best letter he could give them—in the best penmanship, using the stationery upon which thousands of Union soldiers, white as well as black, communicated with their families—and he surely did not mind if Kitty Diggs noticed the difference. That imprint of official backing—Rice writes the letter, the Christian Commission sends it "as the soldier's messenger"—echoes the "powrer and autherity" with which Rice pledges to arrive and reclaim his daughter, the force of "this Government" that "gives chear" to his cause, and the army of "thoughsands" that backs him up.[43]

Both Bowmen and Rice derive confidence from the Union occupation and their own military identity; both use the written word to make a show of power. Meanwhile, Bowmen's wife remains nameless in the documentary record. No writings by Rice's daughters survive, although Caroline— the canny back channel of Kitty Diggs's enmity—apparently was literate. (Rice's daughter Mary was among the elderly former slaves interviewed as part of the Federal Writers' Project in the 1930s, and she told her interviewer stories of her father's life prior to his escape from slavery and enlistment.) Based solely on these letters, the prospect of freedom for these women would appear to be a subject for negotiation between their owners and their would-be male protectors—not a matter of their own initiative. All across the South, enslaved and freed women did not have military enlistment as a path to freedom, education, and power, and they suffered on behalf of husbands who did take that path. As Jane Coward of Kentucky reported to her soldier-husband, two white men "beat me nearly to death," and one of them "says that he will kill every woman that he knows that has got a husband in the army." African American women could not always protect themselves against such vengeance, and rarely did they feel, as Spotswood Rice did, that thousands of blue-clad warriors supported them.[44]

Nevertheless, they could and did testify to their traumas and, in so testifying, work out the meaning of emancipation. They were more likely to register complaints in person than in writing, and the contrast between spoken and written expression reveals how fraught the act of writing could be. The strictures of propriety made literacy, for those who had it, a difficult weapon to wield, and the blank page presented a rough landscape, as daunting as it was filled with possibility. The small number of women's petitions to authority figures display considerable tact and decorum. Edith Jones, enslaved in New Orleans, wrote to General Nathaniel Banks in March 1863 using impeccable script and genteel language: "I earnestly request of your honour to grant a hearing." A freedwoman in coastal Virginia complained of her husband's impressment into the army in the politic terms of health and household, not the political terms of justice and freedom: "he is not competent to bee A Soldier. he is verry delicate. . . . if they, keep him, they leave me, and 3 children, to get along, the best we can." When it came to brutal violence, especially sexual violence, few avenues of expression could pass between Victorian propriety and epistolary decorum, and little evidence survives that women reported beatings and rapes in writing, except in largely euphemistic ways.[45]

A Missouri slave named Martha Glover was one of the women left behind when her husband went to Benton Barracks. When she made an appeal for protection against her owner's assaults, she wrote—as befits a woman's supposed place—not to a public official but to her husband. Even in this ostensibly private letter, Glover does not venture many details: "I have had nothing but trouble since you left. You recollect what I told you how they would do after you was gone. they abuse me because you went & say they will not take care of our children & do nothing but quarrel with me all the time and beat me scandalously the day before yesterday." Though she addressed herself to "My Dear Husband," Glover no doubt expected—probably, in fact, hoped—that he would show the letter to his military superiors, who in turn could intervene to help her. In effect, her letter charges her husband to speak for her, to fill in what she feels enjoined from using in writing. Near the end of the letter, she again veils the abuses she has suffered: "Remember all I told you about how they would do me after you left—for they do worse than they ever did & I do not know what will become of me." Glover's sentence sends her husband the equivalent of a knowing look: my "trouble" is unspeakable, but *you know* what I am talking about.[46]

Outside the confines of the written page, women were perfectly willing to name white men's despicable acts. As the Freedmen's Bureau fanned out across the occupied South, many women visited these local outposts of federal authority to tell of the crimes they suffered, and through the early years of Reconstruction, they vigorously exposed white men's depredations. In the testimony bureau agents transcribed, these women—either urged on by the agents' questioning or disinclined themselves to hold anything back—offered up the graphic details that seemed to have no place in writing.[47]

Patsey Leach of Kentucky attested in 1865 that her owner beat her because her husband had enlisted and because she had watched as a regiment of black soldiers passed near her home. "[H]e took me into the Kitchen," Leach told her examiner, "tied my hands tore all my clothes off until I was entirely naked, bent me down, placed my head between his Knees, then whipped me most unmercifully until my back was lacerated all over, the blood oozing out in several places so that I could not wear my underclothes without their becoming saturated with blood." In a Freedmen's Bureau office in Georgia, Rhoda Ann Childs narrated a barbaric attack in horrifying detail. A gang of eight men seized her and took her from her house after nightfall, threw her across a log, and beat her mercilessly, and then they turned more vicious still: "I was thrown upon the ground on my back, one of the men Stood upon my breast, while two others took hold of my feet and stretched My limbs as far apart as they could, while the man Standing upon my breast applied the Strap to my private parts until fatigued into stopping, and I was more dead than alive. Then a man, supposed to be an ex-confederate Soldier, as he was on crutches, fell upon me and ravished me. During the whipping one of the men ran his pistol into me, and Said he had a hell of a mind to pull the trigger, and Swore they ought to Shoot me, as my husband had been in the 'God damned Yankee Army,' and Swore they meant to kill every black Son-of-a-bitch they could find that had ever fought against them."[48]

Women in nineteenth-century America did not write such things down. Certainly no black women disclosed them in letters addressed to white men. (One wonders how many squeamish Freedmen's Bureau agents themselves declined to commit every detail of such testimony to paper.) For these women, imagine the potential emotional torment in the act of writing: how unlike a simple matter of expressing thoughts and feelings, when memories of such trauma might smolder in the mind of a woman who sets pen to paper—fettered by propriety if not also marginal literacy, by anguish if nothing else—and composes words doomed to fall short of reality.[49]

We will never know exactly what lay secreted within Martha Glover's words to her husband, "Remember all I told you." When she describes receiving a "scandalous beating"—her letter's only explicit betrayal of physical abuse—her adjective suggests a particular violation of personal integrity. The word seemed essential, in the Civil War South, for articulating the outrage of violence against women. A marginally literate white woman in North Carolina, reporting the abuses of Confederate militiamen hunting deserters, strained for it to describe their treatment of her—the men "drug me a Bought scanless," she wrote—and "scanless," in turn, became a part of southern vernacular connoting affronts to women.[50]

All we know for sure about Glover's ordeal we know from General William Pile. Glover's husband, Richmond, did show the letter to one of his unit's officers, who passed it up the chain of command. Ten days after Martha Glover composed her letter, it had made its way to Pile's desk, and he wrote upon it, "Lt. Hussey is directed to send the man to whom this letter was sent, to me that I may get his Masters name &c in order to redress the wrongs complained of." By the next month, Pile had interviewed Richmond, sent a letter of reprimand to Glover's owner, George Cardwell, and seized Glover and her children when the owner attempted to take them to Kentucky. When he wrote a report on the matter, he revealed, finally, the scandal as he knew it. Not only had Glover's owner whipped her "most cruelly"—he had done it "when she is Pregnant and near confinement."[51]

Glover may have been surprised by her owner's treatment of her, or she may have read it as writing on the wall. At an earlier time, her pregnancy might have shielded her from abuse, if only because her offspring added to George Cardwell's wealth. With slavery crumbling and emancipation imminent, Cardwell would have seen matters differently. Many slaveholders, if not in denial about the passing of the old order, began at least to feign slight respect for their male slaves—for even when free, black men would remain the region's labor force. But black women mattered little to southern planters if they could no longer hold the deed to their bodies. As one historian writes: "Out of patience with the pregnant, the recently pregnant, the potentially pregnant, and the very young—people who had been reckoned 'a heavy Expense' in bondage but tolerated for the value they had added to a slaveholder's purse—planters turned their backs on the distaff and diminutive portions of their former slaves."[52]

The compound injustice of Glover's violation is that her gender, even after it ceased to shield her from a slave owner's violence, did not easily translate into protection by benevolent federals. Though perfectly able to express herself in writing, Glover found the pathways of empowerment narrowed by a different dimension of literacy—the accepted bounds of women's expression, a culture's shame in speaking of women's bodies. She had to send her petition on a detour, via her husband, beyond the written page. As we will see, her letter would yet do its office in the bureaucratic world of white men.

For freedmen like Sam Bowmen and Spotswood Rice, the combination of written literacy and an army uniform galvanized a self-image of free manhood. They expected emancipation to spell an end to their families' separation and suffering, and they spelled out that demand in clear and adamant language. But many confronted a sobering miscarriage of their expectations. For some black soldiers, military service did not enliven but rather undermined their identity as providers and protectors. Not only for black women did it sometimes seem that emancipation preserved or even intensified the agonies of slavery. Enlisted men's separation from families understandably provoked as much grief and frustration as anger and resistance. And although to some extent freer than Martha Glover to write about the delicate and the unspeakable, African American men were nevertheless reluctant to name the particularly appalling abuses women suffered. Their petitions on behalf of wives and children often show a novice writer's unsteadiness magnified by doubts about their own rectitude and power.

John Dennis moved north to Boston after his liberation, but even from this literal and symbolic perch of freedom, he reflected, "I have been in troble for about four yars." In a letter to Secretary of War Edwin Stanton, Dennis devotes one muted sentence to his emancipation amid a longer narrative that revolves around his family:

> my Dear wife was taken from me Nov 19th 1859 and left me with three Children I being a Slave At the time Could Not do Anny thing for the poor little Children for my master it was took me Carry me some forty mile from them So I Could Not do for them and the man that they live with half feed them and half Cloth them & beat them like dogs & when I was admited to go to see them it use to brake my heart. . . . what I went too know of you Sir is is it possible for me to go & take my Children from those men that keep them in Savery if it is possible will you pleas give me a permit from your hand then I think they would let them go I Do Not know what better to Do but I am sure that you know what is best for me to Do.

The same sense of helplessness that suffuses Dennis's letter—all that he "Could Not do" for his children, his turn to Stanton for aid—appears in the abiding troubles of his post-slavery life. "[A]s I have been recently freed," he tells Stanton, "I have but letle to live on." Dennis's powerlessness becomes poignantly literal in his letter's concluding lines, when he reveals that, on top of it all, he is a "Criple."[53]

Although the recourse to a written petition itself bespeaks a hope that wrongs can be righted, some writers betrayed little optimism about life after slavery. For an anonymous member of the First U.S. Colored Cavalry, the nominal end of the war proved to be little cause for celebration. While white soldiers were being mustered out and heading home, many black regiments were dispatched to Texas to stamp out the last embers of rebellion. The First Colored Cavalry, which had served in Virginia ever since it was organized there in 1863, met with a strange and forbidding landscape at the mouth of the Rio Grande, and the men found themselves farther away from family members than they had ever been. In a letter sent to Washington in December of 1865, this soldier wrote, apparently on behalf of his comrades, "our wifes sends Letters stateing thir suferage saying that they are without wood without wrashions without money and no one to pertect them." With a fervent national discussion underway about whether African Americans should be granted voting rights, this soldier had become familiar with the word "suffrage" (black soldiers stationed in Texas themselves weighed in on the debate through letters to black newspapers). His conflation of "suffrage" and "suffering" suggests more than an imprecise grasp of vocabulary. Given the bleak view of the new order his experience warranted—"never was wee any more treated Like slaves then wee are now in our Lives"—he may genuinely have interpreted talk of "Negro suffrage" more as a warning than a wish.[54]

Black soldiers could write plainly about their wives' and children's material deprivation, but more sensitive forms of "trouble" and "suffering" proved almost as challenging for uniformed men to articulate as for enslaved women. A Kentucky soldier, complaining that his enslaved family's owner refused to clothe them, managed not only to document their mistreatment but even to capture the owner's mean spirit: "he dos not giv them a rage nor havnot for too yars . . . he says let old Abe Giv them Close." When it came to instances of violence, though, writers trod hesitantly. A group of freedmen in South Carolina wrote to Abraham Lincoln with a series of complaints about conditions in the Sea Islands, most of them economic matters discussed in plain language. Of one last concern, though, they wrote, "Thiss is shamefull, wee blush write or send it you but the truth must be told." Overcoming their blushing, the authors explained that a northern labor agent had "turn'd the cloths of a Colard Girl over her head turned her over a Barrel, & whipd her with a Leathern Strap."[55]

George Johnson, a black sailor serving in the Mississippi River delta, could speak for himself with the confidence of Sam Bowmen and Spotswood Rice, but he struggled mightily—through blushes, anger, and his own limitations as a writer—to articulate the plight of his sister. Evidently well versed in public discourse about the war, shrewd in applying the new, post-slavery logic of contract and rights, Johnson nevertheless faltered as he wrote his way into the realm of suffering and emotional distress. When he sat down in early January 1863 to compose a letter to a Union official in Louisiana, he began with a clear account of the case he wished to make:

> Dear Genarl Franch Genarl Butler Promest Me if i Went in the Sivest that My Fambely Should be taken Car of by the Govenment but i dou not think that it is so For My Sister has been in Jail now vere nere a Month Suffern and i Would Wish to Gite her out if there is any Possibely Chance of douingin so i think that it is hard that she has been Keep in there so For nothingin For as hard as tames is at the Prasent no one Could Pay Wages house Rent For it is as Mouch as pepel Can dou to Gite somthingin to Eate less payingin Rent. Wages her Master put her in there on that Corse this Case Cane be prove by White. Black so I will ask of you intessede of Giten her out if you so pleas For i think that she has been in there Most Longe or nouff Suffern.[56]

Nothing is known about twenty-five-year-old George Johnson's history, but his writing suggests the sort of hardscrabble education a resourceful young black man might come by in the streets of New Orleans or among new friends aboard ship. Much of Johnson's spelling is phonetic ("fambely," "pepel"), but a tendency toward hypercorrection shows he has received a few lessons—even if he has not fully assimilated them—in the vagaries of written English. He knows about silent *e*'s, for instance, though not when to use them ("Gite," "Eate," and "Cane"). Someone evidently instructed him that, in the case of words he pronounced *nothin'* or *somethin'*, he ought to add *-ing*, but he did not understand exactly how or where to insert this seemingly arbitrary syllable: "nothingin," "somethingin," "payingin." The word *suffering* stands apart: perhaps felt more than thought, or simply so central to his letter that he insisted on writing it exactly as he would say it, the word twice leads Johnson to buck the obscure rule about *-ing* and instead write "suffern."

Though matters of spelling give him pause, Johnson does not waver in his argument. The linear syntax of his opening sentence reflects the logical mood of a contractual claim, as he strings together, with geometric precision, dependent clauses articulating axiom and deduction, axiom and deduction: "Genarl Butler Promest . . . *if* i Went in the Sivest *that* My Fambely Should be taken Car of . . . *but* i dou not think that it is so *For* My Sister has been in Jail." His commanding tone suggests familiarity with the civic realm of wartime rhetoric and recruiters' promises—a discourse to which he surely had exposure, both orally and in print. Such a keen observer of the Union occupation was Johnson, in fact, that he enlisted in the Union navy barely a week after General Benjamin Butler first called for, and began making promises to, black volunteers. Four months later, when Johnson began his petition by reviewing the terms of his enlistment, he either misinterpreted or shrewdly restyled those promises.

It was Butler who pioneered the designation "contraband," more than a year earlier, when enslaved men sought refuge with Union forces at Virginia's Fortress Monroe. Answering to an administration as yet unwilling to sanction emancipation, yet hesitant to return able-bodied African American men to rebel owners, Butler struck upon an inelegant but functional solution: the army would decline to send slaves back to their putative owners, Butler decreed, because any "property" left behind by the enemy was "contraband of war."[57] Butler's 1861 decision ultimately proved to be a crucial step toward emancipation, and by the end of the war he had become an ardent advocate of African Americans in the military. In 1862, though, as he tried to establish federal authority in southern Louisiana, Butler dragged his feet on black enlistment. Commanding a small Union force deep in Confederate territory—communication with Washington took twenty days— Butler aimed to preserve order and strengthen the occupation. He began recruiting volunteers from the loyal white population in July. Not until September did he accept African Americans into the army and even then, to keep peace with local slaveholders, he called for volunteers only from "the free colored population." These he invited to "defend the Flag of their native country" and "protect their wives and children and kindred from wrong and outrage."[58]

However conservatively worded, Butler's August 22 order sounded like a clarion call to black men in New Orleans. The city's pro-Union newspaper, the *Daily Delta,* which already was advocating black enlistment in its columns, reprinted the text of Butler's order multiple times in the ensuing days, alongside the recruiting advertisements that had been targeting white men for weeks. Without delay, recruiting ads for black soldiers began to appear in the same pages, often directly adjacent to the now-familiar appeals to white recruits. Reading across the paper's columns, one could find identical

promises of bounties and wages for men of both races (although equal pay
for black soldiers would prove to be a false promise). The ubiquitous and
prominent assurances that had been appearing in the white ads—"RELIEF
TO FAMILIES"; "SOLDIERS' FAMILIES WELL PROVIDED FOR!"—were somewhat
tepidly replicated, in smaller type, in the notices addressed to "patriotic colored citizens": "Families of Volunteers Supplied with Rations, &c."[59] Nonetheless, the message was clear: what the U.S. Army had been saying to white
men it now was saying to black men, too. Neither freed people nor Union
recruiters seemed punctilious, either, about Butler's restrictions on enlisting
enslaved men. One of the recruits later recalled, "Any negro who would
swear that he was free, if physically good, was accepted, and of the many
thousand slave fugitives in the city from distant plantations, hundreds
found their way . . . into the ranks."[60]

On September 1, 1862, ten days after Butler issued his order, even as the
newspaper pages rapidly filled with talk of black recruitment, George Johnson shipped aboard the U.S.S. *Pampero* off Pilottown, Louisiana. Strictly
speaking, General Butler had not promised him anything—the army commander's order had no bearing on terms of service in the navy—but Johnson clearly had internalized the spirit of the summer's recruiting campaign.
(Nor was he the only one. Another Louisiana soldier, even near the end of
the war more than two years later, still understood the terms of his enlistment as a contract with Butler: "Gel Buttler promas my regt $13.00 per
month $58.00 Bounty and I suppose his promasses should have been kept.")
Undeterred that the government's promises to black soldiers seemed thin
compared with those for whites, or perhaps willfully appropriating white
soldiers' benefits as the black sailor's right, Johnson appeals to a mainstay of
political philosophy: military service entitles a person to full citizenship.
For Johnson to swear himself to the nation's service, in the rhetorical heat
of southern-Louisiana recruiting, was to take on the new identity of a "patriotic colored citizen."[61]

That identity proves a boon not only to his self-image but also to his
writing. In listening to the talk of recruitment, and most likely reading of it
in newspapers, Johnson evidently received an education in the diction and
grammar of contracts and claims. To begin by invoking what "Genarl Butler Promest Me" is to build his act of writing on a foundation of civic identity. When Sam Bowmen repeated what "General Pile says," he might have
referred to an actual conversation with William Pile, who oversaw black

soldiers fairly directly. Johnson, on the other hand, almost certainly never laid eyes on Benjamin Butler. He understands that Butler's name is synonymous with federal authority.

When Johnson's letter shifts from that civic realm to a more private one in speaking about his sister, the syntax of his writing begins to break down. Without extant models for articulating family matters, he proceeds falteringly: "so i Will ask of you intesede of Giten her out if you so pleas For i think that she has been in there Most Longe or nouff Suffern She has not Got very Good health For hes has not been Longe Sence been out of her Clild bad way taken and put in Jail." As it proceeds, this sentence becomes almost incomprehensible. Working at the outer limits of what he knows how to express in writing—what he has the vocabulary for, what he believes he is authorized to say—Johnson briefly flounders in the daunting space of the blank page, the uncertain form of his incipient citizenship.

The meaning of this garbled sentence becomes clear only later in the letter, when Johnson has rallied and remounted his effort to bear witness to his sister's suffering. First, as if at his wit's end in trying to explain her "not . . . very Good health," he follows up the fractured sentence by retreating to the safer ground of official business. He writes down a simple list of known information: his sister's name and address, the number of the "Wachman that taken her," and his own name and station: "her Brother George W. F. Johnson border of the U.S Ship Pampero Gulf Squrd off Pilot town." Johnson apparently means this line to be his signature, although he runs it in with the letter text, rather than setting it off at the bottom of the page. In any event, this declaration of his name and military identity somehow enables him to launch a new formulation. Having committed to paper the station he now holds, perhaps recalling the revolution it symbolizes, he reiterates his request more emphatically. In a kind of postscript, after his signature, he delivers the letter's clearest peal: "also you Will Pleas to answer this Letter and if I Can Gite her out you Will beso Kinde as Give Me a permit to Go in and See her For I Lern that the ponish them slily in Jail and i Woulden For to be ille treted What Sowever because She has Misscarred a Childe."

The difficulty of writing almost quelled the claim Johnson most wanted to make: that his sister merits accommodation not only because a promise was made to Johnson when he enlisted, not even only on grounds of justice, but out of compassion for what this woman has recently endured. The reemergence

New Orleans Feby 7/1863

Dear Genarl Franch ...

George W. F. Johnson to Genarl Franch, January 7, 1863, Miscellaneous Records, ser. 1796, Department of the Gulf, Record Group 393 Part I, National Archives, Washington, D.C.

of this claim, evidently possible for Johnson only after he has written his way
through the others, transforms the letter. The words "What Sowever" sit at
the bottom right corner of the manuscript page, written in very tall letters,
twice as high as the rest of the line. In placement and size they resemble the
signature the letter appears to lack. In fact, the clerk at military headquarters
who received this letter was fooled by it: he evidently did not read closely
enough to notice Johnson's name, and—not finding the document signed in
the usual way, in an obvious place—he labeled it "No Name," filed it, and
presumably took no further action. The clerk's misapprehension has an element of truth to it. Johnson's name and station may form the underpinnings
for his contractual claim to justice but not for his most urgently felt plea.
They are one kind of signature but not the letter's principal one.

The unequivocal line Johnson draws, his private fear and appeal to a
moral absolute—*no ill treatment whatsoever*—marks the climax of his com-
positional drama, as well as the real signature of his petition. Not because
an enlisted man requests it, not because General Butler promised it, but
because humane sympathy demands it, the particular pain of a woman's
body and her particular loss—the suffering authorities never notice, that
usually goes unnamed—must here be written and respected. Well might
such unbureaucratic reasoning stand above a signature out of protocol, a
mark not of outward identity but of the inner resolve to which the slow act
of writing could lead. As his hand moves down the page, Johnson's mind
ventures toward a new idea: this new era's promise extends beyond the
name-and-rank freedom a white general might grant a black man, reaching
toward a whole race's admission to human rights. It is unsurprising that the
letter lay unread, as the promise was long unrealized.

Nine months later, Johnson wrote another letter, and by now he could envision a new role for himself in the post-slavery era. Though it is not known
how his sister's imprisonment was resolved, one way or another Johnson
retained his faith in written petitions. Still aboard the *Pampero,* he wrote to
a Union general, "i am douing Well Where i am" but "Would Rather be in
the army For i do actley think it is My Duty to go and Fight For My Freedom unless i do i dont desirve having it." Johnson requested more than a
simple transfer to another branch of the military. With a year of service
under his belt, he now could write, "[I] think that i am Capabel of

Commading a Squard i Would haft to be in stuckted alittle. after that i Would beabel to Lede a Company i Would wish to try it any Way." Johnson's entry into literacy may have shown him how much he could learn when "in stuckted alittle." He still struggled with signatures: at the bottom of this letter, he scratched out an abortive one and tried again. But the insight and audacity he could achieve while immersed in acts of writing—the one in January, perhaps others in the intervening months—evidently fired his self-confidence. He now could see himself as a leader.[62]

Something of the same sort happened to Abram Mercherson. Like Johnson, whose fluency and resolve rallied in a postscript, Mercherson continued writing after he signed his name to his letter about the assault on a Mitchelville woman. Having reached the bottom of the sheet with his firm concluding sentence, "i think a Stop aught to Put to it," he turned the page and wrote, "Gen I Have the Honer to Remain your obediant Servant, Rev[d] Abram Mercherson." Reaching the end of the letter represented an accomplishment, not at all inevitable, for the marginally literate preacher. With his task completed and his signature affixed, though, he found the verso open before him, a new blank page. Either the idea came to him in that moment, or his inhibitions about writing it down fell away: "i genl Several of the 2nd US Batery men col here & thay Stand Redy to assist me in Keeping order in the Village if you will grant Promission i Dont think that eny officers or Saler aught to have these Night Pass to come over to the Villag for thay will not Behave them Selves as men these col Soildier over here gen are faithfull in the Discharge of there Duty Sum of them i have none ever Since i arive on the island Your obd. Servent Revd A Mercherson."[63]

In a double-barreled volley of radicalism, Mercherson argues that he should command a police force and that African American soldiers should be charged with "Keeping order"—that black men should have the authority to patrol and discipline white soldiers. It was an extraordinary proposition to make, on South Carolina soil, under the military rule of a nation that had insisted only a few years before that this was a "white man's war." Conceived at a writing desk, redoubled in the flush of a postscript, the petition accrued its ambition as Mercherson wrestled with the words at his command, discovering what he could express and what he believed he could justly demand. By October, Union officials had directed black soldiers at Mitchelville "to arrest persons whom *Father Murchison* (magistrate) may designate for any riotous or disorderly conduct."[64]

Pages 2 and 3 of Abram Mercherson to Major General J. G. Foster, August 12, 1864, M-268 1864, Letters Received, ser. 4109, Department of the South, Record Group 393 Part 1, National Archives, Washington, D.C.

Martha Glover's letter secured no position of leadership for her, but it had farther-reaching impact than either Johnson's or Mercherson's. When it made its way to General William Pile's desk, and her husband's testimony filled in her text's silences, it had found a sympathetic audience. As a Methodist minister, Pile no doubt thought Glover's appalling treatment deserved compassion. As a high-ranking officer charged with filling up regiments of Missouri freedmen, Pile had other commitments, too, and Glover seized upon them. In drawing her letter to a close, she turned attention from her own plight to its broader implications for military recruitment: "Tell Isaac that his mother come & got his clothes," she wrote; "she was so sorry he went. You need not tell me to beg any more married men to go. I see too much trouble to try to get any more into trouble too—Write to me & do not forget me & my children—farewell my dear husband from your wife Martha."[65]

Though no doubt genuinely felt, Glover's parting remarks show a kind of tactical brilliance, too. Writing at the end of December 1863—during the flood tide of enlistment at Benton Barracks, but before General Pile had sent a single black regiment into the field—she shows an awareness of both the early signs of Union recruitment's success and the undeniable contingency of the federal emancipatory project in Missouri. She knows that many black men in her neighborhood have traveled the hundred miles southeast to St. Louis—some of them, like Isaac, apparently, even if it meant leaving by night without clothes. She also knows some men who have not left, and she claims for herself a role in their eventual decision. Her announcement that she will not "beg any more married men to go" may be intended less for her husband than for her letter's other audience—the military officials to whom she expects him to show it. To them she says, in effect, the trouble she has seen is their trouble, too. Unless they concern themselves with the welfare of black women, they should not expect many more recruits.[66]

Her point was well taken; her letter, not easily forgotten. It remained on Pile's desk for over a month. He had read it by January 9, and when he talked with Richmond Glover he made notes about Martha's owner in the blank space beneath her signature. Meanwhile, what Glover first called to his attention seemed to be growing into an urgent problem of vast proportions. On January 20, an editorial in the *Missouri Democrat* had commended Pile and his recruits but noted that "the soldiers frequently receive intelligence that their wives and children, left behind, are subjected to severe maltreatment." On February 6, a white officer in one of the Benton Barracks black regiments told Pile about two enlisted men whose wives were whipped by their owners simply for receiving letters from their husbands. Pile still had Glover's letter at hand on February 11, when he forwarded it to head-quarters "for the consideration" of the commanding general of the depart-ment, William Rosecrans. He had not failed to grasp the implications of Glover's closing words: "Hundreds of able bodied men," he wrote, "are de-terred from enlistment by fears of their families being abused or sold to Kentucky." It was about a week afterwards that Pile caught Martha Glover's owner trying to carry her away to Kentucky. Having received word that the owner had brought her and her children to St. Louis, Pile "went in person immediately" to the house where they were held and "took possession of the woman and children."[67]

Glover had become, for Pile, the paradigm of enslaved women's suffering in Missouri, and he used her story as the hallmark of a campaign to protect soldiers' families. On February 23 Pile wrote directly to General Rosecrans, urging him to stop slave owners from taking slaves out of the state. He cited Glover's case as "only a sample of many Similar ones that have occurred during the last two months." Three days later, he wrote to one of Missouri's congressmen, again citing "as a sample of many others, a statement of one case"—Martha Glover's. Pile reported that "the treatment, which the fami-lies of colored soldiers are receiving at the hands of their masters in this State, has almost suspended enlistment." In early 1864 nearly everyone understood, whether they said so or not, that the war effort now depended on a supply of black soldiers, and that supply, Pile told the congressman—as Martha Glover had told him—was in jeopardy so long as black women were. "[T]here is no remedy," he concluded, "but *emancipation immediate and unconditional*"—not just for the men who enlisted but also for all the slaves who could not.[68]

It worked. In March, General Rosecrans issued an order prohibiting the removal of any slave from the state. Slavery in Missouri had effectively come to an end, as its white citizens would acknowledge when they called a state constitutional convention to abolish it later that year. Thus could Sam Bowmen and Spotswood Rice speak out, in May and September, with the force of an army behind them. The rights they asserted were authorized not only by their freedom, their uniform, and a culture's expectations of their gender, but also by Martha Glover's act of writing, by the political changes her letter more or less directly abetted, and implicitly by its method. Glover sent her letter into the hands of people to whom black women did still matter, even if they did not matter enough that they could write freely for themselves. Though less free than Abram Mercherson to spell out the meaning of "trouble," she understood trouble's implications and could call attention to them—if only by enlisting her husband to speak of what her written words could not, if only in resignation that her gender diminished the blessings of literacy and the dawn of freedom.

With her soldier-husband and the Union military as channels of distribution, the work of Martha Glover's pen made its way into the public record. As emancipation progressed, the writings of other ordinary African Americans would likewise find new and broader audiences.

chapter six

Black Ink, White Pages

THE NEEDS of families and the imperatives of justice were among the most immediate and important motives for freed people in their acts of writing, and the travail and oppression that provoked their letters of petition and protest would not soon abate. While written literacy conferred the freedom to demand white leaders' attention, it also would prove necessary for the tense and thorny negotiations that ensued when their petitions fell on deaf ears, when protests gained no sympathy. As emancipation progressed, more and more freed people were learning to write, but they were also finding that the written medium involved many of the same challenges, restrictions, biases, and perils as the social and political world to which it granted them access. As the war's dust settled and the destruction of slavery was formally accomplished, African Americans in the South had to reckon not only with displacement, separation, racism, and violence, but also with the dawning reality of a social revolution. Racial identity and race relations would never be the same.

Freedom held the promise of strengthened African American communities on a large scale, even of black nationalism, and it inevitably would entail new relations with white people—from the southerners who formerly owned slaves to the northerners now cast as protectors of the newly freed. The two transformations, in intra- and interracial relations, were necessarily intertwined, since blacks' status in white-dominated society was the central problem of African American politics, the subject of blacks' internal discussions and of the century-long struggle for civil rights that lay ahead. Plenty of African American community building, as well as tactical maneuvering through the minefields of white oppression, occurred in the oral realm, just as it had during slavery.[1] But toward the end of the war and in its wake, the act of writing took on special importance. Under federal occupation and in a potentially reconstructed South, freed people explored the possibilities for interracial alliances through writing—and sought participation in a realm from which they always had been marginalized, in which written words were the currency. They would find cause for both hope and dismay, for they would find literacy indispensable but also often insufficient. In facing one of the fundamental challenges for all writers—how to define and relate to an audience—they contended with particular problems of racial identity and race relations.

Garland H. White of the Twenty-Eighth U.S. Colored Infantry devotedly read the *Christian Recorder,* and when he picked up the issue for April 22, 1865, he looked with excitement to see whether the editors had printed something he himself had written. The official publication of the African Methodist Episcopal (AME) Church, the *Recorder* was "the most consistently published and widely distributed African American newspaper of the nineteenth century," and it proved especially popular among black soldiers during the Civil War. Arguably the first black periodical to achieve a national audience, the *Recorder* had readers ranging from free-born and well-educated northerners to barely literate former slaves in the South. Each week its four large, tightly packed pages presented a tapestry of African American life. Heralding the rise of African American letters, the *Recorder* printed national news and war dispatches from black soldiers alongside fiction and poetry by black writers. As White's eyes scanned each column of the April 22 number, looking for the words of his pen transfigured by the dignity of print, they encountered a memorial poem on the death of President Lincoln; the text of a sermon preached on "Universal Liberty" at a church meeting in New York; the latest installment in a serialized novel called *The Curse of Caste,* written by a black Pennsylvania woman named Julia C. Collins; more paeans to the martyred president; a traveler's description of the all-black town of Mitchelville, South Carolina; and, in the fifth column of the second page, White's own "Letter from Richmond," forming a part of this kaleidoscopic representation of African Americans' religious, cultural, and political activities.[2]

No less significant were the *Recorder's* practical uses for a readership that, although beginning to develop a unified consciousness in the wake of emancipation, remained scattered by the disruptions of slavery and the war. The paper's backers billed it as a way for African Americans to "communicate with your friends in the army and elsewhere," and, beginning in 1863, they regularly devoted space to personal notices under the heading "Information Wanted." Here, in the columns of the paper's third page, men and women tried to forge anew, in a public arena, the connections some enslaved and freed people sustained through private letters. Those who had been separated by the slave trade or the upheavals of the war tried to find their long-lost family members, each of them telling a single tale out of emancipation's collective drama.[3]

Fannie Robinson of Iowa twice ran a plea for news of her husband, "who left Liberty, Clay County, Missouri, about four years ago, to join the Union army at Wyandotte, Kansas; and he has not been heard from since." Fanny Frazer broadcast an appeal "to ascertain the whereabouts of her six children, who were owned by a family of the name of Bailey." To some former slaves, this far-reaching new communications network offered hope that even the slave trade's oldest wounds now might be healed. Thomas Henry tried to locate his son, "who was sold from Hagerstown, Maryland, to Tallahasse, Florida, in 1838," and had last been heard from in 1847, almost two decades earlier. Thomas Allen of Savannah sought information about a wife and sons from whom he had been separated "for some forty years." Like other African American newspapers of the time, the *Christian Recorder* sought to foster racial unity and progress—its editors implored readers "to make political alliances that will most advance our interests educationally, financially, and politically"—but its message-board elements tacitly acknowledged that a national community's political and cultural solidarity would be slow in coming if individual black families remained fragmented.[4]

Garland White's letter, written at the very conclusion of the Civil War, on April 12, presented a consummate narrative of jubilee, of emancipation's most exhilarating effects both communal and personal. It wove together precisely the themes that perspicacious readers of the *Christian Recorder* regularly pondered: black national unity and the restoration of African American families. His fifth letter to be published in the newspaper, it was, in a way, his masterpiece—a captivating, brief narrative that crystallized the meaning for African Americans of the Union's Civil War triumph.

When the Confederate capital of Richmond fell to Union forces on April 4, the Twenty-Eighth U.S. Colored Infantry was among the first regiments to march victorious through the downtown streets. Garland White, the unit's chaplain, walked "at the head of the column" and witnessed one of the most dramatic, exultant scenes in all African American history: "A vast multitude assembled on Broad Street, and I was aroused amid the shouts of ten thousand voices. . . . [A]ll the slave pens were thrown open, and thousands came out shouting and praising God, and Father, or Master Abe, as they termed him. In this mighty consternation I became so overcome with tears that I could not stand up under the pressure of such fullness of joy in my own heart." By the afternoon, Lincoln himself had arrived from Washington, and "it appeared to me that all the colored people in the world had collected," White wrote, to parade through the streets of the city with the "Great Emancipator." "I never saw so many colored people in all my life, women and children of all sizes running after Father, or Master Abraham, as they called him."[5]

In White's narration of this jubilant mass demonstration, his tableau of a rising black citizenry, one small scene forms the centerpiece—a story of a reunited family. Some of White's fellows in the Twenty-Eighth hail him in the crowd and lead him to a "broken-hearted" woman they have met in the streets. The young chaplain and the old woman come face to face, and she begins to question him. White represents their meeting in unadorned dialogue:

"What is your name, sir?"
"My name is Garland H. White."
"What was your mother's name?"
"Nancy."
"Where was you born?"

"In Hanover County, in this State."

"Where was you sold from?"

"From this city."

"What was the name of the man who bought you?"

"Robert Toombs."

"Where did he live?"

"In the State of Georgia."

"Where did you leave him?"

"At Washington."

"Where did you go then?"

"To Canada."

"Were do you live now?"

"In Ohio."

"This is your mother, Garland, whom you are now talking to, who has spent twenty years of grief about her son."[6]

Though just one among countless war dispatches to appear in the papers, White's narrative of jubilee and euphoric serendipity was an august achievement for a man who had been, only a few years earlier, among the legions of marginally literate former slaves sending halting petitions to white authorities. As recently as 1862, White had offered his services to the war effort in a timid, unsolicited missive to the secretary of war: "please excuse my bad writing as I never went to school a day in my left. I learnd what little I know by the hardest. yet I feel that the simplist instrument used in the right direction sometimes accomplishs much good. I pray you in gods name to consider the condition of your humble speaker in the distant." Now, at the war's end, White's literacy had advanced, and the range of his uses for it had expanded. No longer "the simplist instrument," White and his pen could produce a sophisticated narrative of emancipation, tailored for a newspaper's columns. His clipped dialogue depicts Nancy White dispatching a real-time "Information Wanted" notice in Richmond's noisy, elated streets, their bustle and diversity mirroring the pages of the *Christian Recorder*—a place where broken families can reassemble, where a newly free African American community can come into being.[7]

Newspapers were not exactly new to southern African Americans—they were, in fact, precisely what many enslaved people had first learned to read—but prior to emancipation few could expect to see their own writings printed there, or anywhere else.[8] A small number of escaped slaves in the

North, with the aid of white benefactors or a little money of their own, had seen their autobiographies published and sold to an audience of antebellum northerners increasingly interested in slave narratives, and free blacks established multiple newspapers in northern cities. But for ordinary African Americans in the South, especially those still enslaved, written literacy at first meant primarily the ability to send a private letter—to a husband, a wife, a child, or occasionally a white owner—or, as for Dave the Potter and Adam Plummer, to record one's own experience. The progress of emancipation disclosed new uses for literacy, and new audiences. John Washington, avid reader of *Harper's* magazine, could write a story of his life in the style of a popular romance. William Gould, subscriber to the *Weekly Anglo-African* newspaper, could imagine his personal diary as the chronicle of a burgeoning African American community on a national scale. Freed people could address written petitions to public figures, and Martha Glover could imbue a letter with multiple messages for multiple audiences.

For all these writers, literacy entailed more than learning to spell and to make sentences. It involved, as for every neoliterate writer, learning how to translate thoughts into written language. As for every literate member of any culture, it meant learning the ways of writing considered appropriate to different contexts, from letters to diaries to newspaper columns, and different audiences. And for the large community of people coming en masse out of slavery, it encompassed learning how writing might shape their place in a transformed society. While many freed people, bold to petition those in power, used writing to assert their rights and their own vision of post-emancipation America, others found the written word to be a conservative realm, inhospitable to change, where assumptions of racial inequality were preserved in a language that had largely belonged to white people.

Garland H. White learned to write his inspirational story of the Richmond jubilee, and to harmonize with the tone of the newspaper that had become his window on the world, only after years of practice in conforming his acts of writing to the terms of white politics. Every form of education is both technical and ideological. In freedmen's schools, black children not only acquired literacy but also imbibed the Christian messages of missionary teachers. White, who "never went to school a day," got his schooling from the politics of black enlistment and Washington patronage. His textbooks and lessons were polite correspondence with governors and cabinet members. For him, as for A Colored Man, the act of writing was no pure invention of unalloyed thought but rather an accommodation of individual expression to the verbal world as he found it. A Colored Man found in the U.S. Constitution some words he wished to embrace as his own and some he wished to resist and reinterpret. However ambivalent he was about the logic and rhetoric of that document, he could not have written his declaration without it. Likewise for White, the act of writing was a negotiation with the entrenched politics of white America—an act sometimes of strained conformity, sometimes of cooperation, sometimes of shrewd manipulation.

Emancipation helped foster the literate black public sphere epitomized by the *Christian Recorder,* which in turn enabled a literary turn in the writing of an untutored former slave, but neither sprang spontaneously into being with the fall of slavery. The case of Garland White's journey from slavery and marginal literacy to freedom, military service, and publication in a newspaper—accomplished by extensive written interaction with white audiences—displays the complexities of freed people's collective entry into the citizenry of letters. It exposes the fractures in the dream of a unified African American public sphere. And it shows how freed people, in becoming literate, not only acquired a skill but also labored through the central problems of post-slavery race relations. In the realm of the written page they felt the push and pull of imitation and originality—as they did, in social and political life, the tension between accommodation and integration on the one hand, protest and racial solidarity on the other.

After the war, the professional black writers who produced what we now call African American literature regularly contended with difficult, often unfair questions about how they ought to write—in southern black dialect and folksy styles, or in the supposedly more serious manner of the white writers who dominated the pages of books and periodicals? Before such questions emerged in the realm of literary aesthetics and cultural politics, during Reconstruction and the era of Jim Crow, they characterized the emancipation-era experience of ordinary freed people who had to figure out, at the same time they had to figure out how to live free in America, how the written word worked; how, and whether, to assimilate their thoughts to the norms of literate culture; how to make themselves known in writing to a interracial public.

In April of 1865, a freedman's letter shared space with reports of former slaves governing themselves in the South, news of a white electorate's assassinated president, and a free black northerner's novel about an interracial marriage. With the war over and slavery abolished, the constituencies that mingled in that newspaper's pages would begin to interact in new ways off the page. Frederick Douglass famously asked, "If war among the whites brought peace and liberty to blacks, what will peace among the whites bring?" Emancipation brought education and literacy to countless freed people who had gone without, and they used the act of writing to figure out—and try to influence—that uncertain future. The newspaper's printed columns evoked a complex and diverse national community, but it was in pen and ink on the manuscript page that many newly literate black writers shaped that community and sought a place in it for themselves.[9]

Before becoming the author of a small but stirring piece in a national newspaper, Garland White practiced his writing in a series of letters to public officials. In 1862, when he wrote his earliest letter of the more than twenty that survive, he was an escaped slave living in Canada, and he stood somewhat apart from the mass of freed people who petitioned Union officials: he had a name to drop. His letter to Secretary of War Edwin Stanton arrived unsolicited, but it did not come from a complete stranger. When White was sold away from his mother in his youth, he was taken, like many Virginia slaves, deeper south—to Georgia, where he was purchased by Robert Toombs, one of that state's most prominent politicians and, later, fiercest secessionists. Toombs was elected to the U.S. Senate in 1852, and he brought White with him to Washington, D.C. As a household servant in Toombs's pied-à-terre at the capital, White had occasion to meet other statesmen who came to visit—perhaps taking their coats and pouring their tea—and among the acquaintances he made was the senior senator from New York, William Seward, who lived two doors down. In 1859 White escaped north, and by the time the Civil War broke out he had become a minister of the A.M.E. church in London, Ontario. Meanwhile, his old acquaintance Seward had joined Stanton in Abraham Lincoln's cabinet, as secretary of state. White now knew someone in a high place.[10]

White's time in Washington had introduced him not only to individual white politicians but also to the ways of the white political world—to the nature and importance of networks, alliances, influences, and egos. His letter to Stanton suggests that his political acumen and skills of persuasion outpaced his fluency as a writer. Although he faltered at times in producing the letter—his misspellings prompted him to append an apology for his "bad writing," and heavy drops of ink smudged parts of the page—White knew the currency in which politicians traded. He introduced himself by saying, "My name is G. H. White formerly the Servant of Robert Toombs of Georgia." Undoubtedly aware that Toombs was not an ideal character reference—he had become Seward's opposite number in the Confederacy, Jefferson Davis's secretary of state—White quickly shifted his letter's focus toward his prior relationship with Seward. "Mr Wm H Seward knows something about me," White wrote, and a second time insisted, "Mr Seward & many other of both white & colored know me in Washington."

White's particular reason for writing to Stanton was to make a bold proposition. He offered to serve as the head of a black regiment which he would recruit from among the members of his congregation in Ontario and perhaps in nearby states across the border. Publicly, the War Department and the Lincoln administration contemplated no such thing in May of 1862, and White seemed to know his plan faced long odds. Not only was it disallowed as a matter of federal policy; he also worried, apparently, that his residence in Canada might render him ineligible for the mission he envisioned. "It is true I am now stoping in canada for awhile, but," he assured Stanton, "it is not my home." He offered his service, furthermore, not for "self interest" but for "love for the north & the government at large" and in hope that Union victory would lead to "an eternal overthrow of the institution of slavery."[11]

If White began his letter with two objectives—to establish his Washington connections and declare his patriotism—he nevertheless felt it necessary, as his act of writing proceeded, to change his argumentative tactics. Having filled the front side of a sheet of paper with his complete letter—introducing himself, describing his plan, and explaining his motivations—he signed off at the bottom of the page: "please let me hear from your Hon soon your most humble servant, Garland H. White." Then, as if realizing that the verso provided him a new blank page, he began again. Like Abram Mercherson, White turned the paper over and began composing a postscript in which, evidently emboldened by the accomplishment of the finished letter on the front, he ventured into different rhetorical and political territory.

The letter on the front of the page—which White clearly reread after finishing it, making small corrections and squeezing in words and letters he had omitted—is chiefly about himself and his capabilities: whom he knows,

what he intends, why Stanton ought to hear him out. I know William
Seward, I am a minister, "I am certain of raising a good no" of recruits, "I
am aquainted all thro the south for I traveled with Senator Toombs all over
it nearly," and "I am quite willing to spend my life in preaching against sin
& fighting against the same." On the back of the page, evidently writing
more spontaneously, White tries a new way of relating to his audience.
Rather than speaking solely for himself, he now speaks to and about Stanton, even flattering the statesman's ego: "as simple as this request may seeme
to ᵞᵒᵘ yet ⁱᵗ might prove one of the greatest acts of your life. an act which
might redown to your honor to the remotest generation." The postscript
draws a contrast between White's own lowly station and Stanton's power—
quite possibly a posture he had learned to perform when he interacted with
the white men in Robert Toombs's parlor. On the back of the page, White's
only references to himself are his apology ("please excuse my bad writing as
I never went to School a day in my left") and two descriptions of himself
and his plan as "humble." From there, his language rises to the fever pitch
of his appeal to Stanton's pride and historical legacy. This rhetorical ascen-
sion, and his successful application of lofty phrasing gleaned from spoken
language ("an act which might *redown* to your honor"), seems to buoy
White's confidence. He closes the postscript with surprisingly unhumble
firmness: "I shall not be happy till I hear from you on this very important
subject & not then if I am denied. . . . now may the good lord help you to
make a faverorable desition."

The two sides of White's written page reveal two ways of trying to participate in the white political world. On the first page White says, in effect,
I am of your world. We have acquaintances in common, and I share your
commitment to the "triumph of the north." On the second he says, on the
contrary, I am *not* of your world. Born a slave and still beset by slavery's disadvantages, set apart from you by my less advanced literacy, I am no player
in Washington; as a "humble speaker in the distant," I cast into relief your
greater power and can only entreat you to use that power on my behalf.

The tension between White's letter and his postscript defines what would
become—long after the Civil War, during the nadir of the Jim Crow era—
the central argument within the African American political struggle, and
between that struggle's two great icons. W. E. B. Du Bois would call on
blacks to "strive for the rights which the world accords to men," to insist
upon the kind of equal standing with white people that Garland White's

first page tacitly assumed. Meanwhile, Booker T. Washington stood as the icon of the "accommodationist" position—that blacks had to recognize that racial inequality would take many years to overcome; that they ought to behave agreeably, even obsequiously, toward white people, standing by them "in our humble way," as Washington put it in his most famous speech, in 1895; and that they should appeal, like Garland White in his postscript, to whites' benevolence. In 1862, at the very dawn of emancipation, Garland White began exploring the political system that soon would claim to welcome former slaves as citizens. During the remaining three years of the war, and well into the postbellum era, White would continue his efforts to be both a leader among black Americans and a collaborator with powerful white Americans. As his writing practice migrated among different venues and audiences, he would experiment with—and struggle with the tension between—the assertiveness later associated with Du Bois and the deference associated with Washington.[12]

Although black military service was officially precluded when White wrote to Stanton, it would soon begin in earnest. Abram Mercherson already had held a recruitment meeting at Hilton Head. On the very day White wrote his letter, General David Hunter detailed a junior officer to organize a regiment of the former slaves to whom Mercherson appealed. In July, Congress passed the Second Confiscation Act; in August, Stanton authorized General Rufus Saxton "to arm, uniform, equip, and receive into the service of the United States such numbers of volunteers of African descent as you may deem expedient." Stanton furthermore reminded Saxton, "By recent act of Congress all men and boys received into the service of the United States who may have been the slaves of rebel masters are, with their wives, mothers and children, declared to be forever free." In the fall of 1862, Lincoln released the preliminary Emancipation Proclamation, and the enlistment of African American soldiers soon would become a signal feature of the Union military effort—one of the most revolutionary and keenly watched developments of the war.[13]

When Garland White made his proposition in May, he could not have known any of this was about to happen. Perhaps his letter contributed, as one trickle to a rising river, to Stanton's growing conviction that the Union should arm African Americans. In any event, White saw his vision vindicated by the year's events. Although he received no reply from Stanton (he may have from William Seward, to whom he wrote separately), White was determined to play a part in the historic battle to destroy slavery, and by early 1863 he had reentered the United States and undertaken to become a military recruiter. He stopped first in Toledo, Ohio, and then, for reasons unknown, moved west to Indiana. Though Indiana was a free state and had been throughout its history, it was hardly fertile ground on which to organize black warriors for freedom. Most Hoosiers neither approved of the Emancipation Proclamation nor welcomed the idea of African Americans in the army.

The state's Republican governor, Oliver P. Morton, supported the Lincoln administration's move toward black enlistment—and, besides, knew that African American regiments would help him meet Indiana's federally imposed draft quota—but found himself hog-tied by the local politics of his state. As he explained in a letter to Lincoln, his constituents included "a larger proportion of inhabitants of Southern birth or parentage—many of these, of course, with Southern proclivities—than any other free state." Put more bluntly, racism ran deep in Indiana. While broadsides across New England screamed, "Men of Color, to Arms!"; while Frederick Douglass implored his newspaper's readers to seize their "golden opportunity"; while Bostonians of all races cheered the black men of the Fifty-Fourth Massachusetts marching off to war—white residents of Indiana remained overwhelmingly convinced the conflict was "a white man's war." On the Fourth of July, 1863—the Union's most triumphant day, when Robert E. Lee's army slunk from Gettysburg in defeat and Ulysses S. Grant's men seized Vicksburg to take control of the whole Mississippi River—Governor Morton found himself pleading in a speech to the people of Centerville, Indiana, to accept what many northerners had long since embraced: "Suppose one of those who say, fight it out without the negro or not fight at all, were drafted, and the choice given to him to go or send a negro in his place," Morton offered, "I think he would succeed in conquering his prejudices and say, *let the negro go.*" To audiences that never would be swayed by lofty appeals to human equality, Morton spoke with coarse pragmatism: "I am in favor of using anything to put down the rebellion, even dogs and tomcats, if they could be of any use."[14]

Even these appeals to white Hoosiers' self-interest were slow to gain traction. As summer turned to fall, still no black volunteers were being counted toward Indiana's draft quotas. Garland White had been busily recruiting from a base in Terre Haute, Indiana, but all the men he signed up were sent off to join the regiments of northeastern states. By Morton's cold calculus, each black Hoosier who enlisted was sparing a white New Englander from the draft instead of someone from Indiana. White, though still not a fluent writer, could shrewdly read the political scene, and he wrote to Governor Morton in November with his observations and advice:

> To his Excellency the gov of Indiana Sir as a canvasser among my people namely those of the colored I find one grand objection prevelent among the colored inhabit ants of your state. that is they have no objection to inlist to serve their country but it is that other free states can send their blacks from home to represent ^{them} & your state will not allow it. this objection is put to me at almost every meeting. I cant give the proper answer therefore pray you will. I have been doing business of this kind evry since colored inlistments became a matter of popular recognition & I always thought that a man ough to enlist in his own state if at all. tho I have sent as many men from this state to Rhode Island as any one colored man imploy ed in this business yet I must confess that I should much prefer helping to fill a colored regiment for Ind than to send them against their will to other states I mean that by the power of argument upon an unenlight en mind causes it to act without any refference to pre consived opinion—[15]

In this opening portion of his letter, White reinforces Morton's publicly stated view of the matter, but from another angle. The governor's principal aims are to contribute to the war effort and, more immediately, to fill Indiana's recruiting quotas. Predictably, his politicking has addressed prospective white soldiers, asking them: Do you want to go to war, or would you rather a black man go in your place? White explains that prospective black soldiers, though for different reasons, want the same thing the governor wants. If they go to war, they wish to go under the banner of the state they call home—which of course, as White explicitly acknowledges later in the letter, would reduce the number of white Hoosiers to be drafted.

White's letter puts him in a complex, double-edged relationship with Morton. He writes as a spokesman for the African American men of Indiana, presenting their otherwise neglected point of view to the governor. At the same time, White delivers, only in different terms, a message Morton wants to hear. He is a black community leader lodging a protest, as well as an obliging supporter—a "very humble servant," as he signs himself in the conventional but perhaps not disingenuous valedictory.

This subtle tension in White's self-presentation, and in his purported relationship to the governor, becomes clearest in the letter's most unclear sentence—the one that concludes the section above. Trying to say something that may have exceeded the limits of his literacy, or perhaps became garbled in an effort at euphemism or obliquity, White produces the barely intelligible statement, "I mean that by the power of argument upon an unenlight en mind causes it to act without any refference to pre consived opinion." Whose unenlightened minds are in question, which arguments and preconceived opinions, is difficult to say. Following on his remark about the number of men he has enlisted for Rhode Island and his assurance that "I should much prefer helping to fill a colored regiment for Ind than to send them against their will to other states," White may have felt the need to backpedal slightly or clarify. It is not that I have sent any man anywhere *against his will,* he perhaps wishes to make clear to Morton; I simply have used the "power of argument" to overcome black men's preconceived ideas that they should serve for Indiana, and signed them up for Rhode Island.

Alternatively, White's strained sentence may offer a suggestion for Morton's own political use. Thus can you soften the intractably unenlightened minds of your white racist constituents, White intimates: if you tell them Rhode Islanders are getting the benefits that are rightfully theirs—effective reductions in the number of whites to be conscripted—they may abandon their preconceived opinions about blacks in the military. Indeed, it is from this point in the letter that White proceeds to discuss explicitly the potential of black regiments "to help to fill up the quota of Ind under the last call." Both interpretations have unsavory implications. In one, White speaks of his fellow African Americans as "unenlight en" targets for a manipulative recruiting pitch. In the other, White reprises Morton's pandering, racist argument from the Fourth of July: better to let a Negro go into the line of fire than a white man.

If the sentence is plainly about persuading less intelligent people of something, the agents and terms of that persuasion remain ambiguous. That ambiguity yokes White and Morton together: both are engaged in the work of political persuasion. Just as he had addressed Edwin Stanton as from one acquaintance of William Seward to another, White speaks to Morton as an indirect peer, a fellow beleaguered leader trying to accomplish a worthy goal. Throughout its final page and a half, White's letter leaves behind the concerns of black recruits to consider Morton's interests—the draft, the number of Indiana black regiments White thinks he can fill—and concludes with a direct, almost personal pledge to the governor: "rest asure that your humble servant will do you ample service in Lecturing the Colored people of your state. urging them to give you perfect satisfac tion by a speedy enlistment." Rarely did an African American writer ascribe to black military service such an uninspiring goal—not to free the slaves but to give a governor satisfaction. White began the letter as an ambassador for his race, but he ends it as a white politician's collaborator.[16]

His real sympathies and motivations are, of course, impossible to know. His acts of writing to Stanton and Morton may place a mask of black deference over wily efforts to manipulate white audiences. He knew where power lay and, with a pragmatism one can see as craven or ingenious, sought to influence, mobilize, or borrow that power. On the other hand, he may genuinely have desired to build alliances with white leaders. In fact, such may have been the meaning of emancipation to him—the freedom to participate in the kind of work he used to witness in Robert Toombs's house, the opportunity to join and help create interracial coalitions of national leadership in a transformed America.

These possibilities are not mutually exclusive—White might reasonably have seen a little dissembling as a normal part of honorable political business—and they began to converge during wartime emancipation. In the antebellum South, African Americans had been locked in a state of often quiet, occasionally overt warfare with the white people who enslaved them or otherwise sustained the slave-owning regime. Obsequiousness, dissimulation, and cunning were the tools of both survival and resistance. Federal occupation during and after the war brought to the South a new class of white people with whom cooperation might be desirable. Northern whites might in fact be a crucial part of a new phase in the African American struggle: the fight against white supremacist reprisals in the postwar South. A. F. Flood, writing in North Carolina in July of 1865, pleaded with a Freedmen's Bureau official for a greater federal military presence in his town. "I write you secretly in feare of my life," he began, "For in the present condision we can not helpe our Selves. Because this people has every advantage of us. and they are make ing use of it." After detailing incidents of violence and intimidation perpetrated on freed people by southern whites,

Flood praised, by contrast, "the Northren People ł whom I love as my Self. yea I say more then love them Therefore I look to them for protection."[17]

Communities of freed people would develop strategies to resist the burgeoning reign of Jim Crow, independent of white sympathizers. All too often, though, vengeful ex-Confederates had "every advantage," as Flood pointed out, and many African Americans were forced to look to the Yankees for aid. In exploring the possibilities for interracial alliance they explored new ways of writing, and their acts of writing in turn mediated the alliances they forged. If literacy had allowed enslaved people to communicate with each other and to record their private lives; if it gave freed people the means to envision broader communities and to lodge protests and petitions with white authorities; as the Civil War concluded and emancipation was (nominally) accomplished, southern blacks needed the written word to do other kinds of work, too—to negotiate new race relations, to establish trust and forge partnerships, to integrate them into a changed social order. With delicate rhetorical skills that exceeded the basics of literacy, they sometimes had to practice a kind of writing not simply declarative or communicative. They needed to write letters that could shake hands, or nod and wink. Finding ways of doing that could influence the terms of interracial negotiation after slavery.

As the war progressed toward its conclusion Garland H. White continued writing letters to white politicians. He never stopped propounding his connections to powerful individuals, and he proved ever-ready to accommodate their preferences. When he began writing for the African American audience of the *Christian Recorder,* he initially distanced himself from the southern blacks who had been, like him, born into slavery. As he expanded his uses for literacy, though, practicing his repertoire as a writer of letters—some for an audience of white elites, some for the imagined black nation reading the *Recorder*—he also became more deeply enveloped in the political, rhetorical, and intellectual tendencies he learned in those venues. In turn, he confronted the complexities of intra- and interracial politics.

Shortly before White wrote to Oliver Morton, the Indiana governor had at last pushed aside the misgivings of public opinion (perhaps because November elections were over) and asked for federal approval of a black regiment from his state. Two days after White composed his letter urging African American enlistment, Morton received the War Department's authorization to organize what would become the Twenty-Eighth Regiment, U.S. Colored Troops (USCT). As with Stanton the year before, White could not have known that the measures he advocated already were well under way; again, events would seem to vindicate him. White may have begun reading the *Christian Recorder* around this time, for the paper was running occasional dispatches from Indianapolis, and he might have been pleased to see his activities, if not his name, represented in print. "Our city has been favored with several recruiting officers, dressed in full uniform," a correspondent wrote in late 1863, "which was quite a novelty here, to see colored men dressed in such attire." By late March of 1864, when the Twenty-Eighth was filling up and preparing to enter the field, the same correspondent proudly reported, "The Colored Battalion, the 28th U.S. Vols., paraded through the principal parts of our city. . . . Their soldierly deportment while on drill and parade, caused many to inquire if they were not veterans."[18]

White himself enlisted in the new regiment as a private, then began recruiting for it. Given his ministerial credentials, he had hopes, evidently spurred on by Governor Morton, that his efforts would be repaid with an appointment as the Twenty-Eighth's chaplain—the only officer rank open to African Americans. White had tried to become an army chaplain before. When he first returned from Canada, he went to Ohio and began recruiting for the Fifty-Fifth Massachusetts, one of the first black regiments raised in the North. In April 1863 he wrote to his old acquaintance William Seward, seeking "to obtain influence" for an appointment as chaplain of that regiment. Written on one side of a small sheet of lined paper, the letter makes its case clearly and briefly: "I am the ♭ man who wrote you last on this subject from Canada but since then I have moved to Toledo Ohio where I have already inlisted. I am the former servant of Robert Toombs of Georia & am well acquainted pretty much with all the Southern locality & can be of great use to my regement in many respects. I am now busily engaged day & night trying to fill up my regement at an early day & ɫ will if no dificulty arises more than I have had as yet. please present my humble plea to the proper authorities if I my regt come thro Washington I will call & see you." Evidently nothing came of White's petition, nor of his affiliation with the Fifty-Fifth Massachusetts. By the fall, he had decamped for Indiana and started over.[19]

When he saw a second opportunity to become a regimental chaplain, he again sought Seward's influence for the appointment. In the intervening year, White had practiced his literacy and honed his rhetorical tactics for writing such a letter. If he initially thought Seward would remember him well enough that he could presume a measure of familiarity, he would take no chances the second time around. When White wrote to Seward from the Twenty-Eighth USCT's encampment in Washington, D.C., on May 18, 1864, he wrote more thoroughly and formally than before, perhaps with greater determination to accomplish what the previous year's letter did not. Although White now had written to the secretary of state at least twice, he did not take their acquaintance for granted. He addressed Seward as he would a stranger, mustering a more advanced, more polished version of the deference he had always shown in letters to white politicians. "[P]lease parden me for troubling you with business that is not Immediately connected with your office," he begins, "yet it being justice to myself & of interest to my comrads in the military service of the govenment, I hope your honor will at once parden me for the liberty I take in writing you such a letter."[20]

White's first letter, with comparatively blithe directness, had expressed his "hope to obtain your influence" and offered to "call & see you" if his regiment should "come thro Washington." Now, as he writes in a more fluid hand upon a stationer's embossed letter folio, he approaches the matter with delicacy and indirection. He makes no mention of paying a visit, though he has indeed come to Washington; presumably he now understands it to be impolitic or unrealistic for him to call at the secretary of state's office. He exhibits his more refined knowledge of the matters whereof he writes; he knows military appointments are not within the jurisdiction of the State Department. Before expressly asking for Seward's help in obtaining the chaplaincy, White presents what amounts to a résumé, including references: "I have recruited colored men for every colored regiment raised in the north forsaken my church in ohio & canavssed the intire noth & west urging my people to inlist & have succeded in evry instant. . . . I nearly recruited half the men in the 28th U.S. Colored Infrantry Regiment raised in Indiana. . . . I refer you to Gov Andrew of Mass Todd of ohio Morton of Ind Seymore of New York & Spridge of Rhode I———." With a supplicant tone and a touch of flattery, he finally poses his request: "I know you can get me my commission [as chaplain] if any other gentleman in the world can & at the same time feel quite certain that should you vail to give my humble plea due consideration no other will. I pray you will aid me springing from so humble an origin as myself namely that of being the body servant of Robert Toombs."[21]

Garland White had many reasons for going to great lengths in his slightly unctuous petition to Seward. He noted in his letter that Oliver Morton had promised him the chaplaincy of the Twenty-Eighth in return for his recruiting work but, as a governor, was constrained from making an appointment in a federal regiment. White doubtless wished to see this recognition of his efforts consummated. The status and material rewards of the chaplaincy were considerable, too. Fewer than three dozen African Americans were commissioned as officers during the Civil War, fourteen of them as chaplains. (The vast majority of black regiments—more than 130 of them—had white ministers filling that position.) Chaplains were entitled to the same monthly pay as a captain, at a time when black enlisted men's wages were not even equal to those of white privates.[22]

These benefits would have been apparent to Garland White all along, but between the time he first joined the war effort in 1863 and his petition to Seward in mid-1864, something had changed. White had come to see the army and his place in it differently. He explained to Seward that he had "joined the regt as a private to be with my boys & should I fail to get my commission I shall willingly serve my time out." Such protestation notwithstanding, White seemed increasingly loath to be associated with the "boys" (a common term for soldiers, but also a common diminution of black men). His work as a military recruiter, and especially his deployment in the eastern theater of the war, brought White into contact with greater numbers of African Americans, from more diverse backgrounds, than he probably had ever met in his life. From the comparatively sheltered life of a house servant, then a small community of fugitives in Canada, White ventured into a virtual cross section of the national community of African American men—the whole plethora of black soldiers, who included free-born northern blacks, former slaves who (like White) had escaped to the North, and newly emancipated slaves who had gone straight from southern plantations into Union encampments. As a minister, a figure of some authority, and a practiced, if untutored, reader and writer, White stood apart from most of these men—especially the ones most recently enslaved. As his writings during the middle of 1864 reveal, he became increasingly invested in such intraracial distinctions and in his own elevation above the rank and file.[23]

In the summer of 1864, the Twenty-Eighth traveled east, encamped outside Washington, then went into action in northern Virginia. The men, who not long before were standing in the spotlight in Indianapolis, now merged into the brigades, divisions, and corps of the gigantic Army of the Potomac, joining regiments from across the country. The army was segregated even at its highest levels of organization, with African American regiments typically grouped together, but all black regiments were not alike. When White and his comrades were ordered to the outskirts of Petersburg, Virginia, and dug in for one of the most grueling and protracted campaigns of the war, they dwelled among a diverse array of African American men. Other regiments in their brigade included the Thirty-First USCT, which originated in New York and incorporated several companies of volunteers from Connecticut; the Twenty-Ninth, raised on the banks of the upper Mississippi, in Quincy, Illinois; and the Nineteenth, which was organized on the eastern shore of Maryland and included numerous former slaves, many of them fresh from plantations in Talbot County, birthplace of Frederick Douglass. Before the Twenty-Eighth had even left Washington the army had added almost four hundred men to the regiment, which was short of official quotas, and most of them hailed from Maryland.[24]

Though a southerner born, Garland White began to distance himself from the region of his birth, developing a northern bias that he articulated repeatedly as he surveyed the social landscape of black soldiers. Less than two weeks after the Twenty-Eighth decamped from Washington, while waiting at a Union supply base in eastern Virginia, White wrote to both William Seward and Edwin Stanton to report his initial observations from the field. Undoubtedly after rehearsing his missive in rough drafts, White wrote out one of the cleanest manuscripts he had produced to date, neatly fitted to a single sheet of paper, and said:

> I take the liberty to bring before your mind some important facts imbracing the condition of the slaves now falling in our lines. I had hoped that these fugitives when leaving their Rebel masters & coming into our lines were made instrumental in the hands of your honors government to help crush this wicked Rebellion, but to my sad supprise, I am sorry to say that while white & colored men from the north are breathing out their last breath

upon the Battl field in freeing these stupit creatures, they are left Idle to rove over the country like the ox that feed the army. . . . no less than 300 are lying about this place, for you to dispose of in some way they look as tho they would make good soldiers.

Although White never again expressed his opinions in such unsavory terms, he persisted for some time in his bias against newly freed people. If he denigrated the "idle" contrabands he saw in camp, he was kinder to newly freed slaves who had actually enlisted in the army, but even them he was not prepared to account equal to northerners, or to himself.[25]

White's emerging ambivalence about racial solidarity took form amid a great public drama of intraracial division—a contentious debate within the community of black soldiers, conducted in the pages of newspapers and the conversations buzzing through army camps. It was a debate defined by that salient fracture in African American politics, the tension between protesting and accommodating racial inequality. Black enlisted men received lower pay than their white peers—seven dollars per month to a white private's thirteen. Some black soldiers raised vehement outcries, refusing to take any pay unless it be the same as a white man's. In one regiment, soldiers stacked their arms and resigned, and their black sergeant was executed for mutiny. Meanwhile, others counseled patience and acceptance. Most black leaders and soldiers believed African American men's distinguished service in the army would earn them the rights of citizenship after the war. Conciliators feared that loud protests would spoil this chance, alienating the government and distracting the white public from black soldiers' accomplishments. But in the view of the protestors, accepting second-class pay meant accepting second-class citizenship—a deplorable first step into post-emancipation society.[26]

The controversy provoked black soldiers not only to express themselves to white officers and appeal to public opinion, but also to argue with each other about the right way forward for African American politics—about the nature of their relationship with a government that seemed possibly the salvation of their race, possibly also an inscrutable colossus of renewed racial injustice. Much of that argument transpired in the pages of the *Christian Recorder,* and it would lay bare significant fault lines in the national black community—between literacy and illiteracy, between protest and conciliation—as well as those lines' uneven edges. As Garland White took up his pen and ventured into the public sphere of the newspaper, he discovered how difficult it was to define his place in his race, much less in the post-emancipation U.S. more broadly. At the heart of his struggle to shape an identity for himself were his changing ideas about the uses of literacy and about himself as a writer.

White first was moved to write a letter to the editor of the *Christian Recorder* following the Battle of the Crater, a crafty Union maneuver gone horribly awry, in which black regiments suffered the worst casualties. Some northern newspaper reports of the incident blamed the cowardice of African American soldiers, and White took up his pen to contest the "calumny." His long letter (possibly somewhat embellished by the newspaper's editors) is filled with detailed descriptions of the sequence of events, punctuated by grandiloquent tributes to the valor of the men in his brigade, and unremitting in refuting the "slanderous" characterizations in the New York papers—with the exception of a single paragraph's caveat. "I must be plain in my remarks, though it should offend somebody," White writes. "The First Division of Colored Troops, who led the charge, were those who were principally raised in the Slave States. They did not stand up to the work like those from the Free States; for, when the Second Division of Colored Troops went into action, they charged over the First, and carried two lines of rifle-pits."[27]

In discriminating between free-state and slave-state regiments, between free black men from the North and those who enlisted straight out of southern slavery, White draws an overly bright line. Not all regiments were that homogeneous, and the backgrounds of individual soldiers were, of course, diverse and complicated. White himself had escaped from slavery only two years before the first fugitive slaves arrived at Fortress Monroe in Virginia and were termed contrabands. Although he served in a free-state regiment, he had lived all but a few years of his life as a slave in the South. It turns out, though, that White's categorization was based on more than performance in battle. He closes his letter to the *Recorder* with a call to "our young people to come out to teach and write for the troops in the contraband regiments." The contrabands do not just fail to "stand up to the work" of fighting, in White's view; they also are collectively illiterate. (As we have seen, the latter characterization is not entirely true.) What places White in the *us* of "our" young people and the *Recorder*'s readership, and keeps him separate from the contrabands, is not the region of his birth but his literacy. Though formerly a slave, he needs no one to teach him or to write his letters for him.

Even before emancipation, while literacy may have been a nearly universal aspiration in the African American community, its actual achievement could cause divisions. Slaves who became or tried to become literate invariably faced hostility from white people, but occasionally their fellow slaves discouraged them too, if for different reasons. Though most enslaved people considered their literate peers assets to the community—conduits for news, amanuenses for letters, and potential teachers—to some they were lightning rods for danger. George Teamoh, a fourteen-year-old slave in Virginia, was hired out to a brickyard where he labored alongside an elderly slave named Peter. One day while George was hauling bricks, his copy of John Walker's *Critical Pronouncing Dictionary* fell from his pocket, and it was Peter, not a white person, who caught sight of the book and chastised George for it. "He at once inquired of me how came I by it," George recalled, "at the same time ordering me to leave it at home, and under no considerations must I ever be seen with it about my person." Peter may have feared guilt by association if George's literacy were discovered, or he may simply have wanted to protect the boy from punishments Peter thought were inevitable. Either way, George gave up his primer and deferred his studies for three years.[28]

As rapidly as literacy expanded during the era of emancipation, it remained far from universal. As before, illiterate African Americans could benefit from the help of their more educated peers—the literate black soldiers who wrote letters for other men in their squad, the women like Susie King Taylor who taught children in contraband camps—but literacy was also a potent marker of intraracial class divisions. Such divisions already were growing more complicated as free-born, often well-educated northern blacks mingled in army camps and schoolrooms with recently freed southerners.

The controversy over unequal pay inflamed precisely the tensions White's first letter betrayed, between free, mostly northern, blacks and recently freed southerners. When White picked up the August 20 issue of the *Christian Recorder,* eagerly scanning its pages for his letter about the Battle of the Crater, he found it—the handiwork of his pen, for the first time set in type—in the third column of the second page. Directly alongside it, in the second column, was another item of particular interest. There, the *Recorder* reprinted, under the heading "Payment of Colored Troops," a letter that had appeared in the *New York Tribune* a week earlier. Its author, Colonel Thomas Wentworth Higginson, commanded the First South Carolina Volunteers—arguably the first black regiment in the war, composed entirely of newly freed slaves. A former abolitionist and one of the leading white voices in the fight for equal pay, Higginson had written to the *Tribune* regarding a recent War Department order that supposedly resolved the problem of unequal wages. In fact, though, and as Higginson took pains to make clear, the measure fell far short of resolution, much less justice. While it did direct paymasters to give black soldiers "the full pay allowed by law . . . to white soldiers," it first required the commanders of black regiments to undertake an exercise in biographical research: they should "immediately make a thorough investigation and individual examination of the men belonging to their commands . . . with a view to ascertaining who of them were free men on or before April 19, 1861." Only such men would receive equal pay. All other black soldiers—those who remained enslaved at the beginning of the war and, in theory, owed their liberty to the Union army—apparently were to count freedom as part of their compensation. They would continue to receive seven dollars per month.[29]

Higginson had written his letter to the *Tribune* in a spirit of protest. He had campaigned for equal pay for *all* black soldiers, and as the leader of a regiment raised in the Sea Islands, consisting entirely of men just out of slavery, he was particularly galled by the order's discrimination between *free men* and *freedmen*. "In other words," he fulminated, borrowing the reviled phrasing of the *Dred Scott* decision, "a freedman (since April 19, 1861) has no rights which a white man is bound to respect." Despite Higginson's palpable anger, the editors of the *Christian Recorder* remained—or pretended to remain—curiously deaf to his complaint. They reprinted the letter only to convey the happy news that—for some black soldiers, at least—the struggle for equal pay had ended. "To the many soldiers in the field, and to their friends at home, we call attention to the following extract from the Tribune," reads the note prefacing Higginson's letter. "It seems as if it were a voice from one who ought to know, and it will be read with interest by many. Those who complain will do well to note it." At the bottom of the reprinted text, the *Recorder*'s editors offered this further gloss: "Col. Higginson is a model officer; one who is endeavoring to show that if one party fulfils one side of the contract, the other part will endeavor to do its share—that is, when the colored volunteer does what the Government requires of him, the United States, in turn, will satisfy him."[30]

Hardly could there be a more flagrant misreading. As Higginson argued in the reprinted letter (and would continue to argue elsewhere), the War Department had demonstrated precisely the opposite: the government would *not* "do its share" for a great many "colored volunteers," including those in Higginson's own regiment. Rather, it would violate the express contract under which those men enlisted. It was as if the *Recorder*'s editors had read only the first few lines of Higginson's letter—"it is at length ruled that colored soldiers shall be paid the full pay of soldiers from date of enlistment"—and willfully ignored the crucial caveat—"provided they were free on April 19th, 1861"—as well as everything else Higginson wrote. The *Recorder* had spoken out previously for the cause of equal pay; an editorial in the April 16, 1864, issue implored Congress to do what is "right and just" for "our noble and brave colored soldiers" and pay them "the same as all other soldiers are paid." But now, in August, the paper seemed impatient with "those who complain" and entirely indifferent to the enduring injustice afflicting a large portion of black soldiers—the ones who were enslaved at the start of the war.[31]

Garland White may or may not have given much thought to the disjunction between Higginson's letter and the *Recorder*'s spin on it. Given his own bias against contrabands, he may have found the government's discrimination entirely reasonable and considered the newspaper's implicit position neither surprising nor contradictory. But it is hard to imagine that he was not a little struck by a coincidence of the newspaper's layout. Immediately abutting the paragraph of his own letter in which he disparaged slave-state regiments at the Battle of the Crater and lauded free-state ones, White found the paragraph of Higginson's letter that explained that same divide's new meaning: "Under this order, the greater part of the Massachusetts colored regiments will get their pay at last. . . . But toward my regiment, which had been in service and under fire, months before a Northern colored soldier was recruited, the policy of repudiation has at last been officially adopted. . . . If a year's discussion, however, has at length secured the arrears of pay for the Northern colored regiments, possibly two years may secure it for the Southern." Read left to right across the columns, Higginson's line about the government's "policy of repudiation" of freedmen runs directly into Garland White's own repudiation of the same class—his allegation that the soldiers of the slave-state regiments "did not stand up to the

work like those from the Free States." Here were White's words not only
endowed with the gravitas of print but also engaged in a new kind of dialogue with an important white man. For him, it must have been a particularly transfixing first experience of publication.

At the same time, it reveals how restrictive that public realm could be.
From the exhilarating moment of his first publication in the *Recorder,*
White may have begun to sense his own alienation from a version of African American nationhood shaped by a Philadelphia-based newspaper. The
editorial framing of Higginson's letter suggests that the formerly enslaved
counted little in the paper's estimation. Although newly freed soldiers were
literate more often than White or the editors presumed, and although the
paper's content undoubtedly reached even illiterate freedmen's ears from
the mouths of literate friends, black southerners evidently were peripheral
to the *Recorder's* envisioned audience. They had less claim to equal pay, in
the editors' eyes, than the mostly northern, presumably literate soldiers who
had been free in 1861.

But if the paper's editors held the elitist bias of which the black intelli-
gentsia often would be accused in decades to come—a stratified conception of the African American community, in which an embarrassing mass
of rural, uneducated people awaited uplift by a "talented tenth" of race
leaders—then Garland White's evolving beliefs about race relations and the
internal politics of the black community were, however unsavory to begin
with, growing considerably more complicated. Caught astride the crude
division between free northerners and formerly enslaved southerners, White
used his increasingly varied acts of writing—which now included private
correspondence, open letters published in the *Recorder,* and monthly reports to the army—to craft for himself a civic identity not confined to one
side of the fault line between North and South, free and freed, protest and
accommodation. From the springboard of his Petersburg letter's appearance
alongside Higginson's, he began to experiment with his writing as both a
form of participation in national political dialogue and, in turn, a constant
revision of his own potential roles in the rapidly changing nation—race
leader, white ally, military officer.[32]

On September 8, White sat down with at least one recent copy of the *Recorder* and wrote his second letter to the editor. In the August 27 issue

(probably the most recent he had, since the September 3 was unlikely to have reached him yet), the editors had printed several more letters on the equal-pay controversy that had raged all summer. Given the irregularity of the mail's movement to and from disparate parts of a nation at war, letters to the *Recorder* often covered large spans of time, and those printed on August 27 had been written as long before as July 25 (by a soldier in South Carolina) and as recently as August 17 (by another in northern Virginia). Some of the letters had been written before the War Department's August 1 order had been announced, and all were written before news of it appeared in the *Recorder* on August 20. They were, in short, anachronisms, but that did not prevent Garland White from taking up his pen to respond to them.

In his second letter to the *Recorder,* White remains mindful of social groupings based on literacy, touting the ardent newspaper readership among his immediate compatriots ("I sold the papers in half an hour," he told the *Recorder's* editor, "and could have sold as many more") but also betraying his persistent skepticism of the mental abilities of other black soldiers ("I shall try and get a much larger regular subscription for your paper as soon as I can get about from regiment to regiment," White assured the *Recorder,* but "it may take a little time to impress some minds as to its importance"). This letter is not primarily about the supposedly uncouth regiments from the slave states, though. It is a condemnation of the most celebrated black regiment from the North—the Fifty-Fourth Massachusetts. Particularly inflamed, it seems, by a long letter from a writer named J. H. Hall, which appeared on the front page of the August 27 issue under the heading "Letter from the 54th Massachusetts Regiment," White declaimed against the haughtiness of the famed northern soldiers, who "make more fuss, and complain more than all the rest of the colored troops in the nation." He warned: "They are doing themselves and their race a serious injury." Decrying their "spirit of dissatisfaction and insolence," he instead "deem[ed] it the better policy to remain quiet." White asked that the editor "please state, upon my authority, that the treatment of white and colored soldiers is one and the same. . . . The paymaster came here a few days ago, and paid off all the colored troops in this department" at the same rates as white soldiers.[33]

This was a rather cheap rebuke to the complaint from Hall, which had been written before the War Department's order to raise black soldier's pay was implemented. But White seems less concerned with the pay dispute than with the cultural differences between himself and his men, on the one hand, and the Massachusetts men, on the other. "I am glad to say that neither you nor any other man," White writes, "can ever hear of any complaints going up from the colored portion of the army of the Potomac." In a second petty reproof, White suggests that the Massachusetts regiment, then serving in South Carolina, faced fewer hardships than his own regiment and the others of the Army of the Potomac, who were engaged in a brutal campaign through Virginia—unparalleled "in the history of civilized warfare," White writes, and "upon which rests the salvation of the republic." In a chilling bookend to his opening remarks about newspaper readership in the ranks—a celebration of literacy where it prevailed, a tacit lament of it where it did not—White closes his letter by declaring that the Massachusetts men should "cease to write or speak" until they can "behave themselves like men and soldiers." Protest apparently had no place in White's political world.

Though White's admonitions were largely unfair and overwrought, they were not unprovoked. The letter from the Fifty-Fourth, however justified in its (outdated) protests of unequal pay, evinced little solidarity with black soldiers from anywhere besides Massachusetts. "The *educated* negro," Hall wrote in an obvious slight to southern blacks, as well as to the self-taught White, "does not enter into contracts without knowing what recompense he is to receive." And in a stinging aspersion on slaves and former slaves, the northern soldier wrote, "We will not tamely submit to the infliction of wrongs most foul, as did our forefathers, and go back to despondency and submission without even a single struggle." If the appearance of White's earlier letter next to Thomas Higginson's piqued White's interest in the serendipitous and sometimes ironic juxtapositions in newspaper columns, he likely noticed the contrast between Hall's complaint and the letter immediately to its left, from Henry McNeal Turner—one of White's fellow ministers in the AME Church and the chaplain of the First USCT.[34]

Almost exactly the same age as White, Turner became much more widely known. Born free in South Carolina, he learned to read and write as a child, and he became one of the most prolific contributors of war dispatches to the *Christian Recorder*. His politics were similar to White's. An officer himself, Turner counseled obedience to white superiors and, in a letter only a month earlier, had upbraided black soldiers for complaining about racism in the officer corps. In his letter appearing on August 27, Turner reported the carnage following an explosion aboard an ammunition ship docked at a

Union base in northern Virginia. The slightly snobbish tone of J. H. Hall's protest may have struck White as particularly craven when he saw it along-side Turner's description of a "pile of dead men . . . some of whom looked frightfully mangled, while pieces of human bodies lay in terrific profusion in every direction."[35]

As different as Hall's and Turner's pieces were in politics, tone, and pre-occupation, these two writers—sharing the front page of the newspaper White probably had before him on his desk while he wrote his September 8 letter—had something in common that may have seemed noteworthy only to Garland White. He could not, or at least did not, write like them. Turner produced lengthy, acrobatic sentences that reveal a mind plotting out com-plete thoughts faster than a pen can write them, yet confident of corralling them into proper English grammar as they spread across the page. Even Turner's idle comments on the weather show off an elegant style, sophisti-cated diction, and controlled syntax: "The most disagreeable feeling that we now experience is, that which grows out of the protracted dryness of the weather, the intensity of the heat, the clouds of dust, which neither respect eyes nor clothes, and the swarms of flies, some of which, I learn, can draw their ration of vital wine through a fellow's coat, waistcoat and shirt, with-out any apparent encumbrance."

White, at this point in his life, had never written such a sentence. Only sparingly did he use even dependent clauses, and his efforts at unorthodox sentence structure often stumbled in their grammar ("For the flag of our beloved country we are willing to die to defend," he wrote in the September letter). Hall's letter from the Fifty-Fourth Massachusetts, meanwhile, em-ployed florid rhetoric that Garland White no doubt could have imitated had he wished ("Will the vast city of Boston, and the generous and sympa-thizing State of Massachusetts stand by unmoved, and with unpitying eye permit this foul opprobrium and scorn to be cast upon [black soldiers]?"), but he likely viewed such rhetoric as one more sign of the northern man's self-importance.

White found himself betwixt and between, both as an African Ameri-can and a writer. A distinction between "free-state" and "slave-state" regi-ments may initially have made sense to him as a proud member of Indiana's Twenty-Eighth. As he read the news throughout 1864, though, and inter-jected his own acts of writing into it, he discovered that those categories were not synonymous with "northern" and "southern," nor did they reliably predict his affinities with the people whose letters he read in the *Christian Recorder*. The Virginia-born writer from Canada serving among men from the western states, formerly enslaved though free before the start of the war, belonged to no popularly defined subculture of the national black community. White understandably may have felt his status in his race to be—much like his connections to white politicians—at once both distinguished and tenuous.

Throughout the summer of '64, while the pay controversy raged and White tried his hand at newspaper writing, he was waiting for his chaplain's commission to come through. In October, it finally did. Whether owing to White's more sophisticated entreaty or to the altered circumstances of the war, his second letter to William Seward did the trick. Within a day of receiving it, Seward forwarded it with his commendation to Edwin Stanton. "I knew the writer of the within," he wrote on the back of the folded letter, "when he was a slave of Robert Toombs in Washington." Though White never saw the paper trail, he would have learned from his inquiries about the five-month delay that the business of a federal appointment could involve a formidable bureaucratic odyssey.

The processing and transmission of letters received created an accumulating record of clerical notes and official orders, written either on the blank outer face of the folded letter or on a wrapper designed for the purpose. By the time White's petition for the chaplaincy reached Stanton, it bore both Seward's endorsement and a standard annotation by the War Department clerk who opened it ("Hon. Wm. H. Seward refers to War Dept., for favorable consideration, the within letter from Private Garland H. White"). It left the War Department two days later and headed to the Washington headquarters of the Army's Provisional Brigades, for the appointment had hit a snag: "Under existing orders," a military official wrote on the third of the letter's four folds, "Chaplains cannot be appointed until the regiment is full." It was sent down the chain of military command, back to the Twenty-Eighth USCT's encampment, for review by the regiment's commanding officer; then back to Provisional Brigades headquarters with Colonel Charles Russell's certification: "It is the wish of most of the officers that Garland H. White should receive the appointment of Chaplain, he having been very useful as a rectg. officer for the regt."; and finally back to the War Department. Still the appointment was delayed, until the Twenty-Eighth achieved its requisite enlistment totals and a group of soldiers and officers in the regiment circulated a petition expressing their support for White. That petition traveled its own odyssey through military command and the War Department, until finally White was mustered in as chaplain on October 25.[36]

Though a world apart from the *Christian Recorder,* the vertical columns of official epistolary business recorded on White's letter similarly spoke in multiple voices, juxtaposing the powerful and the relatively powerless—in one, a short letter of grievance from an anonymous black soldier is published next to a statement from Henry McNeal Turner or Thomas Wentworth Higginson; in the other, the perfunctory notations of a government clerk are recorded alongside the signed orders of a general or cabinet member. The mingling of disparate voices in a periodical's pages can have equalizing effects—hence the longstanding association of newspapers with democracy—but no public sphere is perfectly egalitarian.[37] Even at an African American newspaper dedicated to providing a venue for those marginalized from the mainstream press, editorial intervention can filter, slant, and exclude certain points of view—quite blatantly in the case of the *Recorder's* treatment of the Higginson letter. The polyphony of bureaucratic writing is not public in the same sense that a newspaper is—widely distributed, visible to all comers—but it is official, the business of the people's government rather than of private individuals. And there the imbalanced scales of interpretive power can be more obvious than in a newspaper's editorial manipulations. A lowly white clerk, deciding that a letter from a black serviceman did not merit the attention of its intended recipient, could consign it to the oblivion of the file.

When Garland White's appointment as chaplain of the Twenty-Eighth USCT was made official, he entered this province of the written realm. As an officer in the U.S. Army, responsible for the spiritual well-being of hundreds of men, he was no longer a petitioner before the government. He had become part of it, a participant in its bureaucratic workings. Among his duties was the filing of monthly reports with the War Department on the activities of his chaplaincy. If White's career as a writer achieved its apex with his published narrative of euphoria in Richmond, its denouement involved the workaday texts of official business.

In their anticlimactic turn, White's writings mirrored his regiment's spirits during 1865. For the men of the Twenty-Eighth USCT, celebrations of victory, freedom, and reunion with lost relatives unfortunately were not the end of the story. White Union soldiers who had volunteered near the beginning of the war—"for three years or the duration"—were discharged shortly after Lee's surrender at Appomattox on April 9, and they headed home. Since black soldiers had not been allowed to enlist until nearly the middle of the war, most of them still had to serve out their three-year terms. It was African American men, therefore, who became the occupying force in still-smoldering areas of the largely extinguished rebellion. The Twenty-Eighth was among several black regiments transferred to Texas. In that staggeringly alien environment, during the sweltering summer months, on what must have struck many as a pointless mission, White and his men had time to contemplate the now-concluded war, the meaning of the peace, and their uncertain future.

Out in Texas after the war's official end, the old categories—northern and southern, free and freed—must have seemed hardly relevant. Facing forward, White and his men were preoccupied with a question sweeping through the postwar nation: Should African American men be allowed to vote? Though scarcely imaginable to most white Americans only a few years before, black suffrage now was under serious consideration, and if it came to pass, it was not likely to be divvied up based on who was free in 1861 and who was not, or who hailed from the slave states and who from the free. In the plan that ultimately became the Fifteenth Amendment, the right to vote would be extended to all black men, of whatever origin, literate or not. (To opponents, such inclusiveness was precisely the problem.) This revolutionary step would not come without considerable agitation, though, and Garland White, though he professed to disdain "complaining," took up his pen to militate for the right to vote. Forming his argument—and, in the process, finding a certain clarity about his identity—involved acts of writing that moved back and forth between two audiences, between the imagined public of the *Christian Recorder* and the public record of White's obligatory bureaucratic reports.

Since 1862, White's writings had ranged from the pleading to the political to the literary. At times they had been in harmony with the course of national events and the concerns of the African American community; at times they set him in a position of discord. Written literacy had proven a hard tool to handle. But from the open vantage of the Gulf Coast landscape, from the harrowed perspective of a devastating war's wake, as White tried mode after mode of written expression, he fashioned a renewed optimism about the African American future that recent travails had almost dashed.

It was the question of black suffrage that prompted White to write to the *Christian Recorder* after a lapse of months since his last dispatch. "I seat myself in a very unpleasant shelter tent," he began, and proceeded to intermingle the leading arguments in support of black suffrage with unsparing accounts of the conditions for black soldiers in Texas. As numerous black leaders had asserted since the advent of black enlistment, military service earned a man the right to a ballot. Moreover, the franchise was the African American community's best protection against repression in the postwar South. "We left our wives and little ones to follow the stars and stripes from the Lakes to the Gulf," White wrote, "with a determination never to turn back until it should be proclaimed from Washington that the flag of the Union waved over a nation of freemen," and they now deserved all the rights of free men. Only the eradication of legal inequities based on race could "wipe from our history this vexed question which has more than once convulsed our land from the Lakes to the Gulf."

In his two uses of that geographical figure, "from the Lakes to the Gulf"— first as the literal itinerary of the Twenty-Eighth from the Great Lakes state of Indiana to the coast of Texas, then as a figure for the expanse and comprehensiveness of the nation-state—White begins to displace regional identities with nationalism. Far from singing notes of patriotism, though, he immediately shifts to stinging indictments of the nation's neglect of black soldiers. In a clear tone of complaint, White writes: "No set of men in any country ever suffered more severely than we in Texas. Death has made fearful gaps in every regiment . . . I have never witnessed such fearful mortality in all my life." Moreover, there were very few other chaplains serving in Texas, and the U.S. Christian Commission, though "a good and glorious institution, gotten up for the express benefit of the soldiers," apparently "like the chaplains . . . , only worked in Virginia." The men lacked food: "I have not seen a lemon, peach, apple or pear, nor corn enough . . . to fatten a six months' pig." And on top of their own miseries, the soldiers were hearing accounts "of the rebels still holding their slaves, and treating them more cruelly than ever." It was a bleak picture of life in the Twenty-Eighth and, coming on the heels of his letter's paragraphs about the vote, more than a little resembled some of the letters about unequal pay written by men of the Massachusetts Fifty-Fourth.

Then, White stopped writing his letter to the *Recorder* and set it aside. He did not complete it until a few weeks later, and by then his outlook evidently had changed. In the final paragraphs of the finished letter as it appeared in the newspaper, immediately following his bitter litany of grievances White writes: "In conclusion, I am pleased to say that the health of the troops is decidedly better, and mortality greatly abating. . . . We send our love to all our friends at home, and beg them to be of good cheer, as the worst is over." Whatever else may have occurred while White waited to finish and send this letter—undoubtedly the health of the troops did improve—one verifiable occurrence that may account for his change of heart was an act of writing.[38]

In the intervening time, White had completed his chaplain's report for the month of August and sent it to the War Department. He must have approached his task with the material in his postponed *Recorder* letter still circulating in his mind, including the many arguments for black suffrage and his obviously strong sense of indignity. It may have been because White did not want to be a complainer in his official capacity, because he felt constrained from writing to unknown white higher-ups at the War Department in the way he wrote to the *Recorder,* that his report paints a decidedly more positive picture than the letter he had just been writing. It may also have been because he understood that black men's right to vote now hung in the balance.

His arguments for the *Recorder's* readers trailed off into complaints about Texas, but in his bureaucratic writing White knew he addressed an official audience, almost the government itself, and he appears to have tried to make the most of the opportunity. While he was required to report only on the "moral and religious condition" of the men in his regiment, he took the initiative to discuss a considerably wider range of topics, painting a comprehensive picture of black soldiers' fitness for citizenship and making an unstated case for black suffrage. As expected, he described the Sunday services and nightly prayer meetings he held in camp, and he also mentioned a "glorious Revival of Religion now going among us" and the number of men he recently had baptized. Beyond reporting the traditional activities of a chaplaincy, though, he reprised the regiment's distinguished service record, including its march into Richmond on April 3; explained that even though "we have never had any facilities for carrying on a School in the Regt . . . yet the men Seem to to Learn very fast"; pointed out that "no one in our Regt has been executed or punished with capital punishment. no mutinous act can be found." He also enumerated the marriages he performed, which certainly are the purview of a chaplain, but whereas he simply tallied up the number of baptisms, here he created a table lining up the names of enlisted men with the names of the women they married— like a household genealogy on a Bible's flyleaf, or a small census roll of nascent black families. By the end of White's report, his remark about the improvements in the men's health—"present indications bids fare for a decided change for the better"—seemed also a fitting prognosis for the larger African American community reflected in his regiment's microcosm. Religiously faithful, law abiding, quickly becoming literate, organized into families: these were men who should qualify to vote.[39]

If White's act of writing about black suffrage for the *Christian Recorder* inspired him to produce a bureaucratic report that implicitly argued for the right to vote, then the composition of the report in turn rekindled his optimism about the future of black Americans. Whether or not his rosy picture began as a feint to please the War Department, the process of writing it evidently led White to embrace that viewpoint in his other writerly voice, for his other audience. With the miserable conditions in Texas now faded from his mind, he could pick up his unfinished letter to the *Recorder* and conclude it by saying, "be of good cheer, as the worst is over." Not literacy alone but his protracted, winding exploration of different kinds of literacy, less of alphabet than of audience, led Garland White to develop a vision of freedom—for him, a vision rooted in faith that white society's government would execute justice; that African Americans, by their demonstrations of virtue and compliance, would earn a place in the political system as it existed.

Of course, the worst was not over. Black men would earn the right to vote, but they would face violent intimidation when they tried to exercise it. Ultimately, the Jim Crow regimes of southern states would strip that right away. The miseries of black soldiers in Texas were as nothing compared with the brutality and oppression many African Americans would face in the postbellum United States. But Garland White's faith in a political system dominated by whites was real. The scant evidence of the later decades of his life suggests that he adhered to it with unfailing vigor—with a stubbornness or blindness, in fact, that could cast Booker T. Washington as a radical by comparison. By the end of Reconstruction, White had committed what many African Americans at the time would consider a betrayal of his race: he had become a Democrat.

In the immediate aftermath of the war White tried to land a civil-service appointment with the Freedman's Bureau, again by appealing to William Seward, but apparently had no success. His old benefactors were passing from the stage. Seward was nearly assassinated by one of John Wilkes Booth's coconspirators. (Sometime after he "first heard of the brutal attempt to murder" Seward, White wrote him a letter wishing for his speedy "restoration to perfect health" and giving thanks that "through your Self & our much Lamented & departed president our country is again Safe from the powers that sought to devide distroy & sink it." White still signed himself "former Servant of Robert Toombs.") Not long after the assassination attempt, Seward suffered a bout of cholera, and he retired from public service in 1869. Governor Morton of Indiana suffered a stroke late in 1865, and his ill health hampered his later political ambitions.[40]

With his connections to powerful white men stretched and severed, White evidently saw the political landscape anew. Perhaps because the old allies were gone, perhaps deciding to embrace his southernness, or perhaps out of sheer opportunism, he forged alliances now not with white men who held power in Washington but with those who held power in the South. In this he exemplified the spirit Booker Washington would advocate a few decades later: "Cast down your bucket where you are." After initially returning to Indiana and Ohio, White went back to the South and took up residence in North Carolina's Second Congressional District. Known as the "Black Second," it was the product of Democratic gerrymandering designed to isolate and minimize the overwhelmingly Republican African American vote. In 1874, Garland White ran for Congress—against a fellow freedman, John Adams Hyman, who was the Republican nominee.[41]

White may have had the encouragement of white Democratic leaders; in any event, they would have been thrilled to see him draw some black voters away from Hyman (who ultimately did win the election). At least one leading Democrat, White believed, might acknowledge a debt of gratitude. Matt W. Ransom, one of North Carolina's two U.S. senators, now filled the role in White's life once occupied by William Seward; it was with him that White now sought to collaborate. In 1875, White wrote to Ransom seeking a "special favor," a patronage appointment for one of his friends—a fellow black Democrat who, just like White, had been the slave of a distinguished secessionist. The friend "rendered me great Service in Stumping a portion of the 2nd district for me against Jon Hyman," White told Ransom; furthermore, "he Was formerly body Servant of A Mr Stephens of Ga"—the former vice president of the Confederate States of America.[42]

Although he lost his bid to go to Washington, White did his adopted political party's bidding: he took to the stump in support of the Democratic presidential nominee, Samuel J. Tilden. Tilden won the popular vote, but the Republican, Rutherford B. Hayes, won the Electoral College through a back-room compromise in which the party of Lincoln abandoned Reconstruction to retain the White House. When federal forces withdrew from the South in 1877, the seeds of white Democrats' recrimination began growing unchecked into the Jim Crow regime. Garland White, not for the first time in his life, had cast his lot with the victors.

Even years later, when southern blacks' rights had been almost entirely smothered by Jim Crow, White held firm to his allegiance with white Democrats. In 1893, he wrote to Matt Ransom proposing a meeting "with you and other gentlemen relative to my organizing Colored Dem associations in our state." It was accommodation to a degree that would have surprised and probably even angered Booker T. Washington. As racial injustice reached its infamous nadir in the 1890s, Washington, though soon to deliver the speech some black leaders would revile as the "Atlanta Compromise," was speaking out about the atrocity of lynching. Henry McNeal Turner, in apparent hopelessness about the prospects for blacks in America, began to support mass emigration to Liberia. Frederick Douglass, nearing the end of his life, reportedly told a young black man who asked how best to spend his life, "Agitate, agitate, agitate!" And Garland White wrote again to Ransom, insisting still, "The best thing for the colored people to do . . . is to unite with the governing class of white people of this section." That such men could diverge so widely over the course of the late nineteenth century shows how little anyone knew, as they celebrated emancipation in 1865, what the future would hold.[43]

That White leagued with a political faction largely bent on reversing emancipation—on consigning black southerners to a status as much akin to slavery as possible—is almost beyond comprehension. There is no moral to his story, no general lesson to be learned from the aspects of White's life and writings that are astonishing anomalies. Precisely because anomalous, though, they remind us that even the truest historical truths are not true in every instance. African Americans in the postbellum South were about as close to unanimity in their political party affiliation as any large group of humans can ever be to unanimity on any matter of consequence, but every community includes outliers, as often deplorable as admirable in their departure from the norm.

They remind us, too, that written literacy can carry human thought in many and unpredictable directions. It was not inevitable that Booker T. Washington, whose first experience with literacy involved the marks on barrels he packed while working in a salt furnace, would later valorize manual labor in his writings; nor that Frederick Douglass's cunning extraction of lessons from white schoolboys was the prelude to a career using his literacy to change white people's minds about slavery and race. If Garland White acquired his modest education in stolen moments within the household of a secessionist slaveholder, it was not for that reason that he later cast his sympathies in similar directions. The same incomparable experience, plumbing one's own brain with pen and paper, that could draw Maria Perkins or Dave the Potter deeper into the interior selfhood that slavery tried to deny; that could inspire John Washington or William Gould to envision new narratives and new communities—that same experience can carry a person away into illusion, and far apart from his fellows, as inexplicable as all the workings of the mind.

Garland White was certainly not the only black writer reckoning with race relations. Countless others—students in freedmen's schools, black teachers (some of them former slaves who were themselves barely educated), migrants from country to city, seekers after jobs and land—likewise used acts of writing to explore the still-uncertain ways they might, or might not, integrate into American society. They would strike many different balances between acquiescence and resistance, develop many different ideas about race relations and black solidarity. None of them held the illusion that whites' political and social dominance would wane anytime soon; all realized they might be forced to conform, at least superficially, to certain systems, institutions, and forms of expression.

In drawing upon the various raw materials at their disposal—letters and words learned in schoolbooks, phrases from newspapers and political speeches, lines of argument practiced in conversation—freed people sometimes bent to white society's constraints, sometimes shrewdly manipulated them. Even within a single letter, a writer could veer between the strident protestations of an activist and the humble pliancy of a political subject: "we ᵂᵃⁿᵗ to know where our wrights is or are ʷᵉ to be Stamp down or troden under feet," Richard Boyle wrote angrily from the freedmen's colony at Roanoke Island, North Carolina, in 1865. Yet he went on to say, "we dont exspect to have the same wrights as white men doe . . . we exspect to obey the rules and orders of our authories and doe as they say."[44] Becoming a citizen, though it promised a new measure of self-determination, also entailed submission to certain "rules and orders." Becoming a citizen, as it were, of the literate community likewise did not always lead to an open field for self-expression. But it certainly did not leave a person unchanged.

Conclusion: Up from the South

AS FREED PEOPLE'S LIVES changed, the culture of American letters was altered, in turn, by the newly literate African Americans who were writing their way into it. For white northerners in the antebellum period, individual slave escapes had been isolated spectacles, and published slave narratives were interesting surprises on the literary scene; their authors, exceptional individuals. Civil War emancipation was a panoramic drama, and the former slaves who were becoming writers, in their countless small ways, were too numerous and too distant for most white northerners to recognize. It was well known in the abstract that thousands of freed people were flocking to schools, reading newspapers, and writing letters. Northerners who had long perceived the slave South as a place of brutality and mental darkness saw this social revolution as an opportunity to export their more civilized ways. Amid their fervor to reform black southerners, they were scarcely disposed to notice the ways their own conceptions of writing and its uses might themselves be transformed by the many African Americans who now shared possession of the written word.

The inaugural issue of the New England Freedmen's Aid Society's monthly publication, *The Freedmen's Journal,* declared that "New England can furnish teachers enough . . . to make another New England of the whole South." To most white teachers of freed people, those words were not hyperbole, and they were no mere figure of speech. When Frances Johnson traveled south in July 1864, she was about to marry into one of New England's most venerable abolitionist families. Her fiancé, Colonel James C. Beecher—Harriet Beecher Stowe's half-brother—commanded the Thirty-Fifth U.S. Colored Troops (originally the First North Carolina Volunteers), one of the first regiments composed of newly freed slaves. Very soon after she disembarked on Hilton Head Island, the couple exchanged wedding vows at army headquarters, amid "tables and desks strewn with despatches and writing materials" and "picturesque groups of colored people looking in from the piazzas at the unusual sight." Frances Beecher accompanied her husband and his regiment for the next two years, and it became her "duty and habit, wherever our moving tents were pitched, there to set up our school." Most of the men in the regiment could not sign their own name when they enlisted, and Beecher initially was none too impressed with the freed people generally. In a letter home to her mother, she declared, "The blacks are more ignorant, and are obstinate and repulsive in appearance,—indeed, they are unable to talk so that we can understand them."[1]

More than three decades later, when Frances Beecher (by then Francis Beecher Perkins) composed a reminiscence of her experiences for the *New England Magazine,* she modestly paid tribute to the progress that her teaching, and northern influence generally, had made possible. As her memory wandered back to Jacksonville, Florida, where the Thirty-Fifth had been stationed for most of its service, she recalled that it had "looked like a New England town, with its white houses and heaven-pointed spires." Of her former students, she reported: "Many a letter have I had since that day from those stalwart colored men, some of them written in a hand laughably like my own, telling me of the education they had gained while in the regiment. . . . Many of them are to-day filling positions of honor and trust, and for my own part I am grateful that I was counted worthy to have a hand in the uplifting of such a race."[2]

She had an interest in seeing these resemblances—of Jacksonville to a New England town, of the black veterans' penmanship to her own—but even if she magnified the similarities, her attention to them reveals the crux of the social project in which she was engaged. Literacy and New England presumably went hand in hand, and it is no coincidence that her "hand" in "uplifting" the race—the part she played in New England's cultural evangelism—mostly involved teaching the men to write in a neat and civilized "hand" based on her own. But the laughter with which she apparently greeted those letters awkwardly covers over—or rather gives away—the fact that her interracial, interregional interactions were not as one-directional as she may have imagined. As a matter of penmanship, the freed people's writing may be very like her own, but its content came from other minds than hers. She saw her own hand's writing come back to her transformed, tracing words not her own—plain evidence that the literate community to which she belonged had many new members, very unlike her and far from New England. Frances Beecher Perkins may have laughed off that realization, but freed people's writing confronted the white public in a variety of ways, and other northern writers would reckon with its implications differently.

Even if many freed people sent letters to their former teachers, relatively few white northerners were receiving such texts in their mail. For most, the phenomenon of freed people's expanding literacy was witnessed second hand—described in the more numerous letters, and especially the published writings, of fellow northerners who had gone south. Just as they had learned about army life and the battle front through letters from their sons and brothers, many people now learned about southern blacks from their sisters and daughters in the growing corps of freedmen's teachers, and nurses in segregated hospitals. Meanwhile, the northern press—eager to satisfy readers' curiosity about the social revolution unfolding in the southern states (not to mention their appetite for exotic descriptions of moss-festooned oaks, stately plantations serving as Union command posts, and the quaint habits of the former slaves)—published numerous articles by teachers, military officers, and government officials.[3]

Dispatches from the Sea Islands of South Carolina fit the bill particularly well. From this frontier of Union occupation and freedmen's education came accounts representing numerous angles of vision. Edward L. Pierce, though retained by the Treasury Department to oversee cotton production on the abandoned plantation lands, was more interested in initiating the first large-scale educational program in the occupied South. As de facto superintendent of more than thirty freedmen's schools, he made the rounds of the islands, visiting classrooms and conversing with students, and he published his observations in the *Atlantic Monthly* in the fall of

1863. The following spring, the same magazine published "Life in the Sea Islands," a two-part series by Charlotte Forten, a black northerner who was among the teachers working in the region. Forten's movements through the islands were more restricted than those of men, but she also was free to spend time apart from official military activities, and her articles offered a kind of amateur ethnography of formerly enslaved men, women, and children. Thomas Wentworth Higginson, the noted abolitionist whose black regiment was raised and encamped near Beaufort, filled a journal with his wide-ranging reflections on the former slaves under his command—their religion, their music, their efforts to acquire literacy, their fitness for military duty—and in the fall of 1864 began publishing essays based on that journal, also in the *Atlantic*. Higginson ultimately wrote nine pieces for the magazine and revised them for publication as a book, *Army Life in a Black Regiment,* in 1870. In 1865, successive issues of the *North American Review* carried long pieces by William Channing Gannett, a freedmen's teacher, and Edward Everett Hale, a writer and education commissioner, titled "The Freedmen at Port Royal" and "Education of the Freedmen." Newspapers ranging from the *New York Times* to the *Christian Recorder* carried wartime dispatches from the Sea Islands. Books and pamphlets began to proliferate: *Slavery in South Carolina and the Ex-Slaves,* in 1862, by Austa Malinda French, the wife of one of Edward Pierce's partners; the journalist Charles Nordhoff's *The Freedmen of South Carolina* in 1863; and, a few years later, Whitelaw Reid's chronicle of an official federal delegation's tour through the conquered South, *After the War: A Tour of the Southern States, 1865–1866.*[4]

Northern witnesses often lamented the freed people's ignorance, but the missionaries almost universally extolled their enthusiasm for literacy and their ability to learn. After all, many philanthropically minded northerners were devoting years of their lives to freed people's education, often under the aegis of organizations that were actively fund-raising back home, and they knew their reports could influence support for the cause. Such writers therefore stressed the necessity for northern aid but also the former slaves' pliability, their receptiveness to New England's educational and cultural intervention, and the consequent likelihood of their mission's ultimate success.

First impressions often were bleak. Like the prim Miss Ophelia of *Uncle Tom's Cabin,* who arrives at her southern cousin's plantation only to bemoan the "shiftlessness" of the slaves and the want of order in Dinah's kitchen,

New England teachers usually considered the freed people ripe for reformation and organization. Elizabeth Hyde Botume, a white teacher from New York, remembered her first glimpse of the Sea Islands freed people this way: "Negroes, negroes, negroes. They hovered around like bees in a swarm. Sitting, standing, or lying at full-length, with their faces turned to the sky. Every doorstep, box, or barrel was covered with them." Laura Towne wrote, "The number of little darkies tumbling about at all hours is marvellous. They swarm on the front porch and in the front hall." Lucy Chase of Worcester, Massachusetts, wrote home to her family that she found the freed people "wholly destitute of clothing, covered with vermin, and extremely ignorant, and incompetent for noble, self-originating action of mind or body."[5]

As in a classic New England jeremiad, though, such condemnatory assessments, implicitly or explicitly racist, usually gave way to hopes of redemption. As dark as the depths were of freed people's ignorance, northern missionaries promised, so quickly would they rise to a state of literacy and civilization—with proper northern guidance. Edward Pierce praised the freed people's "eagerness for knowledge" and "facility of acquisition." Thomas Wentworth Higginson declared that his soldiers' "love of the spelling-book is perfectly inexhaustible," and he expected the men would be easy to teach—both how to read and how to march as an army—because they were "simple, docile, and affectionate almost to the point of absurdity," like "pliant schoolboys." Charlotte Forten wrote, "I never before saw children so eager to learn, although I had several years' experience in New-England schools." Mindful of straining northern readers' credulity, she added: "Of course there are some stupid ones, but these are the minority. The majority learn with wonderful rapidity." Lucy Chase overcame her initial revulsion and began describing her students' "bright faces, bright heads, and bright little ways." She wondered whether "any white child ever leaped into the mastery of the penmanship of his own name with the agility which characterizes my little children." "Books and teachers find the colored man, even if his home is the wilderness," she reflected, and will enlighten them "like blooming flowers in its sandy waste."[6]

The best-publicized aspects of freed people's progress toward literacy, and for a long time the aspects best known to historians, were the North's exports: prim New England "schoolmarms" to head the classrooms, textbooks from northern publishers for the teachers to use, and, accompanying both, a set of cultural values that included order, propriety, and religious virtue, as well as literacy. But despite the ambitions and pretensions of northerners, freedmen's education was largely shaped by indigenous southern enterprise. Northern interventions seldom were as systematic and intense as in the Sea Islands. Elsewhere, southern blacks worked together with northern missionaries and played a large role in determining the dispensation of aid in their local communities. In the many parts of the South where missionary organizations never ventured, freed people created schools of their own and, most remarkably, sustained them in the face of menacing white opposition and frequent violent reprisals. Although the northern missionary teachers dominated public awareness and historical memory because they were so prolific in writing down their experiences, they actually were a small portion of all teachers in freedmen's schools, far outnumbered by their black and white southern counterparts.[7]

In short, the freed people were not passive recipients of northern beneficence. What appeared to many northerners as an opportunity for cultural evangelism, for an infusion of northern progress into a backward South, in fact ran in two directions. In their interactions with teachers, freed people could also shape northerners' understandings of emancipation and the fallen South. In time, their entry into the citizenry of letters would leave its mark on America's northern-dominated literary imagination.

In the case of Elizabeth Harvard James and Peter Johnston, the freedmen's teacher became the freedman's student. Elizabeth traveled from her home in Medford, Massachusetts, to the Roanoke Island Freedmen's Colony, North Carolina, in the fall of 1863, at the special request of her cousin Horace, who was superintendent of the camp. She became the first American Missionary Association teacher stationed on the island. In November 1865 she went ashore to Elizabeth City in search of a site for an orphan asylum, which she hoped would help alleviate overcrowding on Roanoke. There she met Peter, who had been enslaved on the nearby Poplar Plains plantation. Elizabeth never was Peter's classroom teacher; he already was marginally literate when they met, and she was impressed by "his general intelligence, & gentlemanly bearing." "I conversed with him," she recalled, "& found his information quite extensive."[8]

Elizabeth may have thought Peter could help her with what had become her highest priority: improving conditions for the more than three thousand freed people residing in the Roanoke colony. Indeed, Peter had an idea, and either at her urging or on his own initiative, he explained his proposition in a letter to President Andrew Johnson and gave it to Elizabeth to send. Before she did, she recopied it—regularizing his spelling and making a few emendations—and addressed her own letter of petition to the president, endorsing Peter's statement. Peter may or may not have taken seriously the notion that his letter would reach the president's desk. (He was, of course, far from the only freed person ever to direct a petition straight to the top.) He certainly did know that wherever his missive ultimately might go, its immediate audience was Elizabeth James. She made clear in her covering letter, "He conversed with me, then wrote this address and wished me to forward it." In other words, by the time of Peter's act of writing, he knew something about Elizabeth. He had gauged her receptiveness to his proposal and probably understood that, if he persuaded her, she in turn might be able to wield greater influence than he.

Peter's scheme was not original; it was, in fact, the stuff of fervid speculation during the summer and fall of 1865. He proposed that the government distribute five-acre parcels of land to individual freedmen.[9] His particular contribution to the broader idea of land redistribution was to recommend a certain chunk of land—the three thousand-acre plantations of his former owner, James Cathcart Johnston, who had died in May and bequeathed his estate to an already wealthy planter in the same neighborhood, Christopher Wilson Hollowell. In part, Peter made the same arguments about land ownership in a reconstructed South that black leaders and radical Republican politicians had been making all summer. African American slaves had improved this land—had "tilled this soil and raised corn and cotton by the swet of thay brow"—and thereby earned the right to claim it as their own. Their labor was vital to the land's continued productivity, and that productive potential would be squandered if they could not work farms of their own. He also argued that there were good reasons for this land, in particular, to go to former slaves. James Johnston had died unmarried and childless, and "from mere caprice," as Peter put it, he had willed his nearby plantations to Hollowell, "who already had more than he could cultivate." He had also bequeathed plantations in two other North Carolina counties to men "not Relativs," Peter pointed out. In contrast to the dead planter's dearth of kin and the beneficiary's excess of wealth, Peter was, by his own account, "46 years old have a wife and 7 children I am free but without a cent." Many of his fellow freed people were "passed the prime of life" or "infirm unable to support them selves," Peter wrote; "I ask for them,—I ask for myself,—*Jestice.*"

Elizabeth evidently found his case compelling, and having now both listened to Peter make it in conversation and read his written expression of it, she proceeded to write the entire letter over in her own hand. "Allow me to transcribe a few lines for one not accustomed to wield the pen," she begins, though in fact she copies every line of Peter's letter, cutting nothing and preserving a few of his colloquialisms.

Countless other scenes of collaborative writing were playing out across the South, as nurses and freedmen's teachers, as well as literate black soldiers, took dictation from illiterate freed people yearning to send letters to loved ones scattered by the upheavals of the war. The white teacher Elizabeth Hyde Botume recalled writing numerous letters for freed people at Port Royal. She and her fellow teachers "set apart two afternoons in the week for this purpose"—sometimes recopying the faltering efforts of the newly literate, sometimes taking dictation, sometimes ghostwriting—and still could not keep up with demand. One freedwoman sought her help writing a letter to a distant husband. She directed Botume to say that she was well and "mentioned a long list of names" to whom she wished to send greetings. "What else?" Botume asked. "'Why, you know, ma'am,' she said. Evidently to her mind," the teacher reported, "there was but one outline for letters, which I was expected to fill up." "Writing these letters for the freed people was our best means of becoming acquainted with their characters and needs," Botume found. What she learned from the letters that passed, through her, between loved ones was that freed people were capable of "touching . . . exhortations to constancy, and protestations of eternal devotion," and—somewhat less often, she said—of "comprehend[ing] that they had rights."[10]

Elizabeth James was not merely Peter Johnston's secretary, nor did she play the ethnographer. Presumably alone at her desk, under no obligation to return Peter's letter to him, show him what she wrote, or forward it to the president, she could reflect on their conversation and reject or embrace what he had written. And she embraced it. "Her" letter, on the verso of her transcription of "his," does not merely express support for the petition she has just recopied. It includes sentences that almost perfectly echo Peter's. A few minutes after writing out Peter's contention that "had each man 5 acres of land in ten years the cuntry would be vastly richer in agriculture produce then it now is," Elizabeth reaches the impassioned conclusion of her separate plea and insists, "if each invalid could have five acres of land given them, from being paupers they would soon add greatly to the wealth of the country." She voices the same indignation at James Johnston's bequests "to those not relatives." She takes up Peter's particular concern for the "infirm" and those "past the prime of life" and applies his terms to the community in which she is "especially interested"—the Roanoke Freedmen's Colony, where "the aged & infirm" had taken asylum.

As Peter's words flowed from Elizabeth's pen, they became partly her own, and his language infiltrated her act of writing. That small drama of composition reveals a different kind of intellectual movement from the one most northerners presumed was taking place. General William Tecumseh Sherman's Special Field Orders, No. 15, which declared that seized plantations would be divided into forty-acre parcels and given to "respectable negroes," incited rumors among freed people that they would receive "forty acres and a mule." But even as news of Sherman's order trickled down and circulated, an individual freed person like Peter Johnston could instill a political vision of post-war America in a white reader's mind and urge that vision back up the chain of influence—from the northern teacher, who perhaps also would tell her influential brother, up to the president of the United States. Through her interaction with Peter's poorly spelled yet convincing and infectious words, Elizabeth became an emissary less of New England's cultural values to the South than of incipient southern black politics to the North. The White House did not grant Peter and Elizabeth's request, of course, but Elizabeth remained affected by the experience. She headed back north in 1870, taught for years in greater Boston schools, and lived to be eighty years old. She carried with her, to what precise effect it is impossible to say, the influence of Peter Johnston as well as countless other freed people she met and taught.[11]

Elizabeth James may have been quite taken with Peter Johnston's thoughts, but she still held his writing at arm's length. He was "not accustomed," in her view, to wielding a pen, and she considered it necessary to rewrite his letter for the eyes of a president who was himself unaccustomed to reading such texts. Other northern missionaries and observers likewise persisted in seeing black literacy as incomplete, flawed, even comical, at the same time that they trumpeted freed people's educational progress and increasingly came face to face with the work of their pens. The white northern public therefore received conflicting messages about the intellectual lives of former slaves—or, rather, messages that would have seemed conflicting had not most white northerners been predisposed to imagine African Americans as essentially inferior. On the one hand, northerners heard reports of freed people's irrepressible eagerness to learn, their great receptiveness to New Englanders' pedagogical efforts, and their rapid progress from the depths of ignorance toward fitness for citizenship. On the other, they heard quaint and amusing tales that attested to the fundamentally alien nature of southern blacks' relationship to the written word.

Northern whites who declared the freed people quick to learn usually qualified that assessment by pointing out that black students learned by imitation and memorization—faculties of a lower order, presumably, than those of white students. Thomas Wentworth Higginson was filled with adulation for his soldiers' "imitativeness and docility," and William Channing Gannett and Edward Everett Hale reported that former slaves' knack for "memory often surprises persons used to note-books and memoranda. But while they apprehend and hold detached facts easily, they are slow to comprehend them in connection,—are deficient in the more ideal operations, which require reflection and reasoning." Edward Pierce likewise concluded, "The memory is very susceptible in them—too much so, perhaps, as it is ahead of the reasoning faculty." Black students' aptitude for memorization—including, supposedly, their tendency to memorize words without understanding them—often formed the subject of humorous anecdotes in which freed people of all ages were cast as the archetypal child who appears able to read but in fact has only memorized a favorite storybook. Harriet Ware remarked on students who displayed their reading abilities with their primers held upside down. Lucy Chase entertained her family members back home with a sample spelling lesson in her classroom: "What does D i n n e r spell?" Chase asked "my scholars," and the response came back, " 'Dinner.' What does s-u-p-p-e-r spell? 'Supper.' What does H o o d spell? 'Breffust,' screams a little boy."[12]

White observers' preoccupation with racial differences often threatened to undermine their abiding optimism that freed people would learn readily under a New England–style educational regimen. Northern teachers accustomed to staid classrooms expressed vexation not only with the crowded conditions of freedmen's schools but also with the decibel level of their students' voices. The students' enthusiasm for learning understandably manifested itself in a certain boisterousness, and Charlotte Forten remarked politely in the pages of the *Atlantic Monthly* that she found "it was necessary to tax the lungs very severely." In the more confidential venue of a letter to her family, Lucy Chase declared, "All my children scream, and I am forced, as [my sister] Sarah says, 'to outscream the screamiest.'" Besides differences of temperament, Gannett and Hale identified a mismatch between New England educational materials and southern black students' cultural knowledge: "The primers, for instance, contain few words with which a white child is not already more or less familiar; but to the learner here they introduce very many of whose sound and meaning he knows nothing."[13]

Differences of vocabulary were a frequent source of amusement in northern accounts. Teachers frequently mocked the black speech patterns they struggled to understand (especially the Gullah dialect spoken by some in the Sea Islands), and Colonel Higginson told of his soldiers' taking the passwords he issued for guard duty and translating them into words from their own lexicon—"'Carthage' being familiarized into Cartridge, and 'Concord' into Corn-cob." On one occasion that Higginson recalled with particular bemusement, he determined that the password for the night would be "Fredericksburg" but later found that a black sergeant, "being weak in geography, thought best to substitute the more familiar word, 'Crockery-ware.'"[14]

The representations of freed people appearing before northern readers, then, depicted an aptitude for learning but also made that aptitude appear strange and sharply limited. No matter how fervent many white northerners were about "civilizing" former slaves through education, very few actually believed, or suggested in their writings, that southern blacks could or should become whites' intellectual equals. Edward Pierce, after offering enthusiastic accounts of freed people's progress in learning to read, came to the tepid conclusion that "they could read with much profit a newspaper specially prepared for them and adapted to their condition." He followed three pages of meticulously detailed descriptions of reading lessons, in ten different freedmen's schools, with the terse report, "In some of them writing was taught." To him and to many northerners, literacy for former slaves (as for women, too, in early America) really only needed to include reading—the component of literacy that provided access to the Bible and the civic life embodied in newspapers; that was amenable to "imitative" but "unreasoning" intellects; and that enabled no original, potentially dissident forms of expression.[15]

Perhaps because they themselves had been discouraged from writing, particularly for publication, northern women showed more enthusiasm than men for teaching freed people to write. But even they had modest expectations of their students—Lucy Chase hoped that she could "fix their ambition to write by letting them see that they really can write their own names"—and still characterized black writers' manuscripts as queer and difficult to read. Harriet Ware observed an unseemly physicality in her students' use of writing tools—a sign, her choice of metaphor seems to suggest, that African Americans are better suited to agricultural labor than to the pursuits of the mind. "They must learn, by gradually growing familiar with the use of a pencil, not to use it like a hoe," Ware wrote. "There are furrows in the slates made by their digging in which you might plant benny-seed, if not cotton!" Lucy Chase, ardently as she tried, struggled to decipher the letters she received from marginally literate freed people seeking assistance: "A letter from a woman to her 'Dear husband' (who is not here) has been opened, and the woman is discovered to have told her husband that if he does not come to join her, she shall be obliged to get another 'Bough'—Boy, I supposed she meant, but the Dr [Orlando Brown] says 'No, Beau.'"[16]

It was neither a secret nor a surprise that white society would judge African Americans in the post-slavery era by their ability to assimilate into literate culture. As emancipation gathered steam, the African American newspaper *The Christian Recorder* began publishing its own version of a longstanding genre of white society's didactic literature—advice on writing. Frequent editorials propounded the importance of good English composition and offered recommendations for how the paper's readers ought to write. "Short sentences and short words are generally best," the editors wrote, "inasmuch as they are less likely to be misunderstood, and do not require to be read twice." The paper declaimed on the virtues of correct punctuation; reprinted a column from the *Atlantic Monthly* titled "Good Advice to Young Writers"; published a black Indiana teacher's description of his methods for teaching writing; and provided instructions on letter writing ("The commendatory features in writings of a business character, are clearness and conciseness. Items foreign to the subject are not allowable here, and could

be productive of but little good"). A sternly worded "Hints to Contributors" column instructed readers to "send your composition in such a shape
that it shall not need the slightest literary revision before printing" (a standard to which the paper clearly did not adhere, since Garland H. White's
letters to the *Recorder* always were published in a state of orthographic per-
fection that his surviving manuscripts from the same period never exhibited). The newspaper's editors plainly wanted African Americans' public
writing to appear in the best light possible.[17]

In reality, only some readers of the *Christian Recorder* were properly
equipped to heed detailed advice on the proper use of punctuation. For
most southern blacks the ability to write was coming within reach, but full
literacy, by educated whites' standards, was not. The manuscript culture of
freed people, halting and irregular, therefore registered in whites' consciousness slowly and unevenly. Edward Pierce saw it, yet at the same time
failed to see it. He paid almost no heed to writing instruction in the schools
he supervised, even though he had seen evidence that written literacy preceded his and his teachers' arrival in coastal South Carolina. Exploring one
of the islands, Pierce wandered into a slave cemetery, where he found—and
transcribed—the following inscription on a wooden grave marker:

OLd Jiw
de Part his
Life on the
2 of way
Re st frow
Lauer[18]

Like the poems on Dave the Potter's clay jars, this text enjoys a readership
only because it was written on material more durable than paper. Having
survived long enough for Edward Pierce to see it and copy it down, it shows
a glimmer of a larger corpus of writing that has since disappeared. Though
the abolitionist Pierce saw fit to preserve this brief text, he judged such inscriptions "rather illiterate," and he seems to have been a somewhat obtuse
reader of them: although the writer's confusion of *m*'s and *w*'s is entirely
plausible, it strains credulity to think the letter *u* in "Lauer" was not in fact
a *b* on which the writer simply had not fully closed the loop. The Christian

philanthropist may have been less unable than unwilling to recognize the letter that spelled a dismal reality: a slave well might imagine death not as heavenly salvation but simply as rest from labor.

Pierce likewise failed to grasp the ways freed people's conceptions of the act of writing differed from his own. During one of his classroom visits, he encountered a student who had learned quickly enough to become her teacher's unofficial assistant. Elsie, "a full black, and rather ungainly" girl, could read so rapidly that her teacher had to slow her down. When she saw Pierce taking notes as she read from the Bible, "she looked archly at the teacher, and whispered,—'He's putting me in the book.'" Relating this anecdote in the pages of the *Atlantic,* Pierce writes, "as Elsie guessed, so I do." Elsie plainly meant that Pierce had put her in the book—written down something about her in his notebook—at that moment. But Pierce, writing "so I do" in the present tense of his magazine article, betrays a certain bias about the definition of writing. He thinks Elsie has arrived "in the book" only once his notes about her appear in a published work. In the eyes of a well-educated white man, from a highly literate community noted for its rich print culture, newly emancipated African Americans might become literate, but they could enter the domain of *real* writing—published authorship— only when people such as he put them there.[19]

Along with nearly everything white northerners heard about freedmen's education, then, came reminders that black literacy remained far from universal; that the community of writers, as it grew, began to encompass people who struggled with the fundamentals of the craft, whose ideas about the act of writing did not conform to northern expectations, and who produced strange and surprising texts. For white northern writers who reflected on such developments, and especially for actual readers of such texts, African American writing could prove disarming and intellectually transformative.

The Civil War era in general witnessed an array of changes in the ways writing was understood and practiced in the United States. The conflict transfixed the imaginations of literary artists—it became the principal subject of Walt Whitman's poetry, led the novelist Herman Melville to start writing poetry himself—and the exigencies of war and contemporary technological advances radically altered Americans' daily interactions with the written word. Military commanders, government officials, and journalists increasingly enjoyed the convenience, and the pitfalls, of telegraphic communication. Under pressure to issue orders when life and death hung in the balance, plagued by interruptions and truncated transmissions, they chose words carefully and wrote with a conciseness very unlike the elaborate prose style of well-educated Americans. The widely read postwar memoirs of Ulysses S. Grant owed their popularity in part to a lucidity of expression the general had honed in battle, dispatching crystal-clear orders "no matter how hurriedly he may write them on the field," as one military officer recalled. Secretary of War Edwin Stanton's dispatches to the press modeled a terse, direct form of presentation that journalists soon would embrace as their new industry standard—the "inverted pyramid."[20]

Meanwhile, the periodical press responded energetically to the public's insatiable appetite for war news, publishing voluminous and variegated written dispatches—and, thanks to advances in printing, images of the war, too. The rise of photography and the proliferation of battlefield photographs may have appeared liable to obviate the written word (even though their verisimilitude was less than what many supposed), but publishers cannily integrated word and image. *Frank Leslie's Illustrated Newspaper* and *Harper's Weekly* printed artists' illustrations as well as engravings of photographs, pioneering a format that brought events of the Civil War and emancipation before the eyes of countless Americans.[21]

The modern landscape of industrialized print that literate northerners inhabited threw into relief the proliferating descriptions of freed people who could barely write rudimentary texts. Even though pen and ink remained the tools of writing for all Americans, from farmers sending letters to professional authors composing books, manuscript culture increasingly lay outside the cultural spotlight. It could seem downright peripheral, as Edward Pierce intimated—a form of pseudo-writing, preliminary to fruition in print publication—or hopelessly old-fashioned. An aging and ailing Nathaniel Hawthorne complained to his editor, James T. Fields, in 1863, "I have bought what purported to be a first-rate gold pen, but it has a trick of writing as if the paper were greasy." Deeply ambivalent about the Civil War, struggling to make progress on his last, never-finished book—a novel whose plot revolves around a "weary, ugly, yellow, blurred, unintelligible, bewitched, mysterious, bullet-penetrated, blood-stained manuscript" that the protagonist is unable to read—Hawthorne seemed to think his troubles stemmed from the process of handwriting itself. "Do you think it possible that I might write better on some other kind of paper," he asked Fields, "—or with different ink? I wish, if you answer this note, you would do it on a specimen of paper that you think might suit me, and I will make trial of my pen on it. If possible, let the sheet be of the same size as that on which I have written the first chapter. The surface of that seems too much polished."[22]

Most of the time so ubiquitous as to become invisible, manuscript writing mainly attracted attention when it departed from the norm—as in the grave-marker inscription Pierce copied down, or the penmanship of the scores of Union soldiers who suffered the amputation of their dominant arm. In the fall of 1865, a magazine for veterans called *The Soldier's Friend* sponsored a left-handed writing contest that drew hundreds of entries, and a distinguished panel of judges scrutinized the "slope" and "firm[ness]" of these mens' handwriting, searching for "fine specimens of chirographic excellence." At the beginning of his famous correspondence with Emily Dickinson, Thomas Wentworth Higginson formed his impressions of the reclusive Amherst poet chiefly upon the physical appearance of her initial letter: "It was in a handwriting so peculiar that it seemed as if the writer might have taken her first lessons by studying the famous fossil bird-tracks in the museum of that college town. Yet it was not in the slightest degree illiterate, but cultivated, quaint, and wholly unique. Of punctuation there was little."[23]

The kind of writing being done by newly emancipated southern blacks, then, resembled little in the public imagination besides the writing of eccentrics, the disabled, and, most of all, children. Most of the errors and difficulties freedmen's teachers described would have been familiar to any middle-class northerner who had experience teaching a child to read and write, as most mothers did. The trials of mothers who doubled as their children's writing teachers likely animated their laughter at a little joke published in *Godey's Lady's Book,* one of the most widely read women's periodicals, in 1869: "You really ought to learn to write better," an adult tells a young man with bad penmanship; "But if I were to write better," the youth replies, "people would be finding out how I spell." Elizabeth Keckley, a former slave who became the White House dressmaker, recalled teaching young Tad Lincoln how to read: holding open a primer in which "a small wood-cut of an ape" illustrated the word, Keckley asked Tad, " 'What does A-p-e spell?' 'Monkey,' was the instant rejoinder." In a reversal of condescending comic interludes in freedmen's teachers' writings, an African American woman could laugh at the solecisms of a coddled white child, as many black house servants surely did.[24]

In the decade's most famous representation of childhood, Louisa May Alcott depicted an autobiographical heroine's tenacious effort to become a successful author, but filled her novel with reminders of the difficulties of writing. The youngest of the sisters in *Little Women,* Amy March, amuses the others with her overzealous efforts to improve her *"vocabilary"* and with the poor punctuation in her contributions to their homemade newspaper. When the March household gets out of joint, it is the work of manuscript that first shows the strains: Jo "upset an inkstand," Amy's chalk markings are washed out by "the tears that had fallen on her slate," and Mrs. March barks reprimands at the girls while distractedly "crossing out the third spoilt sentence in her letter." When Amy lashes out in anger and retribution at the older sister who occasionally mocks her strained literacy, it is by burning Jo's manuscript of fairy tales, which she had hoped would be "good enough to print."[25]

The one major literary representation of emancipation written by a white American during the 1860s, Rebecca Harding Davis's *Waiting for the Verdict,* is largely preoccupied with fragile scraps of paper, strained acts of writing, and the prospects for black literacy. Though tinged with racism, it is a novel about the plight of African Americans after emancipation—a community "waiting for the verdict" on its status in the postwar nation. The written word at first appears to be a source of black freedom, but its potential slowly fades. A slave named Nathan makes his way behind Union lines as the courier of "a yellow scrap; the back of an old letter, on which were scrawled some numbers." Nathan's father, Hugh, is also enslaved but acquires a measure of power by secreting a "slip of yellow parchment"—a controversial will written by Hugh's owner. Both men, though, are illiterate. Nathan explains: "If you wrote 'Nathan' dar on de wall, I wouldn't know it." Enslaved characters accomplish only the most primitive acts of writing, as when Nathan's son Tom "blotted [a handkerchief] wid pokeberry juice" and said of it, "Dat's my name." Nathan's wife, Anny, initially imagines a bright future for her family after emancipation: "She had planned the pattern of the rag-carpet she would make, and the shelves which Nathan would put up for Tom's books. For Tom would go to school, and at night he could teach her and his father to read." But by the time the whole family, finally free, has reunited in the North, Anny's hopes for literacy have dimmed: "Dar's few schools in de country besides dem kept by de Quakers dat will admit a cullored boy or girl." Of Tom she wonders: "What perfession is free to him? His hands is tied."[26]

Rebecca Harding Davis likely never had seen a piece of writing by a former slave, but she plainly understood that literacy would neither follow automatically from emancipation nor alone secure African American liberty and prosperity. For other white women who had actually read the strained sentences of newly literate freed people, the texts could, with stunning directness, transform their readers' way of seeing the world. We do not know what Frances Beecher Perkins's former students wrote in the handwriting she found uncannily like her own, but another white New England teacher preserved some of the letters she received from former students. Lucy Chase grew up in a Quaker family in Worcester, Massachusetts, and she traveled south in 1863, along with her sister Sarah, to teach in contraband camps and freedmen's schools in Virginia, Georgia, and Florida. Among the numerous letters she wrote and received during the six years she spent teaching freed people is a small trove of letters from her students, written either while she sojourned back in Massachusetts during the hot summers or after she had moved on to schools in other parts of the South. Among them are a pair of letters from Jordan Johnson. His writings may have affected Lucy Chase as much as any other aspect of her remarkable experience as a witness to emancipation.

As in many classrooms then and now, literacy instruction in freedmen's schools sometimes included, among other kinds of writing exercises, the composition of a personal letter. Jordan Johnson's first letter to Lucy Chase was written on June 29, 1868—a day on which his current teacher, Miss Gayle, evidently had coached both him and at least one other student in crafting letters to their former teacher. The letters from Johnson and David Barr—residents of Columbus, Georgia, where Chase had taught for five months in early 1866—follow the standard form of a schoolroom letter. They begin with conventional greetings: "I will now take this pleasure to write you a few lines," writes Johnson; "I take the present opportunity to write to you," writes Barr. Each writer describes what he is studying in school: "third reader seond Geog raphy second a rithmetic webters Dictionary and elementry ˢ pelling Book I have been though four copy Books I have been though 3 No 3 copy Book 1 No 2 copy and I a am also in No 5ᵗʰ copy Book" (Johnson); "I study 3d Geography 3d Reader 2 Arith metic Webseters Dictionary Elementary spelling Book" (Barr). And they both round out their letters with assorted particular observations. Johnson reports that Miss Gayle's class has received singing lessons and plans "to have a consirt the 6 of July." Barr, clearly the better speller and perhaps a more confident writer, ventures a few comments on Reconstruction's conflicts. Evidently worried about racial violence, Barr expresses support for federal occupation: "Suppose you heard of the Death of Mr ~~Asburen~~ Ashburn there is one good thing the Millitary has taken that Case in hand another good thing our City is now under Millitary law."[27]

Miss Gayle may have given Johnson and Barr an assignment, or they may have solicited her help with their own epistolary initiative. Either way, the letters make clear that she looked over their shoulders or sat nearby. Johnson writes, "Miss Gayle says that she Will Write to you soon her ł self," and Barr likewise concludes his letter by conveying a message from the teacher: "Miss G received A letter forom you and was very glad ~~of hearing f~~ you to hear from you nor have I forgot that pretty little speller that you gave me before you went Away Miss Gayle say that she will write to you soon miss Gayle say she would like to see you so would I yours truly David Barr." Although Chase surely was touched to receive these thoughtful missives from her former students, they likely did little to disturb her conceptions of freed people's literacy and their intellectual lives. Johnson's and Barr's faltering letters probably could not have been written without their teacher's help. In their adherence to convention they may have reinforced her presumption that African Americans could learn by imitation but lacked the capacity for original reasoning.

Such were the impressions Chase continued to convey to acquaintances in the North. One of the principal audiences for her own letters during this period was Anna Lowell, a member of the New England Freedmen's Aid Society's Committee on Teachers. Though Chase's correspondence with Lowell had begun as a teacher's businesslike reporting to her supervising organization, it evolved into a friendly and affectionate exchange. By the time she received Johnson's and Barr's letters, Chase was sending Lowell lengthy, almost diaristic reflections on her experience. The one she wrote in June 1868—the same month her former students in Georgia wrote to her—sought to entertain Lowell with comic anecdotes of freed people's verbal imperfections. "I wonder if I ever told you," Chase wrote from her current station in Virginia, "a Norfolk child's definition of irrational—'It's rational when you have rations, and irrational when you do not.'" She described a "very black, thick-lipped, broad-nosed savage looking boy of mine" who was delighted by an illustration in the *Lincoln Primer* and declared, "'*So* glad they're free, dun gone and put it in a book!'" Her recollection of the child's declaration inspired Chase to "decline for you the verb 'Dun' as I hear it daily used," and she wrote out, at full length, the word's conjugation in six tenses, including the second future:

I dun gwine dun it
You dun gwine dun it
He dun gwine dun it
We uns dun gwine dun it
You uns dun gwine dun it
They uns dun gwine dun it[28]

For Chase, casting primitive language in a sophisticated form produced a joke that might amuse her friend in much the same way that Frances Beecher Perkins was amused by the sight of her former students' words in handwriting like her own. Johnson's and Barr's letters, with their adherence to a familiar template for a student's letter to an elder, may have struck Chase similarly.

Freed people's struggles with written English could remain a source of amusement, though, only so long as white readers neglected to look past the words' strangeness to sympathize with their meaning. Lucy Chase's later letters to Anna Lowell contain no jokes at freed people's expense. On the contrary, Chase copies into one of her dispatches two poignant letters from a freedman to the wife from whom he had long before been separated. She even confesses to Lowell that the verb she once found so quaint now has become a part of her own lexicon: "Just now, I find myself singing, 'Ole sheep dun know the road: Young lambs gwine to learn the way.'" Though many things might have occurred between June 1868 and March 1870 to temper Chase's perceptions of freed people, one thing assuredly did: she received a second letter from Jordan Johnson in May 1869.[29]

This time, Johnson wrote on his own. Miss Gayle had gone away to Mobile, Alabama, and Johnson "would have Retten to you before now," but he "did not ~~noo k~~ know how to direct my letter to you." Though lacking a teacher's help, Johnson was determined to send Lucy Chase a letter, and that determination shows through in his struggles both to write the letter and to get it mailed. He frequently crossed out words and wrote in a hand much more erratic than in his 1868 letter. Without an immediate source for answers to his questions, he had to seek help further afield: Johnson reports that he "went to the teachers ~~Rezident~~ sdrelling house ~~afew~~ a few day sense" in the hope of finding Lucy Chase's address.[30]

Having gone to such effort, Johnson remained unsure that Chase even would remember him, and he reintroduced himself via anecdote: "Remember me the one who went to school at the Baptist Church to chool and kept door there the one you call red neck tier and there was one morning I came with out a neck tier and you ask me whare it was I told [you] it was at home and [you] ask me what was the reason I [did not] wareitt I told you the sreasion [it] I didin wareit becaue you call me red neck tier you told [me] to I put it on the nex day and you would [not] call me red neck tier anymore." With that, Johnson reached the bottom of the first page of his letter, having not only refreshed Chase's memory but also rehearsed, in writing, a scene of political action. Angered, or at least embarrassed, that his teacher identified him by an object rather than his name, Johnson had demanded to be treated with respect.

At the time, he perhaps felt unable to express himself except by what he did or did not wear. Now, when he turned his letter over and found the blank verso lying before him, the sight seems to have reinvigorated his act of writing, as it had other marginally literate writers from Abram Mercherson to Garland H. White. At the top of the page, he wrote, "my name is Jordan Johnson the red neck tier"—an act of assertion *(I am a human being, and I am known by my name)* as well as one of reconciliation, in which he accepts Chase's objectifying if playful nickname as a secondary part of his identity.

Having reached that complicated moment of self-definition and assimilation, Johnson finally could broach the subject that probably had driven him all along to write this letter. Next to large, sprawling letters, "P.S.," Johnson writes:

> Remember me I will
> you do you Remember
> David Barr
> Barr
> Barr
> Barr

Johnson's penmanship grows neater each time. The two *r*'s in David Barr's name initially resemble a lazy *m*, but by the fourth try they have become impeccable examples of proper cursive. And having perfected Barr's last name, Johnson moves his hand back up the page, sets his pen down in the white space to the left of his penmanship practice, and resumes:

> hes is ded he went
> to mobile last sept with his teacher
> ~~miss A mary~~ Miss mary A Gayle
> to mobile With her and came Back on
> the 28th ist of december and was taking
> Withh fits a few ~~days~~ ^{days} after and died
> January 1 1869 and was berried on the
> 2 of ~~Ja~~ January
> David Barr is dead
> Death
> You truly friend
> Jordan Johnson

It is impossible to reconstruct Lucy Chase's precise reaction to this letter, but it is equally impossible to imagine that she was unmoved by it—by its reminder of the ways she used to perceive and talk to African Americans; by its unmistakable evidence that, even if freed people could not write well, they had such things to write. On Emancipation Day, David Barr died. Jordan Johnson lost the schoolmate whose name he now copied over in mournful quiet. Alone with feelings for which few writers can find words, he gripped the pen with which he could not even make quite the right letters—filled with the expressive power of literacy yet filled, too, with lessons taught by a white woman who called him a necktie; mindful of her strict standards for the look of his *r*'s; unable to give voice to whatever grief or reminiscence coursed through his mind as he slowly traced the increasingly

miss gates is in Mobile   if you wish to write
            Mrs   her Direct your
                        Letter to mary A Gayle
                        Stone Street
                        mobile

my name is Jordan Johnson
the first neck tier
I will bring my letter to a Close
Your truly Carter of C Johnson
    P.S
        Remember me I will
you   do you Remember
                David Barr
        hes is dead he went Barr
to mobile last sept with her and Barr
miss may   Miss mary A Gayle Barr
to mobile with her and come Back an
the 28th ist of December and was taking
with fits a few days after and died
January 1 1869 and was berried on the
2 of January

                David Barr is dead
                    Death
        You truly friend

            Jordan Johnson

            of C Johnson
the whenever you write to me Direct
    Letter
your to go Jordan Johnson in the
Care of L. H. Hill of Columbus Georgia may 11 1869

Page 2 of Jordan Johnson to Lucy Chase, May 11, 1869, Chase Family Papers,
American Antiquarian Society, Worcester, Massachusetts. Courtesy of the
American Antiquarian Society.

opaque words, almost hopeless of meaning, "David Barr is dead," or the single word insuperable, "Death."

Perhaps, if more white Americans had laid eyes on such texts, the racial divide that plagued the nation for decades might have been bridged more fully, more quickly. As A Colored Man reminded his imagined readers, "the black men has wives and sweet harts jest like the white men . . . God mad all." As Jordan Johnson might add, all are unmade the same, too: black people witness and suffer the mortality every human shares. That some people did read freed people's writing—that Lucy Chase, at least, may have sympathized with what flowed through Johnson's words, however inadequate—perhaps produced for the post-emancipation United States a better history than it otherwise might have had. Almost no way more than through writing does human thought cross the distances between separate minds and separate communities.

Even so, the world of language is a hard place to build bridges of sympathy. Merely a missing *e* or *a* can mark the difference between the familiar and the strange—enough to distract an educated reader from the similarities A Colored Man was trying to point out. Writing has no skin color, but the written page makes much of the difference between "dun" and "done." In written letters and words one sees the "disadvantages," as John M. Washington put it, of African Americans' long exclusion from the community of writers.

Yet it was here, amid the often unforgiving precepts of grammar and spelling, that freed people needed to lay their claims, assert their rights, and make real their identities, opinions, and feelings. Like emancipation itself—as a matter of law, the nation's most honorable yet most tragically unfulfilled act—the expansion of literacy among former slaves represented both incalculable progress toward racial justice and an incomplete, often poignantly imperfect instrument of black self-determination. The strictures of language and the conventions of the written page could prove unforgiving— far, far less so than the rule of the slaveholder, but also peculiarly ineluctable. How could one run away from them, or rebel against them?

If freed people could not break those strictures, they could, within their bounds, make the inventions born of necessity—and kindle the creative sparks sent flying by their own minds' friction with the written world's

walls. If African American literature was begotten "by the necessity of con-
fronting the constraints of the segregation era," as one scholar has argued,
then ordinary freed people did at least some of the begetting, for they lived
and wrote within the medleyed constraints of that nascent era and their
own nascent literacy. It is to their acts of writing that we must listen if we
wish to hear the song of freedom, for it was they who sang it word by word.[31]

Notes

Introduction

1. Statement of A Colored Man, enclosed in Lt. Col. Jas. A. Hopkins to Brig. Gen. James Bowen, 2 September 1863, H-99 1863, Letters Received, ser. 1920, Civil Affairs, Department of the Gulf, Record Group 393 Part I, National Archives Building, Washington, DC [C-704]. A transcription appears as "Statements of an Anonymous New Orleans Black" in *Freedom: A Documentary History of Emancipation, 1861–1867,* ser. 2: *The Black Military Experience,* ed. Ira Berlin et al. (Cambridge: Cambridge Univ. Press, 1982), 153–157. Documents from the National Archives that also are among the papers of the Freedmen and Southern Society Project (FSSP) are cited by their location in the archives, followed by their FSSP control number in square brackets. Those that have been published in the five volumes of *Freedom: A Documentary History of Emancipation, 1861–1867,* include a further reference to their published transcription.

2. Indeed, many rural and working-class white Americans were not a bit more literate than black slaves. Important studies of the Civil War era have cited an archive analogous to the one at issue in this book—namely, the numerous but widely dispersed (and often barely intelligible) writings of marginally literate enlisted men in both armies. See esp. Chandra Manning, *What This Cruel War Was Over: Soldiers, Slavery, and the Civil War* (New York: Alfred A. Knopf, 2007), and

also Drew Gilpin Faust, *Mothers of Invention: Women of the Slaveholding South in the American Civil War* (Chapel Hill: Univ. of North Carolina Press, 1996), 115–116.

3. For a related scholarly intervention, focused on ordinary African American readers rather than writers, see Elizabeth McHenry *Forgotten Readers: Recovering the Lost History of African American Literary Societies* (Durham, NC: Duke Univ. Press, 2002). For recent work on 19th-century American manuscript culture, see Karen Sánchez-Eppler, "Copying and Conversion: An 1824 Friendship Album 'from a Chinese Youth,'" *American Quarterly* 59 no. 2 (June 2007): 301–339, and Sánchez-Eppler, "Practicing for Print: The Hale Children's Manuscript Libraries," *Journal of the History of Childhood and Youth* 1 no. 2 (Spring 2008): 188–209. (Both articles are part of Sánchez-Eppler's longer work in progress, "The Unpublished Republic: Manuscript Cultures of the Mid-Nineteenth-Century United States.")

4. I certainly am not the first to propose an alternative intellectual history centered on ordinary African Americans. Lawrence W. Levine framed his pioneering study of black folklore that way more than thirty years ago; more recently, Davarian Baldwin has directed attention to the "marketplace intellectual life" of African American consumers in twentieth-century Chicago. While I follow the lead of those scholars, I am using a more old-fashioned definition of "intellectual history" in which the written word is the principal register of people's thinking. See Lawrence W. Levine, *Black Culture and Black Consciousness: Afro-American Folk Thought from Slavery to Freedom* (New York: Oxford Univ. Press, 1977), xi; Davarian Baldwin, *Chicago's New Negroes: Modernity, the Great Migration, and Black Urban Life* (Chapel Hill: Univ. of North Carolina Press, 2007), 5–6.

5. For a corrective to the image of benevolent white mistresses who indulged their female slaves, see Thavolia Glymph, *Out of the House of Bondage: The Transformation of the Plantation Household* (Cambridge: Cambridge Univ. Press, 2008).

6. Such a representation of emancipation is consonant with a salient trend in much of the newest research by historians of the period. Increasingly, scholars of emancipation are complicating notions of a stark divide between slavery and freedom, focusing attention instead on the limitations of black freedom and African Americans' continuing struggle, after the Civil War, for rights, power, and justice. This trend was crystallized in a two-day conference, "Beyond Freedom: New Directions in the Study of Emancipation," at Yale University's Gilder Lehrman Center for the Study of Slavery, Resistance, and Abolition, 11–12 November 2011. Video of the conference is available at http://www.yale.edu/glc/emancipation /schedule.htm. An important new study of families separated during slavery, including the role of literacy in preserving familial bonds, appeared as this book went to press. See Heather Andrea Williams, *Help Me to Find My People: The African American Search for Families Lost in Slavery* (Chapel Hill: Univ. of North Carolina Press, 2012).

7. Louis P. Masur, *Lincoln's Hundred Days: The Emancipation Proclamation and the War for the Union* (Cambridge, MA: Harvard Univ. Press, 2012); James Oakes, *The Radical and the Republican: Frederick Douglass, Abraham Lincoln, and the Triumph of Antislavery Politics* (New York: Norton, 2007), 173–208; Mitch Kachun, *Festivals of Freedom: Memory and Meaning in African American Emancipation Celebrations, 1808–1915* (Amherst: Univ. of Massachusetts Press), 103–105.

8. Joanne Pope Melish, *Disowning Slavery: Gradual Emancipation and "Race" in New England, 1780–1860* (Ithaca, NY: Cornell Univ. Press, 1998); Steven Hahn, *The Political Worlds of Slavery and Freedom* (Cambridge, MA: Harvard Univ. Press, 2009), 7–9; Hilary Moss, *Schooling Citizens: The Struggle for African American Education in Antebellum America* (Chicago: Univ. of Chicago Press, 2009), 60; Alexis de Tocqueville, *Democracy in America,* trans. Arthur Goldhammer (New York: Library of America, 2004), 397.

9. Eric Foner, *Reconstruction: America's Unfinished Revolution, 1863–1877* (1988; repr. New York: Harper Perennial, 2002), 1–11. For notable examples of the "self-emancipation" thesis, see Ira Berlin et al., eds., *Freedom: A Documentary History of Emancipation,* ser. 1, vol. 1: *The Destruction of Slavery* (Cambridge: Cambridge Univ. Press, 1985), 1–56; Hahn, *Political Worlds;* and Steven Hahn, *A Nation under Our Feet: Black Political Struggles in the Rural South from Slavery to the Great Migration* (Cambridge, MA: Harvard Univ. Press, 2003). For a critical evaluation of that thesis, see James M. McPherson, "Who Freed the Slaves?" in *Drawn with the Sword: Reflections on the American Civil War* (New York: Oxford Univ. Press, 1996), 192–207.

10. Thomas Wentworth Higginson, *Army Life in a Black Regiment and Other Writings* (1870; repr. New York: Penguin, 1997), quotation on 172; Eric Foner, *Nothing but Freedom: Emancipation and Its Legacy* (1983; repr. Baton Rouge: Louisiana State Univ. Press, 2007), quotation on 72.

11. John W. Blassingame, *Black New Orleans, 1860–1880* (Chicago: Univ. of Chicago Press, 1973), 35–39.

12. Jonathan Goldberg, *Writing Matter: From the Hands of the English Renaissance* (Stanford, CA: Stanford Univ. Press, 1990), 191; Morris quoted in Michael Warner, *Letters of the Republic: Publication and the Public Sphere in Eighteenth-Century America* (Cambridge, MA: Harvard Univ. Press, 1990), 115. For a useful survey and reinterpretation of theories of media and mediation, see Dominic Boyer, *Understanding Media: A Popular Philosophy* (Chicago: Prickly Paradigm Press, 2007).

13. Plato, *The Symposium; and The Phaedrus: Plato's Erotic Dialogues,* trans. William S. Cobb (Albany: State Univ. of New York Press, 1993), 128–137; Eric Havelock, *Preface to Plato* (Cambridge, MA: Harvard Univ. Press, 1963), 36–60. Havelock's argument and the copious work of Walter Ong typify an influential but idealized view of literacy as an engine of " 'progress,' 'civilisation,' individual liberty

and social mobility." Brian V. Street, *Literacy in Theory and Practice* (Cambridge: Cambridge Univ. Press, 1984), 2.

14. Beth Daniell, "Narratives of Literacy: Connecting Composition to Culture," *College Composition and Communication* 50, no. 3 (February 1999): 396. Perhaps the best-known example of such views is Paolo Freire, *Pedagogy of the Oppressed*, trans. Myra Bergman Ramos (New York: Herder and Herder, 1970). On state administration, see the essays in Seth L. Sanders, ed., *Margins of Writing, Origins of Cultures* (Chicago: Oriental Institute of the Univ. of Chicago, 2006).

15. Street, *Literacy in Theory and Practice;* Harvey Graff, *The Literacy Myth: Literacy and Social Structure in the Nineteenth-Century City* (New York: Academic Press, 1979); Carl F. Kaestle, "Studying the History of Literacy," in *Literacy in the United States: Readers and Reading since 1880,* ed. Carl F. Kaestle et al. (New Haven, CT: Yale Univ. Press, 1991), 3–32; David Barton and Mary Hamilton, *Local Literacies: Reading and Writing in One Community* (London: Routledge, 1998); Ramona Fernandez, *Imagining Literacy: Rhizomes of Knowledge in American Culture and Literature* (Austin: Univ. of Texas Press, 2001); Shannon Carter, *The Way Literacy Lives: Rhetorical Dexterity and Basic Writing Instruction* (Albany: State Univ. of New York Press, 2009); Katrina Powell, *The Anguish of Displacement: The Politics of Literacy in the Letters of Mountain Families in Shenandoah National Park* (Charlottesville: Univ. of Virginia Press, 2008).

16. Peter Elbow, *Writing with Power: Techniques for Mastering the Writing Process,* 2nd ed. (New York: Oxford Univ. Press, 1998), quotation on xxiii; K. Nakamura et al., "Modulation of the Visual Word Retrieval System in Writing: A Functional MRI Study on the Japanese Orthographies," *Journal of Cognitive Neuroscience* 14 (January 2002): 104–115; Anne Mangen and Jean-Luc Velay, "Digitizing Literacy: Reflections on the Haptics of Writing," in *Advances in Haptics,* ed. Mehrdad Hosseini Zadeh (Intech, 2010), 385–401, www.intechopen.com/articles/show/title/digitizing-literacy-reflections-on-the-haptics-of-writing; Clive Thompson, "The Pen That Never Forgets," *New York Times Magazine,* 16 September 2010, 46–51; Gerardo Ramirez and Sian L. Beilock, "Writing about Testing Worries Boosts Exam Performance in the Classroom," *Science* 331 (14 January 2011): 211–213; Fredrick E. Hornung, "Finding Impressionist Moments in a Digital Classroom: Writing about van Gogh in an Avatar-Based Environment" (1 January 2007), in *Dissertations Collection for University of Connecticut,* Paper AAI3265824, http://digitalcommons.uconn.edu/dissertations/AAI3265824.

17. Dana Nelson Salvino, "The Word in Black and White: Ideologies of Race and Literacy in Antebellum America," in *Reading in America: Literature and Social History,* ed. Cathy N. Davidson (Baltimore: Johns Hopkins Univ. Press, 1989), quotation on 144; David R. Olson and Nancy Torrance, preface to *The Cambridge Handbook of Literacy,* ed. David R. Olson and Nancy Torrance (Cambridge: Cambridge Univ. Press, 2009), quotation on xiv. Also see Richard Brodhead,

Cultures of Letters: Scenes of Reading and Writing in Nineteenth-Century America (Chicago: Univ. of Chicago Press, 1993), 24; Cathy N. Davidson, *Revolution and the Word: The Rise of the Novel in America,* rev. ed. (New York: Oxford Univ. Press, 2004), 131; Tamara Plakins Thornton, *Handwriting in America: A Cultural History* (New Haven, CT: Yale Univ. Press, 1996), 52.

18. Melville quoted in Elizabeth Renker, *Strike through the Mask: Herman Melville and the Scene of Writing* (Baltimore: Johns Hopkins Univ. Press, 1996), 6. On Adams and Jackson, see Jill Lepore, *A Is for American: Letters and Other Characters in the Newly United States* (New York: Alfred A. Knopf, 2002), 112. On marginalia, see Davidson, *Revolution and the Word,* 145–149; on maps, Larry Freeman, *Louis Prang: Color Lithographer, Giant of a Man* (Watkins Glen, NY: Century House, 1971), 26; on scrapbooks and other creative reuse of printed text, Ellen Gruber Garvey, "Scissorizing and Scrapbooks: Nineteenth-Century Reading, Remaking, and Recirculating," in *New Media, 1740–1915,* ed. Lisa Gitelman and Geoffrey R. Pingree (Cambridge, MA: MIT Press, 2003), 207–227, and Karen Sánchez-Eppler, "Marks of Possession: Methods for an Impossible Subject," *PMLA* 126, no. 1 (January 2011): 151–159; on newspapers, David Henkin, *The Postal Age: The Emergence of Modern Communications in Nineteenth-Century America* (Chicago: Univ. of Chicago Press, 2006), 47. On gender differences in literacy instruction, see Thornton, *Handwriting in America,* chap. 2; Sarah Robbins, *Managing Literacy, Mothering America: Women's Narratives on Reading and Writing in the Nineteenth Century* (Pittsburgh: Univ. of Pittsburgh Press, 2004); and Catherine Hobbs, ed., *Nineteenth-Century Women Learn to Write* (Charlottesville: Univ. Press of Virginia, 1995).

19. On the role of religion in slave literacy, and for the most comprehensive treatment of slaves' literacy acquisition in general, see Janet Duitsman Cornelius, *"When I Can Read My Title Clear": Slavery, Literacy, and Religion in the Antebellum South* (Columbia: Univ. of South Carolina Press, 1991).

20. Frederick Douglass, *My Bondage and My Freedom* (1855; repr. New York: Penguin, 2003), 109. On slave passes, see Christian Parenti, *The Soft Cage: Surveillance in America from Slavery to the War on Terror* (New York: Basic Books, 2003), 21–23, and Sally E. Hadden, *Slave Patrols: Law and Violence in Virginia and the Carolinas* (Cambridge, MA: Harvard Univ. Press, 2001).

21. Henry Louis Gates, Jr., introduction to *The Classic Slave Narratives,* ed. Henry Louis Gates, Jr. (New York: Penguin, 1987), ix; Theresa Perry, "Freedom for Literacy and Literacy for Freedom: The African-American Philosophy of Education," in Theresa Perry, Claude Steele, and Asa G. Hilliard III, *Young, Gifted, and Black: Promoting High Achievement among African-American Students* (Boston: Beacon Press, 2003), 13. For selected variants of the "literacy as liberation" thesis in African American studies, see William Andrews, *To Tell a Free Story: The First Century of Afro-American Autobiography, 1760–1865* (Urbana: Univ. of Illinois Press, 1986); Houston A. Baker, Jr., introduction to *Narrative of the Life of Frederick*

Douglass, an American Slave, by Frederick Douglass (New York: Penguin, 1982); Steven Mintz, *Huck's Raft: A History of American Childhood* (Cambridge, MA: Harvard Univ. Press, 2004), 110; James Olney, "'I Was Born': Slave Narratives, Their Status as Autobiography and as Literature," in *The Slave's Narrative,* ed. Charles T. Davis and Henry Louis Gates, Jr. (New York: Oxford Univ. Press, 1985), 156; Sidonie Smith, *Where I'm Bound: Patterns of Slavery and Freedom in Black American Autobiography* (Westport, CT: Greenwood Press, 1974), 10–11; Christopher Span, *From Cotton Field to Schoolhouse: African American Education in Mississippi, 1862–1875* (Chapel Hill: Univ. of North Carolina Press, 2009), chap. 1; Robert Stepto, "Preface to the Second Edition," in *From Behind the Veil: A Study of Afro-American Narrative,* 2nd ed. (Urbana: Univ. of Illinois Press, 1991), x. The related argument that literacy in the age of racial slavery connoted whiteness and humanity is most fully developed in Henry Louis Gates, Jr., *Figures in Black: Words, Signs, and the "Racial" Self* (New York: Oxford Univ. Press, 1987) and *The Signifying Monkey: A Theory of African-American Literary Criticism* (New York: Oxford Univ. Press, 1988); also see Lindon Barrett, *Blackness and Value: Seeing Double* (Cambridge: Cambridge Univ. Press, 1999), 66–78.

22. For more complicated views of the relationship between literacy and freedom—ideas that have influenced my own—see Karen Sánchez-Eppler, "Gothic Liberties and Fugitive Novels: *The Bondwoman's Narrative* and the Fiction of Race," in *In Search of Hannah Crafts: Critical Essays on* The Bondwoman's Narrative, ed. Henry Louis Gates, Jr., and Hollis Robbins (New York: Basic Books, 2004), 254–275, and *Dependent States: The Child's Part in Nineteenth-Century American Culture* (Chicago: Univ. of Chicago Press, 2005), 3–40; Katherine Clay Bassard, "Gender and Genre: Black Women's Autobiography and the Ideology of Literacy," *African American Review* 26, no. 1 (Spring 1992): 119–129; Dana Nelson Salvino, "The Word in Black and White"; McHenry, *Forgotten Readers,* 13; and Ben Schiller, "Learning Their Letters: Critical Literacy, Epistolary Culture, and Slavery in the Antebellum South," *Southern Quarterly* 45, no. 3 (Spring 2008): 11–29, and "Selling Themselves: Slavery, Survival, and the Path of Least Resistance" *49th Parallel* 23 (Summer 2009), www.49thparallel.bham.ac.uk. Several of these scholars find that the literacy-as-liberation thesis breaks down specifically in the experiences and writings of African American women. For an in-depth study of literacy and black women—mostly well-educated, socially elite women, as opposed to marginally literate slaves and freedwomen—see Jacqueline Jones Royster, *Traces of a Stream: Literacy and Social Change among African American Women* (Pittsburgh: Univ. of Pittsburgh Press, 2000).

23. The foundational work in this vein is Levine, *Black Culture and Black Consciousness.* Also see the discussion of these methodological questions in Barrett, *Blackness and Value,* esp. 73–78 and notes to chap. 2.

24. Robert Pattison, *On Literacy: The Politics of the Word from Homer to the Age of Rock* (New York: Oxford Univ. Press, 1982), quotation on 24. For an excellent discussion of literacy studies' recent attention to the blurring of written and oral discourse, see Royster, *Traces of a Stream,* 43–45.

25. "Writing is thus always in some sense hermeneutic, which means that it is never an original activity but is always mediated by the texts that provide access to the system." Gerald L. Bruns, "The Originality of Texts in a Manuscript Culture," *Comparative Literature* 32, no. 2 (Spring 1980): 122–123.

26. Elizabeth Regosin, "Surnames in the Gap between Orality and Literacy," in *Freedom's Promise: Ex-Slave Families and Citizenship in the Age of Emancipation* (Charlottesville: Univ. Press of Virginia, 2002), 60–67.

27. I avoid the term *semiliterate* because it suggests an inadequacy I do not think characterized the writers discussed in this book. "Marginally literate" differs from Jack Goody's phrase "the margins of literacy," which refers to the condition of people who cannot themselves read and write but are influenced by their proximity to literate people and written texts. The majority of American slaves dwelled on the margins of literacy in precisely this sense—even those who could not read and write gleaned information by, for instance, listening to white slaveholders or literate blacks read aloud from newspapers—but the individuals featured in this book were themselves literate. Jack Goody, introduction to *Literacy in Traditional Societies,* ed. Jack Goody (Cambridge: Cambridge Univ. Press, 1975), 4–5. On methods for studying writings by a different community of marginally literate people— working-class immigrants—see Bruce S. Elliott, David A. Gerber, and Suzanne Sinke, eds., *Letters across Borders: The Epistolary Practices of International Migrants* (New York: Palgrave Macmillan, 2006), 3–4, and David A. Gerber, *Authors of Their Lives: The Personal Correspondence of British Immigrants to North America in the Nineteenth Century* (New York: New York Univ. Press, 2006), 83–84.

28. I am grateful to Ed Heinemann for helping me formulate this view of my own methods.

29. For a recent persuasive definition of African American literature along these lines, see Kenneth W. Warren, *What Was African American Literature?* (Cambridge, MA: Harvard Univ. Press, 2011).

30. Dickson D. Bruce, Jr., *The Origins of African American Literature, 1680– 1865* (Charlottesville: Univ. Press of Virginia, 2001). Notable recent efforts to expand the canon of early African American literature include the work of Xiomara Santamarina (who has brought readers' attention to texts by black writers who were, unlike the authors of fugitive slave narratives, "marginal to abolition") and Eric Gardner (who has studied overlooked writers and editors in the early black press)—though these studies, too, focus on published sources. See Xiomara Santamarina, *Belabored Professions: Narratives of African American Working*

Womanhood (Chapel Hill: Univ. of North Carolina Press, 2005), 18, and "Antebellum African-American Texts Beyond Slavery and Race," in *Beyond Douglass: New Perspectives on Early African-American Literature,* ed. Michael J. Drexler and Ed White (Lewisburg, PA: Bucknell Univ. Press, 2008), 141–153; Eric Gardner, *Unexpected Places: Relocating Nineteenth-Century African American Literature* (Jackson: Univ. Press of Mississippi, 2009). A few twentieth-century discoveries have expanded the early African American literary canon with texts that were not published during their authors' lifetimes, though modern scholars have tended to present and interpret these texts primarily in relation to print publication. *The Bondwoman's Narrative* by Hannah Crafts remained unpublished until 2002, but it was clearly a self-conscious artistic work informed by the conventions of the literary marketplace—a manuscript comprising numbered chapters headed by epigraphs and hand-bound in cloth. Henry Louis Gates, Jr., introduction to *The Bondwoman's Narrative,* by Hannah Crafts (New York: Warner Books, 2002), xxiii–xxv.

1. Black Literacy in the White Mind

1. Josephine F. Pacheco, *The Pearl: A Failed Slave Escape on the Potomac* (Chapel Hill: Univ. of North Carolina Press, 2005), 115.

2. Harriet Beecher Stowe, *Uncle Tom's Cabin,* ed. Elizabeth Ammons (New York: Norton, 2010), 356.

3. Harriet Beecher Stowe, *A Key to Uncle Tom's Cabin; Presenting the Original Facts and Documents upon Which the Story Is Founded* (Boston: John P. Jewett, 1853), 171–172.

4. Stowe, *Key to Uncle Tom's Cabin,* 173, 171. The text of the Ducket letter also appears in John Blassingame, *Slave Testimony: Two Centuries of Letters, Speeches, Interviews, and Autobiographies* (Baton Rouge: Louisiana State Univ. Press, 1977), 89. Blassingame "restored the letter to the original," although even his more faithful transcription regularizes many of Ducket's words (Blassingame silently inserted all the missing terminal *e's*). The technology for rendering handwriting in a printed work, usually involving a woodcut of the manuscript, was not new—see, for instance, David Melville, *A Fac-simile of the Letters Produced at the Trial of the Rev. Ephraim K. Avery, on an Indictment for the Murder of Sarah Maria Lowell* (Boston: Pendleton's Lithography, 1833); Edgar Allan Poe, "Autography," *Southern Literary Messenger* 2 (February and August 1836): 205–212, 601–604; and *Autographs for Freedom* (Boston: John P. Jewett, 1853)—but its use remained relatively costly and infrequent.

5. Stowe, *Key to Uncle Tom's Cabin,* 109.

6. The most thorough study of slaves' literacy is Janet Duitsman Cornelius, *When I Can Read My Title Clear: Literacy, Slavery, and Religion in the Antebellum South* (Columbia: Univ. of South Carolina Press, 1991). Also see Konstantin Dierks, *In My Power: Letter Writing and Communications in Early America* (Philadelphia: Univ. of Pennsylvania Press, 2009), 249–266; E. Jennifer Monaghan, *Reading for the Enslaved,*

Writing for the Free: Reflections on Liberty and Literacy (Worcester, MA: American Antiquarian Society, 2000); Jacqueline Jones Royster, *Traces of a Stream: Literacy and Social Change among African American Women* (Pittsburgh: Univ. of Pittsburgh Press, 2000), 108–143; Thomas L. Webber, *Deep Like the Rivers: Education in the Slave Quarter Community, 1831–1865* (New York: Norton, 1978), esp. 131–139; and Heather Andrea Williams, *Self-Taught: African American Education in Slavery and Freedom* (Chapel Hill: Univ. of North Carolina Press, 2005), 7–29.

7. The phrase "positive good," which became a watchword of pro-slavery thought, was initiated by John C. Calhoun in an 1837 speech before the Senate. For the intellectual history of slavery's defenders during the three decades preceding the Civil War, see George Frederickson, *The Black Image in the White Mind* (1971; repr. Middletown, CT: Wesleyan Univ. Press, 1987).

8. Frederick Douglass, *My Bondage and My Freedom* (1855; repr. New York: Penguin, 2003), 108; Gregory S. Jay, *America the Scrivener: Deconstruction and the Subject of Literary History* (Ithaca, NY: Cornell Univ. Press, 1990), 270.

9. Harriet Beecher Stowe, *Dred: A Tale of the Great Dismal Swamp*, ed. Robert S. Levine (1856; repr. Chapel Hill: Univ. of North Carolina Press, 2000), 311–312. The tale of the cork leg circulated widely in Britain and the U.S. as a folk song; one text appears in John Ashton, *Modern Street Ballads* (London: Chatto & Windus, 1888), 153–155.

10. On antebellum education as a form of religious assimilation, see Hilary J. Moss, *Schooling Citizens: The Struggle for African American Education in Antebellum America* (Chicago: Univ. of Chicago Press, 2009), 21–43.

11. "The Tree of Slavery," in *The Star of Freedom* (New York: W. S. Dorr, n.d.), also available online at *The Antislavery Literature Project,* http://antislavery.eserver .org/childrens/star_of_freedom; Cornelius, *When I Can Read My Title Clear,* 125–134; Frederick Douglass, "Bibles for the Slaves," *The North Star,* 14 January 1848. Also see Victor B. Howard, *The Evangelical War against Slavery and Caste: The Life and Times of John G. Fee* (Selinsgrove, PA: Susquehanna Univ. Press, 1996), 41–42; John R. McKivigan, *The War against Proslavery Religion: Abolitionism and the Northern Churches* (Ithaca, NY: Cornell Univ. Press, 1984), 124; and Peter J. Wosh, *Spreading the Word: The Bible Business in Nineteenth-Century America* (Ithaca, NY: Cornell Univ. Press, 1994), 200–212.

12. Ronald G. Walters, *The Antislavery Appeal: American Abolitionism after 1830* (Baltimore: Johns Hopkins Univ. Press, 1976), 55; Theodore Dwight Weld, *American Slavery As It Is* (New York: American Anti-Slavery Society, 1839), 150.

13. *The Anti-Slavery Alphabet* (Philadelphia: Merrihew & Thompson, 1847); Martha L. Sledge, " 'A Is an Abolitionist': *The Anti-Slavery Alphabet* and the Politics of Literacy," in *Enterprising Youth: Social Values and Acculturation in Nineteenth-Century American Children's Literature,* ed. Monika Elbert (New York: Routledge, 2008), 78.

14. Joanne Pope Melish, *Disowning Slavery: Gradual Emancipation and "Race" in New England, 1780–1860* (Ithaca, NY: Cornell Univ. Press, 1998), 211; Joseph A. Conforti, *Imagining New England: Explorations of Regional Identity from the Pilgrims to the Mid-Twentieth Century* (Chapel Hill: Univ. of North Carolina Press, 2001), 152. White northerners' concern for the welfare of enslaved blacks in the South generally did not extend to free blacks in the North, who virtually nowhere enjoyed access to education equal with whites; see Moss, *Schooling Citizens.*

15. "Southern Literature," *Putnam's Monthly* 9, no. 50 (February 1857): 210; "The Moral of Statistics," *New Englander and Yale Review* 13, no. 50 (May 1855): 199; [Moncure D. Conway], "Then and Now in the Old Dominion," *The Atlantic Monthly* 9, no. 54 (April 1862): 500.

16. Weld, *American Slavery as It Is,* 187; Stowe, *Key to Uncle Tom's Cabin,* 365; "Gov. Hammond's Defense of Southern Slavery," *New Englander and Yale Review* 3, no. 12 (October 1845): 571n (emphasis in original).

17. John Comly, *A New Spelling Book, Adapted to the Different Classes of Pupils; Compiled with a View to Render the Arts of Spelling and Reading Easy and Pleasant to Children* (Philadelphia: Kimber & Sharpless, 1831), 167–168. The historian Edward Ayers writes, "Accent is the closest attribute white Southerners have to a physical marker to separate them from other white Americans; the same is true among blacks." This pseudo-ethnic attribute, Ayers suggests, has long been "a symbol of poor education, low ambition, and reactionary politics." Edward Ayers, "What We Talk about When We Talk about the South," in Ayers et al., *All Over the Map: Rethinking American Regions* (Baltimore: Johns Hopkins Univ. Press, 1996), 71.

18. Robert S. Levine, *Martin Delany, Frederick Douglass, and the Politics of Representative Identity* (Chapel Hill: Univ. of North Carolina Press, 1997), 147. I am not alone in finding a tinge of "crusading self-righteousness" in abolitionism and northerners' attitudes about the South more generally; see Richard J. Ellis, *The Dark Side of the Left: Illiberal Egalitarianism in America* (Lawrence: Univ. Press of Kansas, 1998), 18. Joanne Pope Melish argues that "the construction of New England as the antithesis of an enslaved South had become commonplace by the time of the Constitutional Convention" (*Disowning Slavery,* xiv). It is important to acknowledge, though, that anti-slavery northerners, however self-serving their arguments sometimes were, exhibited real moral courage. At a time when it was very easy to ignore, if not tolerate, the institution of slavery—and the vast majority of Americans did—white abolitionists refused. That their rhetoric aggrandized their own position makes them little different from many other progressive reformers.

19. Stowe, *Uncle Tom's Cabin,* 238. For a convenient survey of such images, see the illustrations reproduced in Henry Louis Gates, Jr., and Hollis Robbins, eds., *The Annotated Uncle Tom's Cabin* (New York: Norton, 2007), 271–273. For an extensive history of the original Hammatt Billings engraving of this scene—"the

most influential picture ever made for *Uncle Tom's Cabin*"—see Jo-Ann Morgan, *Uncle Tom's Cabin as Visual Culture* (Columbia: Univ. of Missouri Press, 2007), quotation on 11.

20. Stowe, *Uncle Tom's Cabin,* 215–216. Tom's use of a slate for his first draft may be Stowe's projection of northern childhood learning, but some archaeological evidence does suggest the use of slates by slaves; see Theresa Singleton, "The Archaeology of Slave Life," in *Images of the Recent Past: Readings in Historical Archaeology,* ed. Charles E. Orser (Walnut Creek, CA: Alta Mira, 1996), 141–165.

21. Stowe, *Uncle Tom's Cabin,* 216.

22. Stowe, *Dred,* 12.

23. Ibid., 130.

24. Ibid., 132.

25. On abolitionism's figurative and literal conjunctions of African American slaves and white women, see Karen Sánchez-Eppler, *Touching Liberty: Abolition, Feminism, and the Politics of the Body* (Berkeley: Univ. of California Press, 1993).

26. Stowe, *Key to Uncle Tom's Cabin,* 50; "How Shall I Learn to Write?" *Hearth and Home,* 16 January 1869, 56; H. B. Stowe to Mary Edmondson, 2 October 1852, Henry Cowles Papers, Record Group 30/27, Oberlin College Archives. For Mary Edmondson's age, see Pacheco, *The Pearl,* 121, 138. On "disciplinary intimacy" in Stowe's representations of education, see Richard Brodhead, *Cultures of Letters: Scenes of Reading and Writing in Nineteenth-Century America* (Chicago: Univ. of Chicago Press, 1993), 35–42.

27. Abraham Lincoln wrote, "He who would *be* no slave, must consent to *have* no slave" (Letter to Henry Pierce, 6 April 1859, in Roy P. Basler, ed., *The Collected Works of Abraham Lincoln,* vol. 3 [New Brunswick, NJ: Rutgers Univ. Press, 1953], 376), and Frederick Douglass's attacks on "the Slave Power" consistently warned of slavery's threat to the moral integrity and the liberty of the North and northerners (David W. Blight, *Frederick Douglass' Civil War: Keeping Faith in Jubilee* [Baton Rouge: Louisiana State Univ. Press, 1989], 40–41).

28. *The North Star,* 14 September 1849. J. E. Cairnes, "The Slave Power; Its Character, Career, and Probable Designs," *The Living Age* 75, no. 963 (15 November 1862): 308. Some twentieth-century historians persisted in characterizing the proscription of literacy as effectively universal. Kenneth Stampp wrote in 1969, "No person, not even the master, was to teach a slave to read or write, employ him in setting type in a printing office, or give him books or pamphlets." Stampp, *The Peculiar Institution: Slavery in the Ante-Bellum South* (New York: Alfred A. Knopf, 1969), 208.

29. Ira Berlin, *Generations of Captivity: A History of African-American Slaves* (Cambridge, MA: Harvard Univ. Press, 2003), 9; Walter Johnson, *Soul by Soul: Life inside the Antebellum Slave Market* (Cambridge, MA: Harvard Univ. Press, 1999), 231n20.

30. James F. McKee to Governor John Owen, 7 August 1830, in *David Walker's Appeal,* ed. Peter P. Hinks (University Park: Pennsylvania State Univ. Press, 2000), 105; also ibid., 74n. William Lloyd Garrison began publishing his abolitionist newspaper, *The Liberator,* the same year, further outraging southern slaveholders.

31. Laura Edwards has demonstrated the importance and persistence of localized law in the antebellum South, long after jurisprudential centralization and "modernization" were previously thought to have been accomplished. See Edwards, *The People and Their Peace: Legal Culture and the Transformation of Inequality in the Post-Revolutionary South* (Chapel Hill: Univ. of North Carolina Press, 2009), 5.

32. Cornelius, *When I Can Read My Title Clear,* 33–34. The two other states were Alabama and Louisiana.

33. Anti-literacy statutes quoted in Heather Andrea Williams, "African Americans, Literacy, and the Law in the Antebellum South," appendix to Williams, *Self-Taught,* 203–213; Peter Kolchin, *American Slavery, 1619–1877* (New York: Hill and Wang, 1993), 129. Also see Thomas D. Morris, *Southern Slavery and the Law, 1619–1860* (Chapel Hill: Univ. of North Carolina Press, 1996), 347.

34. Margaret Douglass, *The Personal Narrative of Mrs. Margaret Douglass, a Southern Woman* (Boston: John P. Jewett, 1854), 9; Cornelius, *When I Can Read My Title Clear,* 34; Sylviane A. Diouf, *Servants of Allah: African Muslims Enslaved in the Americas* (New York: New York Univ. Press, 1998), chap. 4; James Stirling, *Letters from the Slave States* (London: John W. Parker, 1857), 295.

35. Petitioner quoted in Stampp, *The Peculiar Institution,* 212; Stowe, *Key to Uncle Tom's Cabin,* 178, 181, 183. If Ducket remained one of Harrison's slaves, he may later have become something exceedingly unusual: the slave of a fellow African American. Following Harrison's death, a handful of newspapers, curious to observe "Wealthy Colored People in Louisiana," ran notices that "the plantation of the late Samuel T. Harrison, some three or four miles from Bayou Goula, was purchased on the 5th by the son of Cyprien Ricard, a free woman of color." *Lowell (Massachusetts) Daily Citizen and News,* 26 June 1858, 2.

36. *Southern Cultivator* article quoted in James O. Breeden, ed., *Advice among Masters: The Ideal in Slave Management in the Old South* (Westport, CT: Greenwood Press, 1980), 331; Edwards, *The People and Their Peace,* 30; John Belton O'Neall, *The Negro Law of South Carolina* (Columbia, SC: John G. Bowman, 1848), 23 (emphasis in original). On slave owners teaching slaves to read and write, see Cornelius, *When I Can Read My Title Clear,* chap. 5; on white southerners using slaves and ideas about slave management to define themselves and fashion images of their own potency, see Johnson, *Soul by Soul,* 102–115.

37. Tiya Miles, *Ties That Bind: The Story of an Afro-Cherokee Family in Slavery and Freedom* (Berkeley: Univ. of California Press, 2005), 94–95; Cornelius, *When I Can Read My Title Clear,* 66.

38. Carter G. Woodson, *The Education of the Negro prior to 1861* (1919; repr. New York: Arno Press, 1968), 226–228.

39. W. E. B. Du Bois, *Black Reconstruction in America* (New York: Russell & Russell, 1935), 638; Eugene D. Genovese, *Roll, Jordan, Roll: The World the Slaves Made* (New York: Vintage, 1974), 563.

40. Cornelius, *When I Can Read My Title Clear,* 9.

41. Ivan E. McDougle, "The Social Status of the Slave," *Journal of Negro History* 3, no. 3 (July 1918): 289–290.

42. UNESCO statement quoted in David Harman, "Illiteracy: An Overview," *Harvard Educational Review* 40, no. 2 (May 1970): 226. For a fuller account of sources for the quantitative study of historical literacy, see Kenneth A. Lockridge, *Literacy in Colonial New England: An Enquiry into the Social Context of Literacy in the Early Modern West* (New York: Norton, 1974), 109–119, 123n2, and Harvey Graff, *The Literacy Myth: Literacy and Social Structure in the Nineteenth-Century City* (New York: Academic Press, 1979), 326–327.

43. Slave narratives are the subject of a vast scholarly literature; useful and influential starting points include Robert Stepto, *From behind the Veil: A Study of Afro-American Narrative* (1979; repr. Urbana: Univ. of Illinois Press, 1991); William L. Andrews, *To Tell a Free Story: The First Century of Afro-American Autobiography, 1760–1865* (Urbana: Univ. of Illinois Press, 1986); the essays in Charles T. Davis and Henry Louis Gates, Jr., eds. *The Slave's Narrative* (New York: Oxford Univ. Press, 1985); and the essays in Audrey Fisch, ed., *The Cambridge Companion to the African American Slave Narrative* (Cambridge: Cambridge Univ. Press, 2007). For a metacritical reflection on the slave narrative's place in slavery historiography and literary theory, see Ronald A. T. Judy, *(Dis)Forming the American Canon: African-Arabic Slave Narratives and the Vernacular* (Minneapolis: Univ. of Minnesota Press, 1993), 33–48.

44. Frederick Douglass, *Narrative of the Life of Frederick Douglass, an American Slave, Written By Himself* (1845) in *The Frederick Douglass Papers,* ed. John W. Blassingame et al., ser. 2, vol. 1 (New Haven, CT: Yale Univ. Press, 1999), 37.

45. "Narrative of the Life and Escape of William Wells Brown," in William Wells Brown, *Clotel, or The President's Daughter: a Narrative of Life in the United States,* ed. Robert S. Levine (1853; repr. Boston: Bedford/St. Martin's, 2000), 65.

46. The following survey examines antebellum slave narratives that were written, not dictated, by their authors. The exception is Solomon Northrup, whose narrative was recorded by a white editor. Like many scholars, I am greatly indebted to William Andrews for making the complete corpus of American slave narratives available online: "North American Slave Narratives," Documenting the American South, University of North Carolina Library, http://docsouth.unc.edu/neh.

47. Douglass, *Narrative of the Life,* 37; Juan Francisco Manzano, *The Autobiography of a Slave,* trans. Evelyn Picon Garfield (Detroit: Wayne State Univ. Press,

1996), 105; Peter Randolph, *Sketches of Slave Life* (Boston, 1855), 26–27. Also see Cornelius, *When I Can Read My Title Clear,* 72–73.

48. *Experience and Personal Narrative of Uncle Tom Jones, Who Was for Forty Years a Slave* (Boston: H.P. Skinner, [1854–1855]), 15

49. Solomon Northrup, *Twelve Years a Slave,* ed. Sue Eakin and Joseph Logsdon (Baton Rouge: Louisiana State Univ. Press, 1968), 175–176; William Hayden, *Narrative of William Hayden, Containing a Faithful Account of His Travels for a Number of Years, Whilst a Slave, in the South; Written By Himself* (Cincinnati, 1846), 32. Hayden presumably means "walnut bark and *copperas,*" the latter being a common name for ferrous sulfate.

50. Henry Bibb, *Narrative of the Life and Adventures of Henry Bibb, an American Slave, Written by Himself* (1849), repr. in *Slave Narratives,* ed. William L. Andrews and Henry Louis Gates, Jr. (New York: Library of America, 2000), 516–517. On learning to write as an adult, see Jeanne R. Paratore et al., "Writing in Immigrant Families: Parents and Children Writing at Home," in *Learning to Write, Writing to Learn: Theory and Research in Practice,* ed. Roselmina Indrisano and Jeanne R. Paratore (Newark, DE: International Reading Association, 2005), 97–119, and Susan L. Lytle, "Living Literacy: Rethinking Development in Adulthood," in *Literacy: A Critical Sourcebook,* ed. Ellen Cushman et al. (Boston: Bedford/St. Martin's, 2001), 382.

51. Cornelius, *When I Can Read My Title Clear,* 70. Also see Christopher Span, *From Cotton Field to Schoolhouse: African American Education in Mississippi, 1862–1875* (Chapel Hill: Univ. of North Carolina Press, 2009), 37.

52. The "direction" on a letter was the period's customary term for what we call the address.

53. On nineteenth-century readers and composition books, and the differences between them, see Jean Ferguson Carr, Stephen L. Carr, and Lucille M. Schultz, *Archives of Instruction: Nineteenth-Century Rhetorics, Readers, and Composition Books in the United States* (Carbondale: Southern Illinois Univ. Press, 2005).

2. The Private Life of the Literate Slave

1. Letters by currently enslaved writers have been published in John Blassingame, ed., *Slave Testimony: Two Centuries of Letters, Speeches, Interviews, and Autobiographies* (Baton Rouge: Louisiana State Univ. Press, 1977), 1–119; Randall M. Miller, ed., *Dear Master: Letters of a Slave Family* (Athens: Univ. of Georgia Press, 1990); Robert S. Starobin, ed., *Blacks in Bondage: Letters of American Slaves* (1974; repr. New York: Markus Wiener Publishing, 1988); Carter G. Woodson, ed., *The Mind of the Negro as Reflected in Letters Written During the Crisis, 1800–1860* (1926; repr. New York: Russell & Russell, 1969), esp. 511–624. Also see "Slave Letters," Duke University Rare Book, Manuscript, and Special Collections Library, http://library.duke.edu/rubenstein/research/guides/slaveletters.html. For scholarly

examinations of letters written by enslaved people, see Phillip Troutman, "Correspondences in Black and White: Sentiment and the Slave Market Revolution," in *New Studies in the History of American Slavery,* ed. Edward E. Baptist and Stephanie M. H. Camp (Athens: Univ. of Georgia Press, 2006), 211–242; and Ben Schiller, "Learning Their Letters: Critical Literacy, Epistolary Culture, and Slavery in the Antebellum South," *Southern Quarterly* 45, no. 3 (Spring 2008): 11–29.

2. Maria Perkins to Richard Perkins, 8 October 1852, Ulrich B. Phillips Papers (MS 397), ser. I, box 3, folder 47, Manuscripts and Archives, Yale University Library.

3. The modern field of composition and rhetoric has since the 1970s largely centered around the conviction that writing is a "process of discovery through language," and the idea is intuitive to most writers. Donald M. Murray, "Teach Writing as a Process not Product," in Richard L. Graves, ed., *Rhetoric and Composition: A Sourcebook for Teachers* (Rochelle Park, NJ: Hayden Book Company, 1976), 80.

4. Maria's letter to Richard bears no direction, but Edward L. Ayers locates Richard in Staunton. *In the Presence of Mine Enemies: War in the Heart of America, 1859–1863* (New York: Norton, 2003), 22. No official records of Maria Perkins have been found. As a slave, she would not have been tallied in the census until after the war (if she lived to see it), and the 1870 census lists no Maria Perkins in Virginia. Gayle M. Schulman, "Site of Slave Block?" *Magazine of Albemarle County History* 58 (2000): 64–86.

5. William G. Shade, *Democratizing the Old Dominion: Virginia and the Second Party System, 1824–1861* (Charlottesville: Univ. Press of Virginia, 1996), 38; Schulman, "Slaves at the University of Virginia," http://www.locohistory.org /Albemarle/Slaves_at_the_University_of_Virginia.pdf, 10, 29n48, 17–19. On the role of the domestic slave trade in eliciting letters between family members, see Troutman, "Correspondences in Black and White."

6. Tamara Thornton, *Handwriting in America: A Cultural History* (New Haven, CT: Yale Univ. Press, 1996), 32. Late-antebellum spelling books and writing manuals attest to the persistence of the long *s;* see, for instance, *The Fashionable American Letter Writer* (Newark: Benjamin Olds, 1839), 158, and J. E. Worcester, *Pronouncing Spelling-Book of the English Language* (Boston: Hickling, Swan, and Brewer, 1859), 159. On white southerners' involvement in slave education, see Janet Duitsman Cornelius, *When I Can Read My Title Clear: Literacy, Slavery, and Religion in the Antebellum South* (Columbia: Univ. of South Carolina Press, 1991), 105–124.

7. For a description of a typical court day, see Laura Edwards, *The People and Their Peace: Legal Culture and the Transformation of Inequality in the Post-Revolutionary South* (Chapel Hill: Univ. of North Carolina Press, 2009), 75–76.

8. Ronald J. Zboray, "The Letter and the Fiction Reading Public in Antebellum America," *Journal of American Culture* 10 (1987): 28; David Henkin, *The Postal*

Age: The Emergence of Modern Communications in Nineteenth-Century America (Chicago: Univ. of Chicago Press, 2006), 3–4; Charles Morley, *A Practical Guide to Composition* (1839), quoted in Lucille M. Schultz, "Letter-Writing Instruction in Nineteenth-Century Schools in the United States," in *Letter Writing as a Social Practice,* ed. David Barton and Nigel Hall (Philadelphia: John Benjamins, 2000), 115. On letter-writing guidebooks and epistolary conventions, see also Zboray, "The Letter and the Fiction Reading Public," 29, and Henkin, *The Postal Age,* 111–116.

9. Troutman, "Correspondences in Black and White."

10. Titus Shropshire to William McLain, 22 November 1852, in Woodson, *Mind of the Negro,* 59; James Gipson to Dear sir, 6 June 1804, in Starobin, *Blacks in Bondage,* 59; Adam F. Plummer to Emily Plummer, 8 March 1858, in Woodson, *Mind of the Negro,* 524; William Henry to my Dear mis, 3 October 1862, in Starobin, *Blacks in Bondage,* 77; John M. Washington, "Memorys of the Past," in David W. Blight, *A Slave No More: Two Men Who Escaped to Freedom, Including Their Own Narratives of Emancipation* (Orlando: Harcourt, 2007), 173.

11. Abream Scriven to Dinah Jones, 19 September 1858, in Starobin, *Blacks in Bondage,* 58 (also see Decker, *Epistolary Practices,* 87–88); Bruce Redford, *The Converse of the Pen: Acts of Intimacy in the Eighteenth-Century Familiar Letter* (Chicago: Univ. of Chicago Press, 1986), 14, 39.

12. Ulrich Bonnell Phillips, *Life and Labor in the Old South* (1929; repr. Columbia: Univ. of South Carolina Press, 2007), 212.

13. Quoted in John David Smith, " 'Keep 'Em in a Fire-Proof Vault': Pioneer Southern Historians Discover Plantation Records," in *Slavery, Race, and American History: Historical Conflict, Trends, and Method, 1866–1953* (Armonk, NY: M. E. Sharpe, 1999), 142. On Phillips's collection of documents, also see Merton Dillon, *Ulrich Bonnell Phillips: Historian of the Old South* (Baton Rouge: Louisiana State Univ. Press, 1985), chap. 6.

14. On the Newby letters, see Troutman "Correspondences in Black and White," 211, and Blassingame, *Slave Testimony,* 116–119. On Brown, see Troutman, "Correspondences in Black and White," 219, and Blassingame, *Slave Testimony,* 46–47. Hobbs's letter appears in Elizabeth Keckley, *Behind the Scenes: Thirty Years a Slave, and Four Years in the White House,* ed. Frances Smith Foster (Urbana: Univ. of Illinois Press, 1998), 14–15. For a discussion of the contingencies of the "individualized process of retention, collection, and preservation" affecting the correspondence of ordinary people (in this case, immigrants), see David Gerber, *Authors of Their Lives: The Personal Correspondence of British Immigrants to North America in the Nineteenth Century* (New York: New York Univ. Press, 2006), 8–9.

15. It should be noted, too, that enslaved people exchanged many letters they did not write themselves; the number of slaves who communicated by letter was undoubtedly greater than the number with written literacy. A slave might dictate a

letter to a literate fellow slave, or free black person, a friendly white person, or even an owner—who might prefer to act as amanuensis, and thus monitor or censor the communication, than to withhold such favors and give slaves extra inducement to learn to write on the sly.

16. Kenneth M. Stampp, "Rebels and Sambos: The Search for the Negro's Personality in Slavery," *The Journal of Southern History* 37, no. 3 (August 1971): 367.

17. John W. Blassingame, "Using the Testimony of Ex-Slaves: Approaches and Problems," *The Journal of Southern History* 41, no. 4 (November 1975): 480. For an extended discussion of slavery historiography and the study of slave narratives, see Ronald A. T. Judy, *Dis(Forming) the American Canon: African-Arabic Slave Narratives and the Vernacular* (Minneapolis: Univ. of Minnesota Press, 1993), 33–48. A brief sampling of studies of nineteenth-century African American oral and material culture might include Lawrence W. Levine, *Black Culture and Black Consciousness: Afro-American Folk Thought from Slavery to Freedom* (New York: Oxford Univ. Press, 1977); Sterling Stuckey, *Slave Culture: Nationalist Theory and the Foundations of Black America* (New York: Oxford Univ. Press, 1987); Lindon Barrett, "Figuring Others of Value: *Singing* Voices, *Signing* Voices, and African American Culture," in *Blackness and Value: Seeing Double* (Cambridge: Cambridge Univ. Press, 1999), 55–93; Theresa A. Singleton, ed., *The Archaeology of Slavery and Plantation Life* (Orlando: Academic Press, 1985); and Charles H. Fairbanks, "The Plantation Archaeology of the Southeastern Coast, *Historical Archaeology* 18, no. 1 (1984): 1–14. For a discussion of the thematics and performance of slave testimony in literature and culture, as opposed to the evidentiary problems of slavery historiography, see Dwight A. McBride, *Impossible Witnesses: Truth, Abolitionism, and Slave Testimony* (New York: New York Univ. Press, 2001).

18. A record card I once ran across in the Freedmen and Southern Society Project papers carries a researcher's penciled notation: "great doc—would be publishable if writer were more literate."

19. Christopher Clark and Nancy A. Hewitt, *Who Built America? Working People and the Nation's Economy, Politics, Culture, and Society,* vol. 1: *From Conquest and Colonization through 1877* (New York: Worth Publishers, 2000), 505. On gender, marriage, and family structure under slavery, see Herbert Gutman, *The Black Family in Slavery and Freedom, 1750–1925* (New York: Pantheon, 1976); Deborah Gray White, *Ar'n't I a Woman? Female Slaves in the Plantation South,* rev. ed. (New York: Norton, 1999); and esp. Brenda E. Stevenson, *Life in Black and White: Family and Community in the Slave South* (New York: Oxford Univ. Press, 1996).

20. Phillips, *Life and Labor,* 212. For quotations of the Maria Perkins letter relating to issues of family, see Gutman, *The Black Family in Slavery and Freedom,* 35–36; Wilma A. Dunaway, *The African-American Family in Slavery and Emancipation* (Cambridge: Cambridge Univ. Press, 2003), 57; and Linda Kerber and Jane Sherron De Hart, *Women's America: Refocusing the Past,* 6th ed. (New York: Oxford

Univ. Press, 2004), 132. For quotations relating to the domestic slave trade, see Steven Deyle, *Carry Me Back: The Domestic Slave Trade in American Life* (New York: Oxford Univ. Press, 2005), 264; David Brion Davis, *Inhuman Bondage: The Rise and Fall of Slavery in the New World* (New York: Oxford Univ. Press, 2006), 183; Edward L. Ayers, *In the Presence of Mine Enemies,* 22–23; and Ira Berlin, *The Making of African America: The Four Great Migrations* (New York: Viking, 2010), 119. Quotations relating to slaves' property appear in John T. Schlotterbeck, "The Internal Economy of Slavery in Rural Piedmont Virginia," *Slavery and Abolition* 12, no. 1 (May 1991): 177; and Dylan C. Penningroth, *The Claims of Kinfolk: African American Property and Community in the Nineteenth-Century South* (Chapel Hill: Univ. of North Carolina Press, 2003), 79–80.

21. Blassingame, *Slave Testimony,* 96–97. Phillips's transcription of the letter in *Life and Labor* was the source text for several reprintings, including Willie Lee Rose, ed., *A Documentary History of Slavery in North America* (New York: Oxford Univ. Press, 1976), 151; Gutman, *The Black Family in Slavery and Freedom,* 35–36, and David Brion Davis, ed., *Antebellum American Culture: An Interpretive Anthology* (1979; repr. University Park: Pennsylvania State Univ. Press, 1997), 324–325. From 1929 until 1977, only Phillips's transcription was in circulation; from 1977 until the late 1990s (when Edward Ayers included the letter in the online archive *The Valley of the Shadow*), Blassingame's version was the only other available transcription. The deviation between Phillips's "Maria" and Blassingame's "Marie" marks the provenance of later scholars' quotations: before even looking at the endnotes of a book that quotes Perkins, one knows that a historian who calls her "Marie" had Blassingame's *Slave Testimony* open on his or her desk. Every other reprint of the letter has drawn directly or indirectly from Phillips.

22. Kerber and De Hart, *Women's America,* 132. Elaine Tyler May, *Barren in the Promised Land: Childless Americans and the Pursuit of Happiness* (New York: Basic Books, 1995), 57 (ellipses in original).

23. Anthony B. Pinn, *Terror and Triumph: The Nature of Black Religion* (Minneapolis: Fortress Press, 2003), 45; Deyle, *Carry Me Back,* 264. Of course, I do not mean to say that the precise details of Blassingame's or Phillips's transcription swayed any analysis of the evidence. It is entirely reasonable to suppose that these scholars' own historiographical and ideological predispositions influenced both their reading of the Perkins letter and their choice of source text.

24. Phillips silently corrected Perkins's mistake in line eleven (or he unthinkingly transcribed what he expected the text to say), rendering the second "told" as "took." As a result, most subsequent printed iterations of the letter mistakenly use "took."

25. Rose, *A Documentary History,* 151 (emphasis in original); Davis, *Antebellum American Culture,* 322; Stuart Weems Bruchey, *Enterprise: The Dynamic Economy of a Free People* (Cambridge, MA: Harvard Univ. Press, 1990), 247; Debra Newman

Ham, ed., *The African-American Mosaic: A Library of Congress Resource Guide for the Study of Black History and Culture* (Washington, DC: Library of Congress, 1993), 11.

26. On the self as controller and controlled, and for a useful introduction to cultural-studies approaches to interiority, see Joel Pfister, "On Conceptualizing the Cultural History of Emotional and Psychological Life in America," in *Inventing the Psychological: Toward a Cultural History of Emotional Life in America,* ed. Joel Pfister and Nancy Schnog (New Haven, CT: Yale Univ. Press, 1997), 17–59. For a recent critique of twentieth-century thought's general turn away from discussions of interiority, see Marilynne Robinson, *Absence of Mind: The Dispelling of Inwardness from the Modern Myth of the Self* (New Haven, CT: Yale Univ. Press, 2010).

27. George M. Frederickson, *The Black Image in the White Mind: The Debate on Afro-American Character and Destiny, 1817–1914* (1971; repr. Middletown, CT: Wesleyan Univ. Press, 1987), 102.

28. Frederick Douglass, *Narrative of the Life of Frederick Douglass, an American Slave, Written by Himself,* ed. David W. Blight (Boston and New York: Bedford/St. Martin's, 2003), 83.

29. On reading, writing, and access to human interiority, see David Rosen and Aaron Santesso, *The Watchman in Pieces: Surveillance, Literature, and Liberal Personhood* (New Haven, CT: Yale Univ. Press, forthcoming).

30. George M. Horton, *The Poetical Works of George M. Horton, the Colored Bard of North Carolina, to which is Prefixed the Life of the Author, Written By Himself* (Hillsborough [NC]: Heartt, 1845), xiv, viii. On Horton's professional authorship, see Leon Jackson, "The Black Bard and the Black Market," in *The Business of Letters: Authorial Economies in Antebellum America* (Stanford, CA: Stanford Univ. Press, 2008), 53–88.

31. Horton, *Poetical Works,* xvii–xviii (emphasis added).

32. Dave and his work have received brief treatment in numerous overviews of southern and African American art and folk culture, which generally provide the known outlines of Dave's biography and situate his work in the context of South Carolina's Edgefield District, a center of southern pottery production. See Mark Hewitt and Nancy Sweezy, ed., *The Potter's Eye: Art and Tradition in North Carolina Pottery* (Chapel Hill: Univ. of North Carolina Press, 2005), 122–127; John Michael Vlach, *The Afro-American Tradition in Decorative Arts* (Cleveland: Cleveland Museum of Art, 1978), 76–81, and "Arts and Crafts, Slave," in *Dictionary of Afro-American Slavery,* ed. Randall M. Miller and John David Smith (Westport, CT: Greenwood, 1997), 64–70; John A. Burrison, "Afro-American Folk Pottery in the South," in *Afro-American Folk Art and Crafts,* ed. William Ferris (Boston: G. K. Hall, 1983), 332–350. The clearest synthesis of this material is Aaron De Groft, "Eloquent Vessels/Poetics of Power: The Heroic Stoneware of 'Dave the Potter,'" *Winterthur Portfolio* 33, no. 4 (Winter 1998): 249–260. Cinda K. Baldwin studies

Dave's work in the context of an extensive history of pottery production in the Edgefield District in *Great and Noble Jar: Traditional Stoneware of South Carolina* (Athens: Univ. of Georgia Press, 1995). Jill Beute Koverman, ed., *I Made This Jar: The Life and Works of the Enslaved African-American Potter, Dave* (Columbia, SC: McKissick Museum, 1998), is the catalog of an exhibition at the University of South Carolina, the only exhibit that has been devoted entirely to Dave's work. *I Made This Jar* includes several essays on Dave and provides more photographs of his work than any other published source. For an extended, theoretically informed analysis of Dave's poetry and pottery, see Michael A. Chaney, "Throwing Identity in the Poetry-Pottery of Dave the Potter," in *Fugitive Vision: Slave Image and Black Identity in Antebellum Narrative* (Bloomington: Indiana Univ. Press, 2008), 176–208. For a general treatment of Dave's life, work, and context, written by a descendant of Dave's owners, see Leonard Todd, *Carolina Clay: The Life and Legend of the Slave Potter Dave* (New York: Norton, 2008).

33. See Vlach, *Afro-American Tradition,* 77, and "Arts and Crafts, Slave," 66; Burrison, "Afro-American Folk Pottery"; and De Groft, "Eloquent Vessels/Poetics of Power"; as well as Cinda Baldwin, "Edgefield Face Vessels: African-American Contributions to American Folk Art," *American Visions: The Magazine of Afro-American Culture* 5, no. 4 (August 1990): 19. Leonard Todd expresses skepticism of scholars' assertions that Dave was a typesetter for the *Edgefield Hive;* the evidence indeed is not definitive, but neither are Todd's arguments to the contrary fully proven; see Todd, *Carolina Clay,* 39–53. Georgia statute quoted in Heather Andrea Williams, *Self-Taught: African American Education in Slavery and Freedom* (Chapel Hill: Univ. of North Carolina Press, 2005), 204. Slowness and repetition are common to most people's experiences of literacy education, of course, though people who learned as children tend not to remember those experiences as vividly as Jones does.

34. Jill Koverman has explained Dave's process in an interview (Zoe Ingalls, "A Slave, A Poet, A Potter: Preserving the Legacy of David Drake," *Chronicle of Higher Education,* 31 July 1998) and in *I Made This Jar,* 29. Also see Baldwin, "Edgefield Face Vessels," 19. I am additionally indebted to Alison Ehrmann Hager for acquainting me with the ins and outs of throwing large pots.

35. Baldwin, *Great and Noble Jar,* 76; Vlach, *Afro-American Tradition,* 79–80; couplet transcribed from photograph in Koverman, *I Made This Jar,* 62; Todd, *Carolina Clay,* 241.

36. Quoted in Todd, *Carolina Clay,* 238.

37. Quoted in Koverman, *I Made This Jar,* 28, and Baldwin, *Great and Noble Jar,* 195. The latter text is from 1840. "Iterative" denotes a mode of narration "where a single narrative utterance takes upon itself several occurrences together of the same event." Gérard Genette, *Narrative Discourse: An Essay in Method,* trans. Jane E. Lewin (Ithaca, NY: Cornell Univ. Press, 1980), 116.

38. Couplet quoted in Todd, *Carolina Clay*, 240; for description of the vessel, see Koverman, *I Made This Jar*, 97.

39. For images of the unexplained dots and slash marks on many of Dave's pots, see Baldwin, *Great and Noble Jar*, 78, and Todd, *Carolina Clay*, sixth inset page facing 144. Such was also the practice of some ancient Greeks; see Robin Osborne and Alexandra Pappas, "Writing on Archaic Greek Pottery," in *Art and Inscriptions in the Ancient World*, ed. Zahra Newby and Ruth Leader-Newby (Cambridge: Cambridge Univ. Press, 2006), 131–155.

40. Henri Bergson, *Duration and Simultaneity, with Reference to Einstein's Theory*, trans. Leon Jacobson (Indianapolis: Bobbs-Merrill, 1965), 50.

41. Walter Johnson, *Soul by Soul: Life inside the Antebellum Slave Market* (Cambridge, MA: Harvard Univ. Press, 1999), 48–49. In truth, Brady did live in Scottsville; see Troutman, "Correspondences in Black and White," 239n31. Previously unfamiliar slaves became acquainted with one another "in the trade." Kept in the close quarters of coffles, jails, and trading pens, or simply brought together at auctions or on court day, they struck up conversations and exchanged information about themselves and about owners past, current, and potential. See Johnson, *Soul by Soul*, esp. 63–77 and 162–188. On the domestic slave trade in general, see Michael Tadman, *Speculators and Slaves: Masters, Trades, and Slaves in the Old South* (Madison: Univ. of Wisconsin Press, 1989), and Steven Deyle, *Carry Me Back: The Domestic Slave Trade in American Life* (New York: Oxford Univ. Press, 2005).

42. John Boston to Mrs. Elizabeth Boston, 12 January 1862, enclosed in Maj. Genl. George B. McClellan to Hon. Edwin Stanton, 21 January 1862, A-587 1862, Letters Received, ser. 12, Record Group 94, National Archives Building, Washington DC [K-23]; published in *Freedom: A Documentary History of Emancipation, 1861–1867*, ser. 1, vol. 1: *The Destruction of Slavery*, ed. Ira Berlin et al. (Cambridge: Cambridge Univ. Press, 1985), 357–358.

3. Writing a Life in Slavery and Freedom

1. Adam Francis Plummer Diary, Anacostia Community Museum, Smithsonian Institution, http://anacostia.si.edu/Plummer/Plummer_Diary.htm, 14, 137–138 (page numbers refer to the PDF file of the holograph). For an overview of Plummer's life, see The Students of History 429, *Knowing Our History: African American Slavery and the University of Maryland*, University of Maryland, http://www.history.umd.edu/slavery, 27–30.

2. Plummer Diary, 13, 12, 16, 159; Emily Plummer to Adam Plummer, 2 July 1856, in Carter G. Woodson, ed., *The Mind of the Negro as Reflected in Letters Written during the Crisis* (1926; repr. New York: Russell & Russell, 1969), 523.

3. Houston A. Baker, Jr., "Autobiographical Acts and the Voice of the Southern Slave," in *The Slave's Narrative*, ed. Charles T. Davis and Henry Louis Gates, Jr.

(New York: Oxford Univ. Press, 1985), 253. Baker goes on to contend that "the voice of the unwritten self, once it is subjected to the linguistic codes, literary conventions, and audience expectations of a literate population, is perhaps never again the authentic voice of black American slavery" (253). On racialized definitions of personhood, see Henry Louis Gates, Jr., *Figures in Black: Words, Signs and the "Racial" Self* (New York: Oxford Univ. Press, 1987) and *The Signifying Monkey: A Theory of African-American Literary Criticism* (New York: Oxford Univ. Press, 1988), 127–139.

4. William L. Andrews, *To Tell a Free Story: The First Century of Afro-American Autobiography, 1760–1865* (Urbana: Univ. of Illinois Press, 1986), 9. Andrews's book remains the most thorough study of antebellum African American autobiography. Also see Sidonie Smith, *Where I'm Bound: Patterns of Slavery and Freedom in Black American Autobiography* (Westport, CT: Greenwood Press, 1974).

5. Mary J. Bratton, ed., "Fields's Observations: The Slave Narrative of a Nineteenth-Century Virginian," *Virginia Magazine of History and Biography* 88, no. 1 (January 1980): 92.

6. "Memorys of the Past" was published for the first time in David Blight, *A Slave No More: Two Men Who Escaped to Freedom including Their Own Narratives of Emancipation* (Orlando: Harcourt, 2007). It also is available as *John Washington's Civil War: A Slave Narrative,* ed. Crandall Shifflett (Baton Rouge: Louisiana State Univ. Press, 2008).

7. Washington, "Memorys of the Past," in Blight, *A Slave No More,* 169. My quotations from "Memorys" represent my own transcription from the original manuscript in the John Washington Papers at the Massachusetts Historical Society in Boston or from the Library of Congress's microfilm of that manuscript. For readers' reference, all quotations from Washington's post-emancipation narrative will be keyed to the appropriate page number in Blight, *A Slave No More.* On the few occasions when my transcription differs substantially from Blight's, I offer an explanation in the notes. Washington recalls that his mother's journey away happened "about christmas" of 1850, which is in keeping with the common practice of hiring out slaves for yearly terms, with transfer and travel taking place during the "holiday" period between Christmas and New Year's. Here and throughout this chapter, I am indebted for details of Washington's biography to Blight, *A Slave No More,* chap. 1: "The Rappahannock River."

8. Washington, "Memorys," 172, 173. Janet Duitsman Cornelius, in her study of slave literacy, identifies a former slave who cited a similar reason for learning to write—to be able to exchange love letters without a slave owner's knowledge. Cornelius, *"When I Can Read My Title Clear": Literacy, Slavery, and Religion in the Antebellum South* (Columbia: Univ. of South Carolina Press, 1991), 73.

9. Washington, "Memorys," 173–174. Blight and Shifflett both indicate "Cowleys Spelling Book," and Washington's *m* does somewhat resemble a *w,* but

the title in question undoubtedly is a text by John Comly, a Quaker schoolmaster whose *New Spelling Book, Adapted to the Different Classes of Pupils; Compiled with a View to Render the Arts of Spelling and Reading Easy and Pleasant to Children,* was reprinted numerous times during the antebellum era.

10. David Henkin describes the stunning ubiquity of certain stock phrases in the opening lines of nineteenth-century correspondence, and he argues, "Personal letters began with references to taking 'pen in hand,' inscribing 'these few lines,' or having 'an opportunity,' not because such locutions necessarily captured the goals and values of correspondence, but because they marked a piece of writing as properly epistolary." Henkin, *The Postal Age: The Emergence of Modern Communications in Nineteenth-Century America* (Chicago: Univ. of Chicago Press, 2006), 112–113.

11. Washington, "Memorys," 174. William J. Walker led the Shiloh Baptist Church, an African American congregation in Fredericksburg that reestablished itself in Washington, D.C., after emancipation. Blight, *A Slave No More,* 94.

12. See James C. Scott, *Domination and the Arts of Resistance: Hidden Transcripts* (New Haven, CT: Yale Univ. Press, 1992).

13. Washington, "Memorys," 173; Diary, John Washington Papers, Massachusetts Historical Society, 18; Frances E. Percival, ed., *The Angel Visitor; or the Voices of the Heart* (Philadelphia: John E. Potter, 1857), 25.

14. "Scorn Not the Lowly," *Merry's Museum, Parley's Magazine, Woodworth's Cabinet, and the Schoolfellow* 41–42, ed. Robert Merry and Hiram Hatchet (New York: J. N. Stearns, 1861), 177. Washington may have exchanged reading material with his future wife. In one of her letters to him, she copied down four lines from a poem called "Smiles" that had appeared in an old issue of the same magazine; see Diary, Washington Papers, 15, and *Robert Merry's Museum* 5 (1844): 48.

15. Autobiography, John Washington Papers, Massachusetts Historical Society, 7. Some internal references among the Washington Papers refer to "Memorys of the Past" as an "autobiography," as indeed it is. For the sake of clarity, I refer to the 1873 text by the title Washington gave it, "Memorys of the Past," and the earlier, untitled text—the enslaved narrative—as his "autobiography."

16. There is evidence that Douglass's *Narrative* circulated surreptitiously in the South—see Dickson D. Bruce Jr., *The Origins of African American Literature, 1680–1865* (Charlottesville: Univ. of Virginia Press, 2001), 247—but very few slaves would have acquired it in such a way. In certain respects, Washington's autobiography resembles Hannah Crafts's *The Bondwoman's Narrative,* another text that does not fit our general understanding of an early African American genre and that draws upon popular Victorian-era fiction. Unlike *The Bondwoman's Narrative,* though, Washington's autobiography was written by a still-enslaved author. It is possible that both Crafts and Washington were devoted readers of *Harper's.* In 1852

and 1853, the magazine serialized Charles Dickens's *Bleak House,* which strongly influenced *The Bondwoman's Narrative.* (*Frederick Douglass's Paper* serialized the Dickens novel, too.) See Jennifer Phegley, "Literary Piracy, Nationalism, and Women Readers in *Harper's New Monthly Magazine, 1850–1855," American Periodicals: A Journal of History, Criticism, and Bibliography* 14, no. 1 (2004): 63–90; Hollis Robbins, "Blackening *Bleak House:* Hannah Crafts's *The Bondwoman's Narrative,"* in *In Search of Hannah Crafts: Critical Essays on The Bondwoman's Narrative,* ed. Henry Louis Gates, Jr., and Hollis Robbins (New York: Basic Books, 2004), 71–86; and William A. Gleason, *Sites Unseen: Architecture, Race, and American Literature* (New York: New York Univ. Press, 2011), 58–66.

17. Out of twenty-two people named in either the diary or the autobiography, I have located nine in the Fredericksburg census records for 1850 or 1860, all listed as black or mulatto. The census counted only free persons; others may not have appeared in the census for a variety of reasons, but surely at least some, like Washington himself, did not appear because they were enslaved. "1850 List of Free Inhabitants" and "1860 List of Free Inhabitants," Fredericksburg Research Resources, Center for Historic Preservation, University of Mary Washington, http://resources.umwhisp.org/fredburg.htm.

18. Autobiography, Washington Papers, 7.

19. Washington probably discarded pages of the diary as he finished with them, although it is conceivable that there were no previous diary entries—that Washington had not kept a diary prior to July 5, 1858, and that he composed the earlier portions of the autobiography from memory rather than from existing writings. Either way, the overlapping portions of the two texts—roughly the month of July—offer both draft and revision of the same narrative of events. I have several reasons for concluding that Washington did this work while in Richmond in 1861. The autobiography had to have been written sometime after 1858 (the time of the last events it narrates), and the internal evidence of the text is consistent with composition prior to his escape in 1862; even though Washington never discusses his enslaved status, none of the events he narrates, nor any knowledge he betrays, postdates his emancipation. The handwriting of the autobiography resembles that of his October 1861 letter to Annie more closely than it does any of Washington's other surviving writings (which span the period 1858 to 1873). The most convincing evidence for an 1861 date of composition is that an excerpt of poetry Washington added to the autobiography—a stanza of "Scorn Not the Lowly," quoted above—first appeared in *Merry's Museum* in June 1861. Therefore, at least chapters four and five of the autobiography, which follow this poetic epigraph, must have been written no sooner than the second half of 1861, and no evidence exists to indicate that they were written subsequent to Washington's departure from Richmond.

20. John Washington to Annie Gordon, 27 October 1861, John Washington Papers, Massachusetts Historical Society; Blight, *A Slave No More,* 33. On slaves'

knowledge of political and military news, and their anticipation of the coming of their freedom, see Leon F. Litwack, *Been in the Storm So Long: The Aftermath of Slavery* (New York: Vintage, 1979), 27, and Steven Hahn, *A Nation under Our Feet: Black Political Struggles in the Rural South from Slavery to the Great Migration* (Cambridge, MA: Harvard Univ. Press, 2003), 65–68.

21. Washington to Gordon, 27 October 1861; Washington, "Memorys," 186. "Memorys" makes only one oblique reference to Washington's earlier writings. On the first page of the 1873 text, Washington recalls having to leave Fredericksburg when his mother was hired out to another town, "When I was about 2 years of age." He goes on to say: "I will not promise to Narate the incidents of that Jurney as I did not keep a Diary at that age in a Slave State" (165). This peculiar statement (surely Washington knew free two-year-olds did not keep diaries either) becomes explicable only if the writer did keep a diary at *some* age "in a Slave State."

22. Richard C. Wade, *Slavery in the Cities: The South, 1820–1860* (New York: Oxford Univ. Press, 1964), 327; Midori Takagi, *"Rearing Wolves to Our Own Destruction": Slavery in Richmond, Virginia, 1782–1865* (Charlottesville: Univ. Press of Virginia, 1999), chap. 3.

23. Washington, "Memorys," 186 (unmatched quotation marks in original); Washington to Gordon, 27 October 1861.

24. Washington, "Memorys," 187; Blight, *A Slave No More,* 33.

25. Harriet A. Jacobs, *Incidents in the Life of a Slave Girl, Written by Herself,* ed. Jean Fagan Yellin (Cambridge, MA: Harvard Univ. Press, 1987), 201. Although slave marriages could be and often were discouraged, forbidden, and sundered by slave owners, there is considerable evidence—witness, for instance, Maria Perkins's letter—that enslaved people sustained marital bonds even under forbidding circumstances; see Frances Smith Foster, *'Til Death or Distance Do Us Part: Love and Marriage in African America* (New York: Oxford Univ. Press, 2010). By the time of the Civil War, some white politicians and anti-slavery activists had come to see the freedom to love and to marry as an inviolable human right that must be protected from the depredations of slaveholders; Amy Dru Stanley, "Slave Breeding and Free Love: An Antebellum Argument over Slavery, Capitalism, and Person-hood," lecture, Yale University, 27 September 2010, and "Instead of Waiting for the Thirteenth Amendment: The War Power, Slave Marriage, and Inviolate Human Rights," *American Historical Review* 115, no. 3 (June 2010): 732–765.

26. Diary, 13–14, and Autobiography, 15–16, Washington Papers. If the latter passage seems not similar enough to the former one to be regarded as a direct revision, consider that neither the words "encourage" nor "discourage," nor any variants thereof, appear anywhere in all of Washington's writings besides these two excerpts. Additionally, the diary's report of Annie's rejection concludes by saying that his hope had "perished in its bud." Washington might have picked up this commonplace formulation practically anywhere, but it probably is an echo of the

phrase from "Scorn Not the Lowly," the poem Washington found in *Merry's Museum* in 1861—with its opening line, "Many a bright bud perished"—that he decided to copy down as an epigraph to chapter 4.

27. For earlier examples of black writers adopting the prevailing rhetoric of Anglo-American abolitionism, see Bruce, *Origins of African American Literature,* esp. 74–76.

28. Autobiography, Washington Papers, 22, 17, 23.

29. Diary, 2, and Autobiography, 19, Washington Papers.

30. Autobiography, 18, Washington Papers. Race was no doubt a strange and unstable category for Washington, who was so light-skinned that, when he first met Union soldiers, they were "utterly astonished" to learn he was a slave and not a white man (Washington, "Memorys," 193).

31. Diary, 6–7, Washington Papers.

32. Washington, "Memorys," 165. On the conventions of the slave-narrative genre, see James Olney, " 'I Was Born': Slave Narratives, Their Status as Autobiography and as Literature," in *The Slave's Narrative,* ed. Charles T. Davis and Henry Louis Gates, Jr. (New York: Oxford Univ. Press, 1985), 148–175.

33. Washington, "Memorys," 189, 194–195.

34. Michael Fried, *Realism, Writing, Disfiguration: On Thomas Eakins and Stephen Crane* (Chicago: Univ. of Chicago Press, 1987), 146–147.

35. Eric Foner, *Free Soil, Free Labor, Free Men: The Ideology of the Republican Party before the Civil War* (1970; repr. New York: Oxford Univ. Press, 1995).

36. Washington, "Memorys," 198.

37. The ink sections of the manuscript include corrections made in Washington's hand (some in pencil, some in ink). A struck-through line, discussed below, strongly suggests that he drafted some early sections of "Memorys" before copying them into the composition book in ink.

38. Washington, "Memorys," 203, 205, 207, 208.

39. Ira Berlin et al., eds., *Freedom: A Documentary History of Emancipation, 1861–1867,* ser. 2: *The Black Military Experience* (Cambridge: Cambridge Univ. Press, 1982), 567–570.

40. Washington, "Memorys," 209, 210. Jane E. Schultz, *Women at the Front: Hospital Workers in Civil War America* (Chapel Hill: Univ. of North Carolina Press, 2004), 151; Kate Masur, *An Example for All the Land: Emancipation and the Struggle over Equality in Washington, D.C.* (Chapel Hill: Univ. of North Carolina Press, 2010), 28.

41. A small shred of a separate leaf of paper, as well as some residual binding material, adheres to the lower left corner of manuscript page 129, the page that contains the "interrupted soliloquy." That scrap of paper does not match any torn corners elsewhere in the manuscript, indicating that it is from a page that has not survived—yet the manuscript's pages are complete and numbered sequentially.

Though it is technically possible that Washington ripped out a page because, say, he needed paper to make a grocery list, it would be surprising if he chose for that purpose a page at the very climax of his 100-page manuscript; more likely, he wanted to redo something. There is no evidence that a page has been torn out at any other place in Washington's composition book.

42. Washington, "Memorys," 211–212. The transcription of this passage in Blight, *A Slave No More,* begins with "I then came back," but the word in the manuscript more clearly resembles "out."

43. On slave narratives' role in the rise of American literary realism, see Andrews, *To Tell a Free Story,* 287–290, and Augusta Rohrbach, *Truth Stranger than Fiction: Race, Realism, and the U.S. Literary Marketplace* (New York: Palgrave, 2002), esp. 29–50.

44. Julia A. Stern, *Mary Chesnut's Civil War Epic* (Chicago: Univ. of Chicago Press, 2010).

45. Washington, "Memorys," 174. For Mary Chesnut, proper spelling demonstrated southern gentility and defined the boundaries of social class; she savaged the "atrocious" spelling in letters by Union soldiers and mocked the solecisms of an aspiring young southern lady. *Mary Chesnut's Civil War,* ed. C. Vann Woodward (New Haven, CT: Yale Univ. Press, 1993), 170; and Stern, *Mary Chesnut's Civil War Epic,* 109–110. On Melville, see Elizabeth Renker, *Strike through the Mask: Herman Melville and the Scene of Writing* (Baltimore: Johns Hopkins Univ. Press, 1996), 6–7. In the present quotation, both Blight and Shifflett show "education," but my comparison of that word in the manuscript with other usages of *o* and *u* confirms that Washington spelled it with an *o.* I should note that, in all my transcriptions of Washington's manuscripts (and those of other writers under discussion elsewhere), I give him the benefit of the doubt—that is, I represent his prose as conforming with standard English spelling and usage unless I am entirely convinced, based on careful examination of the manuscript, that it does not. I have been particularly circumspect about attributing misspellings or other errors to a text when to do so, as here, bolsters my interpretation.

46. Washington, "Memorys," 174. Jacobs, *Incidents in the Life of a Slave Girl,* 745.

4. The Written We

1. Allen Guelzo, *Lincoln's Emancipation Proclamation: The End of Slavery in America* (New York: Simon and Schuster, 2004), 171. Many northern army units saw action both near Fredericksburg between April and August and at Antietam in September; see Alan D. Gaff, *On Many a Blood Field: Four Years in the Iron Brigade* (Bloomington: Indiana Univ. Press, 1996).

2. William B. Gould, *Diary of a Contraband: The Civil War Passage of a Black Sailor,* ed. William B. Gould IV (Stanford, CA: Stanford Univ. Press, 2002), 15–17.

3. Susan L. Blake, Review of *Diary of a Contraband, African American Review* 37, no. 2/3 (Summer–Autumn 2003): 453; William B. Gould, Diary, 3 October

1862; *Diary of a Contraband,* 105. The original manuscript of the diary—which was edited by Gould's great-grandson William Gould IV and published in 2002 as *Diary of a Contraband*—resides at the Massachusetts Historical Society. High-resolution images of the manuscript are available at http://goulddiary.stanford.edu. Subsequent citations will provide the date of the diary entry, if not indicated in the main text, followed by the relevant page(s) of the published edition.

4. Gould, *Diary of a Contraband,* 104.

5. Ibid., 8 March 1863, 137.

6. See, for example, Allison Dorsey, *To Build Our Lives Together: Community Formation in Black Atlanta, 1875–1906* (Athens: Univ. of Georgia Press, 2004); Elizabeth McHenry, *Forgotten Readers: Recovering the Lost History of African American Literary Societies* (Durham, NC: Duke Univ. Press, 2002); and Elsa Barkley Brown, "Negotiating and Transforming the Public Sphere: African American Political Life in the Transition from Slavery to Freedom," *Public Culture* 7 (1994): 107–146. The most famous theorization of print culture's role in forging collective consciousness is Benedict Anderson, *Imagined Communities: Reflections on the Origin and Spread of Nationalism,* rev. ed. (New York: Verso, 1991); also germane is Jürgen Habermas, *The Structural Transformation of the Public Sphere: An Inquiry into a Category of Bourgeois Society* (1962), trans. Thomas Burger (Cambridge, MA: MIT Press, 1991), which I discuss further in notes to Chapter 6.

7. Steven Hahn, *A Nation under Our Feet: Black Political Struggles in the Rural South from Slavery to the Great Migration* (Cambridge, MA: Harvard Univ. Press, 2003), quotation on 73. On literacy acquisition among African American soldiers, see Dudley Taylor Cornish, "The Union Army as a School for Negroes," *Journal of Negro History* 37, no. 4 (October 1952): 368–382; John W. Blassingame, "The Union Army as an Educational Institution for Negroes, 1862–1865," *Journal of Negro Education* 34, no. 2 (Spring 1965): 152–159; Robert C. Morris, *Reading, 'Riting, and Reconstruction: The Education of Freedmen in the South, 1861–1870* (Chicago: Univ. of Chicago Press, 1976), 14–15; Ira Berlin et al., eds., *Freedom: A Documentary History of Emancipation, 1861–1867,* ser. 2: *The Black Military Experience* (Cambridge: Cambridge Univ. Press, 1982), 611–632; and Keith Wilson, *Campfires of Freedom: The Camp Life of Black Soldiers during the Civil War* (Kent, OH: Kent State Univ. Press, 2002), chap. 4. All these accounts focus on more or less organized schooling conducted under military auspices. For black soldiers cooperatively learning to read and write on their own, see Heather Andrea Williams, *Self-Taught: African American Education in Slavery and Freedom* (Chapel Hill: Univ. of North Carolina Press, 2005), 45–56.

8. Susie King Taylor, *Reminiscences of My Life in Camp: An African American Woman's Civil War Memoir* (1902; repr. Athens: Univ. of Georgia Press, 2006), 5, 9.

9. Frances Beecher Perkins, "Two Years with a Colored Regiment: A Woman's Experience," *New England Magazine* 23, no. 5 (January 1898): 536; hospital visitor

quoted in Williams, *Self-Taught,* 51; Christopher Looby, ed., *The Complete Civil War Journal and Selected Letters of Thomas Wentworth Higginson* (Chicago: Univ. of Chicago Press, 2000), 172; Elijah Marrs, *Life and History of the Rev. Elijah P. Marrs* (Louisville: Bradley & Gilbert, 1885), 23; [William Channing Gannett and Edward Everett Hale], "The Freedmen at Port Royal," *North American Review* 101 (July 1865): quotation on 3.

10. Looby, *Complete Civil War Journal,* 182; Zack Burden to Mr. Abebrem Lenken, 2 February 1865, B-110 1865, Letters Received, ser. 360, Colored Troops Division, Record Group 94, National Archives, Washington, DC, [B-118], published in *Freedom,* ser. 2, 647–648; Warner Madison to Genral C. B. Fisk, 13 September 1865, enclosed in Bvt. Brig. Gen. N. A. M. Dudley to Capt. Clarke, 30 September 1865, D-66 1865, Registered Letters Received, ser. 3379, Tennessee Assistant Commissioner, Record Group 105, National Archives, Washington, DC [A-6108], published in Steven Hahn et al., eds., *Freedom: A Documentary History of Emancipation, 1861–1867,* ser. 3, vol. 1: *Land and Labor, 1865* (Chapel Hill: Univ. of North Carolina Press, 2008), 270.

11. Quoted in Williams, *Self-Taught,* 205, 209, 207.

12. On white-sanctioned religious gatherings of slaves, see Erskine Clarke, *Dwelling Place: A Plantation Epic* (New Haven, CT: Yale Univ. Press, 2005), which details the life and work of Charles Colcock Jones, a wealthy Georgia planter and minister who was among the most active proponents and practitioners of Christian missionizing among slaves. On slave communities in general and the resilience of their cultural traditions, see John Blassingame, *The Slave Community: Plantation Life in the Antebellum South* (New York: Oxford Univ. Press, 1972); Charles W. Joyner, *Down by the Riverside: A South Carolina Slave Community* (Urbana: Univ. of Illinois Press, 1984); and Herbert Gutman, *The Black Family in Slavery and Freedom* (New York: Pantheon, 1976). For examples of barbecues and balls, respectively, see Clarke, *Dwelling Place,* 328–329, and Julia A. Stern, *Mary Chesnut's Civil War Epic* (Chicago: Univ. of Chicago Press, 2010), 236–238. On maroon colonies in the late eighteenth century, see Ira Berlin, *Many Thousands Gone: The First Two Centuries of Slavery in North America* (Cambridge, MA: Harvard Univ. Press, 1998), 328–329; on maroons in comparative perspective (they were more plentiful in Spanish colonies of the Americas), see Richard Price, ed., *Maroon Societies: Rebel Slave Communities in the Americas* (Baltimore: Johns Hopkins Univ. Press, 1979); and for a somewhat overstated account of maroon colonies in North America, see Herbert Aptheker, "Maroons within the Present Limits of the United States," *Journal of Negro History* 24, no. 2 (April 1939): 167–184.

13. For accounts that stress the vulnerability of slave families and community relations, see Brenda E. Stevenson, *Life in Black and White: Family and Community in the Slave South* (New York: Oxford Univ. Press, 1996), and Clarke, *Dwelling Place,* 322–324, 413–416.

14. "Colored Soldier" to A. Lincoln, 26 February 1865, Beaufort, SC, box 111, A-137 (1865), Letters Received, ser. 360, Colored Troops Division, Record Group 94, National Archives [B-114]. The writer of the letter, who worked in ink, wrote the letter *g* by starting at the top of the letter and forming a circle counterclockwise, before dropping down to make the tail; the novice with the pencil makes *g's* out of two clockwise loops.

15. *Freedom,* ser. 2, 661–663.

16. Ira Berlin et al., eds., *Freedom: A Documentary History of Emancipation, 1861–1867,* ser. 1, vol. 2: *The Wartime Genesis of Free Labor: The Upper South* (Cambridge: Cambridge Univ. Press, 1993), 166; *Freedom,* ser. 2, 725, 642–643; unsigned letter to Edward M. Stanton, 7 March 1866, A-52 1866, Letters Received, series 360, Colored Troops Division, Record Group 94, National Archives [B-207], also published in *Freedom,* ser. 2, 515–516.

17. Zacharia Jefferson to editors of the *Lyceum Observer,* [30] July 1864, and [James] H. Freeman to Madam, 19 August 1864, both enclosed in Rebecca Guy to the Adjutant General of the Army, 11 March 1865, G-42 1865, Letters Received Relating to Recruiting, ser. 366, Colored Troops Division, Record Group 94, National Archives [B-348]. The Freeman letter is transcribed and published in *Freedom,* ser. 2, 600–601.

18. Gould, *Diary of a Contraband,* 13 April 1863, 143; 14 March 1863, 138; 21 March 1863, 140; 27 March 1863, 142; 25 May 1863, 143; 10 December 1862, 120.

19. Xavier Pla, "The Diaries of Josep Pla: Reflections on the Personal Diary, Draft Diary, and Elaborated Diary," in *Marginal Voices, Marginal Forms: Diaries in European Literature and History,* ed. Rachael Langford and Russell West (Amsterdam: Rodopi, 1999), 128. Philippe Lejeune enumerates four functions of diaries: "to express oneself," "to reflect," "to freeze time," and "to take pleasure in writing"; see "How Do Diaries End?" *Biography* 24, no. 1 (Winter 2001): 99–112. For further definition of the diary genre, see Felicity A. Nussbaum, "Toward Conceptualizing Diary," in James Olney, ed., *Studies in Autobiography* (New York: Oxford Univ. Press, 1988), 128–140; Alain Corbin, "Backstage," in *A History of Private Life,* vol. 4: *From the Fires of Revolution to the Great War,* ed. Michelle Perrot, trans. Arthur Goldhammer (Cambridge, MA: Harvard Univ. Press, 1990), 497–502; and Steven E. Kagle, "The Diary in Nineteenth-Century America," in *Early Nineteenth-Century American Diary Literature* (Boston: Twayne, 1986).

20. See editor's annotation in Gould, *Diary of a Contraband,* 120.

21. See manuscript entries for 18 May and 11 September 1865.

22. Gould, *Diary of a Contraband,* 153, 151.

23. Ibid., 1–2 July 1864, 199; for the minister's visit, see Gould, "A Portion of the Cruise of the U.S. Steam Frigate 'Niagara,'" in *Diary of a Contraband,* 77.

24. Ibid., 16 February 1863, 133.

25. Brown, "Negotiating and Transforming the Public Sphere," 125.

26. Gould, *Diary of a Contraband,* 19 October 1862, 108; 6 November 1862, 111; 13 November 1862, 113. Identical passages appear elsewhere in the first months' entries.

27. Ibid., 16 October 1862, 107; 12 February 1863, 132; 18 and 21 November 1862, 115–116; 27 December 1862, 123. The *Cambridge* was rated for a complement of ninety-six, according to the U.S. Navy's *Dictionary of American Naval Fighting Ships,* http://www.history.navy.mil/danfs. Classical scholars have analyzed the protean *we* of Herodotus's *Histories,* with one interpreter offering a distinction between "an ethnographic *we,* and an authorial *we*"—that is to say, a *we* that refers to a distinct group of actors within the history narrated, and a *we* that denotes a narrating presence or voice. David Chamberlain, " 'We the Others': Interpretive Community and Plural Voice in Herodotus," *Classical Antiquity* 20, no. 1 (April 2001): 8–9. As the examples above demonstrate, Gould's *we* generally tends more toward the ethnographic than the authorial, but, as we will see, it takes Gould some time to define the *ethnos* to which he belongs.

28. If Gould's plural voice is a way of speaking *for* his fellow sailors, it is, in these early portions of the diary, more desirous than political; it bespeaks an interest in becoming one with them, not in representing them. Robert S. Levine has studied the ways two major African American leaders conceived the relationship of an individual to his (racial) community; see *Martin Delany, Frederick Douglass, and the Politics of Representative Identity* (Chapel Hill: Univ. of North Carolina Press, 1997). But Gould's grammar of affiliation more closely resembles the modes of "representation" at issue in Jay Grossman's analysis of Walt Whitman in *Reconstituting the American Renaissance: Emerson, Whitman, and the Politics of Representation* (Durham, NC: Duke Univ. Press, 2003). Though certainly with less explicitness (or panache) than Whitman's 1855 *Leaves of Grass,* Gould's diary presents a speaker—an *I*—who is virtually connected with many others, and although Gould's understated diary never gestures toward the erotic possibilities of such connection, it is easy to imagine him in the role of Whitman's "twenty-ninth bather." The famously homosocial setting of a ship's close quarters likely intensified, even if it did not inspire, the communal outlook of the diary. Of course, and as we shall see both with Gould and in Chapter 5, such an outlook inevitably becomes political, even if it does not begin that way.

29. Gould, *Diary of a Contraband,* 113.

30. Donald L. Canney, *Lincoln's Navy: The Ships, Men and Organization, 1861–65* (Annapolis, MD: Naval Institute Press, 1998), 122. During its days as a receiving ship, the *Ohio* was rated for a complement of 840 men *(Dictionary of American Naval Fighting Ships).*

31. *Lowell (Mass.) Daily Citizen and News,* 29 May 1863, quotation on 2; *Liberator,* 5 June 1863, quotation on 91; "immense number" quoted in Luis

Fenollosa Emilio, *A Brave Black Regiment: The History of the Fifty-Fourth Regiment of Massachusetts Volunteer Infantry, 1863–1865* (1894; repr. New York: Da Capo, 1995), 33; *Christian Recorder,* 30 May 1863; Russell Duncan, *Where Death and Glory Meet: Colonel Robert Gould Shaw and the Fifty-Fourth Massachusetts Infantry* (Athens: Univ. of Georgia Press, 1999), 83–88; Harriet Jacobs quoted in Jean Fagan Yellin, *Harriet Jacobs: A Life* (New York: Basic Civitas, 2004), 168–169.

32. Quoted in *Douglass' Monthly,* August 1863, 852.

33. Thomas H. O'Connor, *Civil War Boston: Home Front and Battlefield* (Boston: Northeastern Univ. Press, 1997), 140; Barnet Schecter, *The Devil's Own Work: The Civil War Draft Riots and the Fight to Reconstruct America* (New York: Walker, 2005), 202–203. Also see David R. Roediger, *The Wages of Whiteness: Race and the Making of the American Working Class* (New York: Verso, 1991), 167–181.

34. Initial reports of the assault on Fort Wagner began appearing in newspapers around 23 July. By 30 July the Boston papers were running obituaries for Colonel Shaw; see, for example, *Boston Daily Advertiser,* 27 July 1863 and 30 July 1863. For casualties, see "Fifty-Fourth Massachusetts Casualty List," National Archives and Records Administration, http://www.archives.gov/exhibits/american_originals /54thmass.html.

35. Gould, *Diary of a Contraband,* 25 May 1863, 143. Gould's entry for this date actually was written on or about 13 October 1863. His recollection of the men's names can be confirmed: Henry Burrows died of inflammation of the brain at Chelsea Naval Hospital on 24 August 1863, and Lewis B. Hoagland died of consumption on 17 September. See Joan Dixon, ed., *National Intelligencer Newspaper Abstracts, Special Edition: The Civil War Years,* vol. 2 (Westminster, MD: Heritage Books, 2000), 34; and "Appendix B: Correspondents of William B. Gould," Gould, *Diary of a Contraband,* 315.

36. Howard University Black Sailors Project and the National Park Service, "Union African American Sailors Index," Civil War Soldiers and Sailors System, www.itd.nps.gov/cwss/; hereafter cited as CWSS.

37. As Jane Schultz demonstrates in the definitive study of the subject, Civil War hospitals could be spaces of surprising racial integration, but racial divisions did affect life in northern hospitals (much more than in southern ones, in fact). Even if Gould was not forbidden to minister to white sailors, and white nurses did not refuse outright to attend blacks, doctors and hospital administrators may have been quite glad to circumvent tension by assigning a black nurse to black patients. Schultz's archive does not reveal significant conflict over race in such settings, but that probably is less because it did not occur, she notes, than because "racist workers would have avoided working at black hospitals." Schultz, *Women at the Front: Hospital Workers in Civil War America* (Chapel Hill: Univ. of North Carolina Press, 2004), 4–5, 99.

38. Gould, *Diary of a Contraband,* 14 and 16 October 1863, 146; ibid., 149, 150, 152.

39. Ibid., 3 and 8 December 1863, 155; 22 October 1863, 148; 7 November 1863, 151; 31 October 1863, 150. For excerpts from Boston newspapers on the *Niagara's* recruiting troubles, see the annotations in ibid., 154–157. The ship finally sailed from Boston in mid-December, despite being shorthanded. In mid-March 1864, it reportedly was operating with one quarter of its necessary crew ("Perilous Voyage of the Niagara," *New York Times,* 5 April 1864, 2). Recruiting problems afflicted the entire U.S. Navy during the Civil War, which is largely the reason contrabands like Gould were accepted into the service even in the early years of the conflict; see Steven J. Ramold, *Slaves, Sailors, Citizens: African Americans in the Union Navy* (DeKalb: Northern Illinois Univ. Press, 2002), chap. 2.

40. Gould, *Diary of a Contraband,* 18 and 23 March 1864, 174–175; 9 March 1864, 172; 12 January 1864, 164; 17 March 1864, 174; 9 April 1864, 181.

41. Ibid., 26–27 March 1864, 177.

42. Ibid., 14 March 1864, 173.

43. Ibid., 24 January 1863, 129.

44. Ibid., 23 November 1863, 153; 24 April 1864, 183; 1 June 1864, 191; 24 October 1863, 148. Ross, who indeed was born in New York and enlisted there in June 1863, and Scott, who was from Connecticut, both were among the men transferred from the *Sabine* during Gould's first week on the *Niagara*. They were twenty-three years old in 1863, a few years younger than Gould; see CWSS.

45. William B. Gould IV, "An Introduction to William B. Gould: In the Service of 'Uncle Samuel'," in Gould, *Diary of a Contraband,* 23. Also see manuscript entry for 18 October 1863.

46. William H. Belt—or Henry Belt, in the diary (ibid., 193)—and Charles Johnston (206) were waiters; Henry Smith (190), Hutchinson Allen (191), and William Morris (243) were cooks; for their occupations, see CWSS.

47. Gould, *Diary of a Contraband,* 1 and 5 November 1863, 150–151; 3–4 January 1864, 163; 15 February 1864, 168.

48. According to W. Jeffrey Bolster, "If able seamen's skill mitigated racial differences and provided opportunities aboard ship to men of color, jobs as cook or steward reinforced racial stereotypes. Black mariners were both beneficiaries and victims of role assignments in the hidebound world of the ship"; *Black Jacks: African American Seamen in the Age of Sail* (Cambridge, MA: Harvard Univ. Press, 1997), 82. On racialized roles and segregation in the Civil War navy in particular, see Ramold, *Slaves, Sailors, Citizens,* chap. 4; Barbara Brooks Tomblin, *Bluejackets and Contrabands: African Americans and the Union Navy* (Lexington: Univ. Press of Kentucky, 2009), chap. 7; and Joseph P. Reidy, "Black Men in Navy Blue during the Civil War," *Prologue: Quarterly of the National Archives and Record Administration* 33, no. 3 (Fall 2001): 160.

49. Naval records indicate sailors' "complexions." Designations are not consistent, but all the men I have mentioned are listed as "negro," "black," or, like Gould, "mulatto." Their names appear in Gould, *Diary of a Contraband,* on pages 148, 174, 183, 190, 191, 193, 206, 230, 242, and 243. Gould spells a few of their names slightly differently than the Navy does (e.g., Johnston for Johnson, Hutcheson for Hutchinson), but muster rolls confirm that these same men were aboard the *Niagara* with Gould; see CWSS.

50. Gould, *Diary of a Contraband,* 16–17 April 1864, 182. Many details of what happened at Fort Pillow are lost in the fog of war, but Confederate forces unquestionably gave no quarter to surrendered Union troops, and it is difficult to dispute that at least some southern soldiers massacred black soldiers in brutal retribution for what they saw as the unpardonable offense of slaves taking up arms against masters. Certainly that is the story that captured the attention of northerners, the northern press, and Gould's cohort. For accounts of the massacre, see Richard L. Fuchs, *An Unerring Fire: The Massacre at Fort Pillow* (Rutherford, NJ: Fairleigh-Dickinson Univ. Press, 1994), and Andrew Ward, *River Run Red: The Fort Pillow Massacre in the American Civil War* (New York: Penguin, 2005).

51. Gould, *Diary of a Contraband,* 18 May 1864, 188; 25 May 1864, 190; 21 March 1865, 230.

52. Ibid., 30 March 1864, 179.

53. Such is the classic argument in Anderson, *Imagined Communities.*

54. Twentieth Regiment: Gould, *Diary of a Contraband,* 5 March 1864, 171. Visits to the *Anglo-African:* 5 April 1864, 180; 11 April 1864, 181; 7 May 1864, 186; 11 May 1864, 187; and 14 May 1864, 188. Lectures: 11 March 1864, 172; 30 April 1864, 185. Performance: 15 March 1864, 173, and Eric Lott, *Love and Theft: Blackface Minstrelsy and the American Working Class* (New York: Oxford Univ. Press, 1995), 235. Galloway delegation: 11 May 1864, 187. Ann Hoagland: see "Appendix B," Gould, *Diary of a Contraband,* 314.

55. A section of the diary, apparently spanning September 1864 to February 1865, has not survived, and the portion that covers February 1865 through the end of the war survives as a fascicle of unbound pages that have partly deteriorated. In quotations from the diary's 1865 entries, then, missing letters do not necessarily indicate Gould's misspellings but often reflect the fact that words have been cut off at the ragged edges of the pages. See Gould IV, prologue to ibid., 4–5.

56. Ibid., 26 July 1864, 204; 27 May 1865, 248. Regarding minstrel performances, Gould writes on one occasion, "this evening the 'Saccramento' Etheopeon Troupe are to have A performance. and several of our crew"—apparently Gould was not among them—"have gone over to enj[oy] the fun" (28 March 1865, 233). Elsewhere Gould writes, "Our Minstrel Troup gives one of thair entertainments this evening. I wish them success," and afterward reports that the performers "acquited themselves creditabley" (30–31 May 1865, 249). Ramold presents a

benign picture of minstrelsy in the navy, concluding "It is difficult to call minstrel shows racist when African American sailors themselves enjoyed performing in them" (*Slaves, Sailors, Citizens,* 113, 176). But as Reidy points out, "Only a thin line may have separated voluntary from involuntary participation in the ritualized merriment"; furthermore, black spectators sometimes were relegated to a "Colored Gallery" during minstrel performances ("Black Men in Navy Blue," 163–164). Gould gives no obvious signs of feeling offended by minstrel shows, and he may have found them a pleasant reminder of life in the South, but it is equally plausible, to take Reidy's suggestion, that Gould felt obliged, if not to participate in the performances themselves, at least to let on that he enjoyed them.

57. Gould, *Diary of a Contraband,* 15 April 1865, 239; 7 March 1865, 227; 6 May 1865, 242; 16 June 1865, 252; 11 July 1865, 256; 14 June 1865, 251.

58. Conceivably, Gould's *we* may have referred since the beginning only to African American sailors. The "we" who "finished Coaling" off Beaufort could have been all contrabands, whom the navy commonly used as laborers (and the majority of the crew on the *William Badger,* the supply ship mentioned in Gould's very first diary entry, was black; see Reidy, "Black Men in Navy Blue," 158–159). Even if so, it would remain true that, over the course of the war, Gould turned an unannounced definition into an explicit statement. The racial identity of the first-person plural pronoun, at first either unworthy of mention or too obvious to remark, became a matter of self-conscious consideration.

59. Gould, *Diary of a Contraband,* 15 July 1865, 257; 16 August 1865, 263; 17 September 1865, 271. Variants on "Nothing of importance" appear in entries for 15, 22, and 23 May 1865, 246–247; 3 June 1865, 249; 8, 13, and 28 July, 256–259; and 12 September 1865, 270. "Just killing time" appears at 11 and 19 August 1865, 262 and 265.

60. Ibid., 2 September 1865, 268; 10 April 1865, 237; 11 August 1865, 262.

61. Ibid., 22 September 1865, 273.

5. Petition and Protest in the Occupied South

1. Revd. Abram Mercherson to Maj. Gen. J. G. Foster, 12 August 1864, M-268 1864, Letters Received, ser. 4109, Department of the South, Record Group 393 Part 1, National Archives, Washington, DC [C-1327], published in Ira Berlin et al., eds., *Freedom: A Documentary History of Emancipation, 1861–1867,* ser. 1, vol. 3: *The Wartime Genesis of Free Labor: The Lower South* (Cambridge: Cambridge Univ. Press, 1990), 314–316.

2. See letters reproduced in Ira Berlin et al., eds., *Freedom: A Documentary History of Emancipation, 1861–1867,* ser. 1, vol. 1: *The Destruction of Slavery* (Cambridge: Cambridge Univ. Press, 1985), 239–240, 384, 386; ibid., ser. 2: *The Black Military Experience* (Cambridge: Cambridge Univ. Press, 1982), 654–655; and Steven Hahn et al., eds., *Freedom: A Documentary History of Emancipation,*

1861–1867, ser. 3, vol. 1: *Land and Labor* (Chapel Hill: Univ. of North Carolina Press, 2008), 719.

3. Researchers at the Freedmen and Southern Society Project, which produces the *Freedom* series, attempted to locate replies and follow-ups to many of the freed people's letters they have published. In some cases they found documentation of an official response to a freed person's protest, in some cases they found nothing, and in some cases they found affirmative evidence that a letter was filed away without action being taken. For an example of the latter circumstance, see *Freedom,* ser. 1, vol. 1, 608n.

4. Merrill D. Peterson, ed., *Thomas Jefferson: Writings* (New York: Library of America, 1984), 1434. For white anxieties about emancipation, see Forrest G. Wood, *Black Scare: The Racist Response to Emancipation and Reconstruction* (Berkeley: Univ. of California Press, 1968), chap. 2; George M. Frederickson, *The Black Image in the White Mind: The Debate on Afro-American Character and Destiny, 1817–1914* (1971; repr. Middletown, CT: Wesleyan Univ. Press, 1987), esp. chap. 5; Paul D. Escott, *"What Shall We Do with the Negro?": Lincoln, White Racism, and Civil War America* (Charlottesville: Univ. of Virginia Press, 2009); Stephen V. Ash, *When the Yankees Came: Conflict and Chaos in the Occupied South, 1861–1865* (Chapel Hill: Univ. of North Carolina Press, 1995), chap. 5. For an eloquent summary of these anxieties, see Frederick Douglass, "What Shall Be Done with the Slaves If Emancipated?," in *The Life and Writings of Frederick Douglass,* ed. Philip S. Foner, vol. 3 (New York: International Publishers, 1952), 188–191.

5. Although colonization was advocated and supported by many white Americans, it was not exclusively so. Some African American leaders, most notably Martin Delany, believed emigration to Liberia held greater promise than any future in the United States. See Robert S. Levine, ed., *Martin R. Delany: A Documentary Reader* (Chapel Hill: Univ. of North Carolina Press, 2003).

6. Steven Hahn, *A Nation under Our Feet: Black Political Struggles in the Rural South from Slavery to the Great Migration* (Cambridge, MA: Harvard Univ. Press, 2003), 74–75; Escott, *"What Shall We Do with the Negro?"* 74–79. Henrietta Stratton Jaquette, ed., *South after Gettysburg: Letters of Cornelia Hancock from the Army of the Potomac, 1863–1865* (Philadelphia: Univ. of Pennsylvania Press, 1937), 32, 41, 44. On northern soldiers' changing opinions about slavery as they witnessed life in the South firsthand, see Chandra Manning, *What This Cruel War Was Over: Soldiers, Slavery, and the Civil War* (New York: Alfred A. Knopf, 2007).

7. *Freedom,* ser. 2, 725; Leon F. Litwack, *Been in the Storm So Long: The Aftermath of Slavery* (New York: Random House, 1979), chap. 3.

8. Hahn, *A Nation under Our Feet,* esp. 60–61; Laura F. Edwards, *The People and Their Peace: Legal Culture and the Transformation of Inequality in the Post-Revolutionary South* (Chapel Hill: Univ. of North Carolina Press, 2009).

9. *Freedom,* ser. 2, 453, 666. Even in the many parts of the South that Union forces never penetrated, African Americans witnessed and adjusted to a shift away from individual slaveholders' sovereignty and toward the centralized authority of a nation-state—the Confederate States of America, that is. For obvious reasons, slaves and freed people generally did not appeal to that government for aid; in fact, they found shrewd and effective ways to weaken it. See Stephanie McCurry, *Confederate Reckoning: Power and Politics in the Civil War South* (Cambridge, MA: Harvard Univ. Press, 2010), 283–284.

10. John Blassingame, ed., *Slave Testimony: Two Centuries of Letters, Speeches, Interviews, and Autobiographies* (Baton Rouge: Louisiana State Univ. Press, 1977), 4.

11. Much has been written about the trickster tradition in African American culture and its roots in slaves' reliance on shrewdness and duplicity. To begin, see Henry Louis Gates, Jr., *The Signifying Monkey: A Theory of African-American Literary Criticism* (New York: Oxford Univ. Press, 1988), and Rafia Zafar, *We Wear the Mask: African Americans Write American Literature, 1760–1870* (New York: Columbia Univ. Press, 1997). On the shift to contractual logic, see Amy Dru Stanley, *From Bondage to Contract: Wage Labor, Marriage, and the Market in the Age of Slave Emancipation* (Cambridge: Cambridge Univ. Press, 1998). Historians Elizabeth Regosin and Donald Shaffer have noted that pension applications following the war—of which African American veterans and their families filed many—represented "perhaps the greatest encounter between ordinary Americans and the federal government in the nineteenth century"; Regosin and Shaffer, *Voices of Emancipation: Understanding Slavery, the Civil War, and Reconstruction through the U.S. Pension Bureau Files* (New York: New York Univ. Press, 2008), 7. Not all pension applications were filed in writing, though. For a related discussion, from a different historical period, of marginalized people petitioning government officials via letter, see Katrina Powell, *The Anguish of Displacement: The Politics of Literacy in the Letters of Mountain Families in Shenandoah National Park* (Charlottesville: Univ. of Virginia Press, 2007).

12. *Freedom,* ser. 2, 424, 647; Ira Berlin et al., eds., *Freedom: A Documentary History of Emancipation, 1861–1867,* ser. 1, vol. 2: *The Wartime Genesis of Free Labor: The Upper South* (Cambridge: Cambridge Univ. Press, 1993), 239; *Freedom,* ser. 2, 754; Abraham E. Lohman to the honerable Sectry of War, [?] September 1865, L-1249 1865, Letters Received, ser. 127, Record Group 99, National Archives [CC-6]; *Freedom,* ser. 1, vol. 1, 239; *Freedom,* ser. 2, 655, 798–799, 83, 641.

13. John Q. A. Dennis to Hon. Stan, 26 July 1864, D-1049 1864, Letters Received, Record Group 107 [L-51], published in *Freedom,* ser. 1, vol. 1, 386.

14. Anonymous to unnamed official, 18 October 1864, A-400 1864, Letters Received, Colored Troops Division, ser. 360; Records of the Adjutant General's Office, Record Group 94, National Archives [B-81], published in *Freedom,* ser. 2, 642.

15. *Freedom,* ser. 1, vol. 2, 166; *Freedom,* ser. 2, 428–429.

16. Joseph P. Reidy, "Coming from the Shadow of the Past: The Transition from Slavery to Freedom at Freedmen's Village, 1863–1869," *Virginia Magazine of History and Biography* 95, no. 4 (October 1987): 403–428.

17. Sally Brown to A. Lincoln and John Robertson to A. Lincoln, [November 1864?], enclosed in Capt. J. M. Brown to Major C. H. Raymond, 31 December 1864, W-2 (1865), Letters Received, ser. 360, Colored Troops Division, Record Group 94, National Archives [B-132].

18. Brown to Raymond, 31 December 1864.

19. Eric Lott, *Love and Theft: Blackface Minstrelsy and the American Working Class* (New York: Oxford Univ. Press, 1993). In earlier periods, white writers had used "fake documents written in [black] dialect" as a tactic for discrediting political opponents. Dickson D. Bruce, Jr., *The Origins of African American Literature, 1680–1865* (Charlottesville: Univ. of Virginia Press, 2001), 95. In an interesting twist, George Teamoh recalled in his postbellum slave narrative that he once mimicked the writing of a marginally literate white man. To assist a needy fellow slave, he forged a letter, supposed to be from a labor foreman, that began, "i sete miself to write you these fu lines," and ended, "excuse my pure spelin for i am a stone mason here by the day." F. N. Boney, Richard L. Hume, and Rafia Zafar, eds., *God Made Man, Man Made the Slave: The Autobiography of George Teamoh* (Macon, GA: Mercer Univ. Press, 1990), 76.

20. *Freedom,* ser. 1, vol. 2, 235.

21. *Freedom,* ser. 1, vol. 1, 242–243. For slaveholders' reprisals against African Americans during transient or partial Union occupations, see Litwack, *Been in the Storm So Long,* 172–187.

22. *Freedom,* ser. 2, 654.

23. Prince Murrell to Gen. Swain, 17 December 1865, Alabama Assistant Commissioner, Freedmen's Bureau, ser. 9, Record Group 105 [A-1632].

24. Willie Lee Rose, *Rehearsal for Reconstruction: The Port Royal Experiment* (New York: Oxford Univ. Press, 1964). Also see Julie Saville, *The Work of Reconstruction: From Slave to Wage Laborer in South Carolina, 1860–1870* (Cambridge: Cambridge Univ. Press, 1994), 32–45.

25. "Gen. Mitchell's Speech to the Contrabands," *The Liberator,* 31 October 1862; *Freedom,* ser. 1, vol. 1, 19–20; "The Pioneer Negro Colony in South Carolina," *The Liberator,* 12 May 1865. For a comprehensive articulation of the questions emancipation raised, see Steven Hahn, foreword to Eric Foner, *Nothing But Freedom: Emancipation and Its Legacy* (1983; repr. Baton Rouge: Louisiana State Univ. Press, 2007), xiii.

26. J. M. W., "Emancipation in South Carolina," *New York Times,* 17 May 1862, 3; Benjamin Quarles, *The Negro in the Civil War* (1953; repr. New York: Da Capo Press, 1989), 109–110; Clarence L. Mohr, *On the Threshold of Freedom:*

Masters and Slaves in Civil War Georgia (Baton Rouge: Louisiana State Univ. Press, 1986), 84–85; Thomas Wentworth Higginson, *Army Life in a Black Regiment and Other Writings* (1870; repr. New York: Penguin, 1997), 1, 211–215.

27. Benson J. Lossing, *The Pictorial Field Book of the Civil War in the United States of America*, vol. 3 (Hartford: Belknap, 1874), 189; Frederic Denison, "A Chaplain's Experience in the Union Army," No. 20 in *Personal Narratives of Events in the War of the Rebellion*, 4th ser. (Providence: Rhode Island Soldiers and Sailors Historical Society, 1893), 28–29; Baptist Wriothesley Noel, *The Rebellion in America* (London: James Nisbet, 1863), 365.

28. Charles Carleton Coffin, *The Boys of '61, or Four Years of Fighting; Personal Observation with the Army and Navy, From the First Battle of Bull Run to the Fall of Richmond* (Boston: Page, 1896), 230; J. M. W., "A Negro Conventicle," *New York Times,* 19 April 1862, 2; "A Colored Preacher," *Christian Watchman & Reflector,* 14 August 1862, 1.

29. Melvin Patrick Ely, *Israel on the Appomattox: A Southern Experiment in Black Freedom from the 1790s through the Civil War* (New York: Vintage, 2004), 291; Ronald Wardhaugh, *An Introduction to Sociolinguistics,* 6th ed. (Malden, MA: Wiley-Blackwell, 2010), 170–171; *Freedom,* ser. 1, vol. 3, 407, and ser. 2, 692.

30. The editors of *Freedom* transcribe the word as "to rape," but a careful look at Mercherson's handwriting throughout the manuscript—especially a comparison with other words with leading *w*'s ("which," three lines above "wrape," and "wife" in the line below)—makes clear that the initial mark is a *w,* not a *t.* It also is clear from the manuscript that Mercherson added the *w* during a subsequent pass through the letter: he originally wrote "rape" (with a capital *R,* such as he uses elsewhere exclusively for the initial letters of words) and later squeezed in a *w,* leaving almost no space between "commited" and "wrape." In other words, his hypercorrection seems to have stemmed from reflection on his choice of words. On the physical elements of handwriting and nineteenth-century penmanship pedagogy, see Tamara Plakins Thornton, *Handwriting in America: A Cultural History* (New Haven, CT: Yale Univ. Press, 1996), 53–55, 68–69.

31. *Freedom,* ser. 1, vol. 2, 517; ser. 1, vol. 1, 242; ser. 2, 756, 696. On violence against black women, see Litwack, *Been in the Storm So Long,* 129–130. There are numerous possible explanations for statistical measures of word usage, but it is suggestive to note that, according to Google's massive dataset and Google Books Ngram Viewer, the frequency of the word *trouble* in books published in the United States increased by 50 percent between 1860 and 1900 and did not subside to pre-1860 levels until roughly the end of the civil rights movement.

32. Frances Smith Foster, *'Til Death or Distance Do Us Part: Love and Marriage in African America* (New York: Oxford Univ. Press, 2010); Amy Murrell Taylor, *The Divided Family in Civil War America* (Chapel Hill: Univ. of North Carolina Press, 2005), 191–208; Laura Edwards, *Gendered Strife and Confusion: The Political*

Culture of Reconstruction (Urbana: Univ. of Illinois Press, 1997), 24–65; Amy Dru Stanley, *From Bondage to Contract: Wage Labor, Marriage, and the Market in the Age of Slave Emancipation* (Cambridge: Cambridge Univ. Press, 1998). On the complicated effect of marriage on property relations, and its upheaval upon emancipation, see Dylan Penningroth, *The Claims of Kinfolk: African American Property and Community in the Nineteenth-Century South* (Chapel Hill: Univ. of North Carolina Press, 2003), 176–185.

33. See Hahn, *A Nation under Our Feet,* 40; McCurry, *Confederate Reckoning,* 319–320; and Stanley, *From Bondage to Contract,* esp. 47–51. Although women's distinctive experiences of slavery and emancipation were long neglected, a rich and fast-growing body of scholarly literature explores women's side of the history of emancipation. See especially Stephanie McCurry, "War, Gender, and Emancipation in the Civil War South," in *Lincoln's Proclamation: Emancipation Reconsidered,* ed. William A. Blair and Karen Fisher Younger (Chapel Hill: Univ. of North Carolina Press, 2009), 120–150, and also Leslie Schwalm, *A Hard Fight for We: Women's Transition from Slavery to Freedom in South Carolina* (Urbana: Univ. of Illinois Press, 1997); Susan Eva O'Donovan, *Becoming Free in the Cotton South* (Cambridge, MA: Harvard Univ. Press, 2007); Nancy Bercaw, *Gendered Freedoms: Race, Rights, and the Politics of Household in the Delta, 1861–1875* (Gainesville: Univ. Press of Florida, 2003); and Diana Paton and Pamela Scully, eds., *Gender and Slave Emancipation in the Atlantic World* (Durham, NC: Duke Univ. Press, 2005).

34. Mary Farmer-Kaiser, *Freedwomen and the Freedmen's Bureau: Race, Gender, and Public Policy in the Age of Emancipation* (New York: Fordham Univ. Press, 2010).

35. Edwards, *Gendered Strife and Confusion,* chap. 1; McCurry, *Confederate Reckoning,* 94–96, 226–233.

36. William E. Parrish, *Turbulent Partnership: Missouri and the Union, 1861–1865* (Columbia: Univ. of Missouri Press, 1963), chaps. 1–3.

37. United States War Department, *The War of the Rebellion: A Compilation of the Official Records of the Union and Confederate Armies* ser. 3, vol. 3 (Washington, DC: Government Printing Office, 1899), 1034–1036. For the history of Benton Barracks, and Missouri recruitment and emancipation in general, I have relied on *Freedom,* ser. 1, vol. 1, 395–489; ser. 1, vol. 2, 551–622; and ser. 2, 12, 188–89, 226–251; Louis S. Gerteis, *Civil War St. Louis* (Lawrence: Univ. Press of Kansas, 2001), chap. 9; and Margaret Humphreys, *Intensely Human: The Health of the Black Soldier in the American Civil War* (Baltimore: Johns Hopkins Univ. Press, 2008), 86–93.

38. *Freedom,* ser. 2, 241, 189.

39. Emily Elizabeth Parsons, *Memoir of Emily Elizabeth Parsons* (Boston: Little, Brown, 1880), 89; Jane Schultz, *Women at the Front: Hospital Workers in Civil War America* (Chapel Hill: Univ. of North Carolina Press, 2004), 25; Gerteis, *Civil War*

St. Louis, 275–276; J. G. Forman, *The Western Sanitary Commission: A Sketch of Its Origins, History, Labors for the Sick and Wounded of the Western Armies, and Aid Given to Freedmen and Union Refugees, with Incidents of Hospital Life* (St. Louis: R. P. Studley, 1864), 95, 134.

40. *Freedom,* ser. 1, vol. 1, 484–485. Wilson notified Union officials of Bowmen's threats and requested protection, and the military officer who investigated the matter cast doubt on Bowmen's authorship of the letter. According to the officer's report, Wilson "says that the negro previous to his enlistment always bore a good character" and that "as the negro can neither read or write" the letter probably "was written by some designing person." Though it is plausible that someone else wrote the letter pretending to be Bowmen, it is hard to imagine what "designing person" would have greater interest in the fate of Bowmen's wife than Bowmen himself. Bowmen would have had ample reason to keep his literacy a secret before now, and Wilson would not have been the first slaveholder to find that a slave's docility ("good character") changed to assertiveness after he escaped and enlisted. Furthermore, Wilson found the letter a sufficiently credible and alarming threat to bring it before Union authorities, which a Confederate sympathizer in a border state would not have done lightly. He may have believed in Bowmen's authorship more than he let on. Bowmen's letter and Spotswood Rice's (see below) are also discussed in Louis Gerteis, "Slaves, Servants, and Soldiers: Uneven Paths to Freedom in the Border States, 1861–1865," in *Lincoln's Proclamation: Emancipation Reconsidered,* ed. William A. Blair and Karen Fisher Young (Chapel Hill: Univ. of North Carolina Press, 2009), 186–187.

41. *Freedom,* ser. 2, 690.

42. Ibid., 689.

43. [Private Spotswood Rice] to My Children, [3 September 1864], enclosed in F. W. Diggs to Genl. Rosecrans, 10 September 1864, D-296 1864, Letters Received, ser. 2593, Department of the Missouri, Record Group 393, Part I, National Archives [C-154]; Drew Gilpin Faust, *This Republic of Suffering: Death and the American Civil War* (New York: Alfred A. Knopf, 2008), 107.

44. George P. Rawick, ed., *The American Slave: A Composite Autobiography,* ser. 2, vol. 11, *Missouri Narratives* (Westport, CT: Greenwood, 1972), 25–31; *Freedom,* ser. 2, 697.

45. *Freedom,* ser. 1, vol. 3, 429; ser. 2, 138.

46. Martha to My Dear Husband, 30 December 1863, enclosed in Brig. Genl. William A. Pile to Maj. O. D. Greene, 11 February 1864, P-91 1864, Letters Received, ser. 2593, Department of the Missouri, Record Group 393 Part I, National Archives [C-159], published in *Freedom,* ser. 2, 244–245.

47. Hannah Rosen, *Terror in the Heart of Freedom: Citizenship, Sexual Violence, and the Meaning of Race in the Postemancipation South* (Chapel Hill: Univ. of North Carolina Press, 2009), 222–241. For a long time, historians of Reconstruction and

the Jim Crow era believed freedwomen were somewhat less susceptible to violence than freedmen, because the victims of high-profile lynchings usually were men. On the contrary, women in the wartime and postwar South suffered relentless if less visible brutalization; see Elsa Barkley Brown, "Negotiating and Transforming the Public Sphere: African American Political Life in the Transition from Slavery to Freedom," *Public Culture* 7 (1994): 112n8. For sexual violence against black women before the Civil War, see Joshua D. Rothman, *Notorious in the Neighborhood: Sex and Families across the Color Line in Virginia, 1787–1861* (Chapel Hill: Univ. of North Carolina Press, 2003).

48. *Freedom*, ser. 2, 269, 807.

49. For a discussion of black women's reluctance to speak about being raped, see Darlene Clark Hine, "Rape and the Inner Lives of Black Women in the Middle West: Preliminary Thoughts on the Culture of Dissemblance," *Signs: Journal of Women in Culture and Society* 14, no. 4 (Summer 1989): 912–920. On the larger problem of the dearth of written sources by nineteenth-century African American women, see Deborah Gray White, "Mining the Forgotten: Manuscript Sources for Black Women's History," *Journal of American History* 74, no. 1 (June 1987): 237–242.

50. Quoted in McCurry, *Confederate Reckoning*, 129. Also see Rosen, *Terror in the Heart of Freedom*, 231. Trudier Harris recalls her mother using the word "scanless" a century later in Alabama, to express varying "degrees of intensity of outrage"; more "scanless" than anything else, in the mother's usage, was a man who groped a teenage girl; Harris, *Summer Snow: Reflections from a Black Daughter of the South* (Boston: Beacon, 2003), 120.

51. Brig. Gen. Wm. A. Pile, 9 January 1864, endorsement on Martha to My Dear Husband, 30 December 1863; *Freedom*, ser. 2, 245–246. Pile's letter names "Richard Glover," but only Richmond Glover appears in the records of the Sixty-Fifth U.S. Colored Troops, originally organized as the Missouri Volunteers, Second Regiment Colored Infantry; he served in Company A, as did Lieut. Lutellus Hussey. National Park Service, "Names and Records of Union and Confederate Troops," Civil War Soldiers and Sailors System, http://www.itd.nps.gov/cwss (hereafter CWSS).

52. O'Donovan, *Becoming Free in the Cotton South*, 159.

53. *Freedom*, ser. 1, vol. 1, 386.

54. *Freedom*, ser. 2, 725. On movements of the First Colored Cavalry, see CWSS. On the suffrage debate and black soldiers in Texas, see Edwin Redkey, ed., *A Grand Army of Black Men: Letters from African-American Soldiers in the Union Army, 1861–1865* (Cambridge: Cambridge Univ. Press, 1992), 196–203.

55. *Freedom*, ser. 1, vol. 1, 608; ser. 1, vol. 3, 298.

56. George Johnson to Genarl Franch, 7 January 1863, Miscellaneous Records, ser. 1796, Department of the Gulf, Record Group 393 Part I, National Archives [C-1062], published in *Freedom*, ser. 1, vol. 3, 407–408.

57. On the explosion of the term into broader cultural usage, see Kate Masur, "'A Rare Phenomenon of Philological Vegetation': The Word 'Contraband' and the Meanings of Emancipation in the United States," *Journal of American History* 93, no. 4 (March 2007): 1050–1084.

58. "General Orders No. 63," in *Freedom*, ser. 2, 65–67. Also see *Freedom*, ser. 2, 41–44; Howard C. Westwood, "Benjamin Butler's Enlistment of Black Troops in New Orleans in 1862," *Louisiana History: The Journal of the Louisiana Historical Association* 26, no. 1 (Winter 1985): 5–22; and John David Smith, "Let Us All Be Grateful That We Have Colored Troops That Will Fight," in *Black Soldiers in Blue: African American Troops in the Civil War Era*, ed. Smith (Chapel Hill: Univ. of North Carolina Press, 2002), 1–77.

59. "The Colored Soldier Question," *Daily Delta*, 22 August 1862, 2; "Let Us Argue the Point," *Daily Delta*, 23 August 1862, 2. Butler's order ran on page four of the 27 and 29 August 1862 issues. Quotation from *Daily Delta*, 30 August 1862, 4.

60. Joseph T. Wilson, *The Black Phalanx: A History of the Negro Soldiers of the United States in the Wars of 1775–1812 and 1861–'65* (Hartford, CT: American Publishing, 1890), 195; also see John W. Blassingame, *Black New Orleans, 1860–1880* (Chicago: Univ. of Chicago Press, 1973), 36.

61. *Freedom*, ser. 2, 384. As McCurry observes in *Confederate Reckoning*, "The nexus of manhood, military service, and citizenship was so tight in the nineteenth century" that even Jefferson Davis could not fathom admitting slaves into the Confederate army without emancipating them and conferring upon them at least some of the rights of citizens (336). Butler would make a notable promise of government protection for enlisted freedmen's wives and children, but that promise was still a year away, in December 1863, in a different theater of the war; see *Freedom*, ser. 2, 659.

62. George Willford Johnson to Genarl, 9 September 1813 [1863], J-41 1863, Letters Received, ser. 360, Colored Troops Division, Record Group 94, National Archives [B-35].

63. Mercherson to Foster, 12 August 1864.

64. *Freedom*, ser. 2, 316.

65. Martha to My Dear Husband, 30 December 1863.

66. For the dates of organization and troop movements of Missouri black regiments—the Sixty-Second, Sixty-Fifth, Sixty-Seventh, and Sixty-Eighth U.S. Colored Troops—see CWSS. Glover's claim makes her similar to some Confederate soldiers' wives in the seceded states, who also asserted political power by appealing to the needs of the army, namely by trading on their influence over whether or not their soldier-husbands deserted to return home; see McCurry, *Confederate Reckoning*, chaps. 3 and 4.

67. *Missouri Democrat* quoted in Gerteis, *Civil War St. Louis*, 288; Capt. A. J. Hubbard to Brig. Genl. Pile, 6 February 1864, enclosed in Brig. Genl. William

A. Pile to Maj. O. D. Greene, 11 February 1864, P-91 1864, Letters Received, ser. 2593, Department of the Missouri, RG 393 Part I, National Archives; Brig. Genl. William A. Pile to Maj. O. D. Greene, 11 February 1864; *Freedom,* ser. 2, 245–246.

68. *Freedom,* ser. 2, 245–246, 248–49; ser. 1, vol. 1, 411–412.

6. Black Ink, White Pages

1. See, for example, Susan Eva O'Donovan, "William Webb's World," *Disunion* series, www.nytimes.com, 18 February 2011, and Steven Hahn, *A Nation under Our Feet: Black Political Struggles in the Rural South from Slavery to the Great Migration* (Cambridge, MA: Harvard Univ. Press, 2003), 41–42.

2. Mitch Kachun, "Interrogating the Silences: Julia C. Collins, 19th-Century Black Readers and Writers, and the *Christian Recorder," African American Review* 40, no. 4 (Winter 2006): 652. On the general history of the *Christian Recorder,* see Gilbert Anthony Williams, *"The Christian Recorder," Newspaper of the African Methodist Episcopal Church: History of a Forum for Ideas, 1854–1902* (Jefferson, NC: McFarland, 1996). On the paper's literary content and its role in African American nationalism and culture, see Eric Gardner, *Unexpected Places: Relocating Nineteenth-Century African American Literature* (Jackson: Univ. Press of Mississippi, 2009), 56–91; Frances Smith Foster and Chanta Haywood, "Christian Recordings: Afro-Protestantism, Its Press, and the Production of African-American Literature," *Religion & Literature* 27, no. 1 (Spring 1995): 15–33; P. Gabrielle Foreman, "The *Christian Recorder,* Broken Families, and Educated Nations in Julia Collins's Civil War Novel *The Curse of Caste," African American Review* 40, no. 4 (Winter 2006): 705–716; and Elizabeth McHenry, *Forgotten Readers: Recovering the Lost History of African American Literary Societies* (Durham, NC: Duke Univ. Press, 2002), 130–140. On the paper's circulation in black army regiments, see Keith P. Wilson, *Campfires of Freedom: The Camp Life of Black Soldiers during the Civil War* (Kent, OH: Kent State Univ. Press, 2002), 74–80, 112, and William Seraile, *Fire in His Heart: Bishop Benjamin Tucker Tanner and the A.M.E. Church* (Knoxville: Univ. of Tennessee Press, 1998), 20.

3. "Speech of Dr. Armstrong," *Christian Recorder,* 24 December 1864. On the "Information Wanted" notices, see Jean Lee Cole, "Information Wanted: *The Curse of Caste, Minnie's Sacrifice,* and the *Christian Recorder," African American Review* 40, no. 4 (Winter 2006): 731–742. Efforts to reunite families after emancipation, including through "Information Wanted" notices, are a principal subject of Heather Andrea Williams, *Help Me to Find My People: The African American Search for Families Lost in Slavery* (Chapel Hill: Univ. of North Carolina Press, 2012), which appeared too late to inform the present discussion.

4. "Information Wanted," *Christian Recorder,* 1 July, 22 July, 16 December, 3 June, and 29 April 1865; editors quoted in Williams, *"The Christian Recorder,"* 127.

5. "Letter from Richmond," *Christian Recorder,* 22 April 1865, 2. This dispatch has been reprinted in Edwin S. Redkey, ed., *A Grand Army of Black Men: Letters from African-American Soldiers in the Union Army, 1861–1865* (Cambridge: Cambridge Univ. Press, 1992), 175–178.

6. Ibid.

7. Garland H. White to E. M. Stanton, 7 May 1862, W-561 1862, Letters Received, ser. 23, Record Group 107 (also microfilm 221, roll 208), National Archives, Washington, DC [L-160], published in Ira Berlin et al., eds., *Freedom: A Documentary History of Emancipation, 1861–1867,* ser. 2: *The Black Military Experience* (Cambridge: Cambridge Univ. Press, 1982), 82–83.

8. Free blacks in the North, on the other hand, had early seized the power of the press to advance the anti-slavery cause and combat the white public's racism. For a discussion of "what made a newspaper 'colored,' " see Robert Fanuzzi, *Abolition's Public Sphere* (Minneapolis: Univ. of Minnesota Press, 2003), 103.

9. Quoted in David Blight, *Race and Reunion: The Civil War in American Memory* (Cambridge, MA: Harvard Univ. Press, 2001), 98.

10. For an overview of White's known biography, see Edward A. Miller, Jr., "Garland H. White, Black Army Chaplain," *Civil War History* 43, no. 3 (September 1997): 201–218. Also see Christopher Hager, "The Freedman and the Politician: Emancipation and the Letters of Garland H. White," *Traces of Indiana and Midwestern History* 22, no. 3 (Summer 2010): 26–31, and Budge Weidman, "Black Soldiers in the Civil War," National Archives and Records Administration, http://www.archives.gov/education/lessons/blacks-civil-war/article.html. White's extant writings include four letters to William Seward, Edwin Stanton, or both, as well as two chaplain's reports, housed at the National Archives (three of those letters are published in *Freedom,* ser. 2, 82–83, 141, and 348–349); three letters to Seward, held in the Seward Papers at the University of Rochester; one letter to Oliver Morton, housed at the Indiana State Library; eight letters printed in the *Christian Recorder* (no manuscript originals survive and the authorship of one of these letters, published 24 September 1864, is questionable); and four letters in the Matt W. Ransom Papers at the University of North Carolina.

11. White to Stanton, 7 May 1862.

12. W. E. B. Du Bois, *The Souls of Black Folk,* ed. David W. Blight and Robert Gooding-Williams (Boston: Bedford/St. Martin's, 1997), 72; Booker T. Washington, *Up From Slavery,* in *Three Negro Classics,* ed. John Hope Franklin (New York: Avon, 1965), 148. On tensions between protest and accommodation in early post-emancipation black politics, see Eric Foner, *Reconstruction: America's Unfinished Revolution, 1863–1877* (1988; repr. New York: Harper Perennial, 2002), 113–119.

13. Edwin Stanton to Rufus Saxton, 25 August 1862, in United States War Department, *The War of the Rebellion: A Compilation of the Official Records of the*

Union and Confederate Armies ser. 1, vol. 14 (Washington, DC: Government Printing Office, 1885), 377–378.

14. Letter to Lincoln quoted in Walter Rice Sharp, "Henry S. Lane and the Formation of the Republican Party in Indiana," *The Mississippi Valley Historical Review* 7, no. 2 (September 1920): 94n4; "Men of Color, To Arms!" *Douglass' Monthly,* March 1863, 1; speech in Centerville quoted in William R. Forstchen, "The 28th U.S. Colored Troops: Indiana's African Americans Go to War, 1863–1865," PhD diss., Purdue University, 1994, 40, 39. On northern whites' racist reactions to emancipation in general, see David R. Roediger, *The Wages of Whiteness: Race and the Making of the American Working Class* (New York: Verso, 1991), 167–181.

15. Garland White to Governor Morton, 28 November 1863, Anna Wright Papers, Manuscript Division, Indiana State Library, Indianapolis.

16. White's interactions with Morton are the source for a scene in a historical novel that appeared as I was completing this book. A fictionalized Garland White becomes the protagonist of a story much more about battlefield exploits (of which the real Garland White probably had few) than about writing and politics. See Newt Gingrich and William R. Forstchen, *The Battle of the Crater: A Novel of the Civil War* (New York: St. Martin's, 2011), 177–179.

17. A. F. Flood to [Wilson?], 16 July 1865, ser. 2633, Records of the Subassistant Commissioner, Goldsboro, NC, Field Office, Record Group 105, National Archives [A-961].

18. Forstchen, "The 28th U.S. Colored Troops," 42–60; *Christian Recorder,* 12 December 1863, 2; 9 April 1864, 1.

19. Garland H. White to Wm. H. Seward, 27 April 1863, William Henry Seward Papers, Department of Rare Books, Special Collections, and Preservation, Rush Rhees Library, University of Rochester, Rochester, NY.

20. Garland H. White to Wm. H. Seward, 18 May 1864, service record of Garland H. White, 28th USCT, Compiled Military Service Records of Volunteer Union Soldiers Who Served with the United States Colored Troops, microfilm 1824, roll 52, Record Group 94, National Archives [N-6], published in *Freedom,* ser. 2348–349.

21. Ibid.

22. Wilson, *Campfires of Freedom,* 109–126; Edwin S. Redkey, "Henry McNeal Turner: Black Chaplain in the Union Army," in *Black Soldiers in Blue: African American Troops in the Civil War Era,* ed. John David Smith (Chapel Hill: Univ. of North Carolina Press, 2002), 336–360; Miller, "Garland H. White, Black Army Chaplain."

23. White to Seward, 18 May 1864.

24. Miller, "Garland H. White, Black Army Chaplain," 210. Although military policy on black recruitment in Maryland was not always clear, the men who were recruited by William Birney to become the Nineteenth Regiment, USCT, did

include not only slaves of rebel masters but also those of loyal ones; see *Freedom,* ser. 2, 199–200, 203; and L. Allison Wilmer et al., *History and Roster of Maryland Volunteers, War of 1861–5,* vol. 2 (Baltimore: Guggenheimer, Weil & Co., 1899), 206. On the organization of black regiments and the role of the Twenty-Eighth USCT in the siege of Petersburg, see Henry Goddard Thomas, "The Colored Troops at Petersburg," *Century Magazine* 34, no. 5 (September 1887): 777; Forstchen, "The 28th U.S. Colored Troops," 151n79; and Richard Slotkin, *No Quarter: The Battle of the Crater, 1864* (New York: Random House, 2009), 92–95. On the Thirty-First USCT, see *Annual Report of the Adjutant-General of the State of Connecticut* (Hartford: A. N. Clark, 1866), 226. For regimental origins and movements, see National Park Service, "Regiments: Union and Confederate Histories," Civil War Soldiers and Sailors System, http://www.itd.nps.gov/cwss.

25. Acting Chaplain Garland H. White to Hon. Edwin M. Stanton and Wm. H. Seward, 14 June 1864, W-309 1864, Letters Received, ser. 360, Colored Troops Division, Record Group 94, National Archives [B-70], published in Ira Berlin et al., eds., *Freedom: A Documentary History of Emancipation, 1861–1867,* ser. 2: *The Black Military Experience* (Cambridge: Cambridge Univ. Press, 1982), 141.

26. On the struggle for equal pay, see Wilson, *Campfires of Freedom,* 44–58; *Freedom,* ser. 2, 362–405; Joseph T. Glatthaar, *Forged in Battle: The Civil War Alliance of Black Soldiers and White Officers* (New York: Free Press, 1990), 169–176; Thomas Wentworth Higginson, "Appendix D: The Struggle for Pay," *Army Life in a Black Regiment and Other Writings* (1870; repr. New York: Penguin, 1997), 217–227; James M. McPherson, *The Negro's Civil War: How American Blacks Felt and Acted during the War for the Union* (1965; repr. New York: Vintage, 2003), 200–207. On the issue's divisive effects within the community of black soldiers, and the cultural differences within that community, see especially Wilson, *Campfires of Freedom,* 51–53, and Glatthaar, *Forged in Battle,* 175–176. Among the best-known examples of black soldiers' protests against pay inequity are the letters of Corporal James Henry Gooding, a free-born northerner serving in the Fifty-Fourth Massachusetts; see Virginia M. Adams, ed., *On the Altar of Freedom: A Black Soldier's Civil War Letters from the Front* (Amherst: Univ. of Massachusetts Press, 1991).

27. "Letter from the Rev. Garland H. White, Chaplain of the Twenty-Eight United States Colored Regiment, Raised in Indiana," *Christian Recorder,* 20 August 1864, 2.

28. F. N. Boney, Richard L. Hume, and Rafia Zafar, eds., *God Made Man, Man Made the Slave: The Autobiography of George Teamoh* (Macon, GA: Mercer Univ. Press, 1990), 72–75.

29. *Official Records of the War of the Rebellion,* ser. 3, vol. 4, 565. The plan to equalize white and black soldiers' pay, but to exclude freedmen, had been in the works for some time. In June, Congress passed an appropriations bill that included funds to raise the pay of black soldiers who were free on April 19, 1861; in July,

Attorney General Edward Bates provided the War Department with an opinion on the law. The exact plan became widely known and official, though, only when the War Department finally announced it on August 1 (*Freedom,* ser. 2, 367–368). Although any single date would make a specious and arbitrary dividing line between free blacks (who deserved equal treatment with whites) and enslaved ones (who evidently did not), April 19 (a week after the eruption of hostilities at Fort Sumter) was distinctly strange. It is technically the date of the Civil War's first bloodshed: a street riot in Baltimore involving Confederate sympathizers and a Massachusetts regiment on its way to catch a train to Washington—which had little bearing on the course of the war and certainly did not liberate any slaves.

30. "Payment of Colored Troops," *Christian Recorder,* 20 August 1864, 2. The letter also appears in Higginson, *Army Life in a Black Regiment,* 224–226.

31. "Congress and the Pay of Colored Troops," *Christian Recorder,* 16 April 1864, 2.

32. On the familiar paradigm of "black masses" or a "black majority" in tension with "black conservative nostalgia," see Houston A. Baker, Jr., "Critical Memory and the Black Public Sphere," *Public Culture* 7 (1994): 3–33.

33. "Letter from the Front," *Christian Recorder,* 17 September 1864, 2.

34. J. H. Hall to the Editor, "Letter from the 54th Massachusetts Regiment," *Christian Recorder,* 27 August 1864, 1 (emphasis added).

35. Redkey, "Henry McNeal Turner," 346; "Letter from Chaplain Turner," *Christian Recorder,* 27 August 1864, 1.

36. White to Seward, 18 May 1864.

37. Numerous scholars in a variety of fields have both expanded on and critiqued Jürgen Habermas's famous account of a somewhat idealized open marketplace of ideas in eighteenth-century European salons, *The Structural Transformation of the Public Sphere: An Inquiry into a Category of Bourgeois Society* (1962), trans. Thomas Burger (Cambridge, MA: MIT Press, 1991). Study of the print public sphere in the pre-1900 United States revolves mainly around two landmark works: Michael Warner's *Letters of the Republic: Publication and the Public Sphere in Eighteenth-Century America* (Cambridge, MA: Harvard Univ. Press, 1990), which finds Habermas's ideas applicable to the development of a coherent, proto-national discursive community in colonial North America, and the more recent revision by Trish Loughran, *The Republic in Print: Print Culture in the Age of U.S. Nation Building, 1770–1870* (New York: Columbia Univ. Press, 2007), which argues that the centrifugal force of print's volume and diversity fragmented rather than united the early nation. Unsurprisingly, scholars of the literature and history of minority and marginalized groups tend to be deeply skeptical of the classic Habermasian idea of an open and equal public sphere—which, they point out (and which Habermas himself actually acknowledged), was open and equal only for the propertied white men who counted as full citizens. For discussions of

the public sphere and the press in African American studies in particular, see Baker, "Critical Memory and the Black Public Sphere"; Elsa Barkeley Brown, "Negotiating and Transforming the Public Sphere: African American Political Life in the Transition from Slavery to Freedom," *Public Culture* 7 (1994): 107–146; Fanuzzi, *Abolition's Public Sphere;* and the essays in Todd Vogel, ed., *The Black Press: New Literary and Historical Essays* (New Brunswick, NJ: Rutgers Univ. Press, 2001), esp. Vogel, "Introduction," 1–14, and Robert Fanuzzi, "Frederick Douglass's 'Colored Newspaper': Identity Politics in Black and White," 55–70.

38. "An Interesting Letter from the 28th U.S.C.T.," *Christian Recorder,* 21 October 1865, 1.

39. Garland H. White, Chaplain's Report, 28th U.S. Colored Troops, 30 August 1865, microfilm M619, roll 440, 1871, National Archives.

40. Garland H. White to Wm. H. Seward, undated [April (?) 1865], William Henry Seward Papers, Department of Rare Books, Special Collections, and Preservation, Rush Rhees Library, University of Rochester, Rochester, NY.

41. Washington, *Up From Slavery,* 147; Frenise A. Logan, *The Negro in North Carolina, 1876–1894* (Chapel Hill: Univ. of North Carolina Press, 1964), 21–22; Eric Anderson, *Race and Politics in North Carolina, 1872–1901: The Black Second* (Baton Rouge: Louisiana State Univ. Press, 1981), 43–44; "John Adams Hyman," Black Americans in Congress, http://baic.house.gov.

42. Garland H. White to Matt W. Ransom, 10 December 1875 and 10 March 1876, Matt W. Ransom Papers, 1845–1914 (#2615), Southern Historical Collection, Louis Round Wilson Special Collections Library, University of North Carolina.

43. Garland H. White to Matt W. Ransom, 3 November 1893, Matt W. Ransom Papers; Robert J. Norrell, *Up from History: The Life of Booker T. Washington* (Cambridge, MA: Harvard Univ. Press, 2009), 115, 117; Philip S. Foner, *The Life and Writings of Frederick Douglass,* vol. 4: *Reconstruction and After* (New York: International Publishers, 1955), 149; Garland H. White to Matt W. Ransom, 11 April 1894, quoted in Logan, *The Negro in North Carolina,* 22. White was not unique in aligning himself with the Democratic Party, but he was part of a very small minority. The most famous African American to make common cause with the Democrats was Martin Delany; see Robert S. Levine, ed., *Martin R. Delany: A Documentary Reader* (Chapel Hill: Univ. of North Carolina Press, 2003), 380–381. There is no comprehensive study of black Democrats during the Reconstruction and Jim Crow periods, but their existence is evidenced by other African Americans' often strenuous efforts to bring them within the Republican fold; see Nell Irvin Painter, *Exodusters: Black Migration to Kansas after Reconstruction* (1977; repr. New York: Norton, 1992), 13–14, and John C. Rodrigue, *Reconstruction in the Cane Fields: From Slavery to Free Labor in Louisiana's Sugar Parishes, 1862–1880* (Baton Rouge: Louisiana State Univ. Press, 2001), 170–172.

44. Roanoke Island NC to [Secretary of War], 9 March 1865, B-2 1865, Letters Received, ser. 15, Washington Headquarters, Record Group 105, National Archives [A-2966].

Conclusion

1. *The Freedmen's Journal* 1, no. 1 (January 1865): 3; Frances Beecher Perkins, "Two Years with a Colored Regiment: A Woman's Experience," *New England Magazine* 23, no. 5 (January 1898): 533–544; quotations on 534, 536, and 542.

2. Perkins, "Two Years with a Colored Regiment," 536, 543.

3. For discussions and examples of northerners' letters about slaves and freed people in the South, see Chandra Manning, *What This Cruel War Was Over: Soldiers, Slavery, and the Civil War* (New York: Alfred A. Knopf, 2007), 73–78, for letters from soldiers; Jane Schultz, *Women at the Front: Hospital Workers in Civil War America* (Chapel Hill: Univ. of North Carolina Press, 2004), 103–104, for letters from hospital workers; and, for letters from teachers, Rupert Sargent Holland, ed. *Letters and Diary of Laura M. Towne, Written from the Sea Islands of South Carolina, 1862–1884* (Cambridge, MA: Riverside, 1912); Elizabeth Ware Pearson, ed., *Letters from Port Royal, 1862–1868* (1906; repr. New York: Arno, 1969); and Henry L. Swint, ed., *Dear Ones at Home: Letters from Contraband Camps* (Nashville, TN: Vanderbilt Univ. Press, 1966).

4. Edward L. Pierce, "The Freedmen at Port Royal," *Atlantic Monthly* 12 (September 1863): 291–315; [Charlotte Forten], "Life on the Sea Islands," *Atlantic Monthly* 13 (May–June 1864): 587–596 and 666–676; R. D. Madison, introduction to Thomas Wentworth Higginson, *Army Life in a Black Regiment and Other Writings* (New York: Penguin, 1997), xviii; [William Channing Gannett and Edward Everett Hale], "The Freedmen at Port Royal," *North American Review* 101 (July 1865): 1–28, and "Education of the Freedmen," *North American Review* 101 (October 1865): 528–550. For examples of newspaper correspondents' reports from the Sea Islands, see "Emancipation in South Carolina," *New York Times,* 17 May 1862, 3, and "Editorial Correspondence," *Christian Recorder,* 15 April 1865, 2. For an extended discussion of Reid's book, *After the War: A Tour of the Southern States, 1865–1866,* see Lori Robison, "Writing Reconstruction: Race and 'Visualist Ideology' in Whitelaw Reid's *After the War*," *JNT: Journal of Narrative Theory* 29, no. 1 (Winter 1999): 85–109. For a comprehensive account of education in the Sea Islands and the Port Royal experiment's place in the public eye, see Willie Lee Rose, *Rehearsal for Reconstruction: The Port Royal Experiment* (New York: Oxford Univ. Press, 1964). White northerners also formed impressions of the freed people in the Sea Islands from popular songs; see Michael C. Cohen, "Contraband Singing: Poems and Songs in Circulation during the Civil War," *American Literature* 82, no. 2 (June 2010): 271–304.

5. Elizabeth Hyde Botume, *First Days amongst the Contrabands* (Boston: Lee and Shepard, 1893), 31–32; Holland, *Letters and Diary of Laura M. Towne,* 11; Swint, *Dear Ones at Home,* 24.

6. Pierce, "The Freedmen at Port Royal," 304–305; Higginson, *Army Life in a Black Regiment,* 18, 8; Forten, "Life on the Sea Islands," 591; Swint, *Dear Ones at Home,* 61–62, 119.

7. Heather Andrea Williams, *Self-Taught: African American Education in Slavery and Freedom* (Chapel Hill: Univ. of North Carolina Press, 2005); Ronald E. Butchart, *Schooling the Freed People: Teaching, Learning, and the Struggle for Black Freedom, 1861–1876* (Chapel Hill: Univ. of North Carolina Press, 2010). In addition to these two essential volumes, there are several valuable studies of wartime and postbellum education for freed people, including Robert C. Morris, *Reading, 'Riting, and Reconstruction: The Education of Freedmen in the South, 1861–1870* (Chicago: Univ. of Chicago Press, 1981); Jacqueline Jones, *Soldiers of Light and Love: Northern Teachers and Georgia Blacks, 1865–1873* (Athens: Univ. of Georgia Press, 1980); Adam Fairclough, *A Class of Their Own: Black Teachers in the Segregated South* (Cambridge, MA: Harvard Univ. Press, 2007); and Christopher M. Span, *From Cotton Field to Schoolhouse: African American Education in Mississippi, 1862–1875* (Chapel Hill: Univ. of North Carolina Press, 2009).

8. Patricia C. Click, *Time Full of Trial: The Roanoke Island Freedmen's Colony, 1862–1867* (Chapel Hill: Univ. of North Carolina Press, 2001), 82, 153. Peter Johnston to his Excellency the President, 23 November 1865, enclosed in Elizabeth James to Andrew Johnson, 23 November 1865, J-48 1865, Letters Received, ser. 88, Land Division, Washington Headquarters, Record Group 105, National Archives Building, Washington, DC [A-62]. Peter's and Elizabeth's letters (but not Elizabeth's transcription of Peter's letter) appear as "North Carolina Freedman to the President, and a Northern Teacher to the President," in Steven Hahn et al., eds., *Freedom: A Documentary History of Emancipation, 1861–1867,* ser. 3, vol. 1: *Land and Labor* (Chapel Hill: Univ. of North Carolina Press, 2008), 723–725.

9. Steven Hahn, *A Nation under Our Feet: Black Political Struggles in the Rural South from Slavery to the Great Migration* (Cambridge, MA: Harvard Univ. Press, 2003), 128–31, 142–146.

10. Elizabeth Hyde Botume, *First Days amongst the Contrabands* (1893; repr. New York: Arno Press, 1968), 151, 145, 152.

11. Ira Berlin et al., eds., *Freedom: A Documentary History of Emancipation, 1861–1867,* ser. 1, vol. 3: *The Wartime Genesis of Free Labor: The Lower South* (Cambridge: Cambridge Univ. Press, 1990), 339; Click, *Time Full of Trial,* 195.

12. Higginson, *Army Life in a Black Regiment,* 23; [Gannett and Hale], "The Freedmen at Port Royal," 2; Pierce, "The Freedmen at Port Royal," 307; Pearson, *Letters from Port Royal,* 180; Swint, *Dear Ones at Home,* 62.

13. Forten, "Life on the Sea Islands," 592; Swint, *Dear Ones at Home,* 63; [Gannett and Hale], "The Freedmen at Port Royal," 3–4.

14. Higginson, *Army Life in a Black Regiment,* 38, 25.

15. Pierce, "The Freedmen at Port Royal," 307, 306.

16. Chase quoted in Swint, *Dear Ones at Home,* 62 and 37; Ware quoted in Pearson, *Letters from Port Royal,* 149.

17. *Christian Recorder,* 22 Feb 1862, 19 April 1862, 14 March 1863, 17 December 1864, 19 April 1862.

18. Pierce, "The Freedmen at Port Royal," 302.

19. Ibid., 306.

20. Randall Fuller, *From Battlefields Rising: How the Civil War Transformed American Literature* (New York: Oxford Univ. Press, 2011). Edmund Wilson, *Patriotic Gore: Studies in the Literature of the American Civil War* (1962; repr. New York: Norton, 1994), 131–158; quotation on 143. David Mindich, "Edwin M. Stanton, the Inverted Pyramid, and Information Control," in *The Civil War and the Press,* ed. David B. Sachsman, S. Kittrell Rushing, and Debra Reddin van Tuyll (New Brunswick, NJ: Transaction Publishers, 2000), 179–208.

21. Alan Trachtenberg, "Albums of War: On Reading Civil War Photographs," *Representations* 9 (Winter 1985): 1–32; Alice Fahs, *The Imagined Civil War: Popular Literature of the North and South, 1861–1865* (Chapel Hill: Univ. of North Carolina Press, 2001), 55–60; Andrea G. Pearson, "*Frank Leslie's Illustrated Newspaper* and *Harper's Weekly:* Innovation and Imitation in Nineteenth-Century Pictorial Reporting," *Journal of Popular Culture* 23 (Spring 1990): 81–111.

22. Hawthorne to James T. Fields, 9 December 1863, in *The Centenary Edition of the Works of Nathaniel Hawthorne,* vol. 15: *The Letters, 1857–1864,* ed. Thomas Woodson et al. (Columbus: Ohio State Univ. Press, 1987), 619–620; *The Centenary Edition of the Works of Nathaniel Hawthorne,* vol. 13: *The Elixir of Life Manuscripts,* ed. Edward H. Davidson, Claude M. Simpson, and L. Neal Smith (Columbus: Ohio State Univ. Press, 1977), 58.

23. Lacey Worth, "'Getting the Bodies of Boys into Order': Nationhood and the Wounded Body in Louisa May Alcott's *Hospital Sketches,*" paper presented at Midwest Modern Language Association Convention, Chicago, November 2010; "Exhibition of Left-hand Penmanship," William Oland Bourne Papers, New-York Historical Society, Civil War Treasures from the New-York Historical Society, http://memory.loc.gov/ndlpcoop/nhnycw/af/af01/af01008/001v.jpg; Thomas Wentworth Higginson, "Emily Dickinson's Letters," *Atlantic Monthly* 68 (October 1891): 444.

24. Sarah Robbins, *Managing Literacy, Mothering America: Women's Narratives on Reading and Writing in the Nineteenth Century* (Pittsburgh: Univ. of Pittsburgh Press, 2004); *Godey's Lady's Book,* July 1869; Elizabeth Keckley, *Behind the Scenes: Thirty Years a Slave, and Four Years in the White House,* ed. Frances Smith Foster (Urbana: Univ. of Illinois Press, 2001), 158.

25. Louisa May Alcott, *Little Women* (1868; repr. New York: Penguin, 1989), 2, 102, 35, 75.

26. Rebecca Harding Davis, *Waiting for the Verdict* (New York: Sheldon, 1868), 262, 255, 168, 170, 275, 354.

27. Swint, *Dear Ones at Home,* 7; Jordan Johnson to Lucy Chase and David Barr to Lucy Chase, 28 June 1868, box 4, folder 4, Chase Family Papers, American Antiquarian Society, Worcester, MA.

28. Swint, *Dear Ones at Home,* 236–237, and Edward E. Hale, *Mrs. Merriam's Scholars: A Story of the "Original Ten"* (Boston: Roberts Brothers, 1878), 99.

29. Swint, *Dear Ones at Home,* 242–243, 246.

30. Jordan Johnson to Lucy Chase, 11 May 1869, box 4, folder 4, Chase Family Papers.

31. Kenneth W. Warren, *What Was African American Literature?* (Cambridge, MA: Harvard Univ. Press, 2011), 7.

Acknowledgments

While a book such as this may bear the name of a single author, creation depends on communities and institutions. Libraries and archives preserve knowledge and make it accessible. Formal and informal gatherings of scholars, at conferences and on campuses, catalyze new understandings of what's preserved. An individual author's mentors and colleagues model the work of research, interpretation, and writing, while friends and loved ones support the whole time-consuming process. Colleges, foundations, and government agencies provide funding for it. Editors and publishers, braving economic headwinds, bring the outcome to readers. No list of names can fully document the professional and personal advantages I have enjoyed in writing this book, but several people and organizations, in my experience, represent especially well the vast and vital human infrastructure that supports the pursuit of knowledge.

I am indebted, first of all, to Curtis Askew, whom I barely know and have not seen in years but who suggested, while we stood in line one day at the Unicorn Café in Evanston, Illinois, that I take a look at Ira Berlin's *The Black Military Experience*. Later that afternoon, as I leafed through the book on the floor of the 973 aisle in Northwestern University's library, my eyes fell upon a document unlike anything I had ever read.

My effort to make sense of the writings of an anonymous New Orleans "Colored Man" initiated years of research, during which I benefited from the careful assistance of librarians and archivists at the American Antiquarian Society, the Indiana Historical Society, the Indiana State Library, the Massachusetts Historical Society, the Oberlin College Archives, and the National Archives; the Southern Historical Collection at the University of North Carolina; the Rare Books, Special Collections and Preservation Department of Rush Rhees Library at the University of Rochester; and the Manuscripts and Archives Department of Sterling Memorial Library at Yale University. I owe special gratitude to the staff of the Watkinson Library at Trinity College. This book could not have been written, or even imagined, were it not for the monumental work of the Freedmen and Southern Society Project. I especially thank Steven Miller, who welcomed me as a researcher in the project's papers at the University of Maryland.

Much of my research travel was funded by the English Department at Trinity College, and an extended leave to complete the book was made possible by the ACLS Fellowship Program of the American Council of Learned Societies; a full-year fellowship from the National Endowment for the Humanities; and the support of the Dean of Faculty's Office at Trinity. At Northwestern University, a grant from the provost's Residential College program and the dynamic research assistance of Amber North helped get this project off the ground. (Any views, findings, conclusions, or recommendations expressed in this book do not necessarily reflect those of the National Endowment for the Humanities, nor any other agency, organization, or person other than myself.)

Numerous colleagues at Trinity College, present and past, shared their knowledge, sharpened my thinking, critiqued portions of my work in progress, and provided encouragement as I worked on this book over the past five years: Davarian Baldwin, Barbara Benedict, Sarah Bilston, Thora Brylowe, Dario Del Puppo, Jack Dougherty, Sheila Fisher, Rena Fraden, Scott Gac, Cheryl Greenberg, Joan Hedrick, Dutch Kuyk, Gene Leach, Bill Mace, Kevin McMahon, Diana Paulin, Milla Riggio, Clare Rossini, Seth Sanders, Barbara Sicherman, Ron Spencer, and Chloe Wheatley. I must give special mention to three Trinity colleagues whose confidence in my work has buoyed me all along the way. Paul Lauter's support for this project has been especially valuable. I have benefited in countless ways from Lou Masur's guidance and encouragement, not to mention his shrewd reading of a draft of the manuscript. And David Rosen made time to read the manuscript when there was little time to be had. I am grateful as well to my students, especially the members of my Fall 2009 Literacy and Literature seminar; my advisees in the Class of 2011, whose senior year I missed while working on this book; and Stephanie Chan, who provided conscientious research assistance.

I have been frequently astonished by the intellectual generosity of scholars of American literature and history from throughout the country, many of whom took time to aid, inspire, and constructively humble me during the course of my work on this book. Edward Ayers and John David Smith fielded research questions, and John Stauffer offered a helpful response to an early presentation. David Blight shared his expertise on John M. Washington, and William B. Gould IV shared his on William B. Gould. Kathleen Diffley's conference-panel orchestrations and sharp questioning kept my work moving forward. Katy Chiles, Marcy Dinius, Karen Sánchez-Eppler, and Jane Schultz read portions of the manuscript, and their incisive feedback helped me find the life in my material. Elizabeth Renker's comments on chapters in progress were exacting and heartening at the same time, and they made the whole book better. Bob Levine gave the manuscript a keen and careful reading, as did another reader for the press, and both reviewers provided eye-opening feedback.

I am grateful to my editor, Joyce Seltzer, for helping me see my own writing in new ways, and to Brian Distelberg, Julie Ericksen Hagen, and Lisa Stallings, among others who carefully shepherded the book through the process of publication.

I have been exceedingly fortunate in the teachers who brought me up to do the kind of work that went into this book; I will mention just three of many. Almost everything I have thought or written in the past fifteen years shows the influence of the late Gilbert Sorrentino. Julia Stern showed me it was possible to be an imaginative thinker and a responsible scholar at the same time (and by so doing, kept me in graduate school); still my mentor, she read the manuscript with at least as much care as when reading my work was her job. Likewise Jay Grossman, whose percipience never ceases to amaze me, the more for going hand in hand with good humor and devotion.

Least tangible, entirely irreplaceable: the interest and support of my friends and family. I am grateful to dozens of friends and relatives for their genuine curiosity about what I've been working on and for the motivation they have given me in countless conversations. Michael O'Donnell and Ed Heinemann deserve special mention for venturing into the manuscript with their red pens and refreshingly nonacademic eyes. My mother-in-law, Lisa Contino, helped me find time to write in hard-pressed times. My parents, Kathleen and Alan Hager, deserve credit for my every accomplishment. No one ever was more committed to any cause than they were to my education, and their continued faith in me means the world. My father read every word of this book, many of them several times; he was always enthusiastic but never too impartial to help me improve. Young Josephine Hager arrived in the middle of this book's composition, and she did everything she could not to disrupt it too much. To her mother, Alison Ehrmann Hager, my partner in struggle and in joy, who believes in me when I don't, I owe gratitude far beyond words.

Index

Turner, Henry McNeal, 208–209, 217

Turner, Nat, 41

Twenty-Eighth U.S. Colored Infantry (USCT), White as chaplain of, 182, 184, 197–199, 209, 210–212

Uncle Tom's Cabin (Stowe), 26, 27, 36–37, 223

UNESCO, definition of "literate," 46

U.S. Constitution: A Colored Man's written juxtaposition of personal experience with, 1–4, 13–15, 186–187; Morris and unimpeachable clarity of text, 16

U.S.S. *Cambridge,* Gould's diary as collective chronicle of community life on, 110, 118–125, *120,* 130–131

U.S.S. *Niagara,* Gould's diary of individual place in community life of on, 110, 128–137

U.S.S. *Sabine,* 129

Virginia: anti-literacy laws, 41, 42; slave assembly prohibited in, 41, 114

Virginia, University of, 57–58

Waiting for the Verdict (Davis), 236–237

Walker, David, 40–41

Walker, John, 203

Walker, Wm. I., 85

Wallpaper, as writing paper, 85–86

Ware, Harriet, 229, 231

Washington, Booker T., 191, 216, 218

Washington, John M., 59, 107, 115, 186, 243; emancipation narrative "Memory of the Past," 83, 95–106, *98;* literacy education of, 83–87; enslaved narrative,

diary revisions, 87–91, *90;* enslaved narrative, imaginative connection between romance and emancipation, 91–95, 106; Gould's writing compared, 108, 110, 118, 136

Watts, Isaac, Washington's copying of hymn of, 86

Webster, Noah, 18; *American Spelling Book,* 51

Weekly Anglo-African, 119, 133, 134, 186

Weld, Theodore Dwight, 34, 35

Western Sanitary Commission, 161

West Virginia, secession and, 159

Wheatley, Phillis, 23

White, Garland H., 181–219, 232, 240; letter to *Christian Recorder* celebrating end of war, 182, 184–185, 186–187; literacy instruction and, 185, 186, 218; letters to Stanton, 188–192, 195, 200–201; letters to Seward, 192, 197–198, 200–201, 210; letter to Morton, 192–199; letter to *Christian Recorder* and ambivalence about action versus accommodation in racial equality struggle, 202–210, 215–219; letter to *Christian Recorder* about black suffrage, 212–215

Whitman, Walt, 233

Wilson, Goodridge, 161–162

Winthrop, John, 151

Women: literacy instruction and, 6–7; gendered concepts of marriage and family, letters of petition and protest, 156–164

Woodson, Carter, 44–45

Wright, Rufus, 116